DSL Survival Guide

LISA **LEE**

Osborne/**McGraw-Hill**

New York   Chicago   San Francisco
Lisbon   London   Madrid   Mexico City
Milan   New Delhi   San Juan
Seoul   Singapore   Sydney   Toronto

About the Author

Lisa Lee has written several best-selling computer books and is the technical editor for *How to Do Everything with Your Palm Handheld*, and *How to Do Everything with Your Visor*. She has several years of experience working with DSL networks, and setting up and maintaining test networks for large and small companies.

Lisa is an R&D engineering test manager for Microsoft. Over the past decade she has worked with hardware and software developers to create computers, handheld devices, and network products for companies such as Apple, 3DO, WebTV, and Microsoft.

In her spare time, she is an amateur photographer, cartoonist, painter, and Web designer. Visit www.flatfishfactory.com to send her an e-mail, or view her latest project, paintings, and sketches.

Osborne/**McGraw-Hill**
2600 Tenth Street
Berkeley, California 94710
U.S.A.

To arrange bulk purchase discounts for sales promotions, premiums, or fund-raisers, please contact Osborne/**McGraw-Hill** at the above address. For information on translations or book distributors outside the U.S.A., please see the International Contact Information page immediately following the index of this book.

DSL Survival Guide

1234567890 DOC DOC 01987654321

ISBN 0-07-219310-7

Publisher
  Brandon A. Nordin

Vice President & Associate Publisher
  Scott Rogers

Acquisitions Editor
  Jane Brownlow

Project Editor
  Elizabeth Seymour

Acquisitions Coordinator
  Emma Acker

Technical Editor
  Martin Jackson

Copy Editors
  Robert Campbell, Cynthia Putnam

Proofreaders
  Linda Medoff, Paul Medoff

Computer Designer
  Lucie Ericksen
  Melinda Moore Lytle

Illustrator
  Michael Mueller
  Lyssa Wald

Series Design
  Lucie Ericksen

Cover Design
  Gorska Design

621.382
LEE

This book was composed with Corel VENTURA™ Publisher.

This book is dedicated to Mike Neil

Contents

v

Acknowledgments

Thanks to Jane Brownlow, Emma Acker, and the production team at Osborne/McGraw-Hill for being such a great group of people to work with and for making this book possible. I'd also like to thank all the folks who have worked so hard to create the network products that make networking so easy to use today. Finally, thanks to all my friends, family, and work associates for all your love, support, patience, and kindness.

Introduction

I remember when digital subscriber lines became available a few years ago. Many of my co-workers jumped at the opportunity to work from home, and signed up to be the first DSL users on their block. I remember how practically every person would recount a long story about how many visits the phone company had to make, and how the voice phones might stop working after one visit, and get fixed after another visit. And how, after weeks of making appointments with the DSL provider, the Internet connection would not work.

Despite all the time involved to set up the DSL service in its early days, everyone was happy to add a fast Internet connection to their home. I was fortunate to have a successful DSL installation with the first visit from both the phone company and the DSL provider. This book is designed to help DSL subscribers set up, run, and troubleshoot their DSL network.

Overview

Oh, the joys of networking! In many ways networks are still in their infancy, especially if you've witnessed the rise and fall of the dot com community, and the constant improvements of new hardware and software for desktop and laptop computers. What to buy, when to buy, and how to put them all together so each can communicate with each other over a network can be a wonderfully simple experience, or a tedious, problem-filled exercise in futility.

This book focuses on star network hub topologies, and the latest Windows, Mac, and Linux operating systems. It shows you how to put together a network, and expand it with a wireless access point, such as an Apple Base Station, with AirPort cards installed in one or all of the client Macintosh computers. Each chapter walks you through common network and computing concepts you'll encounter on a computer connected to a DSL modem and a fast broadband connection to the Internet. Problems for a particular concept are explained, along with solutions you may implement.

Who this book is for

This book was written for anyone who has subscribed to a DSL service and wants to find out how to set up, run, or troubleshoot a network that's connected to a DSL modem. I'm assuming you're either home-based or renting an office and have already subscribed to a DSL service, or are about to choose a DSL service.

I wish this book could explain every computer and network gizmo in great detail—it does not. I assume you have some computer expertise and some familiarity with computer hardware, software, and network connectivity. If hearing the term "Ethernet" makes you feel like a deer standing in front of car headlights, this book may not be for you. If you are a newbie to computers and networks, you might want to read through this book a little more slowly, and possibly use this book side-by-side with a beginner's book on the Windows, Mac, or Linux operating systems, and possibly a beginner's guide to networking.

How to use this book

This book is about many computer and network technologies and processes, and can be used in many ways. By nature, networking delves into every aspect of computing. If you already have a solid background with computers, but not necessarily with networks, and you have a particular task you want to accomplish such as setting up a Windows computer to surf the Internet, you can skip directly to Chapter 5. If you're a beginner at computers and networks, you might want to read through this book to familiarize yourself with the computing concepts involved with setting up and running a network before deciding how you want to configure a computer. On the other hand, if you've already set up your network, and want to learn about troubleshooting or improving network performance, you may only want to read the last chapters of the book that focus on troubleshooting networks.

There are several tips, notes, cautions, and sidebars you'll find scattered throughout this book. Each contains a different tidbit of information, such as a hint, or factoid that pertains to the discussion at hand. Some chapters also contain tables of information, and step-by-step examples that show you how to install or configure a particular hardware or software component. The following list provides a brief description of the conventions used in this book.

SURVIVAL TIP Tips contain helpful information, such as a shortcut, or an easier way for performing a particular task.

NOTE Notes are brief messages that contain related information about a particular topic in a chapter.

CAUTION Cautions inform you of potential problems that may occur for a particular chapter topic. A workaround or troubleshooting tip may also be included in a caution.

How this book is organized

The DSL Survival Guide describes the basic components of digital subscriber line technology and client-side networking and applications, and focuses on setting up, running, and troubleshooting a local area network connected to a DSL service provider. Other topics covered in this book include network design and server-side software and hardware. Peer-to-peer and point-to-point network connections are also introduced and explained in the context of setting up, running, and troubleshooting a local area network in a home or office. General concepts, such as network processes, are introduced with diagrams, and some of the technologies, such as network interface cards, and wireless network products are presented accompanied with photographs. Each chapter presents common problems and solutions for each chapter topic. Each chapter also provides a list of additional Web site resources if you want to find out more about a particular DSL or network topic.

This book is divided into four parts. It begins with an introduction to DSL, explaining how DSL, networks, and network topologies work. The second part, Setting Up DSL, shows you how to set up networking software and applications on a Windows or Macintosh client computer to access e-mail and browser services on the Internet. The third part, Working with DSL, shows you how to set up a server, add users and groups, wireless networks, and handheld devices to work with two or more client computers connected to a local area network. The fourth part consists of six troubleshooting chapters, exploring network, computer, and VPN troubleshooting, and network performance troubleshooting.

Part I: Introduction to DSL

There are several varieties of digital subscriber line services available as well as different types of DSL modems. The type of DSL modem and service you choose will depend on how many computers you want to connect to the Internet. The chapters in this part explain some fundamental DSL and network technologies and components. It is a brief primer on DSL, network components, and network topologies.

Part II: Setting Up a Computer to Access the Internet

Most computers that access the Internet will do so as client computers accessing services, or Internet servers. The chapters in this part take a closer look at some of the different kinds of DSL services you may have to connect a computer to. You will learn how to configure the network settings for Windows, Mac, and Linux computers, and access e-mail, play streaming media, and participate in interactive chat or instant messaging sessions on the Internet.

Part III: Working with DSL

The chapters in this part explore ways you can run a local network, including setting up a Windows 2000 server. Expanding a local network with a wireless access point, and wireless access cards, is another topic explored in this part of the book. Find out how to set up a wireless access point, create user and group accounts on client computers and servers on the local network, access a wireless access point with a laptop computer, and work with handheld devices on a local network.

Part IV: Troubleshooting DSL

Trouble inevitably follows a network. If hardware problems do not occur, software problems may occur, or network performance may slow down. The chapters in this section describe some of the more common computer, network, network peripheral, virtual private network, and network performance problems and troubleshooting methods that may help you keep your home or office network running smoothly.

Part I

Introduction to DSL

Chapter 1

What Is DSL?

Broadband is a general term used to describe a high-speed connection to the Internet. DSL is one of three possible broadband solutions that can help many homes and businesses acquire fast Internet access. Cable modems and two-way satellites are the other two broadband solutions that are available today. Within the last two years, DSL has become the most popular broadband solution, beating the other two broadband solutions by providing lower cost and better performance. In fact, DSL has become so popular that DSL service providers (which include local phone companies) can't keep up with the demand. The chapters in Part I will introduce you to the concepts and technology behind DSL and will also discuss network concepts, technologies, and planning.

DSL is an acronym for *digital subscriber line*. A digital subscriber line is a type of networking service that is brought to your home or business via telephone lines. It brings fast Internet access to your computers and Internet devices. What's fast? The fastest analog modems can connect to the Internet at up to 56 kilobits per second (Kbps). If your home or office is located near a local phone office (which may not be easy to determine visually), your home or office network may be able to access the Internet at 1 megabit per second (Mbps) using DSL. Each DSL service provider may provide different kinds of DSL services, which may or may not restrict the speed of the DSL network connection. The following list briefly describes three distinguishing characteristics of a DSL service.

+ **Broadband connection**   DSL provides a fast, always-on connection to the Internet.

+ **Internet connection over phone line**   A DSL connection to your home or office is transmitted over existing telephone lines. Depending on the type of services available in your area, a DSL service provider may need to work with your local phone company to bring an Internet connection to your home or office.

+ **Internet and Web access**   Signing up and subscribing with a DSL service provider enables you to access Internet-based e-mail and web browsing. The faster Internet connection can also enable you to view animation and video, and play games over the Internet.

Basic Concepts: Phones, Connectivity, and the Internet

Combining the words "telephone" and "Internet" usually conjures up images of a traditional 56 Kbps modem making odd sounds as it connects computers to the Internet. When an analog modem makes those sounds, it is creating a point-to-point connection with an Internet service provider's modem. Most analog modem connections are used to connect one computer to the Internet. However, it is possible to use a special analog modem to allow computers connected to a local area network (LAN) to dial in to the Internet. Each computer on a LAN can also have its own phone line and analog modem to establish a connection to the Internet.

Some DSL service providers use a similar point-to-point connection to enable a computer to access the Internet. Depending on the type of DSL service to which you subscribe, you can connect one computer or all the computers on a LAN to the Internet via one DSL modem. Figure 1-1 illustrates how a DSL service provider works with your local phone company to bring the Internet into your home over existing phone lines. DSL service providers and the phone company use the term "copper" to refer to the phone lines.

The biggest difference between a DSL modem and an analog modem is that the DSL modem requires a high-bandwidth connection to the copper in order to access the Internet. Analog modems rely on the lower frequency ranges of the phone line to transmit voice data over the copper to another modem. If you subscribe to a DSL service that requires your phone line to be modified with a splitter, you will need to have the DSL service provider

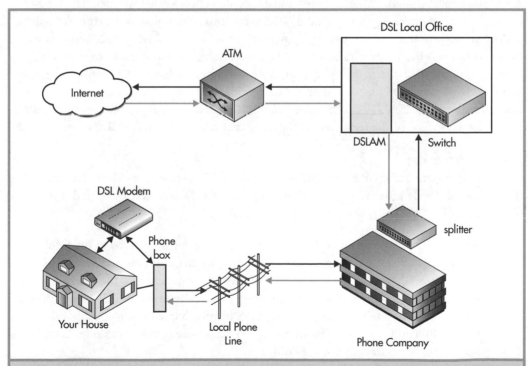

Figure 1-1. A DSL service provider enables you to subscribe to a service package to bring Internet services into your home.

schedule the phone company to visit your home or office. Once a splitter is installed on the copper, the DSL service provider can activate the DSL modem on the DSL provider's network, and activate your e-mail account and any other network services to which you have subscribed. Some DSL services don't require the phone company to install splitters to the copper wire, but usually require any voice phone devices to have a special filter attached to each non-DSL line. The top portion of Figure 1-1 shows how you can access the Internet with a DSL modem, and how data from the Internet gets routed back to your computer.

**SURVIVAL
TIP**

To find out more about splitter and splitterless DSL services, go to Chapter 4.

A Few Phone and Network Terms and What They Mean

A DSL modem is designed to maintain a constant connection to the Internet. The type of modem you use depends on the type of DSL service to which you subscribe. A basic service subscription for one or two computers may only require a DSL modem that uses Point-to-Point Protocol over Ethernet (PPPoE) to establish a connection to your DSL service. Additional services, or support for more computers over the DSL connection, will most likely require a DSL modem that creates a bridge or router connection to the Internet. Bridges and routers are discussed in more detail in Chapters 2 and 3. The following sections briefly explain some of the terms and technology that will be covered in this chapter.

Service Providers

Different terms are used to describe different kinds of DSL service providers. The following list contains brief definitions of some of the more frequently used acronyms and terms associated with DSL service providers and DSL networks.

◆ **Internet service provider (ISP)**   Most analog modem connections to the Internet rely on an Internet service provider to manage Internet accounts and several modems (see Figure 1-3 later in the chapter) and a network connection to the Internet. A DSL service provider replaces the traditional Internet service provider (ISP) and brings a direct connection to the Internet to the LAN in your home or office. Some ISPs, such as Earthlink and AOL, have partnered with DSL service providers to offer faster DSL network services to your home or office.

+ **Competitive local exchange carrier (CLEC)**   A local phone company or DSL company providing DSL services for your home or office; synonymous with the term "DSL service provider"

+ **Incumbent local exchange carrier (ILEC)**   A U.S. telephone company that provides local phone service; usually refers to the baby bell companies that resulted from the breakup of the nationwide Bell system in the early 1980s

+ **Local exchange**   The local office of the local exchange carrier (LEC)

+ **Central office (CO)** A general term used to describe the local telephone company office

+ **Local access and transport area**   An area that consists of several interconnected local exchanges

+ **Interexchange carrier (IXC)**   A term describing a long-distance voice or data carrier such as AT&T, MCI, or Sprint

+ **POTS**   Plain Old Telephone System. The copper, or phone line, connected to your home or office

+ **DSL modem**   A hardware device that can establish a connection between your local network and the Internet

+ **Splitter**   A small hardware device that connects to your phone line to split the voice and data signals

+ **Local area network (LAN)**   One or several networks located in the same building

+ **Router**   A hardware or software network device capable of routing network information between two networks

Open Systems Interconnection Reference Model

The DSL modem, network cables, and computers rely on hardware and software to communicate with each other. The International Standards Organization (ISO) defined the Open Systems Interconnection (OSI) model to create a network design framework to enable different computer platforms to exchange data communications over a network. Every Windows, Linux, or Macintosh computer runs network software that follows an OSI standard.

The OSI model consists of seven layers of protocols, or rules. Starting from the Physical layer, each successive layer relies on the preceding one to propagate network communication.

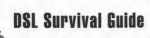

✦ **Physical layer**   The network cables, network interface card (NIC), and general network hardware required to establish a connection to the network

✦ **Data Link layer**   Responsible for encoding the network signal of the network device, and acknowledging or rejecting inter-device network communications

✦ **Network layer**   Defines how data is transferred between computers on a local network and how data is routed across networks

✦ **Transport layer**   Works with the Session layer to define how a complete set of data is exchanged across networks

✦ **Session layer**   Manages the flow of data that moves into and out of the computer via the Transport layer

✦ **Presentation layer**   Provides a translation service for data moving to and from different computer systems

✦ **Application layer**   Enables a browser or other network application to transfer files over a network; relies on protocols that work with all the other layers in the OSI model

DSL Modems

There are three different ways a DSL modem can connect a computer or local network to the DSL provider's network, and to the Internet. Each type of connection usually requires a particular type of DSL modem. The DSL provider will most likely determine which modem to use with the DSL service package you choose.

NOTE

In order to subscribe to a DSL service, a home or office will most likely need to subscribe to an existing phone line service. Some DSL providers may not have this requirement. However, if you don't currently use a telephone, you may need to sign up with a local phone company so that the home or office has an account with the local phone system that will also be bringing the DSL connection into your home or office.

The DSL provider can also limit the download speed of each account. If you are close enough to the central phone office, but are seeing 400 Kbps download rates on an ADSL subscriber line, you can ask your DSL provider to remove the cap on the service and see whether the network throughput rates improve. The following list describes each of the three different DSL modems, and DSL service connections available.

✦ **Point-to-Point**   Most commonly used to connect a single computer to the Internet. A point to point connection enables a DSL modem to connect to the DSL provider's network in order to access the Internet. This type of connection may time out and may require you to re-enter your login in order to restore access to the Internet on a computer.

✦ **Router**   A feature in a DSL modem intended to connect a network of computers to the DSL provider. This kind of DSL modem provides a 24/7 connection to the Internet and may have additional features, such as a firewall, DHCP server, or network filters.

✦ **Bridge**   A type of DSL modem that connects your local network to the DSL provider's network by creating a bridge between the two networks.

NOTE

Line Sharing is a term used to refer to a Competitve Local Exchange Carrier (CLEC) such as Covad. Line sharing enables a CLEC to install a DSL service without requiring the local telephone company (Central Offfice, or CO) to install a second phone line in your home or office. Not all CLECs provide line-sharing services, so check for line-sharing availability with each service provider to find out whether line sharing is available your area.

Good Old Modems and Phone Lines

Why do modems have a 56 Kbps limit connecting to the Internet, and not DSL? The main reason is that analog modems use the voice portion of the phone line. DSL modems work with higher frequencies transmitted over the same phone line.

Phone lines (also referred to as POTS, which stands for Plain Old Telephone System) use analog technology to broadcast information. There are several modulation technology specifications for transmitting signals over a wire. Signals transmit data in a wave format, similar to the way television is broadcast over the air or over cable lines. Analog technology relies on wave modulation to carry signals from point A to point B. Analog technologies work best with shorter, rather than longer, distances.

The Internet transmits information in the form of digital data, which is represented by ones and zeros. The term "modem" is an acronym for MOdulator DEModulator. In order for digital data to be sent over the phone network, the modem converts digital data from the Internet into analog data. When data is sent to your computer from the phone network, the modem converts the analog data back into digital information.

Analog modems plug into existing phone jacks in your home or office. These lines are dedicated to transmitting voice, roughly equivalent to 56 Kbps, over the copper wire. However the copper wire can support up to 8 Mbps of analog data transmission. Figure 1-2 compares the data and voice bandwidths in a plain old telephone system (POTS) line. If you translate kilobits of data into kilohertz of bandwidth on the copper wire, voice data occupies about 4 KHz of bandwidth. DSL modems can occupy up to 500 KHz of bandwidth—

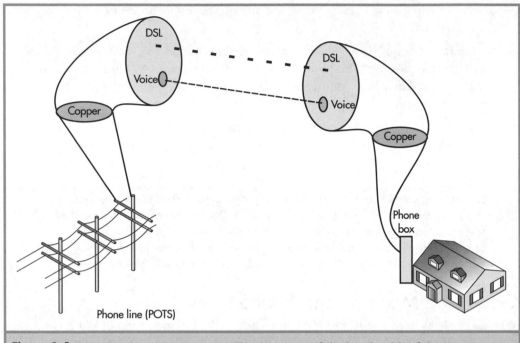

Figure 1-2. Voice data occupies a small percentage of the bandwidth of the copper connecting the phone company to your house.

approximately 125 times more bandwidth than voice. Both DSL and traditional 56 Kbps modems use sophisticated digital techniques to process analog signals.

NOTE Another reason that 56 Kbps modems can't take full advantage of copper phone cable lines is that the chip set in these modems can't work beyond an 8 KHz bandwidth. The full bandwidth of the copper line, which DSL can take advantage of, can modulate up to 64 KHz.

How a Modem Connects to the Internet

Analog modems are designed to use a voice phone line to create and sustain a connection to the Internet. The analog modem dials into another modem, hosted by your Internet service provider (see Figure 1-3). The ISP manages its own network of computers that authenticate your account information and, if valid, complete your connection to the Internet. The ISP assigns an IP address to one of its Internet-connected computers, which interacts with the ISP modem. As your computer communicates with other computers on the Internet, the computer and modem on the ISP network send and receive data using the assigned IP address.

The following list outlines how an analog modem allows your computer to access the Internet.

✦ The modem receives a local number to dial.

✦ The modem dials in to a local modem rack.

✦ A connection speed is negotiated between the two modems.

✦ The account information from your computer is authenticated with a name server.

✦ If the login and password account information are correct, the modem is granted access to the network servers on the Internet.

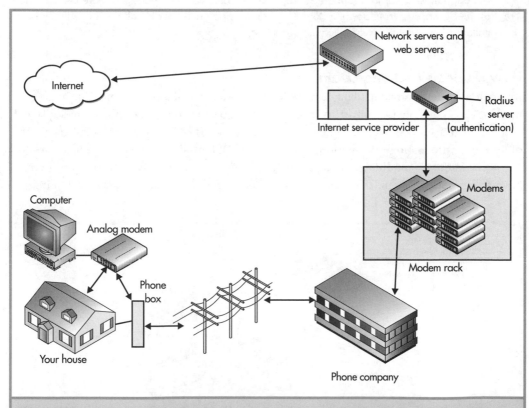

Figure 1-3. When you dial into the Internet with an analog modem, your computer must connect to another modem in order to communicate with computers located on the Internet.

Handshaking with Other Modems

In order to establish an Internet connection, a 56 Kbps modem, attached to a computer, must be able to communicate with another 56 Kbps modem on the ISP's modem rack. The quality of the phone line going into your house can affect the overall speed of the 56 Kbps modem. External factors, such as electrical or magnetic generating sources, may also affect the quality of the phone line.

The two modems may connect at about 52 Kbps. If the modems cannot establish a connection at the highest possible rate, both modems will re-train to a slower connection rate until a connection is established. Once the two modems connect, the ISP/Internet-based modem may encounter additional network traffic resulting in a slower data rate.

> Although most major ISPs support 56 Kbps connections, your computer will more likely connect at 48–52 Kbps or *train down* to 33.6 Kbps, depending on the quality of the phone line (also called a *land line*) that is installed in your home.

NOTE

How Modems Exchange Data

An analog modem transmits data over the voice frequencies of a phone line. The analog modem is responsible for converting the digital data on the computer into an analog signal that can be transmitted over the phone line (see Figure 1-4). A DSL modem can also convert digital data into analog information. However, the DSL modem can communicate over higher frequencies modulated on a phone line. Computers, like many network routers, have an operating system that can run programs to read the packet information being

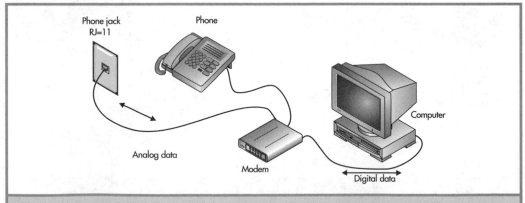

Figure 1-4. Analog modems convert digital data into analog signals, and then convert analog signals back into digital data, enabling a computer to connect to the Internet.

sent to a modem or received from a modem. As network data is sent or received, the computer processes it.

The OSI reference model is followed by companies who make network devices, computers, and computer operating systems and software. As explained earlier in the chapter, the ISO uses this model to define seven layers of protocols that computers follow to communicate with each other over a network. In addition, the Institute of Electrical and Electronics Engineers (IEEE) has defined many hardware and software standards for Ethernet, broadband networks, and wireless networks. The following list provides a brief description of the network components associated with the OSI layers. To find out more about how computers communicate over a network, see Chapter 2, "What Is a Network?"

✦ **Physical layer**   Cables, network interface cards, and modem-related hardware are part of the first layer of the OSI model. They help deliver the data sent between your computer and other computers on the remote network.

✦ **Data Link, Network, Transport, Session, and Presentation layers**   Protocols are used to process data sent over the network. Some protocols can filter other computers out of a network, while other protocols are responsible for breaking up data into packets. Some protocols are designed to confirm that all the packets in a transmission have successfully been sent or received between the source and destination computers. Packets contain the core information being sent between two computers, such as a web page, e-mail, and so on.

✦ **Application layer**   A browser or other network-savvy application can interact with the other layers of the OSI model to send data to another computer on the local network or across the Internet to a computer on the other side of the planet.

SURVIVAL TIP

Creating a network of computers involves not only correctly configuring hardware devices and cabling, but also setting up software. For more information about networks, see Chapter 2.

How a DSL Connection Works

If you have more than one computer online, access your e-mail or web pages frequently, or plan to eventually host your own web server, you'll like the 24/7 access that DSL services will bring to your network. The phone lines are modified at the local phone company and at your home or office. A splitter is connected to the phone company's end, so that the larger bandwidth of the cable can be passed on to the DSL service provider's network.

If you subscribe to one of the more traditional DSL services, the first thing most service providers will do is schedule the phone company to visit your home. The phone company

will modify the phone line that goes into your home with a connector that splits the voice portion of the line from the Internet connection. The DSL portion of the phone line connects to a DSL modem. The type of DSL modem you get will vary depending on the service you subscribe to. The DSL modem will establish a connection to the DSL provider via a point to point over Ethernet, router, or bridge connection. In addition to the Internet connection, the DSL modem has a connector for Ethernet. You can connect one computer directly to the Ethernet port on the DSL modem, or you can plug a hub into the Ethernet port, enabling multiple computers or a couple more hubs to extend the local area network in your home or office.

You can connect a computer to a network in several ways. You can set up a LAN in your home or office by connecting each computer to a central Ethernet hub, and then connecting the DSL modem to the Ethernet hub to allow any computer connected to the hub to access the Internet. You can also connect a computer directly to the DSL modem.

To find out more about how to plan a network, see Chapter 3.

SURVIVAL TIP

Both the DSL modem and computer rely on Ethernet to establish the network connection to the Internet. If you have a computer that does not have a built-in Ethernet port, but has a peripheral component interconnect (PCI) expansion port, you can install a 10 Base T, 10/100 Base T, or Gigabyte Base T Ethernet PCI card into a PCI expansion slot. The PCI card is an internal card interface, similar to built-in Ethernet chip sets that are installed on a computer. If the computer has a universal serial bus (USB) connection port, you can attach a USB-to-Ethernet adapter to the computer's USB connection port. The USB Ethernet device is an external peripheral interface, and the Ethernet connection will only be as fast as the USB connection on the computer. For example, if the USB port can process data at 7 Mbps, the Ethernet connection may be 5–7 Mbps, but it will not be as fast as a 10 Mbps network connection. Also, if you install a PCI card or USB Ethernet device, you will need to install an Ethernet software driver for each card or external device.

You can take a Windows or Macintosh computer with two or more Ethernet cards or portss and turn it into a DSL router, replacing the DSL modem installed by your service provider. For more information, see Chapter 9.

SURVIVAL TIP

The following list describes the items that are used to create a splitter-based DSL connection from the existing phone line in your home. In some cases, your phone lines may need to be upgraded, or the phone wiring in your house may need to be replaced. The most problematic aspect of this scenario is waiting for the installation person from the phone company to arrive. If your phone box is located inside your home, you must be present to have the phone company modify the phone line. If the phone box is outside the house, you do not need to be present when the phone company modifies your phone line.

✦ **DSL modem or modem/router**   Connects to the DSL phone line in your home and can be accessed from the DSL service provider via the Internet.

✦ **Line splitter**   In-line filter, or micro filter (see Figure 1-5). Plugs into the phone jack and splits the voice and DSL signals. Splitterless DSL services are available from some DSL service providers.

✦ **Y adapter**   Plugs into the phone jack to allow a voice and DSL line to connect to the copper.

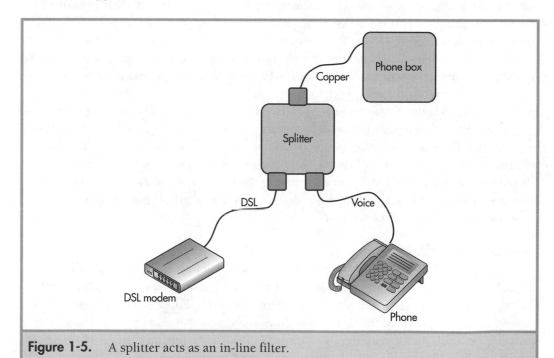

Figure 1-5.   A splitter acts as an in-line filter.

✦ **Phone cable (RJ-11)** A standard phone cable that connects to the DSL modem.

✦ **Ethernet cable (RJ-45)** A standard Ethernet cable that connects a computer to a hub, or a hub to the DSL modem.

Splitters separate copper lines into voice and data signals at the local phone office, and at the phone lines going into your home. Internet data is routed through the DSL service provider, to the local phone company, into your home network.

The DSL service provider can access and configure your DSL modem over the Internet. More specifically, a DSL provider can configure the IP information for your DSL modem over the Internet. Depending on the type of DSL modem installed in your home or office, additional features, such as router, firewall, and Dynamic Host Configuration Protocol (DHCP) services, may also be available in the DSL modem. High-end DSL modems can act as a bridge or router to the Internet.

Most basic DSL modems are only capable of working with Point-to-Point Protocol over Ethernet (PPPoE) to connect one or possibly two computers to the Internet. A PPPoE connection is similar to an analog modem connection to the Internet. This type of DSL account may require you to authenticate your DSL account and computer with the DSL network before you first use your DSL services.

Most DSL modems have a light near each connection port. If the phone line is connected to the DSL modem, and the light is lit near the DSL phone connection port, the connection is active, and the modem has a power source. Most Ethernet hubs also have a light near each port to indicate whether each connection is active. Once the DSL modem has a live connection to the Internet, review your DSL account information. Depending on what type of DSL account you have signed up for, you may need to input the DSL account's IP address information for your computer into the TCP/IP control panel (Mac) or Properties window (Windows) in order to connect your computer to the Internet. Try to load a web page or download your e-mail using the Internet connection to see whether your computer is successfully connected to the Internet.

Translating Digital to Analog

Each DSL phone line is a shared line in the sense that all phone lines originate from the central phone office (CO), and some homes and businesses share some phone lines with other homes or businesses. The network performance of a DSL line does not degrade when more than one person uses the same phone lines simultaneously. However, a DSL service provider can limit the bandwidth of a DSL connection, depending on the type of service to which you subscribe.

Depending on the type of DSL service, the phone company may need to install a splitter to your home or office phone line in order to separate the voice signals from the DSL signals.

Splitterless DSL connections require you to add a splitter to any voice-based phone lines, but not to the DSL phone line connected to your computer. The local phone office gathers each line from each home and connects it to a DSL access multiplexor (DSLAM), which is responsible for connecting each home DSL account to the core network. The local phone office connects the DSLAM lines into an Internet backbone connection, which is a high-speed network connection, such as an asynchronous transfer mode (ATM) line.

A DSL modem converts the digital information from your computer network into analog signals that can be delivered over the copper line to the phone company's local office. The DSL service provider manages the switches and network connections to your home or office, as well as to the Internet. The DSL modem, for example, converts the analog signals from the DSl provider into digital data on your local network. The DSL provider also has a system for converting the analog signals back into digital data, and forwards the information on to the servers and computers on the Internet. The analog-to-digital and digital-to-analog data conversion performed by a DSL modem is a bit more sophisticated, but similar to the way an analog modem translates digital information into analog, and vice versa, over the voice portion of the phone line.

DSL Modem and Local Networks

Except for the faster Ethernet connection, basic DSL modems are comparable to analog modems. More sophisticated DSL modems are capable of performing several tasks over and above what a traditional 56 Kbps modem can do. In addition to providing a 24/7 connection to the DSL service provider, some DSL modems (features vary depending on the type of modem your DSL service installs) can also function as a bridge or a router between your home or office LAN and the Internet. Depending on the features of the modem, it may also be capable of acting as a firewall or assigning network addresses on your LAN.

In order for the DSL modem to sustain a full-time online connection, it must be powered on and connected to both the phone line and your home or office network. The phone company or DSL provider maintains the 24/7 connection to the Internet. In addition to the backbone and DSLAMs, the DSL service provider also has a set of network switches that determine which DSL modem/routers belong to that particular network. You are responsible for making sure that computers on your local network are configured with the appropriate DSL account information if you want one or all of them to access the Internet.

SURVIVAL TIP Most DSL service providers allow you to upgrade your DSL services as your network grows. For more information about network planning, see Chapter 3.

Several computers on your home or office network can simultaneously access the Internet through the DSL modem. Be sure to check with your DSL service provider to ensure that your local network configuration does not conflict with any restrictions that might be associated with the DSL service to which you are subscribing. Some DSL modems can be configured as a DHCP server to allocate local network addresses to enable each computer to access the Internet. DHCP is software or hardware that performs the network administrative task of assigning network addresses to computers connected to the local network, such as the network shown in Figure 1-6. You can also run a DHCP server from a computer connected to your local network.

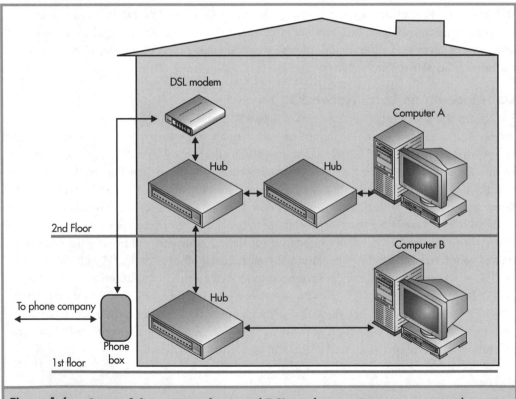

Figure 1-6. Some of the more sophisticated DSL modems can support a network of computers.

One frequently overlooked aspect of using home or business networks is anticipating the number of computers and network traffic on the local network accessing the Internet. Monitor the network connection once or twice a week to identify network performance issues or peak performance times for network usage.

Problems: Choosing a DSL Service

Most DSL service providers offer more than one kind of DSL service. Depending on the location of your home or office, you may be able to choose among several different types of DSL connections. The term "xDSL" describes all the flavors of DSL available: ADSL (asymmetrical DSL), SDSL (symmetrical DSL), IDSL (ISDN DSL), HDSL (high-bit-rate DSL), VDSL (very high data rate DSL), and RDSL (rate-adaptive DSL). Most service providers offer ADSL or SDSL services. However as phone companies and service providers upgrade their phone lines, a wider range of DSL services may become available in the future.

The Many Faces of DSL

If you want to visualize network symmetry, imagine your DSL connection as a four-lane highway to the Internet. If you have three lanes moving traffic from the Internet to your local network, you will be less likely to experience network traffic congestion. However, if you want to send data out, you can expect slower speeds because there is only one lane capable of moving traffic from your local network to the Internet. This three- and one-lane scenario illustrates an asymmetrical network. If the highway had two lanes going in each direction, this example would illustrate a symmetrical network.

ADSL and SDSL are fundamentally different DSL services. If you spend most of your time surfing the web, choose an ADSL network. If you spend time both sending and receiving data, choose an SDSL service.

The best DSL connection is the fastest one. The closer your home or business is to the local phone company, the faster the DSL performance will be. The following list describes general types of DSL services.

Asymmetrical DSL (ADSL)

✦ Faster download time, with a slower data rate for uploading files to the network; an asymmetrical network data design

✦ Data rates: From 1.5–8 Mbps

✦ Pros and cons: Optimal for web surfing, downloading software, and checking e-mail; slow if you want to upload files to a server or send large (2 or more MB) e-mail attachments on this kind of network

Symmetrical DSL (SDSL)

✦ Fairly equal download and upload data rates

✦ Data rates: Up to 2.3 Mbps

✦ Pros and cons: Optimal for networks with a web or file server, as long as faster download times aren't required on the network

ISDN DSL (IDSL)

✦ Symmetrical transmission; usually offered as a replacement for ISDN services, or to homes that are beyond the ADSL or SDSL loops from the phone office

✦ Data rates: Up to 128–144 Kbps

✦ Pros and cons: An alternative to the faster DSL services; can be slightly more expensive

High-Bit Rate DSL (HDSL)

✦ A variation of SDSL; most commonly used to create a DSL network between a corporation and a customer via a phone company

✦ Data rates: Up to 2.3 Mbps

✦ Pros and cons: Fast, symmetrical network but requires two phone lines

Very High Data Rate DSL (VDSL)

✦ A newer implementation of DSL; designed to support very high data exchange rates between short distances

✦ Data rates: 51–55 Mbps

✦ Pros and cons: Faster network speeds, but not widely available.

Rate-Adaptive DSL (RDSL)

✦ Dynamically adjusts the rate at which signals can be transmitted, adjusting the delivery rate of data to match the signal transmission rate

✦ Data rates: From 640 Kbps to 2.2 Mbps downstream, to 272 Kbps to 1.008 Mbps upstream

✦ Pros and cons: Slightly slower than ADSL and SDSL

DSL-Lite or G.Lite

✦ Splitterless DSL; the phone company does not need to install a splitter in your home or business in order for a DSL service provider to install the DSL modem in your home or business

✦ Data rates: To 1.5 Mbps

✦ Pros and cons: Do not need to install a splitter on the copper phone line, only on non DSL phone lines in the home or office. Not available in all areas. This is a newer brand of DSL service.

Advantages and Disadvantages

The DSL service to which you subscribe can affect the way you build out your local network. For example, if you have an ADSL service, you probably won't want to set up a high-traffic server on your local network. However, if you plan to run a networked classroom, where servers are only needed on the local network, ADSL may be the service to get. Table 1-1 compares the advantages of the ADSL, SDSL, and IDSL services.

Matching Services with Network Usage Needs

If you're not sure how you might use a DSL service, consider the things you might do on your local network, as well as what you might do on the Internet. The following list describes some of the tasks or services you might want to take advantage of through your DSL service.

DSL Service	Advantages
ADSL	Multimedia web pages and file downloads
	Fastest one-way Internet access, up to 8 Mbps
SDSL	Faster upload performance
	Web and file server friendly
	Fastest two-way Internet access, up to 1.5 Mbps
IDSL	Internet access faster than a 56 Kbps modem
	Symmetrical upload and download speeds up to 144 Kbps

Table 1-1. Advantages of DSL Services

Local Network Tasks

✦ **Printing**   Share a USB or Ethernet printer with any computer on the local network

✦ **File sharing**   Access other computers over a peer-to-peer wireless connection or over Ethernet

✦ **Web hosting**   Set up a local intranet by adding a Web server or database to your local network

✦ **File server or mail server**   Set up a dedicated file server for backing up your computers; or set up a mail server, if you're running a small business on your local network

Internet Services

✦ **Virtual private network** (VPN)   Log in to a private, firewall-protected network via the Internet

✦ **Web surfing**   Visit millions of Web sites around the world using a web browser program

✦ **Web server**   Set up a dedicated web server on your local network and share it with the Internet

✦ **E-mail and chat**   Set up e-mail or chat with friends and family

NOTE

If you plan to add computers, printers, servers, or other devices to your home or office network within the next few years, you might want to plan connecting them to your DSL network. To account for these possible additions, plan your network to accommodate at least twice as much network traffic as you anticipate to have on the local network.

Location, Location, Location

The proximity of your home or business to the local phone office will most likely dictate which DSL services are available to you. In fact, before you can sign up for a DSL service, you need to find out whether your home or business is within the local phone office's DSL loop. If the signal can't reach your home over the copper line, the phone company won't install the splitters.

How Distance Affects Performance

The farther the phone line extends from the local phone office, the weaker the analog signal strength becomes. Conversely, the closer they are, the stronger the analog signal is likely to be between the two modems. Homes on the fringe of a 5.5 km range of the local phone office (or central office) will probably have a slower DSL connection speed, than homes located within 1 or 2 km of the Central Office(CO). Homes located beyond the 5.5 km radius are not eligible for DSL service. However, homes within the 5.5 km radius are eligible for DSL services. Sometimes you can use the physical proxmity of your home or office to the Central Office to gauge the speed of your DSL connection. However, the best to find out the fastest speed is to contact each service provider and compare the network connection speeds available from the DSL provider's service packages.

Regardless of proximity, a DSL service provider may restrict the speed of any of its network connections, depending on the type of service you choose. The DSL connection is a two-way exchange of analog signals. The DSL modem in your home or business must be able to communicate across the copper that originates from the phone office. Modems that are close in proximity, generally within 5.5 kilometers from the local phone office, benefit from faster network performance because the signal strength is less likely to deteriorate over short distances.

DSL Performance Compared to Modems

If you compare the slowest DSL service (IDSL) with a 56 Kbps modem, DSL performance is faster, hands down. The biggest advantage of using a traditional modem to connect to the Internet is that phone lines are everywhere. You can access the Internet in a hotel room, restaurant, or office using a traditional modem.

DSL is great if you want to add Internet access as you plan or put together a local network for your home or business. Some benefits of DSL service are 24-hour access to the Internet; faster networking speeds; compatibility with Ethernet and Transmission Control Protocol/ Internet Protocol (TCP/IP); and computer platforms that run Windows, Mac OS, Linux, or Unix.

Solutions: Comparing DSL to the Alternatives

Phone lines aren't the only high-bandwidth resources that have been adapted for Internet access. Cable lines and satellite broadcast services also provide many computers with access to the information super-highway. The following sections compare DSL with cable modems, traditional modems, and two-way satellite services.

Cable Modem Services

A popular runner-up broadband service to DSL is cable modem. If you already have a cable TV service, you are likely to have access to cable modem systems. Instead of using phone lines, cable modems rely on cable TV lines that go from your premises to the cable office to connect your home or office to the Internet.

Although cable broadband services rely on a modem router to put your home or office network on the cable network, the cable companies have a different infrastructure for connecting a cable network to the Internet. This difference in infrastructure results in a few differences in the way your computers access the Internet. For instance, most broadband cable services do not support web hosting. The local cable office swaps IP addresses to discourage would-be hackers from trying to access your computer's hard drive. Although the cable modem service is speedy, it can be a bumpy ride, requiring you to check your network software settings in order to refresh your Internet connection. Table 1-2 compares DSL to cable broadband services.

56 Kbps Modems

Traditional voice phone modems are good because phone lines are virtually everywhere. One pitfall of using a 56 Kbps modem is that you have to find the service provider's local dialup number if you want to connect a computer to the Internet. Also, if you dial into a modem that doesn't support 56 Kbps, or if the phone line has noise, the modems will re-train until they negotiate to a slower, reliable connection speed. Table 1-3 compares DSL to 56 Kbps modem services.

T1 Lines

Before broadband became a viable Internet service, most businesses paid a hefty fee to have a T1 network connection relayed into their office site. A computer network can access a full T1 line, or a fraction of a T1 line. A fractional T1 line reduces the network performance from the full speed of 1.5 Mbps to 384 or 256 Kbps per fractional allocation. Table 1-4 compares DSL to T1 services.

Two-Way Satellite

If you live in a remote area, two-way satellite dishes may be the Internet solution for you. Most two-way satellite services cost significantly more than cable or DSL broadband services. Satellite services rely on direct broadcast services (DBS) or digital satellite services (DSS). Each computer or local network may require a small satellite dish to be connected to it in order to access Internet services. The satellite dish must point in the southern direction, preferably from outdoors. Table 1-5 compares DSL to two-way satellite services.

Feature	DSL	Cable
Host	Local phone company	Cable head-end
Media	Phone lines	Cable TV lines
Modem	PPPoE, bridge, or router to the Internet	Router to the Internet
Web hosting	Depends on the type of DSL modem; may require an additional monthly fee or a change to your DSL service	No
Network expansion	Extend network with DHCP server, or pay cost per IP address	Pay cost per IP address
Network performance	144 Kbps (IDSL), or 1.5–8 Mbps	Up to 1.5 Mbps downstream, 300 Kbps upstream; performance depends on the number of neighbors accessing the cable service
Reliability	Location based; depends on phone-line quality	Depends on cable TV lines

Table 1-2.   DSL Versus Cable Broadband Services

Feature	DSL	56 Kbps Modem
Host	Local phone company or DSL service provider	Internet service provider
Media	Higher-bandwidth phone lines	Lower-bandwidth voice phone lines
Modem	PPPoE, bridge, or router to the Internet	Point-to-point connection to an ISP computer modem
Web hosting	Depends on the type of DSL modem; may require an additional monthly fee or a change to your DSL service	Bulletin board service
Network expansion	Extend network with DHCP server, or pay cost per IP address	With additional software, but slow network connection
Network performance	144 Kbps (IDSL), or 1.5–8 Mbps upload speed (ADSL) 128 Kbps download speed. Network speeds may vary depending on the type of DSL service you subscribe to.	48–52 Kbps
Reliability	Location based; depends on phone-line quality	Depends on phone-line quality

Table 1-3.   DSL Versus 56 Kbps Modem Services

Feature	DSL	T1
Host	Local phone company or DSL service provider	T1 service provider
Media	Phone lines	Dedicated network wired into your home or office
Modem	PPPoE, bridge, or router to the Internet	Bridge or router to the Internet
Web hosting	Depends on the type of DSL modem; may require an additional monthly fee or a change to your DSL service	Yes
Network expansion	Extend network with DHCP server, or pay cost per IP address	Yes, but setup may require additional hardware
Network performance	144 Kbps (IDSL), or 1.5–8 Mbps upload speed (ADSL) 128 Kbps download speed. Network speeds may vary depending on the type of DSL service you subscribe to.	Depends on network implementation; fractional T1 lines may have a network bandwidth of only 256 Kbps; a full T1 line will have a network bandwidth of 1.5 Mbps and can cost $700–$1,800 per month
Reliability	Location based; depends on phone line quality	Very reliable

Table 1-4. DSL Versus T1 Services

Feature	DSL	Satellite
Host	Local phone company or DSL service provider	Satellite service provider such as Telocity
Media	Phone lines	Satellite
Modem	PPPoE, bridge, or router to the Internet	Satellite dish
Web hosting	Depends on the type of DSL modem; may require an additional monthly fee or a change to your DSL service	No
Network expansion	Extend network with DHCP server, or pay cost per IP address	With addition of a DHCP server
Network performance	Download/upload 144 Kbps (IDSL), or 1.5–8 Mbps upload speed (ADSL) 128 Kbps download speed. Network speeds may vary depending on the type of DSL service you subscribe to.	300 Kbps or 600–1,500 Kbps, depending on the satellite service provider; some providers use a phone line for uploading data
Reliability	Location based; depends on phone-line quality	Depends on weather, sun spots, and clarity of southern exposure (i.e., if you have a hill blocking southern exposure, you won't be able to use a satellite dish)

Table 1-5.   DSL Versus Two-Way Satellite Services

Additional Resources

DSL is a great broadband solution if your home or business is close to a local phone office, and you want to add fast Internet access to your local home or business network. If DSL isn't available in your area, consider subscribing to a cable or a satellite Internet service provider. DSL is a scalable service. It can support small, medium, and large networks, which you'll learn more about in the next two chapters. To find out more about DSL, visit your DSL service provider's Web site, or go to the following URLs.

✦ cnet.com/internet/0-3762-7-2281939.html

✦ telecom.about.com

✦ www.clec-planet.com

✦ www.dslcenter.com

✦ www.dsl.com

✦ www.isg-telecom.com

✦ www.isg-telecom.com/usa_clecs.htm

✦ www.mysimon.com/ksrch/index.jhtml?c=root&kw=dsl&pgid=list

✦ www.paradyne.com

✦ www.zdnet.com/zdhelp/stories/main/0,5594,914908,00.html

Chapter 2

What Is a Network?

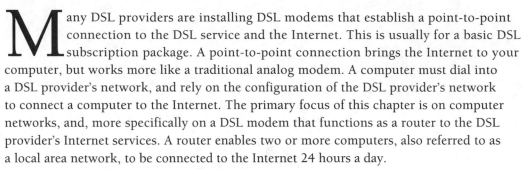

Many DSL providers are installing DSL modems that establish a point-to-point connection to the DSL service and the Internet. This is usually for a basic DSL subscription package. A point-to-point connection brings the Internet to your computer, but works more like a traditional analog modem. A computer must dial into a DSL provider's network, and rely on the configuration of the DSL provider's network to connect a computer to the Internet. The primary focus of this chapter is on computer networks, and, more specifically on a DSL modem that functions as a router to the DSL provider's Internet services. A router enables two or more computers, also referred to as a local area network, to be connected to the Internet 24 hours a day.

There are two aspects to a network: the physical wire layout, or topology, and the more conceptual Open System Interconnect reference model, which helps determine how network traffic flows among the physical components on the network. The physical layout of a network can follow several topologies: point-to-point, star, bus, ring, or mesh. Analog and DSL modem connections are good examples of point-to-point networks, where two computers define the connection.

The star, or hub-based Ethernet network is the most popular network topology. The hub is placed at the center of the network, and each computer is independently connected to it. If one computer loses its connection to the network, the other connected computers are not affected.

To create a star topology network, each computer must have an Ethernet network interface card (NIC) with a cable that connects to a central hub. The cable that connects each computer to the hub will most likely have an RJ-45 connector, which is similar to an RJ-11 telephone connector. Connecting two or more computers to the hub completes a minimum star network configuration.

Ethernet hubs, cables, and network cards for star networks are readily available and are generally more affordable to put together and maintain than a token ring or bus network topology. Bus and token ring topologies are explained in more detail in Chapter 3. Most of the network setup and troubleshooting examples in this book assume your network is configured with an Ethernet star network topology. The following list highlights some of the network concepts and technologies that will be described in this chapter.

- ✦ **Ethernet (802.3) standard**   A network standard defining the hardware and software interface for computers; supports 10 Base T, 100 Base T, or Gigabyte Base T

- ✦ **Network standards**   Specifications for how computers send and receive data over a network

- ✦ **Wireless (802.11b) standard**   A standard for wireless Ethernet, and TCP/IP network communications for computers; supports up to 11 Mbps

✦ **Twisted pair or coaxial cable**   A medium for connecting two computers with Ethernet cards; a Category 5 cable can support network speeds up to 100 Mbps or one gigabit per second (Gbps)

Basic Network Concepts

Each computer on a star network topology has an Ethernet card or chip set, and a connection to a hub. In addition to using an Ethernet cable to connect the hub to a DSL modem, a wired network uses RJ-45 connectors and cabling to connect each computer to an Ethernet port on a hub. You can also attach a wireless access point to the Ethernet hub if you want to enable computers with a wireless access card to connect to the Internet from your local network. This book discusses PCs and Mac computers, along with the most popular operating systems for these hardware platforms: Windows, Mac OS, and Linux. Each of these operating systems supports Ethernet and TCP/IP protocol standards, enabling any of these machines to act as a client or server on the network, as well as exchange data.

The Institute of Electrical and Electronics Engineers (IEEE) defines many hardware and software standards for the computer and electronics industry. This organization, comprised of engineers, scientists, and students, was created in 1963. It is well known for the IEEE 802 standards for local area networks (LANs), which help hardware and software developers create products that enable computers to work with network cables, protocols, and other network devices.

Ethernet was designed by Bob Metcalfe in 1973 when he worked at Xerox Parc research labs. The IEEE organization, which consists of an international group of scientists, companies, and organizations, continued to work with Ethernet and created the 802.3 standard for Ethernet, which is a variation of Xerox Parc's original design. The 802.5 standard defines token ring networks. In addition to all the network hardware standards, the International Standards Organization (ISO) adopted the Open System Interconnect (OSI) reference model for implementing network protocols. As discussed in Chapter 1, the model has seven layers of protocols, each dependent upon the adjacent one, that enable computers to communicate with each other over a network.

A Few Networking Terms

Each computer and network device must follow a certain set of hardware and software rules in order to communicate data over a network. Many of these rules are defined as protocols, which, in turn, are organized according to the OSI model. The ISO manages the OSI model. Many hardware and software networking products also follow IEEE 802 standards. The use of these standards makes it possible for you to connect a PC or Macintosh computer to your home or office DSL network, in addition to other computers on the Internet.

Network-Related Organizations

A few organizations are responsible for bringing network technology into reality. Don't be misled by the simplicity of the names or number of organizations in the following list. Each one is responsible for working with numerous individuals and businesses and a wide spectrum of network issues, designs, and implementations.

✦ **DARPA**   An acronym for the Defense Advanced Research Projects Agency. An organization responsible for the research programs that eventually led to the development of TCP/IP, routers, and other network technologies.

✦ **International Standards Organization (ISO)**   Formed in 1946, this international organization includes members of large organizations, such as ANSI (American National Standards Institute), and is responsible for defining computer standards, such as the OSI standard.

✦ **Institute of Electrical and Electronics Engineers (IEEE)**   Pronounced "Eye-triple-E." An organization was formed to develop standards for the computer and electronics industry. The IEEE charges a fee to individuals who want to obtain copies of these detailed standards. Most of the information for a standard is geared to hardware designers, electrical engineers, software developers, and technicians.

✦ **Internet Assigned Number Authority (IANA)**   This organization is responsible for providing domain name, protocol assignment, and IP address services for the Internet.

Common Network Terms and Protocols

The standards created by network and computer industry organizations have helped the Internet succeed by enabling Windows, Mac OS, and Linux computers to communicate with each other over a network. The standards committees work with hardware and software vendors such as Apple and Microsoft to develop computer hardware and software that can communicate with each other's network protocols and network hardware connected to each network topology. The following terms will be discussed in more detail in this chapter.

✦ **Protocol**   In order for different computers to communicate with each other, they use a common set of communications and networking rules. Protocols used by network hardware and software include IP (Internet Protocol), TCP (Transmission Control Protocol), and HTTP (Hypertext Transfer Protocol).

✦ **802.3**   The IEEE standard for Ethernet networks.

+ **802.11**   The IEEE standard for wireless networks.

+ **Media Access Control (MAC)**   A unique ID number for the network interface card that is used to identify a computer on the local network.

+ **Link Layer Control (LLC)**   Responsible for delivering network data to its destination and verifying that it has reached its destination.

+ **Address Resolution Protocol (ARP)**   A protocol that translates the MAC address of a networked computer to an IP address.

+ **Transmission Control Protocol (TCP)**   A protocol that works with the Internet Protocol (IP) to break up and transmit packets between a point-to-point connection (your computer and the DSL provider's) or between two routers (your DSL modem and the DSL provider's router).

+ **Internet Protocol (IP)**   A network protocol that works with the TCP protocol to track Internet addresses and network nodes, and is responsible for routing incoming and outgoing messages over the Internet.

+ **IPX**   A network protocol created by NetWare. This network protocol will not be covered in this book.

+ **NetBEUI**   A network protocol used by Microsoft's Windows operating systems primarily to share files on a Windows 2000 Professional computer with other Windows computers.

+ **IP address**   Four sets of numbers, grouped as 000.000.000.000, represents the address used by the IP protocol to identify a network device connected to the network. Each network device has its own unique IP address.

+ **Virtual private network (VPN)**   An Internet-connected network that can be accessed via network tunneling protocols; commonly used to allow telecommuters to access their corporate networks over the Internet.

What Is a Node?

In a star network topology, a node is a computer, printer, or other device that contains an Ethernet card and cable that is directly connected to a central hub. A node can process and redistribute network data, or begin or end network data transmission to other nodes. A client node is a computer running a Windows, Mac OS, or Linux operating system with a browser or FTP (File Transfer Protocol) client application. Software on the client node is designed to connect to a server on the network. A server node can run the server versions of the Windows NT, Windows 2000, or Mac OS X operating systems, and is capable of providing network services, such as file sharing or web sharing to client nodes. Most networks consist of client and server nodes, shown in the top portion of Figure 2-1. You can also set up a peer-to-peer network in your home or office; however, a client-server

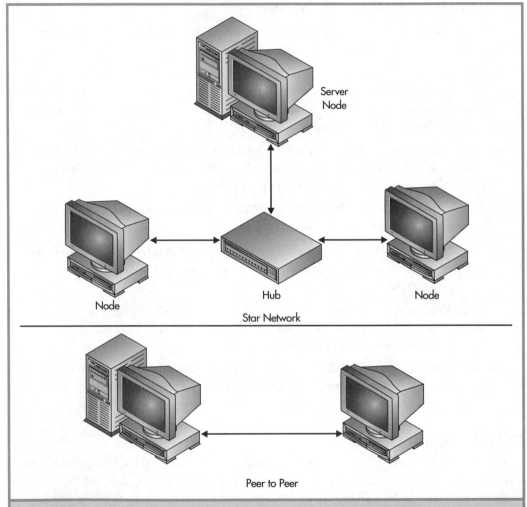

Figure 2-1. Client-server networks consist of two or more nodes connected to the same network: at least one client, and at least one server. Peer-to-peer networks enable two workstation computers to act as both client and server.

network provides full-time access to files, enables all network users to access and share files on a single server, and makes it easier to perform backup and troubleshooting procedures.

A client-server network consists of a group of devices, or nodes connected to a central hub. You can set up one server on a local network and create user accounts to enable several clients to access it simultaneously over the network. The server remains powered on and connected to the network 24 hours a day. This type of network directs network traffic toward the server and permits each client connected to the network to access a public or personal directory of files.

Peer-to-peer networks consist of two or more workstations capable of providing some network services, as well as accessing other services on the network. For example, a network of Windows computers can activate each computer's file-sharing feature. Any Windows computer can log in to any other client, as long as a valid login and password are used to access each computer. A peer-to-peer network is convenient, as long as you don't have to quickly access files on another computer on the network. However, because each computer may not always be connected to the network it can be difficult to create backups and to grow a peer-to-peer network.

How Network Data Moves Between Computer Nodes

Network traffic usually travels between client and server nodes on the network. A computer server is designed to allow multiple clients to connect to it. For example, when you view a web page, the pages are stored on a web server. The client, running a browser, loads the domain name, or universal resource locator (URL) from the web server. The home page is sent from the web server to the client, which displays the home page in the browser window. If you click a link in the browser, the web server will send the client the URL and web page information for the link. While your computer client is connected to the web server, other clients can be connected to the server at the same time.

SURVIVAL TIP

Windows and Mac OS computers have a file-sharing feature that enables other Windows or Macintosh computers to connect to them and share files over the network. This type of connection, where there is no clear client or server, is called a peer-to-peer network. To find out more about peer-to-peer networks, see Chapter 3.

A Closer Look at Ethernet Connections   In order for a client computer to communicate with a server, each computer must have a network interface card (NIC). Your PC or Macintosh computer will probably have some brand of Ethernet NIC installed along with

Ethernet software drivers. The Ethernet NIC and connected cables define the physical connection between two computers on a network. Most of the current model PCs and Macs, have an Ethernet chip set built into the logic board. In addition to network hardware, you also need software to send, receive, and check the data that is sent across the network.

A standard RJ-45 Ethernet cable has the same wiring on each end of the connector. You can connect either end into either a computer's NIC or an Ethernet hub. A crossover cable is a specially wired Ethernet cable that enables you to directly connect two computers. Table 2-1 shows you how to connect the Category 5 wires to an Ethernet connector. Notice that both ends of the cable have the same color of wiring. If you examine both ends of an Ethernet cable, you can see the arrangement of the colored wires that define the Ethernet connection. An RJ-11 telephone connector is similar, except that the white orange/orange wires occupy Slots 3 and 6, and the white green/ green wires occupy Slots 1 and 2. The Ethernet connectors on a hub are wired so that you can use a regular Ethernet cable to connect a computer to an RJ-45 port on the hub. However, the Ethernet connector on the hub is wired a little differently than on a computer.

NOTE   A crossover Ethernet cable can use Category 5 (CAT 5) wiring as a regular Ethernet cable. Eight strands of wiring are routed so that the first six connectors on the right end of the cable reverse the transmit and receive wires from the left side of the cable.

A crossover cable also uses an RJ-45 connector as an Ethernet cable, except the wires for transmitting data are mapped to the wires for receiving data on the opposite end of the cable. A crossover cable can be used to establish a direct Ethernet connection between two computers, preferably running the same operating system, such as Windows or Mac OS. Table 2-2 shows how the transmit and receive wires are reversed on one end of the crossover cable in order to create the special Ethernet connection. To create the network connection, first connect one end of the crossover to the Ethernet port on one computer, and then connect the other end to the second computer. Adjust the network settings on each computer to use Ethernet, and then log one computer to the other to access files or move files between the computers.

Wire Color	Left Connector Pin/Function	Right Connector Pin
White orange	1 transmit +	1
Orange	2 transmit −	2
White green	3 receive +	3
Blue	4	4
White blue	5	5
Green	6 receive −	6
White brown	7	7
Brown	8	8

Table 2-1. RJ-45 Ethernet Cable Wiring Schematic

Wire Color	Left Connector Pin/Function	Right Connector Pin
White orange	1 transmit +	3
Orange	2 transmit −	6
White green	3 receive +	1
Blue	4	4
White blue	5	5
Green	6 receive −	2
White brown	7	7
Brown	8	8

Table 2-2. RJ-45 Ethernet Crossover Cable Wiring Schematic

The Ethernet cable routes data between computers on your local network, as well as data broadcast from the DSL modem. The type of DSL service can determine how much and how quickly data can be sent from or to your local network. Most networks have a half-duplex configuration, in which bi-directional network traffic is supported but not concurrent. This behavior is similar to the way most speaker phones function. A full-duplex connection enables simultaneous transmission in both directions. Full-duplex connections function best on four-wire circuits, which is how long distance calls are transmitted. Most local lines use two-wire circuits, which cannot reliably manage a full-duplex configuration, and function best in half-duplex mode.

NOTE

Each computer's hard disk is responsible for storing the operating system and network applications that process all the network data that the computer sends and receives. Although it's not a requirement, server nodes may be configured to support faster network access or create a redundant set of information on the server. A server node should have a considerably larger hard drive than the client computers that will be connecting to it. The larger the hard drive, the more information that can be stored on the computer.

A MAC Address Becomes an IP Address   Once you have connected the physical network components, you can configure the computer's operating system network settings to connect to the local network. Most of the settings you will need to work with do not correspond directly to any of the layers in the OSI reference model. The following sections explain how a computer sends and receives data to a computer located on a different network.

The Ethernet card and cable define the physical layer of the OSI standard. Each card has a unique MAC address, which is part of the Data Link layer. The Link Layer Control, or LLC is also a part of the Data Link layer and is responsible for ensuring that data reaches its destination on the network. The Data Link layer works with the Network, Transport, Session, Presentation, and Application layers to establish the identity of the computer on the network, break data into packets, and send it to another computer on the network. Figure 2-3 illustrates how a MAC address interacts with the router on a local network, but gets translated to an IP address in order to send data outside the local network. The MAC address information is cached by the Address Resolution Protocol (ARP).

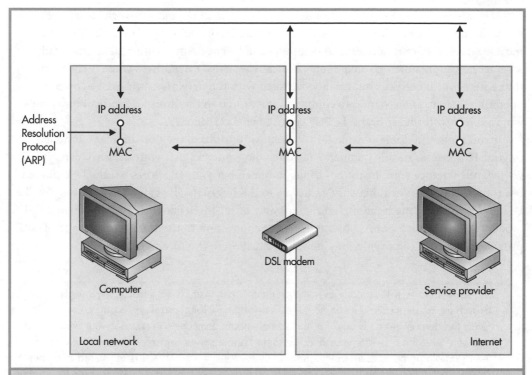

Figure 2-3.   When data is sent from a local network to another network on the
Internet, the Address Resolution Protocol translates the MAC address
into an IP address.

A Closer Look at Internet Protocols   An IP address follows the format of aaa.bbb.ccc.ddd,
where each group of a, b, c, or d can be one to three digits between the values of 0 and 255.
The IP address is one of several network identification settings your computer needs in order
to be properly connected to the network. These settings enable your computer to interact
with TCP/IP protocols on the network.

The Internet Protocol (IP) enables one computer to exchange data with another computer
that supports the IP protocol on a network. The Transmission Control Protocol (TCP) is
responsible for setting up a connection and transporting data between two computers. TCP
uses IP to process data sent over the network. In order for a computer to connect to the
Internet, it must have a unique IP address.

The Internet Protocol works with the Physical, Data Link, and Network layers to define the structure of network addresses. A network address enables your computer to be recognized on different networks. A computer can be configured with a static (manually assigned) IP address or a dynamic (automatically assigned) IP address when it connects to the network. IP address information is stored with the network settings of a computer's operating system. On a Windows computer, it is stored in the Internet Protocol Properties window. You will find it in the TCP/IP control panel on Mac OS.

If you register a domain name for the Web, you can have the domain name assigned to your IP address. In this manner, someone who wants to visit your network can type www.flatfishfactory.com, instead of trying to remember your IP address. If the DSL modem is a router, it is your local network's gateway to the Internet. The gateway IP address for the DSL modem is also the IP address for your home or business network on the Internet. DSL modems that rely on a point-to-point or bridge connection to the Internet rely on the DSL provider's network to provide the gateway connection to the Internet.

NOTE

If you want to register a domain name on the Internet, visit a web site like www.register.com. Search for an available domain name; then decide how long you want to pay to own the name. Once the domain name is paid for, the domain name provider can sponsor your web site, or you can send the provider your IP address and name server information so that it can add your domain name to its list of Internet addresses. After your web site is registered and your IP address is configured on its name servers, wait a few weeks for your domain name to circulate around the network. Once your domain name is regiestered, browsers on the Internet can access your web site.

Network Addressing

Now that some of the behind-the-scenes networking basics have been explained, along with some of the network hardware and computer-related setup options, the following sections will look at how IP addresses can be assigned to each computer connected to a local network. You can choose a static IP address for each computer, or set up a DHCP (Dynamic Host Configuration Protocol) address server that gives each computer a unique IP address as it connects to the local network. There are pros and cons to both types of IP addressing; however, dynamic addressing is the fastest way for you to add a new computer to the network.

Static IP Addressing

Static IP addresses are also called fixed IP addresses. For example, 208.109.80.32 might be an IP address for a computer on your local network. Your DSL service provider will usually give you one static IP address as part of the basic DSL package. Most DSL service providers allow you to purchase additional static IP addresses for a nominal fee. Each static address can be accessed through the gateway via the Internet. This is probably the best feature of using a static IP address; the IP address for a particular computer does not change as long as it's powered on and connected to the network. Static IP addresses can also limit how many computers can be connected to your local network at the same time.

A DSL service provider can assign you one or more static IP addresses for each computer on your local network. As mentioned earlier, each network address follows the 000.000.000.000 format, where 000 is a number between 0 and 255. You must type in each network address exactly as it appears on your account information; otherwise, your computer will not be able to access the Internet via your DSL modem.

To add a static IP address to a Windows 2000 computer, perform the following steps.

✦ Open the Network and Dial-Up Connections window.

✦ Next, open the Properties window for the network interface card on your computer.

✦ Select Internet Protocol, and then click the Properties button in the General components window.

✦ Click the Use the Following IP Address radio button. Then, type the following information in the Internet Protocol Properties window.

  ✦ **IP Address**   The fixed IP address of your computer

  ✦ **Subnet Mask**   The network mask for your computer

  ✦ **Default Gateway**   The IP address of the DSL router or DSL service provider

  ✦ **DNS Server**   One or two IP addresses for the DSL service provider's name servers

In addition to the IP addressing just listed, Windows computers require the following information in order to determine whether they can access the network.

✦ **Host**   The machine name of your computer

✦ **Domain**   The domain of your Windows computer. This information may need to match the domain name of the network to which you want to connect.

✦ **Binding**   The identity of the network interface card on your network that is using the Internet Protocol

✦ **WINS**   The IP address of the Windows name server, if one is used on your local network

✦ **Proxy**   This setting is configured in a browser program. If you have a proxy server running on your local network, you need to set up your browser to access it

A Brief Look at Subnets

A network mask enables you to set up a secondary network on your local network. Each network mask can map to computers connected to the larger local network. The subnet mask setting in the Internet Protocol enables you to configure your computer to connect to a particular network mask. A network mask is analogous to a local area network, in the same way that a local area network is analogous to the Internet. In most cases, you will use the subnet mask IP address provided by your DSL service provider. If you have an IP address of 108.55.10.1, a subnet mask of 255.255.255.0 changes the IP address to 108.55.10 and a node number of 1. Setting the subnet mask to 255.0.0.0 results in a network number of 108 and a node number of 55.10.1. Each computer connected to the local network must use the same network mask configuration in order to make the secondary network valid.

Dynamic Addressing

You can set up a DHCP server to distribute IP addresses on a local network. You can install a DHCP server application on a computer on your local area network; or, if your DSL has this capability, you can configure your DSL modem to assign IP addresses to computers on your local network. Each time a computer connects to the local network, the computer receives a different IP number. For example, an IP address assigned by a DHCP server to a computer might be 10.1.1.1. You can designate which IP numbers to use with the DHCP addresses and use the DHCP server to limit how many clients can access your local network by limiting the number of available addresses in the DHCP server program.

NOTE

IP addresses for a computer connected to a network use numbers between 0 and 255. Zero represents the current host, and 255 usually represents the value for broadcasting to all hosts on the network.

Virtual Private Networks

A virtual private network (VPN) is a term used to describe the network technology that enables you to telecommute to your corporate network over a DSL Internet connection. A virtual private network uses one of several possible network tunneling protocols to establish a connection between the two networks. Once a computer on your network has logged into a virtual private network, it behaves like a computer that is connected to that type of network. You can check your e-mail, view intranet web pages, and work from your home computer as if you were working from your corporate office computer.

Network Address Translators (NAT)

If you try to count the number of computers on the Internet and all the possible combinations of IP addresses, you may discover that there aren't enough IP addresses to support infinite growth of the Internet. A network address translator (NAT) is an RFC (Request For Comment) 1631 specification and is frequently bundled with DHCP servers to create a dynamic NAT solution. This works well for web surfing and checking e-mail, but can be problematic if your computer needs to connect to a virtual private network.

NOTE RFC is an acronym for Request For Comment. This term refers to a type of document that is defined and processed by the IETF. These documents can be proposals, research results, or official protocol specifications, such as TCP/IP. Once the members of the IETF agree upon a set of documents, the Internet Architecture Board (IAB) creates a permanent archive of each RFC.

There are four kinds of NAT routers: static, dynamic, overloading, and overlapping. Overloading is also known as port address translation (PAT) and enables multiple IP addresses to be mapped to one IP address. Overlapping NAT translates unregistered IP addresses into registered ones as data is sent out of or received into the network. A lookup table may need to be created to determine which addresses to substitute for other addresses. Static NAT works similarly, except that a registered IP address is mapped to an unregistered IP address, enabling the computer to be accessed through the DSL modem from another network.

Network Hardware Alternatives

As the number of computers and small networks grows in your office, you may need to purchase additional star hubs to add a new set of computers to your network. Depending on the type of network traffic that will be crossing your network, you may want to consider adding a network switch to reduce network traffic, or a network repeater to strengthen the modulated signal sent across your home or business network.

Some network hardware, such as hubs, can be replaced by switches. Hubs are located at the center of the network and propagate signals across network modes. They do not process packets, whereas switches are capable of isolating port traffic and buffering packets of data to specific network ports, minimizing network traffic.

Moving Data Over an Ethernet Network

Most newer desktop or laptop computers have built-in Ethernet cards. In order to create a proper physical connection from an Ethernet card to a network, you will need to purchase twisted-pair, or possibly coaxial cable, to connect the computer to a network. Purchase a cable that matches the maximum supported speed of the Ethernet card. Many computers offer more than one Ethernet networking solution, depending on how you want to wire your home or business office.

NOTE

Some star hubs have a combination of RJ-45 ports and a coaxial cable connector. Coaxial cable is more commonly used to create a bus topology network. Although you can connect a bus topology network to a star hub, try to preserve the star topology and only attach a single device, such as a printer or computer to the coaxial connector on a star hub.

Almost all Ethernet cards support, at a minimum, 10 Base T Ethernet. Faster cards support 100 Base T or Gigabyte Base T. The IEEE 802.3 standard defines 10 Base T as a twisted-pair wire that supports a 10 megabits per second (Mbps) data transfer rate. The 10 refers to the transmission speed (10 Mbps). Base represents the baseband signaling. In this case, it means Ethernet signals are transmitted in the 10 Base T medium. Finally, the T represents the twisted-pair wiring for the cable that connects an Ethernet card to a network. Ethernet cards can also be connected to a network using media such as fiber-optic cable (10 Base F), thick wire (10 Base 5), or broadband coaxial cable (10 Base 36). In order to take full advantage of the faster Ethernet cards, each card must be connected to a hub and cables that also support 100 or Gigabit Base T; otherwise, the slower 10 Base T data transfer rate will be used to transmit data on the network.

The ANSI/EIA (American National Standards Institute/ Electronic Industries Association) defines standards for many computer components, including cabling categories, also known as CATs. There are five categories of wiring. Category one (CAT 1) supports less than 1 Mbps and is most commonly used in RJ-11 phone-line connectors. The maximum supported throughput rate for each category of cable increases along with each category number. For example, CAT 3 supports 16 Mbps, or 10 Base T Ethernet. Category 5 (CAT 5) supports up to 100 Mbps, or 100 Base T cards. RJ-45 connectors are the standard connectors used to connect Category 5 cables to Ethernet cards.

In addition to the hardware requirements for constructing an Ethernet network, several software settings need to be customized on each computer on the network. Windows, Macs, and Linux operating systems all install Ethernet software drivers, TCP/IP, and other networking software as part of their default, or typical installation options. However, setting up and running each platform will be covered in more detail in Parts II and III of this book.

Operating Systems, Ethernet, and Driver Software

In order to set up an Ethernet card in a computer, you need to install an Ethernet card into the PC box. The operating system installed on the computer's hard drive may already have an Ethernet driver available for the Ethernet card. For example, most Macintosh computers have an Ethernet port built into the logic board. When the Macintosh operating system (Mac OS) is installed onto the computer, the OS installs the Ethernet driver, plus any networking software, such as Open Transport and AppleTalk, so that programs installed on the computer can access the network. Linux and Windows install similar network software and Ethernet drivers.

If you have upgraded a PC or Mac with an Ethernet card, you can download software for the Ethernet card from the vendor's site. Most Ethernet cards are bundled with Windows Ethernet drivers. After you have installed the networking software for the card and the computer's operating system, you can install network applications, such as a browser or e-mail application.

Setting Up Ethernet on a Computer

Each computer will need each of the following hardware or software components in order to connect to an Ethernet network.

✦ **Ethernet card**   This network interface card may be a built-in Ethernet port, a PCI card, USB-to-Ethernet adapter, or wireless PC card installed on the computer.

✦ **Ethernet cables**   Cables are used to connect the Ethernet card to a hub on a star network or directly to a DSL modem's Ethernet port.

✦ **Software drivers**   You will need to install software for the Ethernet card so that the operating system and applications on the computer can communicate with the card, and eventually the network.

✦ **Operating system software**   An operating system manages your computer's hardware, as well as your network connection. You can install Windows or Linux for X86 on a PC, or install Mac OS X, Mac OS 9, or Linux for Power PC on a Macintosh computer.

✦ **Network application**   A browser is the most popular Internet application. You can also run network tools, chat, or instant messaging programs on your networked computer.

A Closer Look at Ethernet Frames

When data is transmitted in an Ethernet packet, each network device reformats the transmitted data with information about where the packet originated on the network, and where it is going. For example, when your computer wants to load a web page on a web server, the browser sends its IP address to the web server.

First, the browser uses TCP to format the URL, and then hands it off to the operating system. The operating system formats the TCP message with the IP address (a unique 32-bit number) of the computer and target. The IP protocol also breaks up the data into smaller IP packets that can be transmitted over the network to the target computer. Each packet is responsible for finding its target on the network. Before the data is sent out to the network (along CAT 5 cables like the ones shown in Figure 2-4), the Ethernet card adds its packet information to the data using a protocol called CSMA/CD (Carrier Sense Multiple Access/ Collision Detect).

Each block of data transmitted over the Ethernet is formatted as a frame. The first 12 bytes of each frame contain the destination (6 bytes) and source address (6 bytes). The operating system or an application can customize the frame information. The remaining frame information indicates how much data is in the transmission. Table 2-3 shows how a TCP/IP Ethernet frame is divided.

Before the data is sent within a local network, the protocol checks the connecting cable to determine whether other nodes are sending data. If the connection appears to be idle, the data is sent over the network. The web server receives the Ethernet message. In some cases, the DSL modem, acting as a router, will disassemble the frame and packet data instead of waiting for the computer to do so. In any case, the web server can disassemble the Ethernet frame and IP information at the operating system level. TCP reassembles the packets created by IP. Then, it hands off the restored data information to the web server, which reads the rest of the data transmission and notifies the source computer that the message is being received.

Figure 2-4. Ethernet devices can work with either coaxial cable or CAT 5 twisted-pair cable.

Ethernet Datalink Preamble	Destinati on MAC Address	Source MAC Address	Ether Type	Data (optional)	PAD (optional)	Frame Check Sequence	Extension (optional)
8 bytes	6 bytes	6 bytes	2 bytes Length and Type may vary depending on the contents of the first byte of the EtherType	46 to 1,500 bytes		4 bytes	

Table 2-3. An Ethernet Frame

Once the web server reads the URL, it sends the HTML page to the client's IP address, formatting the data with TCP. The HTML page is formatted using the TCP and IP protocols, and then formatted once more with the Ethernet protocol. The following lists summarize how data is transmitted between two computers on a network.

Ethertype Field

The Ethertype field consists of 2 bytes, or two octets of information, which can have one of two possible meanings. Think of the term meanings, as a special kind of definition. The contents of the first octet of the Ethertype field helps determine the contents of the Ethernet frame.

The first possible meaning is based on the size of the MAC client data field. The first octet helps determine the length and type of the subsequent contents of the Ethernet frame. If the first octet is the maximum size of the MAC client data field, the Length/Type field indicates the number of MAC client data octets contained in the remaining data fields of the frame.

The second possible meaning relies on the field value being greater than or equal to 1536 decimal. If the value of the first octet is greater than or equal to 1536, the Length/Type field indicates the nature of the MAC client protocol and the Length and Type interpretations of this first octet are incompatible (mutually exclusive).

What does this all mean? The contents of an Ethernet frame are very specific. In order for data to be transmitted over a network, each piece of information sent over the network must meet particular criteria—otherwise, the data will not be capable of being processed between each network device.

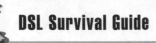
Data Sent from Computer A

✦ Create an e-mail message on computer A.

✦ Type in the e-mail address for computer B and send the e-mail.

✦ The e-mail program formats the message using TCP, and then hands it off to the operating system.

✦ The operating system adds the IP address information for the source computer and sends the data to the target computer on the network.

✦ The Ethernet card receives the message and formats the message as frames, checking the network connection before transmitting the data over the network.

Data Received by Computer B

✦ The Ethernet card on computer B, a mail server, receives a message. It disassembles the Ethernet frames to check the IP information for the message.

✦ The data is received by the operating system. The protocol data is reassembled into the original files sent by computer A.

✦ The mail server program formats the data into a message and stores it in the mail queue for the recipient e-mail account on the mail server.

Data Received by Computer C

✦ An e-mail program starts on Computer C, which is on the same network as Computer B. Computer C logs into Computer B using the same e-mail account as Computer A.

✦ Computer B uses TCP to format the message and hands it off to the operating system, which adds the IP address information for Computer C.

✦ The Ethernet card on Computer C receives the message as frames and passes the data to the operating system to reassemble the network data into its original message.

An Introduction to the TCP/IP Protocol Suite

Several network protocols are responsible for managing communications across networks. These protocols are collectively recognized as the TCP/IP protocol suite. Four layers define the protocols in the TCP/IP protocol suite: the Application, Transport, Network, and Link layers. Starting from the bottom, the device driver and interface card make up the Link layer. Next, the Network layer contains the IP and ICMP (Internet Control Message Protocol).

The UPD (User Data Protocol) and TCP round out the Transport layer. The following list contains a short description of the protocols in the Link, Network, and Transport layers. The Application protocols are listed in the following section.

◆ **ARP**   The Address Resolution Protocol translates the MAC address for each local network device into an IP address and caches the data to each computer.

◆ **IP**   The Internet Protocol is responsible for packaging, addressing, and delivering network data.

◆ **ICMP**   The Internet Control Message Protocol handles error messages, problem reports, and maintenance tasks for the network protocols.

◆ **UDP**   The User Datagram Protocol is a connectionless protocol used to transport data over a network.

◆ **TCP**   The Transmission Control Protocol is a connection-based protocol that works with the Internet Protocol to transport data over a network.

Computers that provide network services, such as a web server or mail server, support an additional set of protocols that must also be running on the client computer. In addition to being able to process protocols, each client and server computer must have access to a name resolution server and, in some cases, a proxy server on the local network. These servers enable the computers on a local network to locate other computers connected to the Internet.

The following list contains a brief description of some common server protocols. In order for a client computer to access a particular network service, the application on the client must be configured to log in to each server with a valid account. The client computer must also be running a compatible version of the server's HTTP, FTP, or other network protocol in order to successfully communicate with the server and establish a connection.

◆ **HTTP**   The Hypertext Transfer Protocol is used by web servers to communicate with client computers running an HTTP-compliant browser application.

◆ **FTP**   The File Transfer Protocol is used by FTP servers and enables client computers to upload and download files to a file server.

◆ **Telnet**   A protocol and a command-line application that provides terminal emulation services on a server and enables client computers to log into a server over a network connection.

◆ **SMTP**   The Simple Mail Transfer Protocol is used to send electronic mail over a network.

✦ **POP3**   The Post Office Protocol is commonly used with POP mail servers to download e-mail to a client.

✦ **IMAP**   The Interactive Mail Access Protocol is an alternative to POP. IMAP enables more than one client computer to access mail and mail settings for a single e-mail account. This works great if you have a laptop and a desktop computer and want to read your e-mail without having to update which messages you have read or not read.

Monitoring Network Traffic

Although Ethernet cards in PCI or PC card form are more or less standardized, not all computers have expansion slots. For example, some computers or Internet terminals may only have a USB port available for network expansion. USB-to-Ethernet adapters are available for PCs and Macs. However, a USB port can only sustain a maximum of 7 Mbps, which is almost half the bandwidth (speed) of a 10 Mbps 10 Base T Ethernet card. Slower network connections can slow network traffic, but they are only noticeable when overall network performance is slow.

If you're responsible for determining what kinds of devices can access your network, be sure to identify slower network nodes, as well as faster ones. Knowing the network capabilities of the devices connected to your network can help you troubleshoot network problems. The following list summarizes a few things to plan for regarding network traffic and design.

✦ **Hardware**   The more reliable the computer and network hardware you use, the more stable and reliable your network performance will be. The hard drive, network card, and cables for each computer must all work properly in order for other computers to work properly on the network. If one computer continually fails by rebooting or crashing while connected to the network, consider removing it from the network or replacing it with a different computer.

✦ **Programs**   Some network programs enable you to monitor network traffic and failed packets sent and received by the program. These programs can help isolate network problems.

✦ **Network planning**   The physical placement of nodes on the network can impact network performance and Internet access. Avoid placing network cable or wiring near sources of interference. For example, you don't want people tripping over network cables, and you don't want to place a network cable near other potential sources of interference.

One way to monitor network traffic is to set up a dedicated computer on your local network. You can purchase and install applications that enable a computer to monitor network traffic and generate reports, or capture a snapshot of data at regular intervals. Many network administrators rely on feedback from those who access or use the network to gather information about potential network problems or system failures.

SURVIVAL TIP

Setting up a network is easy once you've connected a few computers. To find out more about how to configure Mac OS, Windows, or Linux for your DSL network, see Part II.

Networks and Computer Platforms

Connecting a computer, printer, or other device to a network is relatively straightforward, especially if you have already set up a local area network in your home. That is, one that is not connected to the Internet. Most of the popular Ethernet cards, cables, and software are relatively inexpensive. Although most Ethernet cards available today work with the most recent Windows, Mac, or Linux operating systems, it is possible to purchase an 802.3-compliant Ethernet card that does not fit into a PCI card slot, or does not have a compatible Ethernet driver for Windows, Mac, or Linux. Be sure to review the software requirements for an Ethernet card before purchasing one for your computer.

The more time-consuming tasks related to setting up and running networks have to do with each computer's IP address configuration and the applications that run on it. Linux, Windows, and Mac OS have control panel settings that enable you to configure a computer for a network. These network settings can vary depending on what kinds of network services you want your computer to access on the local network, Internet, or virtual private network.

Before you can exchange data with network servers, you need to determine whether a computer needs a static IP address or a dynamic IP address. Both kinds of addresses use the same format. For example, 155.209.85.31 may be used as a static or dynamic IP address on a network.

Static IP addresses remain the same on the computer, no matter how many times you power it off or move it to a different physical location on the network. Dynamic IP addresses are allocated by a DHCP server on the network. Whenever a computer powers on or wakes from sleep, the DHCP server checks to see whether that computer's software is expecting an IP address. If so, the DHCP server assigns an IP address to the computer. You can configure a DHCP server to distribute an unlimited or a fixed number of network addresses.

Each computer must have a unique IP address; otherwise, the router for the local network will not know where to route network packets over the network. This can result

in unnecessary network traffic and slower network performance. Speaking of traffic, most network-bound applications, such as a browser, perform one or more of the following network tasks.

◆ **Receive data** A browser can receive data, such as a web page or a file you want to download from a web server.

◆ **Send data** A browser can communicate with a web server to load a web page, or send data between the web server and your client computer over the network.

◆ **Render HTML information** Each web page uses the HTML language to display text or images in a browser window. A browser, such as AOL's Netscape Navigator, or Micorosft's Internet Explorer, can display text, and if the browser is configured to display these additional items, graphics and animation.

◆ **Interpret JavaScript code** Netscape and Internet Explorer, as well as most browser programs, have an interpreted language, JavaScript, built into them. JavaScript enables a web page to perform some simple tasks, such as enable a button to contain a link and roll over to another web page.

◆ **Show HTML source code** Depending on how a Web page is put together, you may or may not be able to view all the source code for that page in a browser window.

◆ **Provide access to e-mail and news groups** Some browsers, such as Netscape Communicator, build e-mail, and newsgroup access into the browser program.

◆ **Enable additional browser languages** There are many Web-related languages that a web page may use when loaded in a browser window. PHP (Hypertext preprocessor) and Perl (Practical Extraction and Report Language) are interpreted languages that can be installed on a Web server to enhance the capabilities of an HTML web page. Java is a programming language that is compiled to create applets that can run on web pages.

In addition to browser applications, you can use browser editing applications like Microsoft FrontPage or Macromedia Dreamweaver to create web pages that can point to files stored on the web server. You can set up a web server on your local network and share it with the Internet. If you don't want file downloads to slow down the performance of your web server, you can set up a second computer on your network dedicated to storing files for your web server. The best part of putting together a network is that you aren't restricted to using the same hardware, operating systems, or software for every computer on the network.

Multi-Platform Networks

You can connect as many Windows, Macs, or Linux PCs on an Ethernet network as you like, as long as your local network can assign an IP address to each one. What's the catch? Each platform has a slightly different user interface. For example, if you know how to set up a Windows computer on a network, you may need to fumble around to find the same network settings on a Macintosh or Linux computer. The differences between the computer systems increase as you move from one application to another on each platform. For example, Internet Explorer 5.5 on the Mac has a slightly different set of buttons, menu commands, and features than Internet Explorer 5.5 for Windows.

Adding Printers and Other Network Devices

A printer will probably be one of the first network devices you'll add to your home or business network. There are several kinds of printers, in addition to a few ways you can connect a printer to a network. Most ink-jet and non-PostScript printers have USB or parallel port connections. If you have a computer with a USB port, you can share the printer with the computer on a network. Some higher-end PostScript printers have an Ethernet card either built in or available as an add-in. Printers with Ethernet cards can be connected to a network as a standalone device.

Digital cameras, scanners, and handheld devices can also be shared or accessed if connected to a computer on a network. In addition to the hardware needed to connect a device to a computer, you may need to install software to make a camera, printer, or scanner network savvy.

SURVIVAL TIP If you plan to have multiple computers printing to a single printer on the network, it's a good idea to locate the printer in a physical location on the network that doesn't create a bottleneck for network traffic.

Many printers are compatible with more than one operating system. For example, you can set up a printer on a network, and install printer software on a Mac or Windows computer. This enables you to send a print job from a Windows or Mac OS computer to the same networked printer. A computer can be used to configure a printer's network information, whether the printer is plugged directly into a network, or connected directly to a computer's USB, serial, or parallel port. You'll need to install a printer driver and configuration software onto the computer you want to use to set up the network printer.

CAUTION
If you plan to add a printer to a network, check the page-per-minute output for the printer. A fast page-per-minute output rate can help alleviate network bottlenecks that may be created when many computers try to print to the same printer simultaneously.

Adding Wireless Access to Your Network

If you have a relatively small network and do not want to install network wiring in your home or office, consider a wireless network solution. A wireless network requires you to install a wireless access point that functions as a hub for computers that have a wireless network interface card installed. Each computer must log into the wireless access point in order to access your local network or the Internet.

If computing mobility doesn't inspire you to add wireless networking to your home or business, cost and performance might do the trick. Wireless hubs or base stations can be configured with an IP address and can allocate DHCP addresses or network address translation on a local network. Most wireless hubs support the 802.11 standard and work with wireless cards installed on client computers.

Like other Ethernet network devices, wireless hubs are computer agnostic, supporting any platform that can work with Ethernet and 802.11 software. Most wireless client cards come with Windows and Mac software and provide software upgrades on the product's web site. Base stations cost approximately $300; client cards range from $150–$200.

SURVIVAL TIP
Although PCI and PC card Ethernet network solutions are the least expensive way to add a computer to a network, paying the extra money for wireless network solutions can save you the cost of installing CAT 5 networking cables in your home or adding excessive cabling to accommodate additional computers.

CAUTION
Before you decide to set up a full-blown wireless network, check to see whether your home or business is near a source of noise or airwave pollution that could prevent a wireless network from working efficiently. Also, if your home or business has concrete or metal built into the walls, or lead in the paint or undercoating, you may need to add a larger antenna or install a few more wireless hubs to extend the scope of the wireless network. Marble, water, and brick can also inhibit the efficiency of a wireless network. Wood, Plastic, and glass material will have minimal interference with wireless systems.

Depending on the type of DSL modem you have and the type of connection between your home network and the DSL network, one or several computers on your home network can simultaneously access the Internet through the DSL modem. Apple's AirPort base station, can be configured to distribute DHCP addresses over the wireless portion of the network. However, most DSL modems can also act as a DHCP server, allocating local network addresses to enable each computer to access the Internet. DHCP can be software or hardware that provides the network administrative task of assigning network addresses to computers connected to the local network.

A DHCP server can assign an IP number or recognize a static IP number that you configure on your computer. When the computer powers on and connects to the Ethernet network, the DHCP server assigns the computer an IP number. When the computer goes to sleep or powers off, the DHCP IP number is released from the computer, and the DHCP server can assign it to the next computer that connects to the network.

CAUTION

Most wireless network cards and wireless access points support an encryption feature that adds a level of security to data broadcast over a wireless network. If you are thinking about setting up a wireless network, consider activating encryption on your wireless network.

Network Setup and Security Problems and Solutions

With all the news and nightmare stories about worms and viruses attacking computers, you should ask yourself if your DSL network is secure. Network computer security involves tracking two kinds of data on each computer on your network: incoming and outgoing network data. The worms and viruses that have garnered most of the attention in the press are usually distributed over e-mail. Spam is a variant of this type of virus. Network security can require several applications if you want to monitor network traffic flowing through your network routers, as well as on each computer on your local network.

CAUTION

To avoid viruses or other network problems that begin by opening an e-mail, carefully review e-mail and e-mail attachments before reading them. If you do not recognize the e-mail address of an e-mail message that appears in your inbox, you might want to delete it.

Another form of network security helps keep out hackers who want to see what kinds of computers are on your network, and possibly copy data to or from your network. A firewall is usually the first line of defense against network hackers. Although you probably won't find this feature in a low-end DSL modem, some higher-end DSL modem models may have a

firewall security feature activated by default. However, this feature can also prevent you from accessing a virtual private network.

SURVIVAL TIP

To find out more about how to set up applications for monitoring network traffic, see Part IV.

Operating Systems and Network Settings

Although PC and Macintosh computers share many similar hardware components, the Windows, Linux, and Mac OS operating systems each have their own control panels and network settings for connecting a computer to a network. Learning how to work with more than one version of each of these operating systems can be a difficult if not frustrating task. One way to minimize the amount of time required to set up a networked computer is to standardize on one or two operating systems, such as Windows 2000 and Mac OS 9.1. As new operating systems are released, you can adopt the newer system software on one or two computer systems, and then upgrade the other networked computers if no new network problems are introduced as a result of adding the new operating system software to the network.

Keeping Your Network Secure

Network settings enable a computer to process network data that moves into and out of the computer. However network settings do not interact or filter any network data. Some networks install firewall hardware or software on a local network to filter out viruses, trojan horses, and other derelict network dregs from infecting computers on the local network. You can also install personal firewall software to monitor incoming and outgoing network traffic on each computer on a network. Windows XP professional has personal firewall software configured with the operating system as part of the standard installation of Windows XP.

Adding a firewall to your network's gateway to the Internet is like locking the front door to your house. However, some network servers, such as wireless servers, can open potential back doors into your local network. Fortunately, wireless networks support data encryption. You can also create a list of specific 802.11 wireless cards that you will allow to access your network.

In addition to a firewall and data encryption, you may want to set up an alarm system to alert you to unauthorized network visitors. Alarm systems on a network might involve setting up special network hardware or software tools that enable you to sniff packets on a network. You can also check the IP addresses that appear to be attracting the most network traffic, and see whether the heavy network times match up with actual computer use on your local network.

Network Viruses, Worms, and Trojan Horses

Computer hardware and software can have defects, called bugs. These bugs are sometimes unintentionally designed into a hardware or software product. For most commercial computer products, the majority of bugs are fixed before the product is made available to customers.

Viruses, worms, and trojan horses are different types of software programs designed to infiltrate and run on your computer. In most cases, you may not know that the network has brought a guest on to your computer. Many computer viruses and worms sometimes do nothing at all. However, some are malicious and can cause your computer to lose stability, perform slowly, or lose some or all data stored on hard drives. The following list provides a brief description of a virus, worm, and trojan horse.

✦ **Virus**   This program relies on someone to perform a task, such as opening an e-mail attachment, in order to spread the virus to other computers. A virus can sit dormant on your computer until a certain date, such as Friday the 13th. A harmless message may appear, or more damaging tasks may ensue, such as random deletion of files on your hard drive.

✦ **Trojan horse**   Taken from Greek myth, this software program masquerades as an e-mail application or game, but it may contain code to collect keystrokes for a password, or run other tasks on your computer unbeknownst to you.

✦ **Worm**   This network-bound computer program is capable of multiplying and spreading on its own without human or computer interaction. A worm may require disk space to spread to other computers and may also use network bandwidth to move from computer to computer across different networks.

Identifying Internal and External Networks

If you choose to rely on the DSL modem's firewall software to protect your local network, you can log in to the DSL modem to activate this feature. The software on the DSL modem requires a login and password, which can be configured to be accessible from both the local network and external network. If your account information does not include a password, you will need to contact the DSL service provider and request it. If you're not comfortable changing the settings on your DSL modem, you can work with a technical support person to choose the settings for your DSL modem.

Most wireless PC cards can be configured to encrypt data sent to the base station. Encryption can prevent uninvited computers from accessing your network, and can protect the network data. In order for a wireless card to access an encrypted network, each computer must have a software key added to the wireless card configuration. The base station has this same encryption key. If a wireless PC card has the matching number, the computer is permitted to join the network.

Firewalls, Proxy Servers, and Network Performance

You can set up more than one firewall on your network. However, one firewall should be able to keep uninvited guests from accessing your network. You can take several steps to discourage others from accessing your computers or network accounts without authorization.

✦ **Upgrade software**   If you have a computer running Windows 3.0 or Mac OS 7.5, consider upgrading them (hardware, memory, and processor speed permitting) to Windows 2000 and Mac OS 9 or Mac OS X, respectively. Running the most current operating system and software browser can help reduce the likelihood that your network is compromised due to a bug in older software.

✦ **Change passwords**   Use a password consisting of six to eight non-consecutive characters, and change your password once a month or once every two months. If you're the system administrator, you can force users on your network to create new passwords after a certain number of logins.

✦ **Power off computers**   Keep hackers from finding your computer by powering off computers when you're not using them.

✦ **Monitor your network**   Back up critical data on your network, and check each computer and network performance regularly.

Additional Resources

Creating a simple network can be the tip of the iceberg of your DSL network experience. The good news is that hardware and software are readily available for Windows, Mac, and Linux computing platforms. In addition to bringing a fast Internet connection into your home, networks enable network devices and data to be shared among other computers. To find out more about the topics explained in this chapter, visit the following URLs.

✦ IEEE 802 standards, visit http://standards.ieee.org/getieee802/

✦ IEEE organization web site: http://www.ieee.org

✦ IEEE Ethernet document, visit http://standards.ieee.org/reading/ieee/std/ lanman/802.3-2000.pdf

✦ IP address requests, visit http://www.iana.org

Compare prices for network interface cards, hubs, and other network products at the following URLs.

✦ www.cnet.com

✦ www.zdnet.com

✦ www.mysimon.com

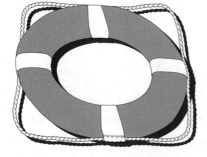

Chapter 3

Planning Your DSL Network

local area network (LAN) can consist of a group of client computers; a combination of clients and servers; or, although rare for a home or office, a group of server computers. Most computers on the local network will be client computers that run browser or e-mail programs. However, you can also set up file, media or mail servers; play music; or host a web server on the local network. A printer, scanner, or camera can also be connected to a computer and shared with other computers on a local network.

If you are setting up the network, or if you're the primary user of most of the computers on the network, you can make yourself—and others, if you like—the administrator of the network. As an administrator, you can set up user accounts on server or client systems. Even if you have only one computer on your DSL network, you may eventually add a printer, or a second or third computer. Setting up user accounts enables you to share files with others over the local network, as well as over the Internet. The following list summarizes three different ways you can set up a computer on a local network. You can set up one computer to do many of these tasks (which is not recommended) or have several computers, each dedicated to hosting a particular kind of service.

+ **Server**   A computer that hosts services or files for client computers to access over a network. You can install file, web, or music servers on your network with Windows, Mac OS, or Linux.

+ **Client**   A computer that can connect to servers on a local network A client can run one of several possible operating systems, such as Windows, Mac OS, or Linux.

+ **External networks**   A network located in a different physical location from the local network. You can access computers on an external network, such as web and file servers on the Internet. You can also create an exclusive external network, such as a virtual private network that requires each user to log in before the computers on the private network can be accessed.

Basic Network Management Concepts

Chapter 1 provided a brief overview of different kinds of DSL services. Chapter 2 explored how networks work, and how computers can communicate with each other over a network. This chapter explores network configurations and managing each computer connected to a local network.

Managing a network involves setting up computers on the network, and then monitoring their performance and behavior as other machines and other users on the network interact with them. The two kinds of generic network accounts are the network administrator, who manages the network, and the network user, who uses the computers on your network. Figure 3-1 shows how the network administrator, known in Unix as "root" or the "superuser"

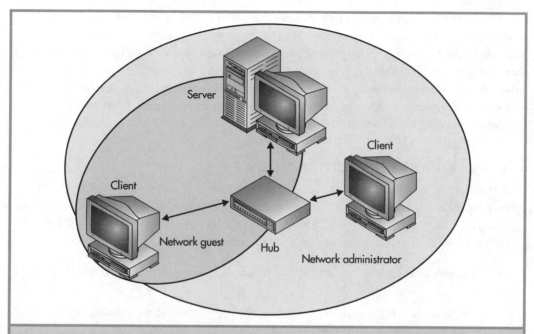

Figure 3-1.   A network administrator can create user accounts, such as a guest account that restricts access to certain directories or files stored on a local client or server.

(su), can have full access to every system on the network. This assumes each computer has been set up for the same administrator account login and password. It is possible to have each computer set up to have its own administrator. However, if you want to manage all computers on the network, you will need to know each computer's administrator user name and login or create separate administrator account on each computer with the same user name and password.

A network user has limited access to a client computer, and possibly also a file server or any other servers connected to the network. Only computers, not network printers or similar devices, can be configured with network access privileges. Setting up a computer on a network involves configuring the network hardware for each computer, and then determining which directories and files can be shared with a user or group of users on each computer.

SURVIVAL TIP

To find out more about how to configure users and groups for Windows, Mac OS, or Linux, go to Chapter 10.

Theoretically, as long as you have the right hardware components, you can create a network that can support as many users, or clients, as you like. Cost, however, is the most limiting factor for both growing your network and accommodating heavy network traffic. For example, you probably won't be setting up an amazon.com web site in your home or office. A typical home network will have one or several client computers. If a local network is set up in the home or office, you may also have one or more servers, plus one or more printers connected to the network.

Network Planning Terminology

An Ethernet hub enables you to connect one or two computers and still leave room for growing your network with more computers and network devices. As you grow your local network, you may consider adding different network devices. The following list gives an overview of network devices that can be used to grow or link local area networks.

- ✦ **Star network** A hub-based topology where each computer on the network connects to the central hub
- ✦ **Bus network** A network of computers, usually connected with coaxial cables, based on a single wire, or bus
- ✦ **Hub** A network device consisting of a power source and RJ-45 Ethernet connectors, enabling you to connect more than one computer to the same network
- ✦ **Switch** A network component capable of creating a dedicated network connection between two computers
- ✦ **Bridge** A network device that can bridge two networks into one enabling the local network to share Internet access with the other network over the bridged connection
- ✦ **Router** A network device that can distinguish one network from the other while connecting the two to each other.
- ✦ **DHCP server** A network server that assigns IP addresses to a computer connected to a local area network. Each local network should only have one DHCP server.
- ✦ **Network address translator (NAT)** Software capable of translating a single IP address to multiple IP addresses on a local network

Network Topologies

A network topology is a map of a network. A network map can help you decide where to place existing computers, hubs, and cabling, as well as help you plan for expansion. A computer connected to a star network will most likely behave as a client, unless you have set it up to behave as a server. Client computers, also referred to as workstations, enable you to connect to computer servers, such as web sites and FTP sites on the Internet. A server can be a Windows, Mac OS, or Linux computer configured to allow one or more users or groups to access the directories and files stores on the server's hard drive. In order to optimize network performance, a server can have a faster Ethernet card, such as a 100 or Gigabit Base T card connected to a fast network connection.

Peer-to-Peer

Computers connected to a star network can also be configured as peers. The file-sharing features on Windows and Mac OS are capable of sharing all or part of the files on your computer with other computers on the network. When one computer hosts sharable files, and then logs in to another computer to access its file, this is a peer-to-peer network. Both computers can act as a client or a server and are peers to other computers on the network.

Peer-to-peer connections can be created by directly connecting a FireWire (1394) cable or an Ethernet crossover cable to a USB Ethernet adapter or Ethernet port between two Mac OS or Windows computers. One of the two computers must have file-sharing software activated, and have at least one folder configured to share its contents with a user account on the computer. The second computer can log in to the file-sharing computer, and copy files from or to the computer over the network connection.

NOTE   If you are upgrading a PC and want to copy the files from one Windows computer to another (or one Mac OS computer to another), you can connect an Ethernet crossover cable between the two computers and copy files between them using the file-sharing feature in Windows (or Mac OS).

The next two figures show two windows related to file sharing on Windows 2000. The window in Figure 3-2 can be opened by choosing Properties for the Ethernet or wireless card installed on your PC. This window enables you to install or configure the file-sharing software for Windows 2000.

If you want to share a file on a Windows 2000 computer, first click a folder icon on the desktop, or in an Explorer window. Right-click the folder icon to access its contextual menu. Then choose the Sharing menu item from a folder's contextual menu to view or set file-sharing options for that directory (Figure 3-3). Click the Apply button to apply your changes to the selected folder. Then click OK to exit the folder's properties window.

To access the files on the Windows computer, go to the second computer on the network and double-click the My Network Places icon. Double-click the Entire Network icon, and then navigate to the Windows 2000 machine name that contains the shared folder. Double-click the computer icon to access the folder on the host computer. If the computer is configured to require each user to log in, type a user name and password if prompted. Then navigate to the shared folder. You can copy files to or from the networked computer.

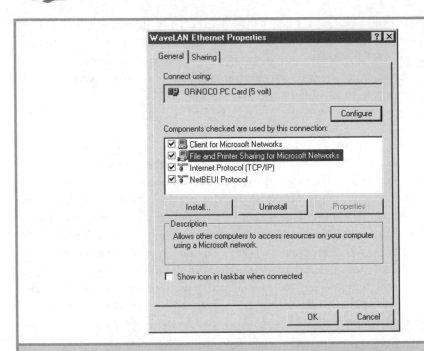

Figure 3-2. File sharing is the most common way to share files on a network. You can install file or print sharing with Windows 2000 Professional.

Choosing Hubs and Routers

Hubs and routers have distinct purposes on a network. A hub enables you to add nodes to a network. A router helps you organize and direct traffic on the network or across local networks. Here's where it gets complicated: hubs and routers can co-exist in the same device. For instance, some DSL modems can also function as network routers.

Regardless of all the network products you can consider for your network, you will want to add a hub to create your first Ethernet network. Connect the hub to your DSL modem and connect computers to the hub. Voila! A network is born!

Hubs come in many sizes, shapes, and flavors. Before opening the Pandora's box of Ethernet hubs, determine what kinds of Ethernet cards or Ethernet ports are on the computers that will be connected to your local network. The majority of Ethernet cards will either use a coaxial cable or twisted-pair cable to connect a computer to a hub. If you know you have network devices, such as a printer or computer, requiring coaxial cable, look for a hub that has one Bayonet Neil-Concelman or British Naval Connector (BNC) coaxial connector, in addition to the standard RJ-45 connector used for twisted-pair Ethernet cables.

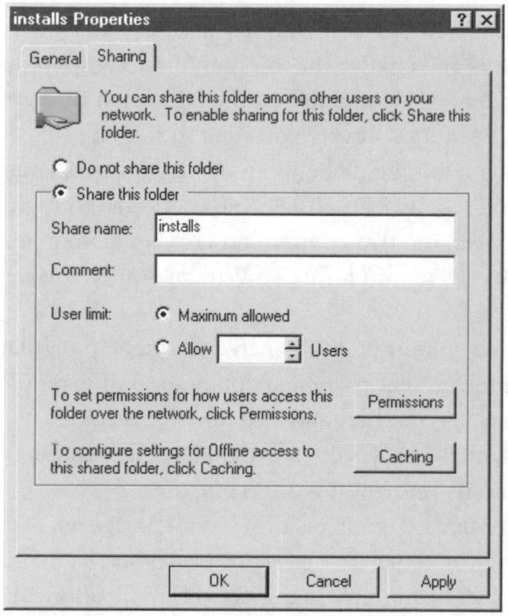

Figure 3-3.   Select sharing settings for a folder you want to share on the network.

Designing your network can be an intimidating task, especially if you don't want CAT 5 cables crawling throughout your home or business. Before you start drilling into walls, check for electronic devices or heat sources and avoid placing a computer or network wiring near potentially dangerous equipment.

Count each network device that will be connected to the network. A network device can be a computer, printer, hub, or other network device that can be connected to a computer, or directly connected to the hub. Double the number of ports (and possibly hubs) you expect to have connected to the network. You may need only one or two Ethernet ports. In this case, connecting a four-port Ethernet hub to your DSL modem will bring your computer online. However, if you plan to have guests who use wireless PC cards and want to access your DSL Internet connection, you may want to expand your network with an AirPort base station.

Computer Placement and Traffic Hot Spots

Don't feel compelled to build your network in a day. Consider the location of each computer in your home or office, and how many people will be accessing your network at any given time. Then, set up one or two computers to see how they fare before growing your network into other rooms or adding new devices. You may need to move the computer to a different room, or keep it where it is and change the location of the computer peripherals. You may also want to upgrade or remove a computer on the network if it has problems with stability or if it's too slow for the network software you want to run on it.

If you need to transfer a lot of data between two computers, you can take them off the main network, and use a crossover Ethernet cable connected to each computer's Ethernet port to transfer data between the two computers. This is a simple peer-to-peer network configuration, and works well if you have two Windows or two Macintosh computers that need to exchange data.

The placement of each computer on the network can help regulate network traffic flow and limit what can be done on that particular computer. For example, if you want to set up a computer to share a few specific files and also function as a CD-ROM station and a game machine, you can install client-only software and place the computer in an easily accessible room so that users can easily find and use this computer.

Computers can be configured as clients or servers, or as peers. A peer-to-peer connection, also known as file sharing (or personal Web sharing on a Mac), enables a client computer to share files with another client computer over a network. The following list highlights some of the files and tasks you can perform with a peer-to-peer connection.

- ✦ **File sharing**   You can use file sharing to make files, such as documents or software updates, easily accessible on the network. The computer will slow down as folks connect to the computer that has file sharing activated.

- ✦ **Documents**   Share text or image files with other users connected to the network.

- ✦ **Web pages**   Set up a Web server and share simple text and graphics on a web page, or create more sophisticated animation or streaming media files that can be viewed over the Web.

- ✦ **MP3**   Listen to music from the latest albums or share music files on the local network, and create a digital juke box that you can control via network access.

- ✦ **Back ups**   Create a copy of the applications and files onto another user's computer. You probably won't be able to schedule regular backups, and the file(s) may not always stay on the other computer. But for the short term, you can share files over a peer-to-peer connection.

- ✦ **CD-ROM or DVD-ROM burners**   Share a computer that has a CD-RW or DVD-RW drive on it. Other computers on the local network can access this CD or DVD burning station.

You can also set up dedicated servers on your network. A dedicated server can be a computer that is configured to only allow users to connect to add or copy files from the file server. Other kinds of servers are mail, Web, and media servers. The primary difference between a client computer and a server computer is that the server computer runs one or more programs dedicated to hosting files on that computer. A server computer is not intended to be used as a client computer. Servers are designed to remain connected to the network 24 hours a day, seven days a week, with no interaction from general users while remaining accessible to network administrators.

Although you can run a server program alongside client software, it's recommended that you run the server on a dedicated machine. Unlike clients, servers need maximum uptime. The more you run client software on a server, the more likely it is to crash. Servers also perform optimally, especially if many users are connected to it at once, if other software is not running concurrently with the server programs. The following list includes several kinds of servers you can set up on your local network.

✦ **Network servers**

    ✦ **Mail server**   A mail server is capable of storing e-mail for a client computer. The mail server can also be used to send and receive e-mail for any client computers that have an e-mail account on the mail server. If you have subscribed to a DSL provider, you probably have an e-mail account on the DSL provider's network.

    ✦ **Name server**   A type of server that collects network domain names and maps them to IP addresses. A name server can help a client computer locate another computer on the Internet.

    ✦ **Firewall**   A hardware or software program that can be configured to filter some or all incoming or outgoing network traffic. In addition to setting up a firewall on a router on the local network, you can also install a personal firewall on each computer. Windows XP Professional has a personal firewall installed with the standard operating system installation.

    ✦ **DHCP server**   A server responsible for allocating IP addresses to any computer that connects to the local network.

✦ **Local file server**

    ✦ **MP3 juke box**   You can install an MP3 program, or use an application such as WinAmp (Windows) or iTunes (Mac OS) to store digital music on a computer, and play songs in your home or office.

    ✦ **Application and document sharing**   Set up a file server on the local network to enable client computers to install the latest software updates, or share text or graphics files with other computers connected to the network.

    ✦ **Game server**   If you like to play games, you may want to set up a dedicated game server for your favorite sports or action/adventure game. Most network games enable you to invite other players on the local network or the Internet to play along with you.

✦ **Web server**   Set up a web server for the local network's intranet, or share web pages on the Internet.

✦ **Backups**   Set up a computer to back up any server or client computers on the local network. Most backup software enables you to schedule backups on a regular basis, and store files on a hard drive, tape, CD, or DVD media.

✦ **Internet server access**

Servers on the Internet enable you to access mail, news, web, game, media, and streaming media servers on the Internet.

Adding Servers

Servers are computers that are dedicated to hosting files or network services for other computers on the network. Both the hardware and the operating system and application software are designed to host multiple simultaneous connections over a network. Regarding hardware, servers should have more memory and hard drive space than the average networked client computer. Regarding software, there may be additional hardware or configuration issues to consider depending on which operating system the server is running, and how many computers you want to host with a server. Most Linux distributions require no additional operating system software in order to support server software.

Windows 2000 has a separate Windows 2000 server product that can be used to set up a wide variety of PC servers on a network. Windows 2000 Professional is the Windows operating system designed for the client computer. Similarly, Apple's Mac OS X server product, shares the Berkeley Software Distribution (BSD) kernel in the Mac OS X operating system, but contains a different operating system bundle than the client operating system software. The following concepts apply to server systems on a network. Mac OS X server is capable of hosting some Windows services, but is primarily designed to host Apple's suite of servers. Most Linux distributions combine FTP and web hosting capabilities in the workstation release of the distribution.

✦ **Domain name**   Domain name servers enable IP addresses to be associated with domain names.

✦ **Platform**   Choosing the right server for your clients depends on what type of network applications each client will be running, and what kind of network services you want the client computers to access on the network. For example, if all the network clients are running applications that require a Windows SQL 2000 server, you will want to set up a Windows SQL 2000 server on your network. On the other hand, if each client needs access to a cross-platform file-sharing server, you may want to set up a Linux-based FTP server on your network. Web, file, print, and mail servers are common types of servers available on a network. Also, choose a server that has minimal downtime and optimal uptime. BSD, a PC flavor of Unix, and Linux tend to host file and Web servers more reliably than Windows or Mac OS computers. However, depending on which computer clients are connected to your network, a Windows or Macintosh computer can also function as a terrific Web or file server.

✦ **Access** Network servers can be accessible only within the local network or on the Internet. If you're setting up a server for the Internet, you can anticipate a significant increase in network traffic that is sent from the server.

The operating system on a server is similar to the operating system on a client. However, you need to configure a few additional network settings in order to allow other computers to access the programs running on the server. For example, you can give the server a local host name to map to its IP address. In addition to configuring the server, you will need to create login accounts, monitor available disk space and network usage, set up a backup system, and make yourself available if the network server should stop working. As the system administrator, you will also need to define how users access files on the server; set up the server to discourage casual visitors from deleting critical system files from the computer; and, possibly, prevent visitors from copying files to the server. For example, you can set up the file server to request a new password once per month or once every three months. As you can see, monitoring and maintaining a server can require a considerable amount of time.

SURVIVAL TIP To find out more about how to set up a Windows, Macintosh, or Linux computer on a DSL network, see Chapter 5.

Outsourcing and Co-located Networks

An alternative to building or expanding a network in your home or office is to consider outsourcing the work to another company for a fee. Outsourcing enables you to connect your local network to the outsourced company's network, co-locating the networks across two distant locations. Co-location sites are usually businesses that have large, high-capacity systems configured to provide optimal network performance, reliable power sources, and speedy network access. The following list identifies some of the network services you may want to consider outsourcing.

Network Services

✦ **Web server access** Physically locate one or more web services outside the local network. This can enable the web site to handle more network traffic without having any impact on the local network.

✦ **Media server access** Host streaming media files on an external computer.

✦ **CD-ROM or DVD-ROM servers**   Set up a file server on an external network to share archives of images and text documents.

Mail Server

✦ Host e-mail services on a computer located outside the local network.

Virtual Private Networks

✦ Remote access to private networks that are also connected to the Internet

SURVIVAL TIP

One limitation of moving part of your network to a co-location facility is that servers in that site will not be easily accessible from your local network. If you know some servers are problematic, or want instant access to a file or mail server, keep it connected to your home or business DSL network.

Designing a Network

There is a method to the madness of putting a network together. Although you can set up a hub near your DSL modem, and then connect desktop or wireless computers to your network, a little network planning can make your network easy to set up and maintain. Network planning can be as simple as deciding on where you want to put your computer and printer. Bigger networks usually require a little more thought. Networks have limits on how network traffic is managed, and larger networks usually require purchasing routers and possibly switches in addition to hubs.

SURVIVAL TIP

Most Ethernet equipment such as hubs and CAT 5 cabling can be purchased at relatively nominal prices. Try to purchase Ethenet network equipment to support more network devices than you currently have on your network. On the other hand, some routers, switches, and other network hardware can be very expensive. Before adding Ethernet equipment to your local network, define exactly what the network will be used for, and make sure you've chosen the right network gear before purchasing and installing it on your network.

Placing Hubs

Ethernet hubs are relatively simple devices. Most hubs do not have dedicated memory and require an external power supply in order to enhance the network connections that extend from them. Each port on a hub has a transceiver capable of transmitting the network signal over a given distance. The most common hub configurations are four- and eight-port hubs. Larger hubs tend to have additional networking hardware, such as a switch or router. The more ports on a hub, the more hardware needed to keep the network signal strong across each network connection. The following list discusses some things you might want to consider as you plan and build your network.

✦ **Server placement** Servers can be located anywhere on the network. If you plan to have several servers connected to your network, you may want to locate them in the same room or shared space. Keep the room at a cool temperature, and try to avoid stacking hardware or confining several computers to a small, unventilated location.

✦ **Server usage** Servers can host many kinds of services, from streaming video to backing up files and hosting web pages. Consider how many computers might access a server connected to your local network or, if applicable, from the Internet. You may want to place a switch or router in this area of the network to ease traffic flow and prevent slow network performance.

✦ **Client placement** Count the number of computers that will access the servers. You may also want to determine peak network usage times, as well as the physical location of each client on the local network.

✦ **Network monitoring system** You may want to set up a computer that is dedicated to monitoring network access to servers and, possibly, clients.

Placing Routers

A router is a combination of network hardware and software that directs network traffic. You can set up a dedicated network router between two star hub networks, or configure a PC to route network traffic between two networks. Regardless of how many networks or routers you have for your local area network, you will need to set up a routing device to separate your local network from your DSL service provider's network. This task can be performed by a DSL modem that has router capabilities, or by a computer set up on the service provider's network with your DSL modem dialing in over a PPPoE connection.

If you have a DSL modem that can be configured as a network router, the IP address of the DSL modem represents the Internet gateway for your local home or business network. Network data destined for any computer in your home or business network passes through the DSL modem/router first. The router is responsible for disseminating and routing Ethernet or IP packet information before forwarding the data on to the target computer.

Computers that share a router can see packets sent to the target computer. For example, if a client computer on the network, tries to download a 10MB file from a local file server, the other computers on the network will review the packets to see whether the data is targeted to that computer. Sending or receiving large files between computers results in slower network access for the other computers that have to interact with the network data.

You can configure the router's software to manage the data flowing through the router. The primary task the router performs is to determine whether the data being sent to it can be forwarded to any machine connected to the router's local network. Connect each PC to a start hub, and then connect the router to the same hub to create a simple local area network. In addition to directing network traffic, you can set priorities for the router, or create special rules for handling traffic from a particular IP address or other server on the network.

You can use routers to separate different kinds of networks that may have heavy or light network loads. For example, if your home has three computer rooms, you might want to put the servers in one room in a small network, and then create two separate networks of clients. Set up a router between each small network.

SURVIVAL TIP

The Internet is a giant mesh of routed networks. It's a perfect example of a mesh network topology. The network path taken to get data from your browser to a web server can change, depending on which router encounters the IP packets sent from your network.

If you want to use a client in network C to print to a printer in network A, you can install and set up the printer software on the client computer. Then send the print job across networks to print the document on network A. Routers enable you to focus network traffic without losing the ability to access any computer on the network.

CAUTION

If you're setting up a router for the first time, be careful to properly configure the network addresses on the router. If you define two separate networks that share IP addresses, the router will get confused when it tries to direct network traffic across its local networks.

Planning for Network Clients

You might think a network would encourage you to have users visit the servers connected to your local network. Realistically, you might not want just anyone logging in to your local file server or viewing all the files stored on your web site, database, and so on. As you add computers to your network, try to create at least three different levels of network access for your servers. You may also want to limit access to each client, or create a pre-configured image of the files and settings for computers added to your network.

The best way to prevent mayhem from occurring on your network is to limit access to files related to the network, such as operating system files, and to the core programs you want to share with computer users. Windows, Mac OS, and Linux support groups and individual login accounts. You can assign a special account to all the individuals who will access the computer, and then put them in a group that has a particular set of privileges for the computer they're using, as well as to other servers and network devices on your home or business network.

SURVIVAL TIP

If you have a DHCP server configured to hand out IP addresses, visitors with wireless-capable laptops can use your network to access the Internet. If the servers and clients on your network require a login and password, visitors can use your network, but they won't be able to access the local computers unless you give them the login and password information.

One way to keep track of all the computers on your network is to draw a simple diagram. You may want to include hardware and software configurations for each computer to identify potential network bottlenecks or server issues before you spend time installing cables and network cards, or configuring network-related software. As you add computers to your network, you can update the diagram.

Network Traffic Problems

The word "traffic," even if associated with the word "network," can have a bad connotation. Traffic on a network can be a good thing, indicating that the connection between two nodes on a network is working properly. Some network problems begin when the network becomes filled with more traffic than it can handle. The most likely cause of this scenario is two computers simultaneously downloading several large files over the network, preventing additional computers from accessing full network bandwidth. A similar situation can be simulated. A denial-of-service attack can be launched from several network computers with the intent of rendering a computer inaccessible over the network. This is considered a malicious attack on a server or router.

Defining Network Workflow

One way to determine how much network data will be flowing to network devices is to determine the average size file that will be transmitted between two devices on the network. If you know that two or more computers will be printing large color images, you may want to place the color printer in a small local network near those computers. A second computer can be added to another router-connected network to isolate the heavy network traffic that will be sent to the color printer. The following lists provide brief descriptions of network workflow, or traffic issues associated with various network devices.

Local Traffic

✦ **Printing** Determine the page-per-minute capability of each printer and the average size of a print job. Then decide how many computers to place on the network that will access each printer. You can use the file size of each document to be printed to determine how much network traffic to anticipate.

✦ **File-sharing servers or file servers** Take a ball park guess at how many files will be sent between two file-sharing computers. Then, decide how often files will be transferred between these computers. If most activity will occur during periods of peak network activity, you may want to create a separate network for these computers.

✦ **Web hosting** Estimate how many local and Internet clients will visit the Web server. If the Web server will be available only to the internal, local network, you probably won't have to create redundant systems or add hardware pieces to support the extra network load.

✦ **Mail server**   Decide how many computers will access the mail server, and how frequently each machine might check for mail. Don't forget that most e-mail applications can be set up to check for e-mail every ten minutes. Also estimate the size of e-mail messages, including any attachment files.

Internet Traffic

✦ **Virtual private network (VPN)**   Accessing a VPN from your home or business network will generate network packets on your local network and can cause network slowdowns.

✦ **Web surfing**   Downloading files from web sites or uploading HTML, scripts, or image files to a Web server can affect network performance if you're working with dozens of files or a few large files.

✦ **E-mail and chat**   Every time you check or download e-mail messages from a server via the Internet, network traffic is created. You may want to monitor network performance while the maximum numbers of users on the network is working in full stride. Chatting with others on the Internet also generates network packets.

Setting Up Local and Global Firewalls

Adding a firewall to your local network can prevent external computers from utilizing your network. You can either install a network hardware device as your network firewall, or install a software solution for your network. Figure 3-4 illustrates how a firewall can act as a doorway between your local network and the Internet. You can also segment a home or business network into smaller networks, using routers to manage traffic between groups of computers. Each smaller network can have its own firewall to determine who can access its computers. However, even if you have set up firewalls, a network can suffer from slow performance, as well as fall victim to a worm, virus, or e-mail attack.

Some network performance problems can be caused by improperly installed cards, cables, or hubs on the network. For example, if the Ethernet connector is not completely connected to the Ethernet card, the connection can generate numerous error packets, increasing network traffic even if little activity is occurring on the network. In addition, some network traffic problems occur when a computer on the network can no longer be found due to a faulty (or broken) cable or port on the hub.

You can install software on your Windows, Linux, or Macintosh computer to monitor incoming and outbound network traffic. Symantec's Norton Personal Firewall enables a Windows or Macintosh computer to log and monitor network data whenever it is connected to a network. If an unidentified computer tries to access a port or send your computer a trojan

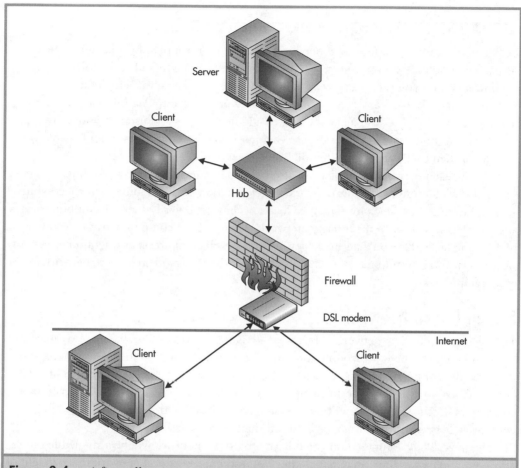

Figure 3-4. A firewall can prevent incoming and outgoing network traffic from entering or leaving your local network.

horse or virus, the Norton Personal Firewall software will reject the packet, and then notify you of the attempted security breach and the originating IP address of the attack. You can use a command-line tool like Traceroute to identify the computer from which the packet originated.

To find out how to use the Traceroute command, see Chapter 15.

SURVIVAL TIP

Solutions: Manage Your Network

Before you set up computers on a network, you can define a plan for managing them. As each computer is set up, you can define how users will log in and access files on that computer. When you set up a server on the network, you can define which files, folders, and services each user can access as an individual or as a group. Defining a consistent method for sharing files can make it easier to add new clients and users to your network, enable you to limit how much disk space each user may have on a server, and enable you to control each user's access to other files on the servers.

Testing each network computer can also help you manage your network. After you have set up a few computers on your network, check whether each computer can successfully access the Internet. Check for e-mail or load a web page to verify that the computer has a working connection to the Internet network. Then use the computers over several days, performing tasks that you'd normally perform with each computer. Pay attention to network slowdowns and intermittent connection issues with the DSL modem or local network for each computer.

Small Local Networks

The best way to build a network, large or small, is to start small. Purchase a few cables and hubs and connect them to a couple computers. Connect the hub to the DSL modem, and then test the connection to the Internet. For example, load a web page or send yourself an e-mail. Check the network performance of the small network. Copy a file between two computers on the network, and then download an HTML or image file from a web page; compare the network performance between the two network servers.

The most likely configuration you'll have for a small network will be a single file server, a printer, and two to four computer clients. You can build the local network independent of the Internet network. Perform a few network tasks, such as printing over the local network. Then, connect the network to the Internet and compare the same print job from the network with the print job from the Internet.

If you're considering adding a computer to control the thermostat, refrigerator, or coffee pot in your home, you may need to install additional software on your network computers to monitor these home devices, or turn off the controlling computer when the power to these devices is off.

Larger Networks

If you were able to set up a small network successfully, your next step might be to create another small network of computers. If you have to set up a large network, you can build several smaller networks, like the ones shown in Figure 3-5, connecting each hub and router, and then test sending data between two devices on two different networks.

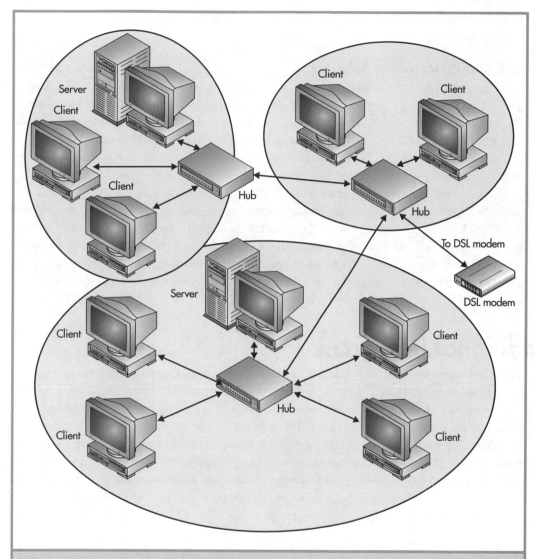

Figure 3-5. You may want to divide busier networks with a router to make network traffic run more efficiently.

Large network servers will require you to install additional network hardware to support a high number of computers accessing those files. For example, if you want to set up an e-commerce web server on your DSL network, set up the server to accommodate the largest number of expected visitors, multiplied by a factor of three. Set up Web server software to handle the worst-case scenario for a network connection. You may need to set up servers that can allow hundreds or thousands of simultaneous users to connect and navigate through the Web site.

Isolating Performance Bottlenecks

Don't be surprised if you stumble over network problems as you test your network. If you notice slow network performance, try to determine which computers on the network are experiencing this problem. You may want to disconnect some of the computers on the network, or check the card, cable, or connectors to see whether the network slowness persists.

Windows, Mac OS, and Linux each has a disk checking application that is installed along with the operating system. You can run a disk checking tool on Linux (called *fschk*), Windows, or Mac OS (Disk First Aid) in addition to other test tools to make sure each computer has properly functioning hardware and software. Similarly, you can run pre-installed network tools on Linux, Windows 2000, or Mac OS X to ping other computers on the network, or to trace packets (using the Traceroute tool) as they move across the network. If you or other users notice network problems, note the date and time that the performance slowdown first occurred, and what each of the computers on the network may have been doing. If the performance slowdown corrects itself, keep an eye out for recurrences.

Additional Resources

There are many cost and design issues to address as you install computers on your home or business network. You'll need to purchase the right network hardware and software and consider which computers, operating systems, and programs you want to run on the computers connected to your network. If you're the system administrator for your network, you may want to dedicate one machine on your network to visitor use, or set up a wireless network so that laptops with wireless connections can access the Internet from your home network. Once computers are up and running on your DSL network, try to monitor network traffic, as well as each computer's uptime on the network. The following URLs provide more information about network management.

- ✦ www.planetdsl.net
- ✦ www.techweb.com
- ✦ www.dslreports.com
- ✦ www.informationweek.com/hom

Part II

Setting Up
a Computer to
Access the Internet

Chapter 4

DSL Network Checklist

The chapters in Part II show you how to review your DSL account information, get a computer set up and connected to the DSL service provider and the Internet, and utilize browser and network applications that take advantage of the fast DSL Internet connection. Depending on the area where you live, there may be more than one DSL service provider, and you may be able to choose from several DSL packages. If you are deciding on a package or if you have already chosen a package, you can review the topics in this chapter to determine how to set up your local network. A DSL service enables a client computer to run Internet programs, such as a browser and e-mail, in addition to tasks that work best with a fast network connection, such as audio or video streaming media, animation, chat, instant messaging, networked games, and so on. The chapters in this part introduce you to some of the Windows, Mac OS, and Linux implementations for these network-media technologies.

There may be more than one DSL service available for your home or office. If several kinds of DSL services are available, compare the speed and cost of each service and choose the one that best fits your current and future network needs. Get the fastest DSL service you can afford. For any DSL service, look closely at the options for that service to see if they match the networking needs of your home or office network.

The DSL provider will most likely determine and install a particular type of DSL modem for the DSL service you choose. Although all DSL modems provide the essential task of keeping your home or office network connected to the Internet 24 hours a day, some modems have additional features that enable you to add a firewall, IP addressing server, or virtual private network (VPN). Other modems, such as a PPPoE modem, provide a more basic connection that may require you to log into the DSL service provider after a period of inactivity.

You may want to find out if a particular DSL service provider will allow you to exchange or purchase the DSL modem; some providers only allow you to rent the modem from them. You may want to swap the DSL modem with another model if the model that is installed with the DSL service has consistent connection problems or compatibility problems with the computer you are using to access Internet services. Exchanging modems may or may not be possible and largely depends on what the DSL provider's policies are for the service package you've subscribed to and whether the DSL provider has another modem model available for install for the DSL service you've selected. No matter which DSL modem is hooked up to your network, the DSL modem can be accessed by both you and your service provider, provided your local network is properly connected to the modem, and the modem is successfully connected to the Internet.

The following list highlights some of topics that will be discussed in this chapter.

✦ **DSL service**   What kind of DSL network will be connected to your home or business?

✦ **DSL modem**   What kind of DSL modem will be connected from your home or business network to the Internet? Does the modem support network and security features?

✦ **Local network design**   What kinds of computers and network devices will be connected to your home or business network?

Matching DSL Services to Your Network

Although there are many ways to set up a network, the speed of the DSL service will affect the number of computers and the total length of Ethernet networking cable that can be used to create the local area network. For example, if only IDSL, a 144 Kbps connection, is available, you may not want to host a file server (FTP) or Web server on your local network. Allowing computers to access a server on the your local network may slow down the local network enough to discourage computers on the local network from accessing the Internet. On the other hand, if an ADSL or fast SDSL connection is available, you will have plenty of capacity to support network growth without slowing down network performance or investing in special networking hardware to optimize performance.

Splitter-Based and Splitterless DSL Services

Some DSL services require modifications to your phone line, while other services allow you to set up your network without waiting for the local phone company to modify your phone line. A splitter-based DSL service requires a visit from the phone company before you can connect a computer on your local network to the Internet. Splitterless DSL services require installation of a filter on any non-DSL phone lines, but do not require a visit from the phone company. Some DSL providers allow you to choose from more than one DSL modem. However, in most cases, the DSL provider will choose and install the modem for a particular type of DSL service (see Figure 4-1).

   The following sections review DSL services, characteristics of DSL networks, and the DSL modems that work with these services. Figure 4-2 shows several DSL services and the average distance supported by each one. The goal of this section is to familiarize you with some of the features that DSL modems may have. If you can match the services you want to use with some or all of the clients connected to the network, you can choose the best DSL modem for your home or business network.

Splitter-Based DSL Services

All DSL services rely on the copper phone line in order to connect your network to the Internet. In this section, the term "phone-based services" refers to the splitter that the local phone company must install on the copper phone line that connects your voice phone services to your home or business. In this context, a phone-based service requires that a phone company (CO) representative visit your home to install a splitter before the DSL modem can be installed by the DSL provider on your local network. The following list provides a brief description of three kinds of DSL networks that require the phone line be modified with a splitter.

✦ **ADSL** Asymmetrical DSL provides a fast connection to the Internet (up to 8 Mbps) for data you want to bring into your network. However, data you want to send out of your network will travel at a much slower rate (up to 1 Mbps). The actual network speed depends on the distance between your home or office and the DSLAM (DSL access multiplexor) and the network rate of your connection, which is set by the DSL service provider.

◆ **RADSL**   Rate Adaptive DSL incorporates technology that can change the rate of the network throughput as the access speed or the condition of the phone line changes.

◆ **VDSL**   Very High Data Rate DSL can support 13–55 Mbps network data transfer rates but requires a shorter distance, usually 1,000 to 4,500 feet, between the local phone office and your home or business.

Dependency on a phone company setup doesn't make DSL services faster or slower than those that don't require the connection setup from the phone company. DSL service providers may offer you more than one modem model, with several features that can be activated on your local network. Most of these features can be set up on a separate network device or computer, but you may prefer to run several network services from the DSL modem instead of spreading them out to different systems on your network.

The DSL modem must be able to support, at a minimum, the network bandwidth of the DSL service it's connected to. The modem can use a router or point-to-point networking protocol (e.g., PPP or PPPoE) to connect a computer on a local network to the DSL service provider's larger network. The DSL provider's network is connected to the Internet through a fast ATM connection.

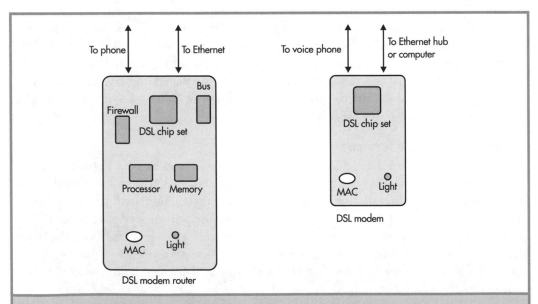

Figure 4-1.   DSL modems offer a basic connection to the Internet. DSL modem routers offer additional features that may enable firewalls, bridges, routers, and virtual private networking.

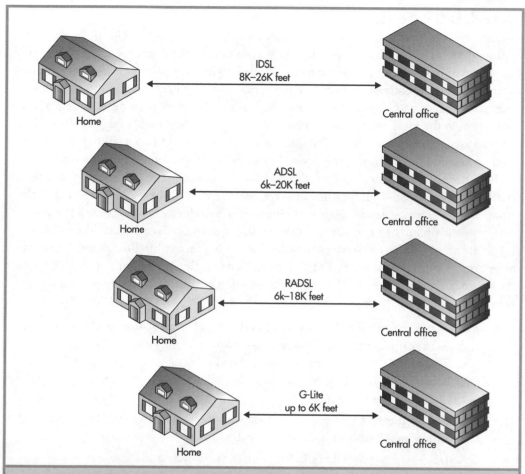

Figure 4-2. Although some DSL services share common data rates and distance limits, newer splitterless high-speed services require a shorter distance between the phone company and your home or office.

To find out more about how a network works, go to Chapter 2.

SURVIVAL TIP

The most important criterion in choosing a DSL modem is to determine whether it will work with the DSL service to which you subscribe. Additional modem features, such as routing network traffic and security, are second in importance.

NOTE

Splitterless DSL Services

Some DSL service providers can split the voice and DSL lines from the local phone office, bypassing the need for the local phone company to modify the copper wiring connected to your home or business. This type of service is called "splitterless" DSL service. It has become a standard only recently. The main difference between a splitter-based and splitterless connection is that with a splitterless connection, the DSL service provider sets up a single connection in the local phone office instead of setting up one at your home or office. A splitter-based service requires the DSL provider to install an additional splitter at the home or office location in addition to the phone line at the local telephone company office (CO).

A splitterless DSL service requires each non-DSL line, such as a voice, fax, or phone-based security line, to have a filter installed between the copper and the cable connected to the phone, fax, or security device. Figure 4-3 illustrates how devices connected to the voice portion of the phone line use filters, while the DSL connection remains unfiltered. ADSL and G.Lite are the only DSL services capable of operating on a splitterless phone line because they permit simultaneous voice and DSL operations on the same copper pair. IDSL and HDSL services can also be considered splitterless services, although each requires a separate copper pair, and both are implemented differently than ADSL and G.Lite DSL services.

- ✦ **ADSL**   Asymmetrical DSL supports a fast download transmission rate of up to 8 Mbps and a slower upload transmission rate of 1.5 Mbps. The splitterless service enables you to access DSL service without having the phone company install a splitter on your home phone line. However, a filter must be attached to any voice-related phone devices in your home or office.

- ✦ **G.Lite (DSL-Lite)**   Based on an ADSL networking model, this service is capable of supporting data download speeds of up to 1.5 Mbps.

- ✦ **G.SHDSL**   High Data Rate DSL, based on the G.991.2 standard, is a new DSL technology begin developed by the International Telecommunication Union (ITU). It is a symmetrical implementation of DSL that can be deployed over a T-1, ATM, and several other kinds of network connections. HDSL can support network speeds between 192 Kbps to 2.3 Mbps.

- ✦ **IDSL**   The slowest DSL service, ISDN DSL service supports a symmetrical data rate of 144 Kbps and can be implemented without splitting the copper line connecting your home to the local phone office.

Big city dwellers typically get to choose from the widest range of DSL services, largely because they are more likely to be located close to a phone company's central office (CO). However, you cannot determine the exact distance between your home or office from the central office (CO) by using a traditional map. Copper phone wires may not necessarily follow the shortest path to connect your home or office to the CO. The type of DSL service you choose will depend on your home or office's proximity to the central phone office, and the service's transmission rate.

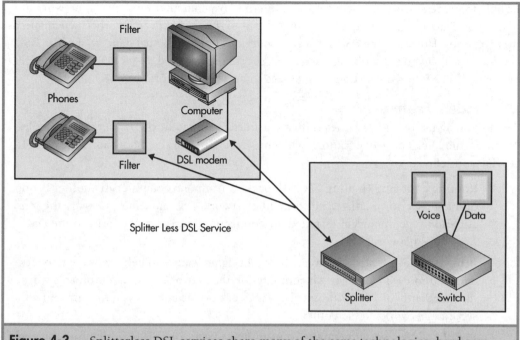

Figure 4-3. Splitterless DSL services share many of the same technologies, hardware, and services of a splitter-based DSL service.

NOTE

G.Lite, or DSL-Lite is based on the G.922.2 standard. Because it is a splitterless service, you can choose a DSL modem from the DSL service provider. Depending on the service provider, you may be able to purchase your own DSL modem. However, check with your service provider before making a decision about which DSL modem to use with your service. G.Lite offers the fast Internet access speeds of other DSL services without requiring you to work with your local phone company to modify your phone line in your home.

Reviewing DSL Modem Features

A wide range of features are available for DSL modems. Some models have a minimal feature set and require at least one other computer or network device if you want to add more than one computer to your Internet connection. Higher-end DSL modems can function as a bridge between the DSL network and the local network or as modem/routers. These models have additional hardware and software that enables them to route network traffic and assign IP addresses in addition to connecting your network to the Internet.

Most DSL modems can support bidirectional data rates that match the download and upload rates of the DSL service. For example, a DSL modem may be able to process an ADSL service at 8 Mbps downstream and 1 Mbps upstream. Technically the DSL modem should be able to process data being sent from the Internet to a computer on the local network at up to 8 Mbps. Data being sent out of the network out to the Internet can be processed at speeds up to 1 Mbps. However, the DSL service provider can limit the actual data rate for the DSL service to which you subscribe. As faster DSL services are created, faster DSL modems will be created. The following section summarizes some general features of DSL modems.

DSL Modem Features

The following list briefly describes software features or capabilities that may be available on a DSL modem. The actual features will vary, depending on the model and type of DSL service your choose.

✦ **Routing**   Moving (routing) TCP/IP packets from one computer to another is one of the most critical tasks to perform on a network. DSL modem routers are the most common type of modem installed for connecting local area networks to the DSL provider's network.

✦ **Bridging**   A DSL modem may include a bridging feature to help translate network data and route it to the correct computer on the network. Bridging protocols work independently of TCP/IP protocols. A network bridge enables you to connect two separate networks to each other.

✦ **PPPoE**   PPP is an acronym for Point-to-Point Protocol. It is typically used to enable modems to communicate with other modems that are connected to computers on the Internet. PPPoE (PPP over Ethernet) is a method that your DSL service provider may use to enable your home network to communicate with the service provider's network. The service provider will most likely authenticate your account information before you connect to its Internet services. A DSL subscriber can choose a connection protocol and modem for each DSL service. Some PPPoE DSL modems do not provide any additional features beyond the capability of establishing a connection with the DSL service provider.

✦ **ATM**   ATM (Asynchronous Transfer Mode) is a Transport layer protocol that supports speeds from 622 Mbps to 2.5 Gbps. It uses fixed-size packets, called cells, to transport services with a defined quality of service. Most DSL service providers rely on an ATM connection to support their DSL customers. The DSL modem must be compatible with the service provider's Internet connection. Most DSL modems have some form of built-in ATM support.

✦ **Security**   There are several levels of security for a DSL modem. First, the DSL service provider must be able to authenticate the DSL modem and user account before allowing the modem to access its connections to the Internet. The DSL service provider is responsible not only for ensuring that its customers can access their network connection, but also for keeping non-subscribers out. The bigger security issue is keeping uninvited computers off your local network. You can activate the DSL modem router's firewall software to set up a simple barrier between your network and the Internet.

✦ **IP address translation**   Most DSL modems can be programmed to recognize specific IP addresses as part of the service provider's network. Most DSL modems can also act as a DHCP server, giving out IP addresses to computers as they connect to your network. Depending on the size of your network, you may want to either rely on the DSL modem to allocate IP addresses, or set up a separate computer on your network to perform this task.

✦ **Virtual private network (VPN)**   You may want to configure your network to allow remote computers to log in to it, or use a computer on your network to log in to a VPN. VPN features are installed with the Windows 2000 Professional workstation and server versions of this software. VPN software is also built into some DSL modems.

Choosing an IP Addressing System

The type of DSL service you choose may depend on how many computers you want to connect to the Internet. Most competitive local exchange carriers (CLECs) have a minimal, single-computer service for a nominal fee. The more computers you want to connect to the Internet, the more expensive the monthly CLEC subscription.

If you have only one computer on your home network, you will probably want to subscribe to a DSL service that provides a dynamic IP address and a basic DSL modem to connect your computer to the Internet (see Figure 4-4). If you have Windows 98, Windows NT, Windows Me, or Windows 2000 running on your computer, you can add a second computer to your network connection by activating the Internet Connection Service (ICS) feature in Windows and connecting the second computer to a second Ethernet port on your computer. ICS enables your Windows computer to act as a router for the second Ethernet card.

SURVIVAL TIP   To find out more about how to set up a computer for a point to point over Ethernet connection, go to Chapter 5.

If you have a local area network that you want to connect to the Internet, you must decide how you want manage IP addressing for each computer on the network. You can choose a DSL service that allocates one or several static IP addresses or a service that allows you to set up a DHCP server and assign IP addresses dynamically. You can also use a static or dymanic IP address for each computer on the network. Static IP addresses are great if you don't plan to move a computer to a different network or don't use any network services that require a computer have the same IP address whenever it connects to the Internet. You have a few different IP addressing options available.

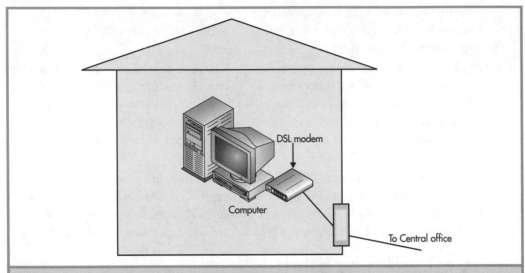

Figure 4-4.   Most basic DSL services, including the PPPoE connection shown here, allow the DSL service provider to assign a dynamic IP address to the computer that uses the DSL modem to connect to the Internet.

The IP addressing system you choose will depend on the network and software needs of those who will be using the local network. You can design the local network to rely solely on dynamic addressing, solely on static addressing, or a combination of static or dynamic addresses. The one thing to avoid is giving two computers the same IP address. If this should occur, network performance problems may occur on the local network.

To find out more about network addressing, go to Chapter 2.

SURVIVAL TIP

CAUTION

You can log into some DSL modems to configure their software settings. Some modems enable you to change settings without permanently saving the changes. If the power to your home or business fails, your DSL modem may reset itself to its default factory settings. Save a backup copy of your DSL modem settings on your PC and use it in case your DSL modem resets itself. Contact your DSL service provider if you want to find out if what features may be available with the DSL modem installed in your home or office.

Designating a Network Administrator

Setting up networking hardware and software can take a lot of time—especially if you include the amount of time you may need to troubleshoot network settings or network performance problems on one or more computers on your local network. To reduce the likelihood of having the network settings, such as a computer's IP address or domain name server settings, changed by accident, you can set up different levels of access on each computer on your network.

You can create as many types of network groups and accounts as you like. One person, for example, can have more than one login account if he or she wants to keep access to some work files separate from access to other files while working on a particular computer. Basically, there should be two kinds of users on your network: a network administrator and regular users.

Network administrators are responsible for setting up new computers and maintaining existing computers on the network. To do this, they need access to most of the computers on the network. In most cases, they need "superuser" access. Superuser is a term that originated with Unix. A super user has access to all files on each computer on the local network. A super user account can add, delete, or change any file on a computer.

Network administrators are usually responsible for configuring and maintaining the software settings for a DSL modem. The following list describes a few common network administrator tasks.

✦ **Account setup**   The network administrator can create, delete, and modify individual or group network accounts.

✦ **Password setup**   The network administrator is responsible for setting up a password system to ensure network security. For example, the network administrator may force all users on the network to change their password once a month. If someone forgets a password, the network administrator can reset the individual's password information or create a new account.

✦ **Network access**   The network administrator is also responsible for setting up network tools to monitor traffic on the network. This account can also set up the firewall and DHCP server software to limit the number of computers that can access the local network.

Figure 4-5 shows the Information window for a folder in Mac OS X. The Read setting for a folder enables you to view or copy all files in a folder. The Write setting enables you to create new documents or delete or modify files in a folder. If you want to share a file on a computer with someone else, you can give that person Read access to a folder. Write access enables a visitor to add or remove files from your computer. You will probably give Write access only to junior network administrators or to network visitors that you trust. You should not give Write privileges to individuals who may abuse their computer access privileges.

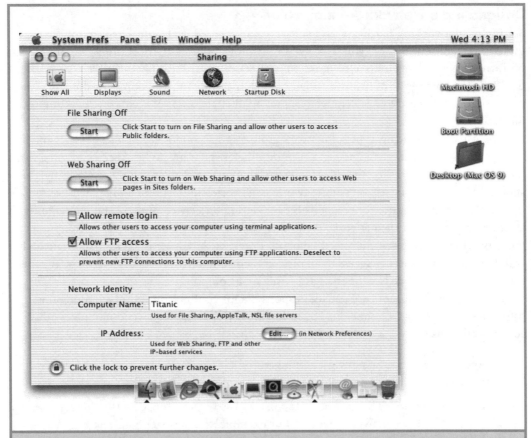

Figure 4-5.   Regular users may not be able to access some directories on a computer, and may only be able to save files in their home directory. If you're an administrator, you can assign access privileges to each folder on your drive.

SURVIVAL TIP

To find out more about how to add, modify, and delete users and groups on Windows, Mac OS, and Linux systems, go to Chapter 10.

You should have a regular user account, whether you're the network administrator or not. Using the regular network account for nonadministrative tasks can help you avoid accidentally erasing a file or moving a critical file to the improper location on a computer. If you create folders and files on a computer as a regular user, other regular users will be able to access those files, too. If you create those files as a superuser, you will need to assign access privileges for the folder containing the files on the computer if you want to share them with another group of network users. Windows and Mac OS 9 computers assign access privileges to folders. Any files in a folder share the access privileges of the folder they reside in. Mac OS X and Linux operating systems enable you to assign access and ownership privileges to files and folders.

Depending on who uses your network, you may want to create different levels of regular users. For example, you may want to create one regular user account for the neighbors who visit your home or office to access the Internet. You may want to give this kind of user browser and e-mail access on your network. However, you may want to create a different, more powerful user account for the people in your home. For example, you may want to create a shared folder on the network so that your roommates or co-workers can share files. If you have an intranet, you may want to give your home users access to a folder on the web server so that each account can have its own web site on the server.

SURVIVAL TIP
Many Unix-based computers, including some of the Linux distributions, include a default guest account. A guest account is usually a minimal level account that enables users to log into the computer and view the files in your home directory. It was originally created as a default access level so that administrators could make sure a very basic user could log into a computer system. However, some network experts see the guest account as a potential security risk to a network. If you want to increase your network security, deactivate or remove the guest account from each computer on your network.

Setting Up a Local Network

The application and networking needs of your network's users will help determine what kinds of clients and servers will be connected to it. For example, if you are a new computer user who wants to access e-mail and surf the Web with a fast Internet connection, you may want to use a Windows or Macintosh computer configured for a single user. On the other hand, if you run a small business and want to several users to connect a small group of networked computers, you may want to set up separate user accounts for each person, and set up a Web or files server on the local network. If you have a Linux computer connected to the network, it might be running an Apache Web server running on it with FTP access, enabling you to add or remove files as the content is updated on the server. The local network may also have several Windows and Macintosh computers that function as client computers with Internet access. You may also want to set up one or two printers on the network.

Before choosing or upgrading a DSL modem, consider the number of network devices that will use the DSL service. It's possible that you may have only one computer connected to the DSL modem. Of course, you can grow your network and add hubs, routers, cables,

computers, and network devices over time. But initially, you must decide how many computers and network devices, such as a printer, will access the DSL modem.

The following list contains a brief description of some of the network-related issues that may affect the DSL modem on your network.

◆ **Number of network devices**   Connecting one computer to the network is much more straightforward than connecting three computers. Count the number of computers and printers that will be connected to the DSL modem. If you have more than one device, consider purchasing an Ethernet hub, and then create a simple map of the network connections you will need to support the computers that want to access the Internet. If you plan to connect only one computer to the DSL network, you can use ICS or Virtual Private Network software on Windows to connect a second PC to the Internet.

◆ **Computer platforms**   Windows, Linux, and Mac OS each have their own networking software and network setup issues. Windows NT and Windows 2000, as well as Mac OS X, have separate operating system products for servers and clients. If you plan to support two or three different computer platforms on your network, choose the one you're most familiar with to bring up your DSL connection to the Internet.

◆ **Workflow**   If you plan to set up a network server, evaluate your network's workflow. If regular user accounts will access servers on the network, make sure the account is set up on the server side before testing the connection on the client side. Once the network is up and running, monitor the workflow of the network and see if you find performance problems.

◆ **Dependent networks**   If you plan to extend your local network by connecting a second local network with a router, decide where you want to install Ethernet cabling, hubs, or routers.

Choosing Computers for Services

Whether you have a heap of old computers waiting to be connected to a network or are planning to purchase new (or used) computers to add to your network, make sure you select computers that are equipped with the hardware and software capable of performing the network tasks you need. For example, if you want to turn a computer into a backup server for the local network, make sure the computer has a small computer system interface (SCSI), USB, or FireWire port that can connect to the tape drive or CD-ROM that you want to use to store backup media. On the other hand, if you need to set up a client computer that is easy to use, you may want to set up a Macintosh computer that has an Ethernet or AirPort card. The following list describes the client and server products and services for the latest Windows, Mac OS, and Linux products.

- ◆ **Windows Me**   Latest, upgraded version of Windows 95, and 98. Windows Me lacks some of more robust internals of Windows 2000, but it is a popular operation system for running networked and non-networked programs on a PC.

- ◆ **Windows 2000**   Upgrade to Windows NT. Windows 2000 is a robust client system and is also used as a operating system to develop software or host network services. Like the Windows Me and XP releases, you can share files over a network and run a browser program or e-mail application using the user-friendly interface.

- ◆ **Windows 2000 Server**   All the same great operating system software as Windows 2000, plus several possible server configurations to choose from. You can configure the PC to host network services, such as DHCP, DNS, Remote Access, or Routing services; host applications such as e-mail, database, terminal, or component services; or be a media, streaming media server, file, or print server.

- ◆ **Windows XP**   The newest realease of Windows, and the latest update to Windows 2000, Windows XP Home edition and Windows XP Pro offer a new, fresh look, or the original classic Windows look.

- ◆ **Mac OS 9**   Classic Macintosh operating system. It runs alongside Mac OS X, enabling you to run any Macintosh application side by side with Mac OS X programs. Mac OS 9 enables you to share files or turn your Mac into a Web server.

- ◆ **Mac OS X**   Apple's latest operating system. It is based on the Berkeley Software Distribution (BSD) and enables you to perform all the same, great file- (file transfer protocol, ftp) and web-sharing features of Mac OS 9, in addition to all the great, new Mac OS X features.

- ◆ **Mac OS X Server**   Enables you to turn a Macintosh computer into a cross-platform file or web server or host some Windows services, such as a Windows name server (WINS)

- ◆ **Linux 68K** (Red Hat distribution)   Enables you to run programs from a command-line interface or from one of two windowing interfaces: Gnome or the K Development Environment. Linux distributions install different combinations of operating system and application software. The Red Hat distribution turns networking features off by default. However, a Linux workstation can host ftp and Web services in addition to supporting regular client tasks, such as text editing, e-mail, and web browsing.

SURVIVAL TIP

Several components on a computer can affect its performance on a network. As long as the computer has an Ethernet card that supports the same speed as the rest of the network, you shouldn't have to worry about the computer affecting network performance. Before adding a computer to a network, copy a few directories to its hard drive and run some programs to gauge its performance off the network. If the computer seems slower after it's connected to the local network, there may be a performance problem.

It may seem that older, slower computers aren't welcome on a network, even when they are equipped with 10 Base T Ethernet cards and cables. Older, slower computers can be added to a network, as helper computers to servers or network devices. For example, you can install print spooling software on a Power PC Mac and then set it up next to a LaserWriter printer on a network, so that it can log print jobs sent to the printer, or you can install Linux for PPC on a Power PC Mac and use it as a network traffic monitoring tool.

CAUTION

A hub or router may seem to be working fine when you first install it on your network. Monitor your network after installing a new hub or other network device. If odd networking behavior ensues, it may be due to some sort of network incompatibility between different network-related chip sets in different network devices.

Evaluating Software for Clients and Servers

If you have installed one of the operating systems listed previously, and have the latest browser or e-mail programs on each computer within the last year or two, you won't need to worry about application compatibility. If you have a computer that has already been successfully configured to access the Internet, chances are it will "just work" when you connect it to your DSL network. The latest Windows, Mac OS, and Linux compatible browsers, e-mail, telnet, and FTP applications are more likely to be incompatible with the operating system that they're running on than the network. However, most folks can't discern whether a problem with their computer is related to an application incompatibility or a network problem.

If you're a network administrator, you can configure each computer with a set of applications of your choice. You can monitor computers on your network and monitor or upgrade applications on each computer platform connected to your network. The following list summarized a few things to keep in mind when reviewing computer configurations, such as memory, disk, network, and operating system requirements for the latest Windows, Mac OS, and Linux operating systems.

◆ **Memory and processor requirements**   How much memory will each application need? You may need to upgrade the computer's memory to support the application that requires the most memory. Mac OS 9, Linux, and Windows 2000 and XP computers can have a minimum of 64 MB of physical memory installed in them. However 128–256 MB of memory is recommended. The more memory each application will need to run on the computer, the more memory you should add to the computer.

◆ **Disk space requirements**   Check the total disk size and the amount of disk space available on the drive. Check the software requirements for each application that you want to install on the computer. Make sure the computer has enough free disk space to create and modify documents for several applications. Mac OS, Windows, and Linux systems usually require approximately 400 MB of disk space for a minimum installation and up to 4 GB, depending on the applications installed along with the operating system.

✦ **Operating system requirements**   What version of which operating system is running on each computer? The latest versions of Mac OS are Mac OS 9.1 and Mac OS X. Apple increments the version number of the operating system as updates are made available. For example, an update for Mac OS 9, is Mac OS 9.0.1.

✦ **Windows XP**   Latest version of the Windows operating system. Windows 2000, Windows Me, Windows 98 Special Edition, and Windows NT 4.0, Service Pack 4, 5, or 6, are all capable of running the latest web browsers and e-mail applications with reliable network performance. As Microsoft updates its operating system software, it releases service packs.

✦ **Linux**   Distribution version numbers may vary from vendor to vendor. Most distributions base their version number on the version of the Linux kernel built into the release. Red Hat, along with SuSE, and most Linux vendors use an incremental number for each new release of the operating system. For example, Red Hat will release Linux 7.0. An update to Linux 7.0 will use version number 7.1.

✦ **Networking requirements**   Evaluate how each computer will connect to the network. Try to install adequate network hardware to maintain consistent network performance for the average number of computers that will be working simultaneously on the network. The latest Windows, Mac OS, and Linux operation systems are generally compatible with most network hardware, driver, and application software, as well as with browser and e-mail programs.

Create a simple inventory of applications and version numbers for each computer platform you want to support on your network. Then check with each software vendor and see whether upgrades are available for the operating system or computer hardware configurations you plan to connect to the network. If you need to install an upgrade, install it before connecting the computer to the network.

**SURVIVAL
TIP**

Each computer system has a limit to how much memory it can recognize. This usually tops out at approximately 1GB of memory. The general rule is to purchase twice as much memory as you think you will need to run the applications installed on your computer. A good ballpark figure for a client computer starts at approximately 128MB and averages between 256MB and 512MB. You may want to install more memory if you plan to use a computer as a file, web, or mail server. Most experts say you can never have enough memory. Buy as much as you can afford.

Problems: Configuring the DSL Modem

The DSL service you subscribe to will largely determine what kind of DSL modem will be installed in your home or office. If you have a basic DSL modem that provides a Point-to-Point over Ethernet (PPPoE) connection to the Internet, you won't have to worry about adjusting additional modem settings for your DSL service. DSL services that support several computers usually install a more sophisticated DSL modem that acts as a bridge or router to the Internet. These more advanced DSL modems may have several features built in to their firmware, such as login software, router configuration settings, firewall software, and the potential to support VPNs. The following sections review some of the issues associated with running services on a DSL modem versus running them on a standalone computer.

Limiting Network Access

Almost all the features on router or bridge-capable DSL modems are designed to provide a constant connection to the Internet. You can work with your DSL service provider to review the network features available on your DSL modem. You may want to set up your DSL modem to provide some form of network security, if that particular feature is available, without preventing computers on your local network from accessing other computers on the Internet.

Firewalls

The term "firewall" is used to describe a network device, such as a computer or network switch, that connects a local network to the Internet, but prevents computers on the external network from accessing computers behind the firewall. Many corporations and schools use firewalls to prevent their computers from being accessed from the Internet.

Firewalls can be created using hardware, software, or a combination of both. You can configure a Linux, Windows, or Macintosh computer, provided you have the right software, to act as a firewall on your network or use the firewall software built into the DSL modem to block Internet surfers from gaining access on your network. Decide whether you want to activate or deactivate this feature on your DSL modem.

CAUTION　Depending on how you set up your network, a firewall may prevent some services, such as a VPN connection, from completing. You may have to set up a separate connection if you want a particular computer to connect to the VPN, or configure a more sophisticated firewall to let specific IP addresses communicate through the firewall.

Static or Dynamic IP Addressing

Before you can connect your local network to the Internet, you need to decide how you want IP addresses to be handed out on your network. As each computer connected to the network powers on, it will need to be assigned an IP address so that it can interact with computer file, mail, and Web servers across the network. If your DSL modem has a DHCP server built in as part of its networking features, you can activate this feature in the DSL modem.

DHCP servers can support static IP addresses. Your DSL service provider will let you know how many static IP addresses are included with your DSL account. One way to encourage network security is to set up a dynamic DHCP server. Having a static IP address gives your computer a constant IP address. Because the static IP address does not change, however, it is possible that someone may try to gain access to it over the Internet. A DHCP server will assign a unique IP address to a computer when it connects to your network. Not having the same, constant computer address can make it difficult for potential network hackers to know which computer they may be trying to access. Most DHCP server software will enable you to choose the number of IP addresses that can be given out on your network. This can help you limit the number of computers that can share your network.

Network Address Translators (NAT)

A network address translator is usually a feature that's combined with a DHCP server. For example, if you have a static IP address, you can combine a DHCP server with network address translation to add more IP addresses to your network. The DHCP server will map the computers that are assigned IP addresses. As network data is sent to the Internet, the NAT will change one of the newer IP addresses into the static IP address. When network packets arrive from the Internet, the NAT will translate them and the DHCP server will route the packets to the appropriate computer on the network.

NOTE

If you plan to use a VPN connection from your local network to a remote network, you may need to deactivate the NAT in the DSL modem or DHCP server. Most VPNs require the connecting computer to have the same IP address that is forwarded by the DSL router. If a NAT is activated, the IP address on the local network will change when it's sent to the remote network. This will result in an unsuccessful connection to the remote network. Before you deactivate your NAT, check to see whether you can connect to your VPN. If you are unable to connect to your VPN, consider trying a different NAT solution for your local network. Some implementations of NAT permit VPN tunnels to pass through them correctly. This can enable your local network to have more than one computer access VPNs without requiring you to use a static IP address for each node.

Reviewing DSL Modem Features

DSL modems can share many of the same router features or vary greatly in capabilities. Check the features available for the DSL modem before choosing a subscriber service. Try to select the DSL modem that offers the features you want to use with your network.

NOTE Some DSL modems enable you to set up the login software. You can require the login to occur from your local network to help prevent computers on the external network from guessing your login name or password.

Solutions: Upgrading Your Office

Choosing your DSL modem and planning your network are the first steps to bringing up a network in your home or office. If you don't plan to use a wireless network, you may need to carve up some of the walls in your home or business to set up the network hubs, cabling, and routers throughout the building. This can be a costly task, which may need upgrading, depending on how quickly your network grows. The following sections review some of the general issues associated with the physical aspects of installing a network in a home or office.

Hub Placement and Cabling

Before you drill holes in a wall, measure how far the network will extend, starting from the DSL modem and moving to the computer that will be located at the farthest physical point on the network. Measure the actual length of the Ethernet cable, and not the shortest walking distance between the two locations. You may need to purchase a hub that strengthens the network signal at approximately 25 feet. The length of the network can affect network performance, as well as extraneous broadcast or magnetic noise located close to the networking cable.

Decide where computers will be located on the network. Then choose how many hubs and routers you'll need to install to support those computers. Create a diagram of the network for each floor of your home or office, and then review your home's or office's blueprint to find out how the electrical wiring is distributed in the walls.

Choose the optimal location in the wall that will hold networking equipment. Make sure that the wall is deep enough to hold the hub or router, plus any cables that will be connected to it. If everything looks like it will fit, choose the wall closest to the DSL modem and connect the equipment. Make sure the network gear works properly before you put it in the wall, and then again after you've installed it. Let the network connection run for a few days (while you're using the computers with the DSL modem) before sealing the wall to make sure all the connections are working reliably.

Setting Up a Simple Network

After you have set up a single computer on the network, set up a second computer and at least one network device, creating a small, simple network. This configuration will test the sending and receiving of data on your local network. You can set up two Windows or Macintosh computers, activate file sharing, and download a folder or file to see if the network can handle the traffic. If you have a printer connected to the network, you can send a print job to the printer from each computer to get an idea of what network performance is like when both computers try to print to the same printer at the same time.

Bringing Up a Server

Many kinds of servers can reside on a network. Some of the popular servers are Web servers, file servers, mail servers, and database servers. However, you can turn any computer into a file server. Windows and Mac OS have file-sharing capabilities built into them. You can share files between two Windows or two Macintosh computers. Alternatively, you can

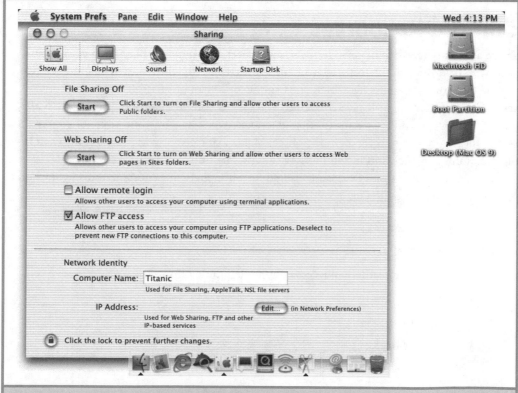

Figure 4-6. Activate file sharing to share data between two computers on your local network. The Mac OS X Sharing window is shown here.

install an FTP or web server on a Linux computer and share files with a Windows or Macintosh. Some operating systems, like Mac OS X, enable you to activate FTP services in addition to file sharing services (see Figure 4-6).

In order to bring up a server on a network, you'll need to install any server-related software, and configure the server's operating system to activate any file-sharing or IP networking software. Then you will need to create at least one login account so that another computer can connect to it over the network. Once you've configured the server software, power on the server and try to access it from a second computer on the network. You can copy files between the client and server to test the local network.

Configuring and adding computers to a network can help test the DHCP services, if they're activated on the DSL modem. You can also test other network services, such as loading a web page, sending e-mail, or accessing a VPN, to see that the network is configured properly for the tasks you want to perform. If network security is a concern, you may want to have a friend try to access your computer over the Internet or access your DSL modem to see whether unexpected problems occur.

Additional Resources

There are many features to consider before and after a DSL modem has been connected to your network. Review the features available for the DSL modem that will be connected to your network. Then decide which ones you want to run on the DSL modem or on a separate computer on your network. Once you have a computer running smoothly with your DSL service, you may want to expand your network or wire your home to support that computer in any room of the home or office. Make a simple network diagram for each floor of your home or office and install hubs or cabling one hub at a time.

To find out more about DSL modems and installing network equipment into your home or office, consult the following resources:

- ✦ www.dslrouters.com
- ✦ www.planetdsl.net
- ✦ www.dsl-modem-internet-access.com/modem/index.htm
- ✦ www.linuxrouter.org
- ✦ www.aquila.net
- ✦ www.csgnetwork.com

Chapter 5

Setting Up Computers

Network devices, such as computers, printers, and digital cameras, populate networks. Computers are the most sophisticated of all these network devices, enabling you to run a wide range of applications or services that can take advantage of a local network or Internet connection. Over the years, computer hardware has evolved from divergent Macintosh and PC hardware slots, connectors, and cables to a more standardized, network-compatible platform. Most video, network connectors, and device slots, such as PCI, USB, Ethernet, and FireWire (IEEE 1394), are identical on Macs and PCs manufactured over the past few years.

Although each computer can support graphics and networking hardware and software standards, each computer can use a different operating system, which results in each computer using a unique implementation of networking software. This chapter takes a closer look at some of the more popular computer, operating system, and network configurations that can populate your DSL home or business network.

✦ **Computers**   Windows, Mac, or Linux computers have many common hardware and software features. Find out how computer hardware, software, and network-related technologies work together to send and receive data with other computers connected to the same network.

✦ **Operating systems**   In addition to managing memory, disk, and input and output on a computer, an operating system is responsible for providing network services, such as routing, for network-savvy applications.

✦ **Network settings**   You can configure the network settings on an operating system so that it can be recognized on your home or office network.

Basic Concepts: Inside a Computer

The latest computer models, including Macs and PCs, share many of the same kinds of hardware components. The basic hardware chip sets—such as a processor, memory, hard drive, USB, FireWire, modem, and Ethernet ports—are virtually identical for both computer platforms. In most cases, both can run the same software.

Despite the similarities, computers vary from one manufacturer to another. Although most of the parts and systems of a computer are standard, there is no right or wrong way for a manufacturer to follow that standard. This can result in small or large software incompatibilities. Although it's rare, it's possible that an Ethernet hub may not be compatible with a particular Ethernet card; network chip set; operating system; or network device, such as a printer. As you put together your network, don't be surprised to encounter software incompatibilities with network hardware.

The following sections provide a close look at how computers work and explain network hardware and software settings for each computer platform. This information will help you understand how each computer on your network functions on its own and on a network.

A Closer Look at Computers

Every PC or Macintosh computer shares some, but not all, of the same core components. For example, every computer requires electricity, so you can expect a power supply on a desktop computer or a battery for a laptop. The processor, memory, and external ports all need to connect to a logic board, which also enables a hard drive, CD-ROM, DVD-ROM, video card, and network card or chip set to be attached to the computer. The final ingredient required to make a computer work is an operating system, which will usually include a few applications. The following sections explain how a computer works and processes network information.

What's in a Computer?

There are many hardware components that make a computer a computer. Some computers have more expansion room for memory, hard drives, PCI cards, and other computer peripherals. Other computers, such as laptops, are smaller, with fewer expansion ports and hardware components. The following list provides a short description of some of the most common components found in today's PC and Macintosh computers.

✦ **Processor**   A chip the provides the horsepower in a computer, the central processing unit (CPU) is responsible for interpreting and running machine code on a computer. A computer can have one or more processors on the logic board. If the operating system can take advantage of each processor, you can run more tasks with applications on that computer.

✦ **Memory**   A set of hardware chips that provides a temporary, fast access storage area for system and application data processed on a computer. When a computer is powered off, the contents in memory are cleared.

✦ **Bus speed**   The speed at which the processor is capable of communicating with the other subsystems, such as the network, memory, disk, and video chip sets on the logic board. Most PC and Macintosh computers have a bus speed of 100 MHz.

✦ **Hard drive**   A storage device on a computer. Most computers have a hard disk size of several gigabytes of data. The hard drive uses a file system to provide a permanent storage area for all the software installed on a computer, such as the operating system and applications.

✦ **CD-ROM, CD-R, CD-RW, or DVD drive**   CD-ROM media is most commonly used to distribute computer content, such as operating system and application software. CD-ROM and DVD-ROM drives enable a computer to read CD-ROM or DVD-ROM disks. CD-R, CD-RW, and DVD-read/write-able disks are a form of removable media that can be used to back up data on a computer's hard drive or to share data with other computers.

✦ **Network interface card or network chip set**   The hardware responsible for processing the network information on a computer and storing the network interface card identification, such as the MAC address.

✦ **Logic board**   The circuit board on a computer responsible for integrating all the hardware components in a computer.

✦ **Monitor**   A tube or flat-screen display that connects to the video or graphics card on a desktop or laptop computer, enabling a computer user to view a command line or graphical user interface, and interact with the computer's hardware and software programs.

✦ **Keyboard**   The primary text input device for a computer. Most desktop keyboards connect to a computer's USB port. Laptops have a keyboard built into the hardware design.

✦ **Mouse or trackpad**   The primary input device used to select items in an operating system that supports a graphical user interface, such as Windows, Mac OS, and Gnome or K Development Environment (KDE) on Linux.

✦ **Modem**   Also called an analog modem. A device responsible for converting digital signals into analog signals, and vice versa, enabling a computer to connect to the Internet over a point-to-point connection created over a voice telephone line.

✦ **Port**   A hardware connector that works with the operating system software installed on a computer to allow a peripheral device to communicate with the rest of the computer. Each port enables an external device to be connected to a computer. Common ports are USB, FireWire (1394), microphone, headphone, and video ports. These ports are used to connect a display, network, keyboard, mouse, printer, or other device to a computer.

✦ **Operating system**   The software code responsible for starting up a computer and enabling an application to communicate with all the hardware components on a computer.

✦ **Applications**   Software that enables you to perform a specific set of tasks on a computer, such as browse web pages, create text documents, draw pictures, or edit video on a computer.

What's a Logic Board?

The logic board of a computer, also called a motherboard, holds all the hardware chip sets that define the heart of a computer. A chip set is a group of custom-designed hardware circuits that is responsible for performing unique tasks, such as processing network data, processing data intended for memory (SDRAM or DRAM) chips, processing data for a USB or FireWire port, and so on. Each hardware chip set can be programmed to work with a computer's operating system software. For example, if the networking chip set on the logic board is designed to be IEEE 802 compliant for Ethernet and IP data, the developer of the logic board should be able to use the IEEE 802 standard to write software that enables the networking chip set to work with IP packets and Ethernet networks.

Desktop logic boards contain many of the same hardware components as a laptop computer, such as a hard drive, processor, memory, graphics card, and external ports for a USB and a modem. Figure 5-1 illustrates how a browser sends data from the Application layer on a client computer down through the operating system, and Network layer and

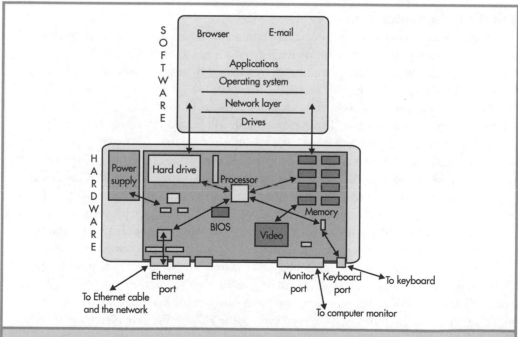

Figure 5-1.   Network application software installed on a hard drive, such as a browser or e-mail program, is routed through the processor and across the logic board out to the network.

drivers to the hardware components in a computer, and then out to the network. Figure 5-1 is a generalization, so each computer system will probably work a little differently than what's shown here.

The logic board is an interface for input devices—such as a keyboard, mouse, monitor, CD-ROM, or DVD-ROM drive—and output devices, such as a monitor or printer. Some input and output devices may have software programmed into them. This code can communicate with the operating system installed on the hard drive connected to the logic board. The operating system manages the data as it is transferred between the device drivers to memory, and then to the hard disk.

NOTE

It's possible to put a fast computer on a network, and observe slow performance on that computer. If the computer connects to a slower computer on the network, the faster computer may appear to be slow while it waits for the networked computer to process its request. It is also possible for the faster computer to generate more network tasks than the network can manage. Of course, a faster processor will be able to show faster overall software performance once the network's performance has been restored.

What's a Computer Monitor?

Although the early computer monitors were monochrome black screens with green or amber text, today's computer monitors range from 15- to 22-inch tube displays, to flat liquid crystal displays (LCDs). A traditional tube-based monitor is usually connected to your desktop computer. However, a growing number of desktops are starting to switch from tube- to flat-screen displays that range in size from 15 to 22 inches to reduce the tabletop footprint of a monitor. The average laptop will have a 10- to 15-inch display.

Most monitors work with either a PC or a Macintosh computer. The two biggest roadblocks to hooking up a monitor to a computer are the cable connector and driver software for the monitor. Almost all desktop PCs and the latest Macs use a 3-row, 15-pin RGB connector. Laptops generally have the best monitor setup: they use an LCD, which is a flat-panel display. An LCD is always connected to the laptop, so you don't have to worry about finding a display that's compatible with a particular video card. Most laptops also have a standard VGA connector, enabling the laptop to connect to an external display or projection system.

In order for a computer monitor to display data on your computer, you must connect a cable to the monitor and to a graphics card or graphic chip set on the computer's logic board. Although most computers have a graphics card or chip set built into them, some models require you to purchase your own card. Some PCs use an Extended Industry Standard Architecture (EISA) graphics card standard, but most desktops support a PCI graphics card. A standard video card will have a chip set enabling graphics to be displayed on a computer, as well as video random access memory (VRAM) that stores graphics in memory for the computer monitor. The more video memory and the more colors the monitor can display, the higher-resolution graphics the computer will be able to display on a computer screen. This doesn't affect the network, unless someone sends huge graphics files to a server on the network.

Most software controls for a monitor are located in the operating system. Windows and Macintosh installation CDs include a bootable version of the operating system so that you can install or upgrade the operating system software on your computer. Most of these bootable CDs will start a computer with some networking capabilities. This can be helpful if you're trying to determine whether the applications or operating system already installed on the computer are the cause of network-related problems on a computer.

If you want to set up a dedicated graphics computer on your network, be prepared to spend some time reviewing graphics card and monitor capabilities and compatibilities before making a purchase. Also, most graphics applications require a considerable amount of computer memory. In addition to the video-related requirement for the software, you may want to upgrade the amount of memory installed in the computer.

NOTE

Computers can work with graphics and video. Graphics can be two-dimensional or three-dimensional. They are used primarily to display the operating system's desktop and applications that run on your computer. The term "video" usually refers to full-motion MPEG or MPEG 2 video that can be created or viewed using a video-savvy application, such as Windows MediaPlayer, or Apple QuickTime.

What's an Operating System?

A computer's hardware components, such as the monitor, keyboard, and mouse, are essential. But a computer needs software in order to interface with hardware components. Different kinds of software enable a computer to perform a wide range of tasks. Most software capabilities depend on the operating system software installed on the computer.

An operating system plays a critical role in initiating and sustaining the network connection on a computer. The network portion of an operating system relies on many other components, such as the file system, graphics systems, and task management system, in order to interact with network applications. The heart of an operating system is the *kernel*, which is responsible for scheduling tasks, managing memory, and handling device drivers. There is no standard design for the operating system kernel. Linux has its own kernel, and Mac OS X has a kernel derived from the Berkeley Software Distribution (BSD) Unix distribution. Windows uses its own custom kernel, and Mac OS 9 also has its own nanokernel.

In addition to the kernel design, each operating system has a different way of handling networking tasks. Linux and Mac OS X build networking into their kernels, while Windows and Mac OS 9 operating systems run networking separately from the kernel. Some people

argue that one operating system design runs better on a network than the other. However, for the most part, Windows, Mac OS, and Linux are fairly reliable, stable operating systems for standalone or network-based computer systems.

NOTE

NIC is an acronym for network interface card. Most computers have an Ethernet network interface card built in. If not, you can either install a PCI or PC card Ethernet solution, or use a USB-to-Ethernet adapter.

Today's operating systems, such as Windows, Mac OS, and Linux, are made up of hundreds of files and small applications. The basic breakdown of the operating system is as follows: The kernel loads first, followed by device drivers; low-level system code, such as the task manager; and high-level code, such as control panels. Applications run at the highest software level and rely on the operating system, or lower software levels, in order to get the computer to start a particular task. Regardless of size, an operating system needs a boot code to enable a computer to run a certain set of software instructions when the computer is first powered on. This startup process checks the integrity of both the hardware and software on the computer. Networking hardware and software is set up in this boot process.

A Computer's Startup Process

PC computers have a Basic Input/Output System (BIOS), and Macintosh computers have a read-only memory (ROM). The BIOS and ROM consist of a hardware chip, and software that stores information for the operating system and hardware devices attached to the computer. All PCs use a BIOS to start a computer. You can boot a PC directly into a BIOS and adjust the settings for the computer's hardware ports. However, you must save your changes and reboot the computer to use the new BIOS settings. Macintosh computers use a ROM to start. Part of the ROM is stored in hardware; the majority is stored as a file on your hard drive. ROM settings cannot be changed; so when you start a Macintosh computer, its ROM boots directly into the operating system.

The startup process on a computer is fairly straightforward and similar, regardless of operating system. When you power on a computer, the ROM or BIOS performs a quick hardware check to make sure that the hardware systems on the logic board are powered on and working. BIOS and ROM do not have the same startup behavior. Next, the core pieces of the operating system—the kernel, core drivers for hardware, and operating system modules—load. These system files are located in a directory of system files on the CD-ROM or on your hard drive. Modular operating system components can consist of code to display graphics on the computer monitor, play sounds on the computer's speaker(s), and interact with a keyboard and mouse.

When the operating system has loaded, a desktop should appear on the computer screen if you're running Windows, Mac OS, Gnome or KDE with Linux, or X Window System on Unix. You can customize settings for the operating system or start applications, such as a browser or mail application, after the operating system has successfully started the computer. Table 5-1 shows the operating system requirements for PCs and Macintosh computers.

NOTE   The BSD kernel, which is part of the Berkeley Software Distribution, was originally designed by students and scientists at the University of California, Berkeley. Universities around the world use it as the operating system for network servers. It is also used as a highly respected, reliable network operating system for hosting web, mail, file, and other data-related servers on the Internet and intranets. Apple liked the BSD kernel enough to incorporate it into the Mac OS operating system.

Computer Platform	Operating System	Requirements
PC	Windows Me	Intel Pentium II processor or equivalent; minimum of 64MB of memory; 1GB of available disk space
	Windows 2000	Intel Pentium III processor or faster; minimum of 128MB of memory; several GB of free disk space
	Windows XP Pro	Intel Pentium III processor or faster; minimum of 128MB of memory; several GB of available disk space
	Linux	Intel x86 processor or equivalent; 64MB of memory; 4GB of disk space
	Net BSD	Intel x86 processor or equivalent; 2GB of disk space, 64 MB of memory.
Mac	Mac OS 9.1	Any Power Macintosh model; 128MB of memory; 500MB free disk space
	Mac OS X	G3 or G4 Power PC processor; a minimum of 128MB of memory; several GB of available disk space
	Linux	603, 604, G3, and G4 Power PC processors; 64MB of memory; 4GB of available disk space
	Free BSD	603, 604, G3, and G4 Power PC processors; 64MB of memory; 4GB of available disk space if you want to install the X Window System, a graphical user interface, and all application bundles

Table 5-1.   Computer Systems and Operating System Requirements

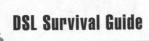

Applications

You may already know that you can't really do much on a networked computer unless you first run a program. You must use an application, or program, to surf the Web, read or send e-mail messages, copy files to and from your computer, or chat with a friend on the other side of the world. Figure 5-2 shows how each network application must interact with the network settings in the operating system in order to create and maintain a connection with another computer on the local or extended network.

Some people, such as developers, refer to applications as high-level code. An application should not need to know what kind of networking hardware is plugged into the computer. The application code relies on the operating system to route the application's request to the correct hardware device. Hardware and device drivers are sometimes referred to as low-level code. The operating system, and its capability to load drivers or low-level code for the hardware components on a computer, should be able to manage network data handed to it from any number of network applications that might be running at once on a computer.

SURVIVAL TIP

To find out more about how to set up e-mail and browser applications on your computer, see Chapter 6.

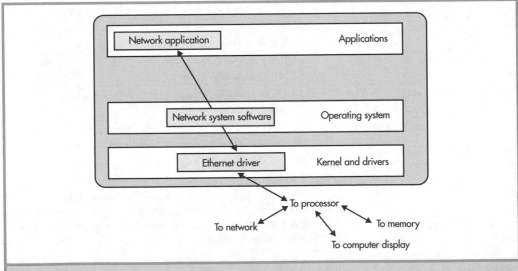

Figure 5-2. Networking applications work closely with an operating system to send and receive data over the network.

How a Client Accesses a Server Over a Network

Network applications, such as a browser or e-mail application, have two basic functions: to send data over the network to a server application, or to receive data sent over the network from a server application. Besides performing these functions, each application has an interface—such as a menu bar, menus, buttons, and windows—that enable you to send and receive data over the network connection, apply a command to the data acquired over the network, or organize the data in a window or as a file stored on your hard drive. The data that can be displayed in a browser or e-mail window, such as an HTML or e-mail file, can be stored either on a server located on the network or on your local hard drive.

Client computers running a browser or e-mail application spend most of their network time receiving data from one or more servers connected to the same network. Each server runs software that may rely on another computer that is also connected to the Internet. The DSL modem enables a computer on your local network to interact with any web or mail server that is connected to the Internet. Servers are designed to interact and manage multiple client connections, serving web pages or e-mail by enabling a client computer to log in or simply load a web page over the network. Servers and clients rely on a computer's IP address to find out where to get or send a web page or e-mail over the network.

How Networking Data Can Find Its Way Around the Network

Several sets of numbers are used to define a computer's location and its identification on a network. Each IP address maps to each computer's MAC or Ethernet address. The router software runs an Address Resolution Protocol (ARP) that translates the IP address into a MAC address. Then the router uses the MAC address to locate your computer on the local network. The computer must also be configured with the router's gateway and name server, so that the software on the computer will know where it should be sent on the local network. If a computer uses file-sharing services, such as File Sharing on Mac OS or NetBEUI on Windows, you will also need to install the appropriate operating system components and set up user login and password accounts on the host, or server computer.

✦ **Name servers** A name server helps a computer convert a name into a number. This enables computers on a local network to locate other file, web, and mail servers on the Internet. Your DSL modem account should have included the name servers for the DSL service provider. You can add this name server information to a Windows, Mac, or Linux computer on your local network if you want it to access other computers on the Internet.

✦ **Gateway** If the DSL modem establishes a point-to-point connection with the provider, the gateway address will be the DSL service provider's gateway address to the Internet. If the DSL router is the gateway for your local network's access to the

Internet, the gateway address will be the IP address of the router. If the DSL service provider does not recognize this IP address, your local network will not be able to receive or send data beyond the local network.

✦ **File sharing**   You can set up a Windows or Macintosh computer to share files with another computer on the network. Most of the file-sharing features built into the operating system enable Windows computers to share with other Windows computers, and Macs to share with other Macs. To share Windows files with a Mac, you may need to convert your PC or Mac into an FTP or web server.

✦ **Access privileges**   You can set up administrator and general user login and password accounts on all server and client computers on the network. Setting access privileges to the computers on your network helps improve the stability of the computer system and can help you monitor network usage. The access privileges may be limited or easy to circumvent on a Macintosh, Windows 98, or Windows Me computer. Linux, Mac OS X, Windows NT, Windows 2000, and Windows XP provide a larger set of access privileges. If you are familiar with these operating systems and you plan to connect many users to your local network, you may want to consider upgrading the computers to these operating systems if each PC or Mac meets the hardware requirements.

CAUTION   Don't misunderstand—sharing is a good thing for a computer to be able to do. However, some operating systems default to sharing all the contents of your hard drive with any guest who connects to your computer. Be sure to check the file-sharing settings on your computer before you connect it to a local network or the Internet.

Cache, Memory, and Other Performance Enhancing Designs

Computers may look alike and have many of the same parts, but some models may be faster than others. The size of the computer's monitor, the amount of memory installed, and the input and output speed of the bus on the logic board all contribute to the overall performance of the hardware on a computer. Some computer makers add specific kinds of memory chips and cache chips to help boost the flow of data through the hardware.

What is a cache? A cache is a small, dedicated amount of hardware or software storage used to store small bits of frequently used filename or system information. Storing this type of data in a cache can give a computer system a small performance boost by not having to load the data into memory every time it needs to be accessed.

A cache, or cache memory, is smaller and faster than main system memory. This enables the system memory to store frequently accessed data in a faster chip, potentially boosting the overall performance of the system. Although you can read about the chip sets from a computer specification sheet, try using a computer for your own needs before purchasing one for your network.

Some operating systems and applications store data in a cache located on the hard drive. For example, on a Macintosh computer, you can set the data cache in the Memory control panel. Internet Explorer on a Macintosh or Windows computer enables you to set the size of the browser cache in the browser's Preferences or Options window. Cached data enables software to quickly access frequently used data. When code is accessed repeatedly, it gets placed in the cache. If the software stops using the code, the operating system or program clears that data from the cache as new data is added.

Problems Setting Up Network Software

Most current operating systems install networking software by default with the rest of the system software. Mac OS installs Open Transport starting from Mac OS version 7.5 and higher and including newer versions of the Mac operating system, such as Mac OS X. Windows 98 Special Edition, Windows Millenium Edition, Windows 2000, Windows NT 4.0, and Windows XP also install network software by default. The most current version of an operating system is not already installed on a computer, and it has plenty of processor power, memory, and disk space available to support a newer version of the Windows, Mac, or Linux operating system, consider upgrading that computer.

Review applications installed on your computers to make sure each is compatible with the new operating system. You may need to upgrade applications in addition to upgrading the operating system. The following sections explain how to configure each operating system to connect to your DSL provider's network and install a browser application.

Adding Network Support to an Operating System

If you want to wait to upgrade your computer hardware so that you can run a newer operating system, visit Apple's or Microsoft's web site to see which version of the latest system update might be available for your computer hardware. If you have a PC running Windows 3.0 or Windows 95, you may want to consider backing up any files on it, upgrading to a new PC, and then installing Linux on the older PC. The following sections familiarize you with the network features and settings available on Windows, Mac OS, and Linux.

Networking Software and Windows

This book provides specific examples for configuring network settings and running applications with Windows 2000, Windows XP, Mac OS 9, Mac OS X, and Red Hat Linux on a personal computer. The general process for bringing a computer onto a network is nearly identical for each computer. First, make sure that the Ethernet hardware is connected to your computer and properly connected to the network. Next, make sure that the software for the Ethernet card is installed with the operating system on the computer. The following sections show you how to configure the network settings for each of these operating systems.

A Short Guide to Windows Network Software

On a Windows 2000 system, open the Network and Dial-Up Connections window to view the network software installed for an Ethernet device on your computer. If the operating system can communicate with the Ethernet card, you can configure the TCP/IP information for the computer. Then, use the Network Identification Wizard to set up a network account, or log in to another computer on the network by visiting Network Neighborhood.

Viewing System Properties   Perform the following steps to view the version of Windows 2000 running on the computer, and the amount of memory installed in the computer.

1. Right-click the My Computer icon on the desktop. The System Properties window will open.

2. View your computer's operating system and memory settings by opening the System Properties window, shown in Figure 5-3. Right-click the My Computer icon, and then choose Properties from the shortcut menu. Select the General tab in the System Properties window. The version information for Windows is located in the top-right

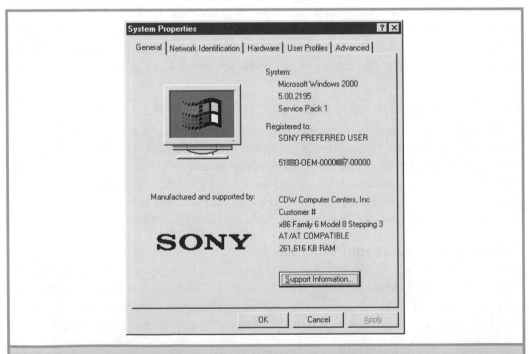

Figure 5-3.   The System Properties window displays the version of Windows running and the amount of memory installed on your computer.

area of the window below the System text. The memory information is located toward the bottom area of the window, just above the Support Information button.

3. Click the Network Identification tab. The network information for the computer will appear in the System Properties window.

4. Click the Network ID button to start the Network Identification Wizard. If a Windows NT or 2000 server requires each client to log into the server, you will need to create a login account on the Windows computer using the Network Identification Wizard to authenticate the client user name and password for the network account.

Viewing Hard Drive Properties   As you use a computer, be sure plenty of disk space is available to download files or create new ones. Perform the following steps to view the available disk space on a Windows computer.

1. Right click the hard drive icon on your computer.

2. Choose Properties. The hard drive Properties window will open. The Local Disk Properties window will open.

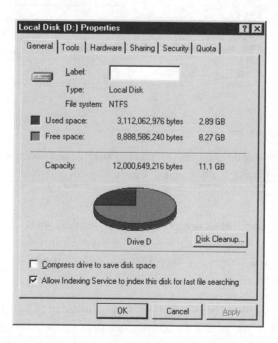

3. View the amount of used and free space for the disk. Make sure you have enough free space to install, create, or store files you may want to use during your computer session.

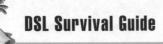
A good way to calculate the amount of disk space you will need is to add up the amount of required disk space for each application, and then double the sum. For example, if your applications require 2GB of disk space, make sure you have 4GB of available disk space before you install the applications.

Navigating Your Network Neighborhood   You can create a new network connection or access other computers on the network by opening the My Network Places window. The following steps show you how to find the other computers connected to your local network.

1. Double-click the My Network Places icon on the desktop to view other computers that are actively connected to the network.

2. The My Network Places window will open.

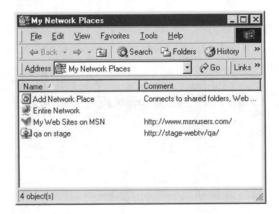

3. If another computer on the network has file sharing activated, you can access files on that computer by double-clicking the Entire Network icon and navigate the network to the computer you want to access.

Viewing Network and Dial-Up Connections   In order to connect a computer to a network, you will need to access the software settings for the network interface card installed in the computer. Perform the following steps to create a network connection for a network interface card that is already installed on a PC.

1. Click the Start button. Choose Settings, and then select Network And Dial-Up Connections. The Network And Dial-Up Connections window will open.

2. Double-click the Make New Connection icon to create a new Ethernet connection for your computer.

3. If a card and its software is already installed in the computer, an icon will appear in the Network And Dial-Up Connections window. The illustration shows the WaveLAN Ethernet icon, which represents the WaveLAN Ethernet PC card inserted in my laptop PC. You can set up each Ethernet network interface card's (NIC) TCP/IP settings from its Properties window. You can use the built-in network wizards to configure traditional Ethernet cards or wireless PC cards to work with Windows.

A Short Guide to Mac OS 9 Network Software

Open Transport is the name for Apple's networking software for Mac OS 8 and Mac OS 9. You can use the Internet Setup Assistant to configure all the control panels and network settings for your computer, or you can manually configure these settings in the TCP/IP and AirPort software. Although Mac OS X does not use Open Transport to manage its networking functions, many of the same settings in the TCP/IP control panel can be found in the Network control panel in Mac OS X.

Locating the AppleTalk Control Panel   If you want to share files between two Macs connected to the same network, you can do so over an AppleTalk file-sharing connection. To open the AppleTalk control panel, perform the following steps.

1. Click the Apple menu, choose Control Panels, and select AppleTalk.

2. Select a network interface card, such as Ethernet or AirPort, in the AppleTalk control panel. If your Mac does not need to access other computers via AppleTalk, you don't need to open the Chooser application to activate AppleTalk. The Chooser application is located in the Apple menu.

Configuring the TCP/IP Control Panel   Open the TCP/IP control panel to access IP address settings on Mac OS 9. The following steps show you how.

1. Click the Apple menu, choose Control Panels, and then choose TCP/IP. The TCP/IP control panel window will open.

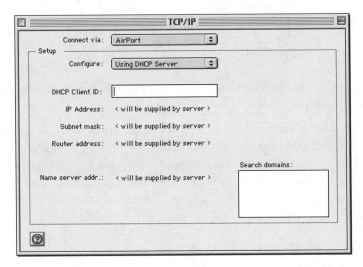

2. View and set the IP address and network information in this control panel. Choose Configurations from the File menu, or press COMMAND - K. The Configurations window will open.

3. By default, one TCP/IP configuration is created by Mac OS. You can duplicate and rename this configuration file if you want to create a new configuration file.

4. Select a configuration file from the window list, and then click the Make Active button to enable a new TCP/IP configuration. You can change TCP/IP configurations without rebooting the computer.

Accessing AirPort Software   If you have a base station or other 802.11b wireless server connected to the local network, you can configure the AirPort software on your Macintosh computer to connect to your local base station. Click the Apple menu and choose AirPort to open the AirPort application, and select a base station to connect your Mac to the wireless network. AirPort hardware and software enables Macintosh computers to access a network, including the Internet, over an 802.11 wireless network.

A Short Guide to Linux Network Software

Linux can be downloaded for free from several distributors. A DSL connection will help you download the average distribution, which fits on a 600MB CD-ROM. The most popular Linux distribution at press time is Red Hat. You can visit Red Hat's web site (www.redhat.com) to find out more about its Linux distributions for PCs. Larger Linux distributions, like the one from SuSE, require four CD-ROM disks in order to complete the installation.

The Linux examples in this book will explain installation, configuration, and troubleshooting for the Red Hat Linux distribution. Other Linux distributions are similar. However, each one uses a slightly different set of administrative tools to configure the network settings. Because networking is part of the Linux kernel, it will be installed by default on a PC or Macintosh computer. Incompatibility between the network card and the version of Linux installed on the computer may be one of the few issues that prevents networking from working on a Linux computer.

Configuring Network Settings

In order for a computer on your local network to work with the DSL modem and access computers on the Internet, you will need to configure the network settings so that the computer can interact with the DSL modem over the network. If you're relying on a static IP address to connect a computer to the network, the IP addresses of the computer, gateway, and name servers must be added to each computer's network settings. If you have set up a DHCP server on your network, you can configure each computer to request an IP address from the DHCP server so that the computer can access the Internet. You can also configure a computer with a static IP address, as long as there are no duplicate IP addresses on the local area network.

Configuring Network Settings on a Windows Computer

An Ethernet hub is a relatively simple device. Most hubs do not have dedicated memory and require an external power supply in order to enhance the network connections extending from the hub. The most common hub configurations are four- and eight-port hubs. Larger hubs tend to have additional networking hardware, such as a switch or router. The more ports on a hub, the more hardware needed to keep the network signal strong across each network connection. Perform the following set of steps to configure the network settings on a Windows computer.

1. Configure the Ethernet device. Click the Start button, choose Settings, and then open the Network And Dial-Up Connections window. From this window, you can install Ethernet drivers for a new card, or view or change the network settings for a network driver that's already been installed on the computer.

2. Open the TCP/IP Properties window. Select the TCP/IP item from the window list. Then, click the Properties button to view the IP information for the selected Ethernet connection.

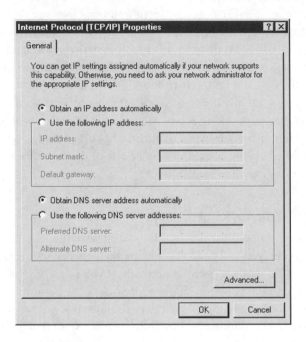

3. Choose the IP addressing format. If the computer uses a PPPoE connection to the DSL service provider, or if you have set up a DHCP server on your local network, choose the Obtain An IP Address Automatically option in the Internet Protocol (TCP/IP) Properties window. To configure a static IP address, choose the Use The Following IP Address button (Windows) or the Configure Manually (Mac OS 9) menu item from the TCP/IP control panel.

4. Type the IP address information. To configure the Windows system with a static IP address, fill in all appropriate IP addresses in the TCP/IP Properties window. The following fields must be filled in to create a static IP address on a computer. The following fields are from a Windows 2000 computer. However, other operating systems will use similarly named text boxes for IP information.

   ✦ **IP address** Type in the static IP address for the computer. This IP address enables your computer to be recognized on the DSL service provider's network.

   ✦ **Subnet mask** Type in the subnet mask for the DSL modem network.

- **Default gateway**   Type the DSL provider's IP address for its Internet gateway. If you have a DSL modem that provides a router connection to the Internet, this IP address represents the IP address for the DSL modem and your local network's gateway to the Internet.

- **DNS server**   Type in one or two IP addresses for the name server for the DSL service provider's network. If the first name server is not available on the network for some reason, the second one will be used to locate other computers on the Internet.

5. Save changes. Click the OK button to save the network changes, or click the Cancel button to exit the window without saving any changes.

6. Right-click the My Computer icon. The System Properties window will open. Select the Network Identification tab. Then, click the Network ID button in the System Properties window. Use the Network ID Wizard to create a login account for your local network.

7. Start the Network Connection Wizard to add a new network interface card to your computer. The illustration shows the first page of the Network Connection Wizard. Click the type of network connection you want to make. Then, follow the on-screen instructions to create a new connection icon in the Network And Dial-Up Connections window.

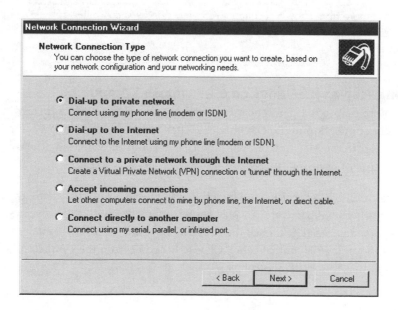

If you have a DSL modem that requires a Point-to-Point over Ethernet (PPPoE) connection, you must dial into the DSL provider. Most DSL service providers will set up the PPPoE software on your computer. Most PPPoE services require you to contact the DSL provider before you can dial into the DSL service.

If your DSL modem serves as a bridge or router, power on your computer; the DSL modem; and any intermediary network devices, such as a hub. If your computer is configured with the correct Internet Protocol information, the network will recognize the computer when it boots to the desktop. If your computer has a web browser installed, you can surf the Web to test your DSL connection.

Setting Up ICS on Windows

Internet Connection Services (ICS) enables a Windows 98, Windows Me, Windows NT, Windows 2000, and Windows XP to piggy-back a second computer off a computer connected to a network. On a Windows 2000 computer, you can use the Virtual Private Networking features combined with the network wizard to configure a computer to act as a router for another computer connected to it via a second Ethernet card. The computer running ICS acts as a router for the second computer system, enabling it to gain Internet access without being registered on the larger network. The primary computer must be connected to the DSL service provider in order for the secondary computer to access the Internet.

SURVIVAL TIP

To find out more about how to configure ICS on a Windows computer, refer to Chapter 10.

Configuring Network Settings on a Macintosh Computer

If you have more than one Ethernet card on your Mac, be sure to select the card that has an active Ethernet connection to the DSL modem. Then, open the operating system control panel and configure the Mac to work with the DSL account information. The following steps explain how to perform this task.

1. Configure the Ethernet device. Open the System folder and make sure the extension for the Ethernet device on your Mac has been installed with the active system folder. If you're using Mac OS 9, click the Apple menu, choose Control Panels, and then open the AppleTalk control panel. Choose Ethernet from the Connect Via pop-up menu in the AppleTalk control panel.

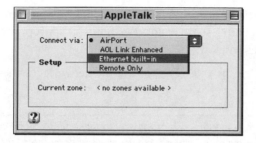

2. Open the TCP/IP control panel. On a Mac OS 9 computer, select the TCP/IP control panel from the Apple Control Panel menu. If you're using Mac OS X, click the Settings button in the dock. Then, click the Network icon in the Settings window and select the TCP/IP tab.

3. Choose the IP addressing format. Click the Choose A Network Format option from the pop-up menu in the TCP/IP control panel (see Figure 5-4).

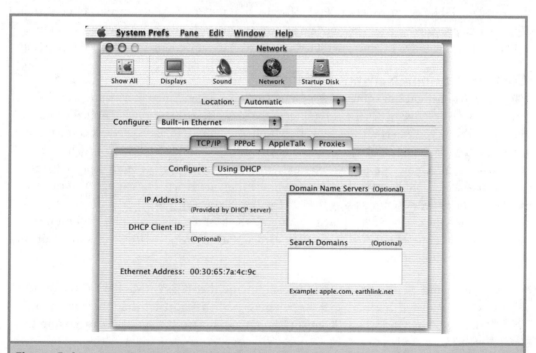

Figure 5-4. Type the network information in the Network Settings window on Mac OS X.

4. Type the IP address information for the computer. If you want to configure the Windows system with a static IP address, fill in all appropriate IP addresses in the TCP/IP Properties window.

5. Save changes. Click the Close box to save the network changes.

CAUTION   Sharing files between computers is a great way to make files on one computer available on your local network or over the network. However, most computers tend to slow down when accessed by another computer on the network. Unless you absolutely must share files on a computer, do not activate File Sharing on your computer or choose any folders to be shared over the network.

After you enter the network settings into your Macintosh computer, you can connect your computer to the Internet. If you have a DSL modem that requires a PPPoE connection, you may need to install the DSL service provider's software first. Some service providers require you to obtain an activation code before you can connect to their DSL service for the first time. After you have installed the DSL provider's PPPoE software, start the PPPoE program and connect to the DSL service provider. If your DSL modem acts as a router or bridge, your Macintosh computer will be connected to the Internet after it has powered on to the desktop or awakened from sleep.

Configuring Linux Network Settings

There are two methods for configuring a Linux computer for an Ethernet network. The first one, which I'll describe in detail, is to configure the network settings from a terminal window. The second way you can configure network settings on Linux is to use a network configuration program that uses a graphical user interface. If you install a windowing system—such as the X Window System, Gnome, or KDE—you can start an application such as Linuxconf, Network Configurator, net config, or netcfg, to configure the computer's network settings. You can also configure the network settings using the Red Hat installation software.

The following steps explain how to configure the host name and IP address for a Linux system from a terminal window. A network card and its network device drivers must already be installed on the Linux system.

1. **Host name**   Type the name of the computer in the HOSTNAME file located in the /etc directory. For example, if the computer name is shortstop, and the domain of your local network is smallcompany.com, type **shortstop.smallcompany.com** in the HOSTNAME file.

2. **Dynamic IP address**   If you have a DHCP server on the local network, check to see whether the Red Hat Program Module (RPM) for DHCP is installed on the Linux system. Red Hat distributions use RPM to install software. If your Linux distribution requires a different method of installing software, look for a DHCP component for the distribution and install it on the computer. When the computer powers on, the DHCP server will assign an IP address to the Linux system.

3. **Static IP address**   Use the ifconfig tool to configure the static IP address for the computer. Open a terminal window. If the IP address of the computer is 10.2.1.1, type the following command at the prompt. Replace *10.2.1.1* with the IP address for your DSL account. You can also add the static IP address to /etc/resolve.conf.

   ```
   >ifconfig eth0 10.2.1.1 up
   ```

4. **Gateway**   The gateway information is stored in the /etc/sysconfig/network directory.

5. **Domain name server**   Type the IP address for the domain name server for the DSL service into the resolve.conf file, which is located in the /etc directory.

Connecting to DSL with Linux

Open a terminal window and type **route** at the prompt. Linux will display the kernel IP routing table. The destination, gateway, netmask, and Ethernet interface information will be displayed in the terminal window. The first line contains the IP address of the computer. The second line contains the base subnet identification for the computer. The last line contains the gateway information for the local network. If any of these settings does not match the network settings for your local network, or the DSL provider's network information, use the commands listed in this section to change the network settings on the Linux system. As an alternative, you can type the following ifconfig command to have your computer broadcast its address. The output will appear in the terminal window.

```
> ifconfig Bcase: output
```

   If you have problems connecting to the DSL service provider with a Linux system, try switching the login user to *root*. Then, check whether you can successfully connect the Linux system to the Internet.

If you make changes to the network settings on your Linux computer, you must restart the computer in order to use the changes. Be sure to save any work before logging out or restarting the computer. Also, make sure network cards and cables are properly connected before powering on the computer.

If your DSL account requires you to use PPPoE, you can download PPPoE software from Roaring Penguin's Web site (www.roaringpenguin.com). To set up rp-pppoe on your Linux computer, log in as the root user, and then open a terminal window. Type **adsl-setup** at the prompt. Press ENTER and answer the questions, typing in your DSL service information as it's requested. Once you have completed the setup, you can initiate the PPPoE connection by typing **adsl-start** at the terminal window prompt. To terminate your DSL connection, type **adsl-stop**. The following list provides a short description of terms related to PPPoE.

✦ **pppoe**   A free ADSL client available for Linux, NetBSD, and Solaris systems

✦ **adsl-setup**   Starts a setup program that enables you to configure PPPoE

✦ **adsl-start**   Starts the point-to-point connection to the DSL service provider's network

✦ **adsl-stop**   Ends the DSL PPPoE connection to the DSL service

✦ **adsl-status**   Reports the status of the DSL PPPoE connection

Roaring Penguin's rp-pppoe also has a firewall option, which it calls IP Masquerading. This feature enables you to connect a second Ethernet card to your Linux box and acts as a network address translator for the other computers on your local area network. If you prefer to use a graphical user interface, you can install Gnome or KDE and log in as a normal user. Type **tkpppoe** in a terminal window, or select Tk:PPPoE from the Internet menu.

**SURVIVAL
TIP**

If you're familiar with using Unix or Linux, you'll probably use your Linux account as a client and as a file-sharing machine. Check your Linux distribution to see whether it installs the inet software module as a default. Many distributions stopped installing this network module because it opened the computer to potential security holes if users were not aware that their computer was easy to access on the network.

Network Solutions: Installing Network Applications

Unfortunately, you won't know whether your computer is set up properly for your network until you install one or two network applications. The obvious program with which to test your network is the most recent browser application, such as Internet Explorer 5 on a Mac (version 6 for Windows) or Netscape Navigator 4.7x. Installing a browser is similar to installing any other application on the network. Fortunately, these particular browsers don't need additional network settings in order to run on a DSL network.

Setting Up a DHCP Server

You can set up static IP addresses on each computer to enable them to access the Internet via the DSL modem. Some DSL modems also support dynamic addressing. If your computer doesn't have an IP address, the DSL modem will assign one. You can also set up your own DHCP server on the local network if you want to manually set how many IP addresses can be assigned on your network. However, you can run only one DHCP server on your network at a time.

If you plan to add a wireless hub to your network, find out whether the wireless access point, or base station, includes DHCP and NAT server software. You can choose from several wireless access point products. Some are bundled with a wireless PC card. If you plan to use one wireless access point for Windows and Mac, be sure to purchase 802.11-compliant PC cards in addition to an 802.11b wireless server. For example, Apple's base station software can be configured with a valid static IP address, that, in turn, can assign IP addresses to other computers that hook up to your network.

SURVIVAL TIP

If you set up a DHCP server on your network, check your DSL modem to make sure that only one DHCP server is set up to assign IP addresses to the computers connected to your local area network.

Installing a Browser Application

Each computer platform has a unique way of installing software onto its operating system. Most applications created for Windows rely on Microsoft's standard installation wizard to guide you through all the installation steps for an application. The Macintosh platform has a number of different installer applications that more or less work the same for installing an application onto Mac OS 9 or Mac OS X. The installation method for a Linux computer will vary depending on which distribution is installed on the computer. The Red Hat distribution and many other Linux distributions that borrow from Red Hat use RPMs to add or remove software modules for each Linux distribution. The following sections explain how to install a browser for Windows, Mac OS, and Linux. If you're able to load a Web page on your computer, the network settings and DSL service have been set up correctly on your computer and local network.

Installing Internet Explorer on Windows

Windows Me, Windows 2000, and Windows XP have Internet Explorer 5 (or a newer version of Internet Explorer) installed as part of the operating system. If your computer runs Windows 95, Windows 98, or Windows NT 4.0, you can also download and install Internet Explorer on your computer. If you don't see an Internet Explorer icon (it's a blue lowercase *e*) on the desktop, Internet Explorer might have been removed from your Windows system.

You can download the latest version of the browser for free from Microsoft's Web site at www.microsoft.com/ie. Click the download link and read any licensing and software compatibility information before you download and install the browser on your Windows computer. Double-click the installer application and follow the on-screen instructions to install Internet Explorer.

Earlier this year, Netscape announced that it is moving out of the browser business. However, you can download Netscape Navigator 4.72 from the Netscape Web site and run this slightly older version of a browser on your Windows computer. You can download the installer application to your PC. Then double-click the installer application and follow the on-screen instructions to install the browser onto your computer.

Most Web pages will appear more or less the same whether you're using Netscape Navigator or Internet Explorer. However, some HTML, JavaScript, and Java code may behave differently in each browser, depending on which version of these Web languages the Web page was written for. When testing your network, pick a Web page that you know will be available on the Internet, such as www.yahoo.com or www.google.com.

Installing Internet Explorer on a Mac

All the latest Mac models, such as the iMac desktop tower, titanium PowerBook, and iBook, have Internet Explorer 5 and Netscape Navigator 4.72 already installed and ready to run on the hard drive. You'll find these applications inside the Internet folder on your hard drive. If your Mac has Mac OS X installed, you can simply click the Internet Explorer (the letter *e*) icon in the dock to start the browser.

To download the latest version of Internet Explorer for a Macintosh computer, visit Microsoft's Macintosh software web pages at www.microsoft.com/mac/ie. You can read about the latest version of Internet Explorer for Mac OS 9 and Mac OS X and download the installer application onto your hard drive. The initial download will place a compressed archive of files on your hard drive. You can double-click this downloaded file to decompress the Internet Explorer files onto your drive. The installer application for Internet Explorer is built into the Internet Explorer application icon. The first time you double-click the application icon for Internet Explorer, Internet Explorer will install the system and application files onto your hard drive before opening a browser window on your desktop.

Installing Netscape Navigator on Linux

Most Linux distributions install Netscape Navigator as the default browser. If you are running KDE or Gnome, look for a shortcut icon (the icon with the letter N) for Netscape Navigator in the menu bar at the bottom of the desktop. Click the shortcut to start Netscape Navigator. It may take a few seconds for the license window to appear.

The default setting for most Linux distributions is to show a local HTML file on the hard drive in the browser window. The SuSE distributions point the browser to their home page. If the computer is properly configured for the Internet, you should be able to type a URL in the Address field and view a Web page in the browser window. Choose Preferences from the Edit menu, shown in Figure 5-6, if you want to customize any of the browser settings.

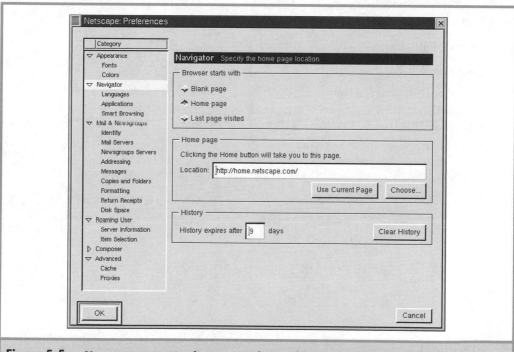

Figure 5-5.   You can customize browser and e-mail settings in Netscape Navigator.

Additional Resources

Plugging your DSL modem into your network is one thing, but the more time-consuming tasks involve getting the network to recognize different computers, operating systems, and network applications. If you have purchased your computer within the past three to five years, you should be able to install an operating system and browser onto it. Then use these software components to check your DSL account, e-mail, and Internet access. Visit one or all of the following Web sites to find out more about each computer platform and what it is capable of doing on a network.

+ www.linux.org

+ www.bsd.org

+ www.dell.com

+ www.compaq.com

+ www.microsoft.com

+ www.apple.com

+ www.dslcenter.com

+ www.roaringpenguin.com

Chapter 6

Setting Up E-Mail

Electronic mail, better known as e-mail, is one of the most popular network-based applications, particularly on the Internet. E-mail applications enable you to send a text message from your computer to any other computer that can connect to the Internet. It is very similar to sending hand-written letters that rely on the post office for delivery. E-mail not only saves trees, but also is relatively inexpensive, and, depending on the speed of your mail server and local networks, can be delivered within a few seconds of being sent.

Other network applications also provide instant communication. Chat rooms and instant messaging software enable you to communicate simultaneously with one or more computers in real time. Some instant messaging programs can show you whether any of your friends are online. E-mail is a form of electronic communication that enables you to exchange long messages that may include file attachments. The e-mail application sends and receives e-mail by accessing a mail server that runs on a separate computer connected to the network. The mail server enables an e-mail application to access a queue of new messages and store any existing messages until you delete them.

✦ **E-mail applications**   Send or receive an electronic mail message from a browser or a dedicated e-mail application, such as Microsoft Outlook, or Outlook Express.

✦ **E-mail account setup**   Configure Outlook to check for e-mail using a POP or IMAP e-mail account on a client computer.

Basic Concepts: Setting Up E-Mail Programs

E-mail is one of the oldest and most popular applications created for networks. It is the most popular program used on the Internet. In order to send or receive e-mail, you need to have an e-mail account on a mail server, and a client computer running an e-mail application that's connected to the same network as the mail server. Most Internet service providers, including DSL service providers, supply an e-mail account for each Internet service subscriber. With DSL services, the user name and password for your e-mail account is usually the login name and password for the DSL account. Some DSL services provide multiple e-mail accounts for a DSL service package, while other DSL providers allow you to create additional e-mail accounts for an additional fee.

In addition to having access to an account on a mail server, you'll need to install an e-mail program on your computer. There are many freeware and shareware e-mail applications from which to choose. Many have the same basic features for configuring and checking e-mail, but each has a different set of buttons, windows, and menu commands.

One of the more popular e-mail applications for Windows computers is Microsoft Outlook. Microsoft's Outlook Express, which is a free e-mail client you can download from Microsoft's Web site, is also a very popular e-mail client program for Windows computers, see Figure 6-1. Outlook Express is also available for Macintosh computers, and is bundled with Internet

Menu bar

Inbox e-mail list

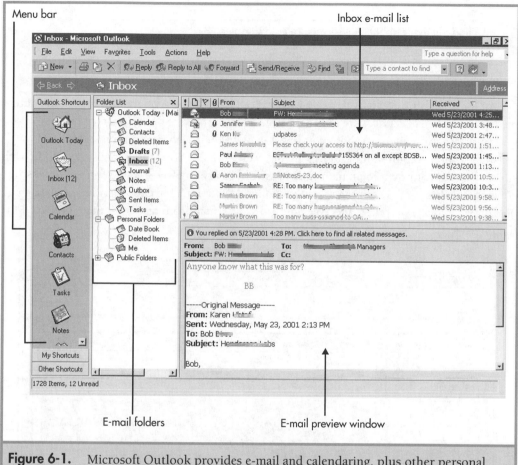

Outlook Shortcuts

Folder List

E-mail folders

E-mail preview window

Figure 6-1. Microsoft Outlook provides e-mail and calendaring, plus other personal organizer features and supports synchronization with handheld devices.

Explorer with every new Macintosh computer. Microsoft Outlook is also available for Macintosh computer, although it can only connect to a Microsoft Exchange Server, and not a POP, SMTP, or IMAP mail server. Entourage is a Macintosh e-mail and organizer program, similar to Outlook for Windows.

Most e-mail clients can track e-mail messages with a mail server. The Post Office Protocol (POP3) and Simple Mail Transfer Protocol (SMTP) method is probably the most common way e-mail clients are configured to send and receive e-mail with a mail server. Internet Message Access Protocol (IMAP) is the other commonly used method for configuring an e-mail client. Windows computers running Outlook can access e-mail from a Microsoft Exchange Server.

To find out more about mail servers, refer to Chapter 13.

An e-mail application isn't the only way you can access e-mail on the Internet. Some of the most popular e-mail services are only accessible from a browser application (see Figure 6-2). For example, Hotmail and Yahoo offer free e-mail on their web sites, and no additional software setup is required for you to send or receive e-mail. You simply register with the web site and create your own login name and password to use the free e-mail services. Accessing e-mail with a browser is convenient and economical. You don't have to worry about managing files on your local computer, and you can read your e-mail from any computer connected to the Internet.

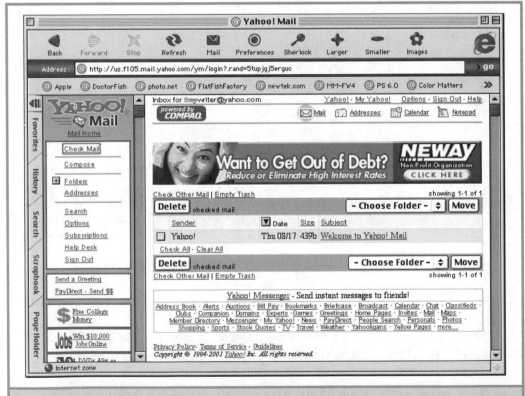

Figure 6-2. Some mail services, like those provided by Hotmail and Yahoo, require you to use a browser to access your e-mail over the Internet.

A Few E-Mail Terms

Electronic mail systems share a few common components. The mail server is the central repository for new mail. An e-mail client that is capable of communicating with the same protocols used by the mail server can log in to a mail server to download and read mail messages from an e-mail account on the mail server. The following list provides a short description of some of the terms that will be used in this chapter.

✦ **Mail server**   A program that provides mail services to e-mail programs that connect to it over a network. Most common mail servers are hosted by DSL service providers or Internet service providers such as Microsoft, Yahoo, and America Online.

✦ **SMTP**   An acronym for Simple Mail Transfer Protocol. This protocol enables an e-mail client to send e-mail to a mail server. The mail client must have an e-mail account in order to send mail from a mail server.

✦ **POP3**   An acronym for Post Office Protocol. This protocol enables an e-mail client to receive e-mail from a mail server. The e-mail client must log in to the mail server in order to access e-mail stored on the mail server.

✦ **IMAP**   An acronym for Internet Message Access Protocol. This e-mail protocol is an alternative to POP3/SMTP mail access for e-mail clients. Accessing a mail server from an IMAP-configured mail client enables the client to view read or unread e-mail messages accessed by the same account but from another computer. If you have a desktop and laptop computer, IMAP access to your mail server can help you keep track of e-mail messages.

✦ **E-mail client**   An e-mail program that is capable of connecting to a mail server. If the e-mail client has a valid account, e-mail can be sent or received from the client application.

✦ **E-mail account**   An e-mail account consists of a user name, password, and mail server information. This account information is created in an e-mail client so that it can connect to an e-mail server.

Installing E-Mail Applications

Some e-mail applications are installed along with a web browser program. Microsoft enables you to install Outlook Express or Entourage with Internet Explorer for the Mac, and Outlook for Windows is part of the Microsoft Office application package. You can also install an e-mail application separately from other applications.

On a Mac, you can simply double-click the Outlook Express or Entourage application icon to start the installation process. The system and program files will be placed in the appropriate folders on your hard drive, and the program will automatically start after all the files have been created on your computer. Outlook and Outlook Express use the standard installation wizard to install these programs on your computer's hard drive. The following sections explain how to install and start Outlook on a Windows and Macintosh computer, and how to install Netscape Communicator on a PC running Linux.

Installing Outlook on Windows

Outlook is Microsoft's "Swiss Army knife" e-mail application. It is a full-featured e-mail program capable of working with POP and IMAP e-mail servers. You can also use e-mail to create, track, and remove calendar events, contact information, notes, tasks, and a journal. If you have a handheld device, such as a Palm handheld or Pocket PC, you can synchronize Outlook to download your e-mail and calendaring information to the mail and calendar programs on these devices.

Before you install applications, you should be logged in to the Windows computer with an account that has administrator privileges. Perform the following steps to install Outlook on Windows 98, Windows NT, Windows Me, Windows 2000, or Windows XP.

1. You can either use the Add/Remove Programs control panel or double-click the installer application. Either method can be used to start the installation wizard for Outlook.

2. Follow the on-screen instructions and choose the Typical installation of Outlook.

3. Wait for the files to be copied to your hard drive and click the Finish button.

4. Restart your computer. Then, double-click the Outlook icon on your desktop to start this program.

The Outlook XP window, shown in Figure 6-3, is divided into three general areas: the menu bar and toolbar area, located at the top of the work area, the shortcut sidebar, and the main window view located in the middle of the Outlook window. Figure 6-3 shows the weekly calendar view in Outlook. Click on a shortcut from the left column to change the window view contents in the middle of the Outlook window. You can customize the information that can be viewed in the main Outlook window. For example, if you want to store e-mail messages on your hard drive, you can add the Folder List, shown in Figure 6-3, to the main window. If you want to preview you e-mail messages in the main window, choose Preview Pane from the View menu.

NOTE   Most e-mail accounts have a preset amount of space you can use to store your e-mail on the mail server. The limit is usually set to 3–4MB of disk space. Send a 2–3MB e-mail message to yourself to determine the maximum size of your mailbox. If your mail queue fills up, the mail server will notify you that your mailbox is full. You can save your e-mail messages on your hard drive to reduce the amount of mail stored on the server.

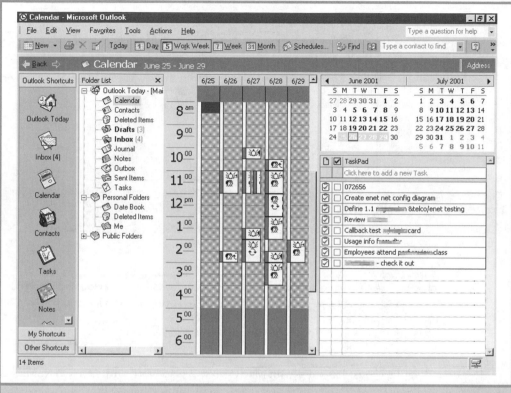

Figure 6-3. Outlook XP combines e-mail with calendaring and other personal information management programs.

Installing Entourage on a Mac

Entourage is bundled with the Macintosh Office 2001 application suite for Mac OS 9 and Mac OS X. Entourage is an e-mail and personal information manager program. You can download Entourage from Microsoft's web site (www.microsoft.com/mac/ie). Perform the following steps to install Entourage on the Mac. The steps are similar for installing Internet Explorer 5 or Outlook Express 5 on a Mac.

1. Copy the Entourage folder from the CD-ROM onto the Macintosh hard drive.

2. Double-click the application icon, shown in Figure 6-4.

3. The first time Entourage starts, it will install the system and applications files onto your hard drive. Wait for the files to install on your computer.

4. When you see the main window appear, you can set up Entourage to access your e-mail.

Figure 6-4. Entourage is Microsoft's most recent Macintosh e-mail application.

Some Web e-mail accounts require you to log in every ten days. If you stop logging in to your e-mail within the predefined time period, the system will remove your account, and you won't be able to log in to get your e-mail.

NOTE

Most e-mail applications that work with Mac OS 9 will also work with Mac OS X. Mac OS X has an emulator for Mac OS 9 software. If an e-mail application is already installed on your Mac, you can continue to run it after you have upgraded it to Mac OS X. However, Apple installs an e-mail program with Mac OS X (see Figure 6-5). You may want to try it to see if you like it more than Outlook, Eudora, Entourage, or any other Mac e-mail program.

Installing Netscape Navigator on Linux

Most Linux distributions that bundle web applications install Netscape Navigator as the browser application. The current versions of Netscape Navigator are compatible with the Linux 2.2 kernel. If you want to download the latest version of Netscape Navigator for Linux, visit Netscape's web site at www.netscape.com to download the latest version of Netscape Navigator. The tar and gzip utilities are used to compress the Netscape Navigator installer application. Use tar and gzip, which are installed with every Linux distribution, to decompress the installation directory onto the hard drive. Perform the following steps to install Netscape Navigator on a Linux system.

1. Start the installer executable.

2. Follow the on-screen instructions to install the browser onto your Linux system. Netscape Navigator for Linux can be installed on x86 PCs. You may need to recompile it to run on a PowerPC Linux distribution.

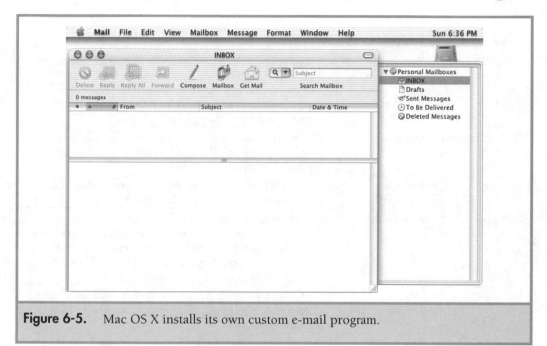

Figure 6-5. Mac OS X installs its own custom e-mail program.

3. Restart your computer after installing Netscape Navigator. If you had a previous version installed, it will still be available to use on your computer.

4. Type the directory path and executable name to start the browser or select its application icon from the start menu if you're using KDE or Gnome.

5. Wait for Netscape Navigator to start. It may take a few seconds. Then, type a URL to check whether the browser can load a Web page over the network connection.

Table 6-1 lists some of the most recent e-mail applications, the platforms they support, and a summary of each program's features.

Setting Up Web-Based E-Mail

Web-based e-mail is a popular alternative to using an e-mail application. Web-based e-mail relies on e-mail services installed on a Web server to send and receive messages over the Internet. Visit Hotmail.com or Yahoo.com to sign up for a free e-mail account. Many DSL providers also enable you to use a browser to access your e-mail account for your DSL service. Perform the following steps to set up an e-mail account and access e-mail with a browser.

1. Start a browser application and visit a Web site that offers access to e-mail over the Web. For example, type **www.hotmail.com** in the browser's Address text box.

E-Mail Program	Platform	Features
Outlook	Windows	Address book, calendar, journal, tasks, reminders, notes, color-coded categories, custom views, links, import from other mail programs, multiple user support, Internet standards support. Support for IMAP or POP e-mail access and MS Exchange server.
Outlook Express	Windows	Address book, custom views, color-coded categories, links, import from other mail programs, multiple user support, Internet standards support
Eudora	Windows, Macintosh	Address book, custom views, import from other mail programs, Internet standards support
Entourage	Macintosh	Address book, calendar, tasks, reminders, notes, color-coded categories, custom views, links, import from other mail programs, multiple user support, Internet standards support. Support for IMAP or POP e-mail access and MS Exchange server
Netscape	Windows, Macintosh, Linux	Browser interface, address book, custom views, import from other mail programs, support for IMAP or POP mail servers
Apple Mail	Mac OS X	No address book; limited features, support for IMAP or POP mail servers
Mail	Unix, Linux	Command-line and text interface, support for IMAP or POP mail servers
Outlook	Pocket PC, Windows CE 3.0	Address book, offline e-mail creation, support for sychronizing with Outlook, and other e-mail applications already installed on the computer.
Mail	Palm	Offline mail creation and viewing, support for sychronizing with Outlook, and other e-mail applications already installed on the computer.

Table 6-1.   E-Mail Programs

2. If this is your first visit to the Web site, look for a New Account, Sign Up Now, or Register button or link on the main Web page.

3. Follow the on-screen instructions and create a user name and password on the e-mail service. Complete the online forms.

4. Return to the login page and type in your user name and password for the e-mail account.

5. The main e-mail page should appear. You should see a summary page listing the number of e-mail messages in your inbox.

6. Click New to create a new e-mail message. Type an e-mail address and a message, and then click Send to deliver the message.

7. To read messages, click the Inbox link and select a message to read. Click the Reply button to send a reply to the person who sent you the e-mail message.

Setting Up E-Mail Accounts

After you have installed an e-mail program onto your computer, you can set up your e-mail account information. Most e-mail enable you to configure the e-mail application with the user name and password information to connect to your DSL service provider's mail server. The following sections explain how to set up Outlook, Entourage, and Netscape to check and send e-mail on your Macintosh, Windows, or Linux computer.

Make sure the DSL service's e-mail account information is nearby. Setting up your e-mail account and accessing e-mail from your mail server is a fairly straightforward process. Your e-mail program must have an account that can locate the send and receive protocols for the mail server. In addition to locating the mail server, the account must have the proper user name and password account information so that you can log in to the mail server and send or receive e-mail.

Adding an E-Mail Account to Outlook

You must first create an e-mail account in Outlook or Outlook Express to send or receive e-mail with other computers on the Internet. Figure 6-6 shows the account information dialog box for Outlook Express for Mac OS 9. The following list summarizes the e-mail settings needed to create an e-mail account in Outlook with an MS Exchange server.

✦ **User Name**   Microsoft Exchange can be configured to link your e-mail address to your account name. You can type your e-mail name in the User Name field. If Exchange Server is set up to recognize your real name as your e-mail name, you can type your real name in the User Name field. The underline indicates that the Exchange e-mail address was found for your account.

✦ **Password**   When you first set up your Exchange e-mail account, you can type your password in the setup wizard.

✦ **Exchange Server**   Microsoft Exchange Server is the name of Microsoft's mail server software. You can install it on a PC, connect it to your network, and set up a local mail and calendar server.

In addition to accessing mail on an MS Exchange server, you can set up Outlook to log in to an IMAP or POP/SMTP mail server. An IMAP server enables you to check your e-mail from more than one computer without actually downloading e-mail to your computer. Each message is downloaded when you select it on the client computer. A POP/SMTP configuration

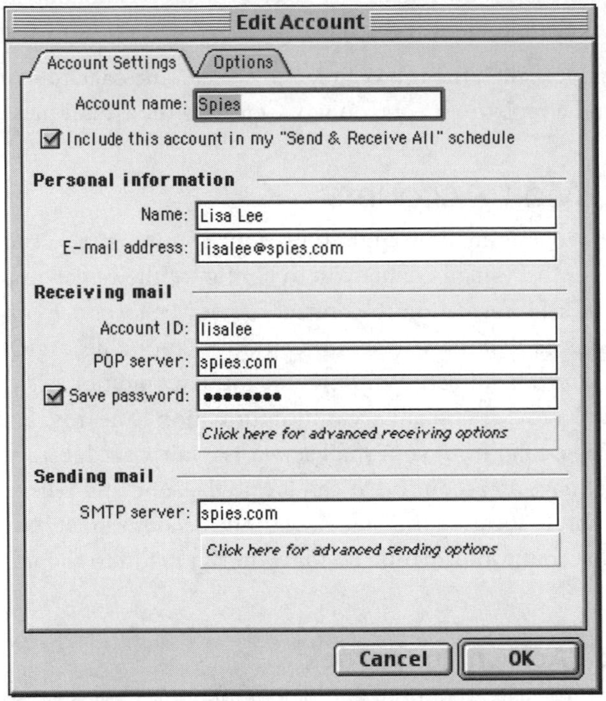

Figure 6-6. Microsoft Outlook enables you to access e-mail using the POP/SMTP protocols, IMAP.

enables you either to leave mail on the mail server or download it all to a computer. Most mail servers enable an e-mail client to use either IMAP and POP/SMTP protocols to access e-mail messages. You can determine which mail protocols the e-mail client uses when you set up your e-mail account in Outlook or another e-mail client application.

SURVIVAL TIP

You can run AOL software on your DSL network, too. Instead of dialing up through a phone line, choose the TCP setting in the connection window. Then type your login name and password into the Welcome window and click Sign On to log into AOL.

Creating an E-Mail Account for Entourage

Entourage is the equivalent of Outlook, but for Macintosh computers. Type your DSL account information in the mail setup windows in Entourage. Your account information allows the e-mail program to determine where your DSL provider's mail server is located on the Internet. The first time you set up an e-mail account, Entourage will run a setup wizard. Type your e-mail account information in each screen. Click the Finish button on the final window of the wizard to create the mail account.

You can modify any mail account in Entourage. Choose Account from the Tools window. The Accounts window will open. Double-click on an e-mail account to modify it. The following list explains the essential fields you'll need to fill in before you can send or receive an e-mail message in Entourage.

✦ **Account Name**   You can create more than one e-mail account in Entourage. You might want to use the name of the DSL service provider for the account name.

✦ **Name**   Type your first and last name in this text box. This is the name that will be sent along with your e-mail address. Whoever receives an e-mail from you will see this name in the From field in their mail program.

✦ **E-Mail Address**   Enter the full e-mail address here. For example, you can type janedoe@hotmail.com.

✦ **Account ID**   This is the login name for the mail account. For example, type **janedoe**, not Jane Doe.

✦ **Password**   Most mail servers require a password in order to enable you to receive your e-mail. Check the Save password checkbox if you don't want to type your password each time Entourage checks for new mail.

✦ **POP Server**   When you receive e-mail, the mail server works with a POP or IMAP server to relay your e-mail to your computer. Some DSL providers use pop.dslservice.com for the POP server account. However, the POP mail server name will vary from provider to provider.

NOTE

Alternatively, you can access e-mail via IMAP using the e-mail account wizard. However do not set up an IMAP and POP account in the e-mail client to access a single e-mail account on the mail server.

✦ **SMTP Server**   If you want to send e-mail, type the SMTP mail server name in this text box.

✦ **Security Settings**   The Account ID and Password enable you to log in to a mail server to receive your e-mail (see Figure 6-7). Some mail servers might also require you to log in if you want to send e-mail. Check the setup information for your DSL service provider to find out whether you need to customize your SMTP security settings. In Entourage, you can click below the SMTP Server text box to view additional login settings that may apply to your DSL provider's mail server.

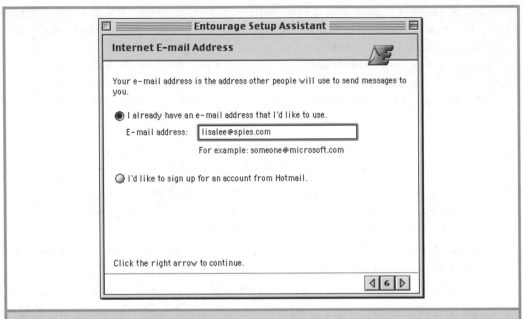

Figure 6-7. Type your mail information in each screen of the Account wizard to set up an e-mail account in Entourage.

SURVIVAL TIP

To access your e-mail from more than one computer, check the Leave a copy of the message on the server checkbox. When you download e-mail, you will see a blue envelope icon appear to the left of each new message. Click the envelope icon to view a pop-up menu. Choose Delete Message From Server At Next Connection if you want to remove that message from the mail server. A red *X* will appear over the envelope icon. The next time you send or receive e-mail messages, Entourage will remove that message from the mail server. Any subsequent mail checks will only download newer e-mail messages.

SURVIVAL TIP

Click the Options tab of the Edit Account window to view more options for each e-mail account.

Setting Up E-Mail for Mac OS X

When you install Mac OS X, Apple installs a mail application onto your hard drive. You can start mail by clicking the mail icon in the dock. Add an e-mail account to the Mac OS X mail application and enter the user name and password to access your e-mail on a POP/SMTP or IMAP mail server. The Mac OS X mail application enables you to send and receive e-mail. It's not a fancy e-mail program, but it gets the job done.

Setting Up an E-Mail Account with Netscape Messenger

Linux users can use Netscape Messenger to check their e-mail messages. Netscape Messenger is the built-in e-mail program that is installed with Netscape Navigator. You can access the mail setup fields from the Preferences window in Netscape Navigator. Choose Messenger from the Communicator menu. The following list describes the fields that must be completed in order to set up your e-mail account for Netscape Messenger.

SURVIVAL TIP

Netscape Navigator is available for Windows, Macs, and Linux systems. Each platform shares almost the same menu and window options, enabling you to easily navigate the setup fields in Netscape Messenger on any computer platform.

◆ **Identity**   Click Identity in the Category area of the Netscape Preferences window to view a list of Mail and Newsgroup options. Assign a name to the e-mail account.

◆ **Login and Password**   Type the account name and password in the fields in the Identity window.

◆ **POP Server**   Choose Mail Server to configure the POP and SMTP mail servers for your e-mail account. Select the mail server in the Incoming Mail Servers window list and click the Edit button to customize the POP server information for your account.

◆ **SMTP Server**   Type the SMTP server name in the Outgoing mail (SMTP) server text box. If your mail server requires you to log in order to send e-mail messages, type your user name in the Outgoing mail sever user name text box, too. Figure 6-8 shows the SMTP server information text fields for the Linux version of Netscape Navigator 4.

SURVIVAL TIP

Because most people use many of the same e-mail programs, some of the more notorious computer viruses that have sprung up over the past few years have been e-mail bombs. With an e-mail bomb, an e-mail attachment is sent as spam to a lot of computers on the network. An unsuspecting person reads the e-mail and opens the attachment. This starts the virus on the computer. Some mail viruses use every e-mail address in your address book to send an e-mail, while others attempt to erase your hard drive. If you do not recognize an e-mail address in your Inbox, you should delete the e-mail message. Avoid opening any e-mail attachments unless you recognize the sender of the e-mail message.

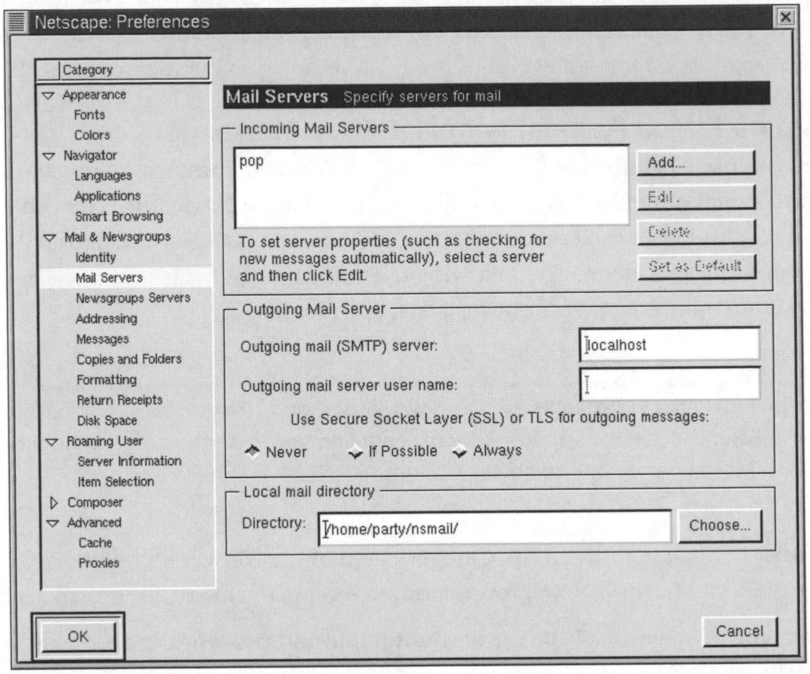

Figure 6-8. Open the Preferences window in Netscape and type your e-mail account information in the Identity and Mail Servers Preferences windows.

Problems Accessing Mail Servers

You may occasionally have problems uploading or downloading your e-mail from the mail server. Mail servers are similar to Web and file servers, except mail servers tend to deal with a much larger load of files that need to be routed to each mail account on a computer or routed to a different mail server on the network. The following sections explain a few common networking problems related to e-mail.

Network Performance and Security Issues

If you have tried to do two or more network-related tasks on a single computer, you may have seen network performance slow down. Slow network performance can occur whether you have one or several computers accessing the network all at once. If your DSL network supports more than one computer and more than one person is tasking multiple computers, you may notice a slowdown in your network's performance. Downloading or sending large e-mail files simultaneously may slow web surfing, or other network-bound tasks of any computers connected to the same network, to the point that a Web page may not load due to excessive network traffic.

You can add hardware devices to your network to help isolate heavy network activity among a few computers on your network. You can also configure the e-mail client to not download attachments or to check for new e-mail less frequently. If spam or mail viruses are an issue, you may want to set up a firewall for your local network or set up a mail filter on the client to prevent mail from unfamiliar accounts from being opened on any computer connected to your local DSL network.

Firewalls

You may want to set up a dedicated PC to act as a network firewall for the local DSL network. A firewall can help prevent uninvited computers from accessing the computers on your local network. It can also be used to filter and monitor network traffic. PC firewall products include Zone Alarm Pro, which is a free download from www.zonelabs.com, and Gauntlet Firewall 6.0, which is a Windows-based firewall program. Microsoft also has another firewall product. Several Web sites, such as www.matrix0.org/firewalls/ and www.yourdoorway.to/firewall-software, are dedicated to reviewing and posting information about firewalls.

You can also set up a personal firewall on each computer on the local network. A personal firewall application enables you to monitor, accept, or reject incoming or outgoing network data on a single computer. Windows XP has personal firewall software available for each network interface card installed on the computer. You can access the personal firewall settings on Windows XP by performing the following steps:

1. Double-click the My Network Places icon on the desktop. The My Network Places window will open.

2. Select the View network connections link from the left column of the My Network Places window. The Network Connections window will open.

3. Right-click the network interface card's (NIC) icon and choose Properties from the shortcuts menu. The properties window will open for the NIC.

4. Click on the Advanced tab of the properties window. The Internet Connection Firewall settings will appear in the Advanced page of the properties window.

5. Check the Protect my computer and network by limiting or preventing access to this computer from the Internet check box to activate the personal firewall software.

6. Click on the Setttings button in the Advanced page of the properties window to customize the personal firewall settings for the NIC.

What Is Spam?

Many people consider e-mail to be the "killer" application for the Internet. As the Internet has become increasingly popular, some individuals have thought it would be great to create the e-mail equivalent of junk mail to send advertisements and offers that are frequently sent to us as regular bulk or junk mail. Spam is the term used to describe electronic junk mail. This type of e-mail isn't only annoying; it can fill up the disk space of mail servers around the world. To deal with this problem, many mail servers filter out addresses that are not usually received by users on the mail server. To reduce the amount of spam in your Inbox, you can create a script to send e-mail messages from individuals who are not in your address book to the Trash folder in the e-mail program.

E-mail Clients and Potential Network Hazards

Some of the more robust e-mail applications such as Outlook (see Figure 6-9) enable you to set up several e-mail accounts, and perform automatic tasks for checking and handling incoming e-mail messages. Outlook and Outlook Express can schedule tasks, such as checking and sending e-mail, in addition to automatically filing e-mail, copying incoming or outgoing addresses into your address book, and placing invitations into your calendar.

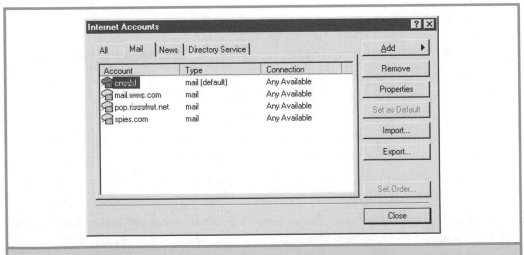

Figure 6-9. You can run several e-mail accounts at once in most e-mail programs.

Taking advantage of these features enables you to download all your latest e-mail. However, each e-mail account can potentially affect the network performance of the local network, and possibly introduce e-mail viruses to the computer.

Outlook, Outlook Express, and Entourage enable you to schedule how frequently each account is checked for new mail. In Outlook Express on a Mac or Windows computer, check the Include this account in my Send & Receive All schedule check box for each e-mail account. The default setting for Outlook Express is to check each mail account every ten minutes for new mail.

You can also use the Rules wizard in the Tools menu of Outlook or Outlook Express to create rules, or scripts that manage your e-mail. Follow the instructions in the on-screen wizard and choose the rules you want to apply to your Inbox or other e-mail folders. Click Finish to save the rule, and then exit the wizard. Click the Apply Now button to run the rule. You might want to create a test e-mail for the rule, for example, to make sure the rule moves the files to the correct e-mail folder.

You can reduce the likelihood of encountering an e-mail virus by creating a rule that checks who sends an e-mail. If the sender's e-mail address does not match any of the addresses in your address book or doesn't fall within a recognizable Internet domain name, you can file the e-mail in a junk mail folder. On occasion, you may want to view the list of mail messages filed in this junk folder. If someone in your address book changes his or her e-mail address, or sends e-mail from a friend's e-mail account, the e-mail may be filed accidentally in the junk mail folder.

Sending E-Mail

Creating a new mail message is fairly straightforward. Perform the following steps to send an e-mail message in Outlook.

1. Click the New mail button in the toolbar or choose File | New | Mail Message from the menu bar.

2. Type the e-mail address in the To field and add a subject to the e-mail.

3. Type your message in the bottom window of the New Message window.

4. Click the Send button when you're ready to send the e-mail onto the network (see Figure 6-10).

Checking and sending e-mail doesn't necessarily create noticeable network traffic. Network performance will usually be slowest when lots of people use the network during peak hours. Of course, if you're the only person using your DSL network, you can schedule network tasks, such as backups, to be performed during periods when you're not using the network.

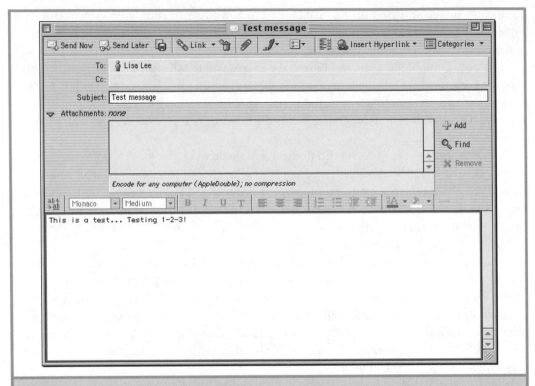

Figure 6-10. You can write one or several e-mail messages. Save your messages in the Drafts folder, or let them queue up in the Outbox.

Solutions for E-Mail Access

There is no right or wrong way to check e-mail. How often you check e-mail will depend on how much e-mail you receive. If you receive a constant flow of mail, you will probably leave your e-mail application running as you work with other programs, such as a browser. However, if you rarely receive e-mail, you may want to start, check, and exit your e-mail application whenever you check for new mail, instead of letting it run all day.

Sending E-Mail to Any Computer

One of the biggest mysteries you will encounter in your e-mail adventures is trying to figure out why someone did not receive your e-mail, or if they received it, why they cannot read it. If you think about this problem, you might realize that two mail servers are involved in sending and receiving an e-mail message. Your DSL service provider's mail server will handle mail messages sent to or from your e-mail account. The other mail server belongs to the other e-mail address involved in the e-mail exchange. If either mail server is not configured to forward a particular type of e-mail message, the message may be delivered, but may not be readable by the e-mail client that downloads the delivered e-mail message.

HTML Versus Plain Text

Most e-mail programs enable you to type your message and send it as text. Some programs also enable you to use Hypertext Markup Language (HTML) to format the color, font, size, or style of the text in your message. In most cases, you don't need to add HTML tags to your e-mail message. This feature is great for creating custom e-mail messages.

If you create an e-mail message using the HTML feature in an e-mail program, the e-mail recipient must have the same e-mail program or an HTML-compatible e-mail program to view the e-mail message as you sent it. Otherwise, the recipient will see only the text message and none of the formatting. In some cases, the stylized text might be converted into unreadable characters, and the text message may get lost in the formatting information of the message.

NOTE

Before e-mail programs were capable of creating fancy-looking HTML messages, computers only used text. In order to distinguish text from a previous message from the current message, an arrow character, such as >, was inserted on the far left of each line of the original message. As others replied to a message, an additional arrow would be added to the left side of each line so that anyone who read the message could interpret the chronological order of each message reply. Some e-mail programs enable you to activate a preference setting that adds an arrow to the left side of each line of a message. However, you can also reply to an e-mail by typing your message at the top of the reply message and then including any previous e-mail messages below it.

Adjusting Attachment Settings

A common problem with e-mail attachments is that the e-mail program is not configured correctly to handle the format of the compressed attachment, or the mail server cannot properly convert the file format of the attachment to another computer platform. If you're sending e-mail from a Macintosh computer, Entourage and Outlook Express enable you to configure how you want your e-mail attachments to be added to an e-mail message. Except in rare cases where compression fails to allow the recipient to open the attachment, all e-mail enclosures should be compressed before being sent to the mail server and the recipient.

Figure 6-11 shows the attachment options for a new e-mail message in Entourage. The zip archive is already compressed. That's why the None radio button is selected in the Compression options for the e-mail message. The default setting for Encoding an attachment is Any Computer (AppleDouble). Although you probably won't have problems sending e-mail from your DSL service provider, some older operating systems may have problems processing an AppleDouble attachment. If the recipient of your e-mail message is unable to decompress the attached file, the compressed file may have been modified by a mail server mistaking the attachment for a BinHex file or another file format.

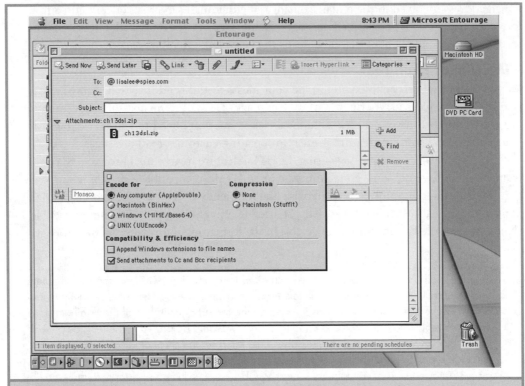

Figure 6-11.   You can modify the attachment settings by clicking below the window list in the new mail message.

If you're using Outlook or Outlook Express running on Windows 98, Windows Me, Windows NT, Windows 2000, or Windows XP, you won't have to worry about configuring your e-mail settings, especially if you're sending the e-mail to another Outlook user. Most problems with attachments sent from Windows computers occur when the recipient is using a Mac or Linux computer and does not have an application that can open the attached file. If you want to send files that are easily opened by any other computer platform, consider converting the file into an HTML or text file. If the attachment is an image, consider converting it to a JPEG or GIF so that the recipient can view the document or image in a browser window.

NOTE   You can also set up a mail server on the local network. If you want to set up a Windows e-mail server, you can install an Exchange server using Windows 2000 Server. Apple's Mac OS X server enables you to set up a POP and SMTP mail server or an IMAP mail server. Linux distributions include a Sendmail mail server that you can install and configure on a Linux computer if you want to add a mail server to a local network. In most cases, you can use a Windows, Mac, or Linux e-mail client to access and e-mail account on any of these mail servers.

Problems Receiving Attachments

Now that you know how to add an attachment to a new mail message, you may want to find out more about the mysteries associated with opening an e-mail attachment. A Mac, Windows, or Linux e-mail client should be able to decompress an e-mail attachment, regardless of the computer platform that sent the original e-mail message. If the e-mail attachment was created by a particular application, such as Microsoft Word or a text editor application, the computer that receives the e-mail must also have an application installed that is capable of opening the attached document in order to open the attached file. If you receive an e-mail attachment that the computer cannot open, you may want to send an e-mail message to the person who sent the e-mail and ask them to save the file in a different file format or find out which application was used to create the attached file.

Decompressing an Attachment

Outlook, Entourage, and Outlook Express have a column in the Inbox area of the main e-mail window to let you know whether an e-mail message has an attachment. A paper clip icon will appear to the left of a message that contains one or more attached files. Opening or saving an attachment is similar on a Windows or Macintosh computer.

On a Windows computer, you can view the name of the attached file by clicking on the paper clip icon in the preview pane of the main window in Outlook Express. Select a file to open it or save it to your hard drive. Choose the Save Attachments command if you want to save all attachments to the same directory on your hard drive. If you're using Outlook 2000, you can access the attachment in the body of the e-mail message. Simply click and drag it to your desktop to copy it to your hard drive. Double-click the attached file to open and view it without downloading it from Exchange Server.

On a Macintosh computer, an attachment section appears below the From and Subject headings in the preview pane of the main window. You can click and drag a file from the Attachments window list and drop it on your desktop to copy the file to your hard drive. You can also double-click the attached file to open and view it.

CAUTION

Before you decompress or open an attachment, check the name of the person who has sent you the e-mail. If the e-mail address is not familiar, the message may be a trojan horse for an e-mail virus. If you're not sure whether to open or delete an e-mail message, you're better off deleting the message instead of opening it. Most e-mail viruses won't do any harm unless you download the attachment from the e-mail message and start the enclosed application on your computer. E-mail viruses can fill up your mailbox with fake messages or use your address book to send themselves to other computers via e-mail.

If the attached file is a zip or stuffit archive, you must decompress it before you can view or open files stored in the archive. You can install a WinZip tool on a Windows computer to open a zip archive. To open a stuffit archive in Windows, you can download and install Unstuffit from Aladdin System's web site at www.aladdinsys.com. Download and install WinZip or Unstuffit on your Windows computer. Then double-click the zip or stuffit archive to open it and view its contents. You can click and drag a file to move it out of the archive. If you're using WinZip, select one or more files and choose the Extract command from the Actions menu.

Unstuffit is preinstalled on any Macintosh computer that shipped with Mac OS 8 or later. You can double-click a zip or stuffit archive on a Mac, and the contents of the archive will be placed in a new folder located in the same directory as the compressed file. If you are unable to decompress an attachment, ask the person who sent it to you what kind of compression program was used to create the archive.

Opening the Attached File

You might be wondering why this chapter has a special section on opening an attachment. How difficult can it be? If I send myself a text file, I can open it in Windows with Notepad, or with SimpleText on a Macintosh computer. The trick to opening an attached file is to have a program installed on your computer that is capable of opening it.

If you're still wondering why this might be so difficult, consider this scenario. You have Linux running on your PC, and you receive an AppleWorks file from a Mac user. If you have an iMac that has AppleWorks pre-installed, all you have to do is double-click the document, and AppleWorks automatically opens the file. However, Apple doesn't publish AppleWorks for Linux.

If you want to view this file, you may be able to find a document conversion program to convert the AppleWorks file into an HTML file. However, not having the application used to create a particular file will prevent most folks from being able to open or view it. To avoid this problem, make sure the recipient of your e-mail message has a compatible application installed on their system. Otherwise, send text, HTML, JPEG, or GIF files if possible. Most computers have a browser application that will be able to view these particular file formats.

Adding a Camera to Your Network

If a digital camera is connected to a computer that is capable of sending e-mail, you can create a script to capture an image and then attach it to an e-mail. You can configure the script to capture and send an image to you, or to someone else, at regular intervals. If you have access to a Web site on the local network or on the Internet, you can upload the image to a web site at regular intervals.

You can use two kinds of digital cameras for this kind of set up. Web cams offer custom software that enables you to capture an image at regular intervals. A digital camera can also be set up and controlled over the network. You will probably need to use more than one application, such as Timbuktu and Photoshop, depending on how you want to control the camera and what type of image you want to e-mail or share on the Web.

Setting Up a Camera on a Network

Choose a camera to connect to your computer. Preferably, the camera will have its own power supply. Some cameras may connect to your computer's serial port, while newer models are more likely to use a USB port. The following steps show you how to connect a digital camera to a computer and install its software on a Windows or Macintosh computer. Check the camera's documentation to find out software is available for Linux systems.

1. Connect the cable to the camera and then to your computer.

2. Install the camera's software, if any, on your computer.

3. Restart your computer and check whether you can view the image viewed by the camera on your desktop. Try taking a test picture with the camera.

4. Set the software settings on the camera so that it will not power off when not in use. Some digital cameras can be configured to go into a low power sleep mode instead of powering off completely.

Capturing Images over a Network

Software for digital cameras varies from camera to camera. Web cams are specifically designed to be controlled by a computer, unlike handheld digital cameras, which require manual interaction in order to capture an image. You can save each captured file to your hard drive. Then create a web page that updates with the latest image. You can also log in to your DSL network over the Internet and use Timbuktu or VNC to access the camera's software and capture an image over the network.

Double-click the application to start the camera's software. Check to see whether you can view live video on your desktop. Capture an image and save it to your hard drive. Then view it in a browser or image viewer application. You may need to adjust the video settings in order to view an image as clearly as possible. To send the image in e-mail, you can add it as an attachment and send it.

Adding an Image to E-Mail

To attach an image file to an e-mail, follow the steps for attaching a text file. Before you attach an image file to an e-mail message, check the image's file size. Image files tend to be larger than regular text files, especially full-color digital images captured by a 2–3 megapixel camera. Depending on the limits of your mail box, you may not be able to send more than 2MB of data from your DSL e-mail account. Consider resizing the image to a smaller size before attaching it to an e-mail message.

NOTE

NetMeeting is an application that comes bundled with Windows operating systems. It is designed to transmit video over a dial-up analog modem connection to another network. If you use NetMeeting connected to a DSL network, you may experience connection problems with a point-to-point or router connection. You may want to request a DSL modem that bridges the network connection between your local network and the DSL provider to enable NetMeeting to work more reliably with the DSL connection.

Additional Resources

E-mail is one of the few network applications that is a no-brainer to install and use on your DSL network. You can use a dedicated e-mail program or view you messages on the Web. In general, using e-mail is relatively trouble-free. The biggest concern is network performance if large attachments are applied to an e-mail, or if many users try to download or send e-mail on the network simultaneously. You may also need to reconfigure your DSL modem settings if you have a mail server that, for some reason, won't work with your firewall setup. Find out more about e-mail and networks by visiting the following Web addresses.

+ www.hotmail.com
+ www.yahoo.com
+ www.microsoft.com/ie
+ www.microsoft.com/mac/ie
+ www.winzip.com
+ www.aladdinsys.com
+ www.download.com
+ www.linux.org
+ www.redhat.com

Chapter 7

Setting Up Interactive Software

C hat, instant messaging, and games enable you to interact with other computer users connected to the Internet . Network games enable you to access single or multi-player games on the Internet. Chat enables you to meet other online visitors or friends. You can type your questions or comments into the chat room window, and you and others can view your comments: sort of like an electronic meeting room. Instant messaging is similar but allows you to have more than one conversation with other people who also have the messaging software installed. Instant messaging is the online feature that made America Online so popular. What better way to find your friends and family online as they log into the Internet with their messaging program?

Each interactive client requires that a server be set up somewhere on the Internet. The server allows participants to create an account and log in. As others who have registered also log in, their names are broadcast on the network, so that other computers running the chat, instant messaging, or game software can see who else has joined the network. Games require the most network bandwidth to run, since graphics, text, and audio must be pumped across the network in order for all players to interact with each other. This chapter shows you how to set up and run chat, messaging, and game client software on the network.

 ✦ **Chat rooms**   Join a large or small group of people and participate in an electronic gathering where you can ask questions or view others' questions and answers online.

 ✦ **Instant messaging**   Set up a buddy list and chat with family and friends whenever they're online. There are over 20 million people online who use instant messaging software to exchange messages over the Internet.

 ✦ **Games**   Log in or sign up for a single-player or multiple player online game. There are many Web sites and network game sites that may provide you with hours of entertainment.

Basic Concepts: Chat, Messenger, and Games

Next to e-mail, chat and instant messaging are two very popular ways people can meet and communicate with each other over the Internet. Chat rooms work more like traditional Web servers. Users can log into a room located on a server on a network and type messages to each other. Each message is broadcast to every computer connected to that chat room. Messaging is a one-to-one format of a chat room. Each messaging client has a unique login name, and each person can create a buddy list of other messaging clients that might be logged into the system. AOL Instant Messenger, shown in Figure 7-1, is the Internet version of AOL's popular instant messaging program.

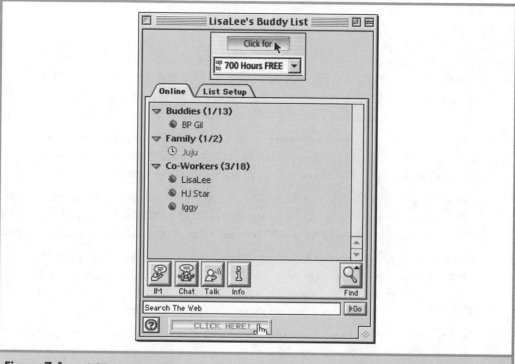

Figure 7-1. AOL Instant Messenger is probably the most popular messaging program used today.

Games are also quite popular on the Internet. Some network games can be played with only a single player. However, many of the more popular games are network games, where other players are interacting with your character over the network. In order to set up a game, chat, or messaging service on a local network, you must set up a dedicated computer, configured with a particular game, chat, or messaging service on the network. The faster the computer, the better. Each client computer must have the chat, messaging, or game client software installed on it before it can connect to the server. The following sections show you how to install, set up, and run a chat, messaging, and game client on your computer.

A Short List of Interactive Product Terms

There are several different client/server applications that enable you to interact with others who are online. You'll probably be accessing chat, instant messaging, and game services using a client application. The following list explains the client and server components of

chat, instant messaging, and network-based games that will be explained in more detail in this chapter.

- **Chat**   The process of exchanging text between a group of client computers that are able to communicate over a network by logging into a common chat server.

- **Chat room**   A virtual room where a chat client can go to exchange messages in real time with other computers running the same chat client software on the chat server.

- **Chat server**   The network computers that host a chat service. The chat server is responsible for relaying messages between chat clients. If the server loses its network connection, the virtual room disappears from the network.

- **IRC**   An acronym for Internet Relay Chat. A type of interactive chat that requires an IRC server to be running on the network. If an IRC client can locate the IRC server, it can participate in a chat session with other IRC clients connected to the same server.

- **Instant message**   A message that is sent through an interactive messaging server between two client computers connected to the same instant messaging server. America Online has the most popular instant messaging service. However, Yahoo and MSN also offer their own instant messaging services for free.

- **Buddy list**   A list of login names of others who use the same instant messaging service. When someone on your buddy list connects to the instant messaging server, your buddy list will update, letting you know they are available for exchanging messages online.

- **Network-based games**   A server- or client-based game. Network-based games enable you to play interactive games in real time on a network.

- **Game server**   A computer that runs the server software for a game.

- **Ping time**   The amount of time it takes to send a ping to another computer on the network. The longer the ping time, the farther away the other computer is from your computer. Adding players with short ping times can help improve the performance of network game play.

Make Friends Online

Chat and instant messaging enable you to exchange messages online. A message reaches the recipient of your online conversation within seconds after you send it. Most messaging software has a buddy list feature. You can add the names of your online messaging friends. If they are online, you will see their names appear in the messaging window, as shown in Figure 7-2. Most messaging services also send news, weather, and stock information while you're connected to the service.

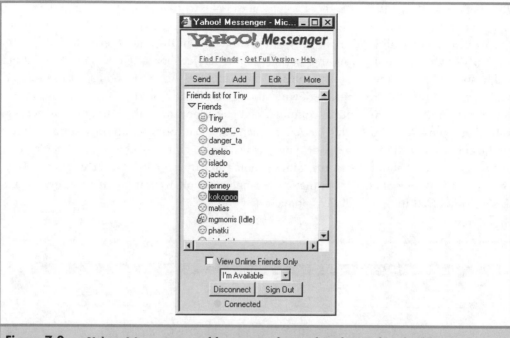

Figure 7-2. Yahoo Messenger enables you to chat with online Yahoo buddies.

Some chat and messaging programs enable you to hook up a digital camera to your computer and send a picture of yourself while you chat. Chat can be used as an online alternative to a telephone conference call. Instead of talking to each other on the phone, everyone can meet in a chat room and attend a meeting. The following sections will show you how to install and set up chat and messaging software on Mac and Windows computers.

Installing Chat Room Software

The good news is that you can chat on the Internet without installing any additional software on your computer. Most Internet chat rooms enable you to chat in real time without having to install a separate application, like the instant messaging programs. One of the most popular chat room Web sites is Talk City (www.talkcity.com).

Before chat rooms became so popular on the Web, Internet Relay Chat (IRC) brought interactive chat to the Internet. You can install an IRC client onto your Windows or Macintosh computer. Log into an IRC server, and chat with one or more IRC clients sharing the same channel. Each channel is like a room, or as the folks who maintain the mIRC (a Windows

IRC client) say, IRC is like CB radio, except you can talk with anyone else around the world. You can download mIRC, Virc, or Pirch to connect to an IRC server with a Windows computer, or download and install Ircle or Homer if you want to use an IRC client on a Mac.

America Online (AOL) is another popular online service, boasting over ten million users and hosting a large number of chat rooms. You can access AOL's chat rooms with a browser, as shown in Figure 7-3, or you can download and install the America Online application onto your Windows or Macintosh computer and pay a monthly subscription fee to access AOL chat rooms. America Online has a fairly elaborate chat room set up. In addition to the public chat rooms, open to everyone, you can also create a private chat room. Each chat room has a limit of about 30 people. More people can gather in an AOL Live session. AOL Live is a special type of chat room that enables more people to participate in a large chat session with celebrities or to discuss popular news topics.

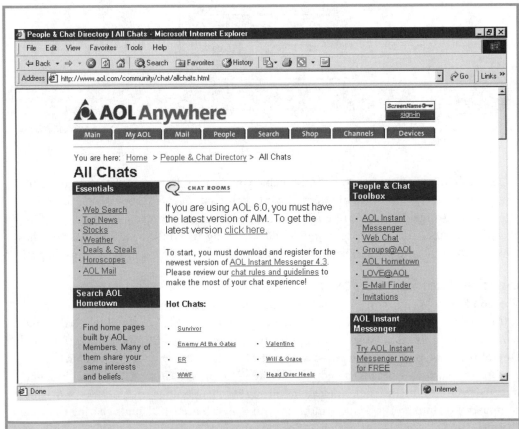

Figure 7-3.   You can use Internet Explorer to visit chat room Web sites, such as AOL's popular public and private chat rooms.

NOTE

When you type and send information to the chat server and to other chat clients, the text is sent without any encryption or security. Although only the intended recipient should see your message, it's also possible for the folks hosting the chat server to read your online conversation. A hacker may able to be able to read your chat. Be careful about what you say online!

AOL also provides message boards online. You can share your thoughts by posting a message to a message board, or read messages posted by others. You'll find hundreds of different topics you can read about on AOL's message boards. Try to find a topic that matches your question, and find a message board that has recent message postings.

Getting Online

The key to using some online chat or messaging services is to create a login account and password. You can use your login name or create a nickname for a chat or message room persona. If you are looking for an inexpensive way to engage in interactive conversation, you can sign up for a free e-mail account on Hotmail.com, and then use that account to log into msn.com online chat sessions (see Figure 7-4). Other chat rooms, like those available on yahoo.com, will use your my.yahoo.com account information to log you into a chat room.

NOTE

In order to join a chat room, you cannot have the same name as someone else who is already registered with the chat service. You may need to spend a few moments to create a unique nickname for yourself before you can join a chat room.

You can join a chat room from msn.com by choosing the People & Chat link. Click a link to pick the chat room you want to join. Then type a nickname for yourself, as shown in Figure 7-5. Each person in the chat room must have a unique name or nickname. If you select a nickname that has already been chosen by someone else, you will be asked to think of another nickname to use before you can enter the chat room. You can use upper- or lowercase letters to create your name, or add numbers to your name, such as Bo3b. Some people type underline characters between each word in their nickname in order to create a unique spelling of that name. For example, if JohnDoe is not available, you might want to try typing **John_Doe** or **John_Doe_1** to see if these nicknames are available.

Chat Room Tips and Tricks

The chat windows for most chat rooms have three common elements you will interact with. A list of other people in the room will appear on the left or right side of the chat window. A large window will fill most of the window. New text typed by anyone else in the chat room will appear at the bottom of the list of text. At the bottom of the window, you can type in

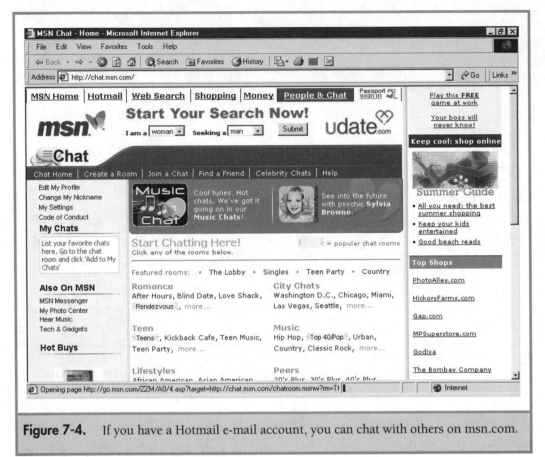

Figure 7-4.   If you have a Hotmail e-mail account, you can chat with others on msn.com.

your own comments. When you press the RETURN or ENTER key, everyone else will view it
in the chat room.

Don't be surprised to see numerous conversations being carried on at the same time
while you're in the chat room (see Figure 7-6). If the chat room is not being run by a host,
anyone can ask any question at any time, although an answer is not guaranteed. Despite the
chaotic nature of the chat room, there are a few syntactical rules that most rooms follow. For
example, if you type in all capital letters, this is the online equivalent of shouting. Also,
profanity and derogatory language are usually discouraged.

In addition to typing in a text message, you can add an emoticon to the end of a message.
Emoticons are sideways faces created by typing combinations of characters. For example, the

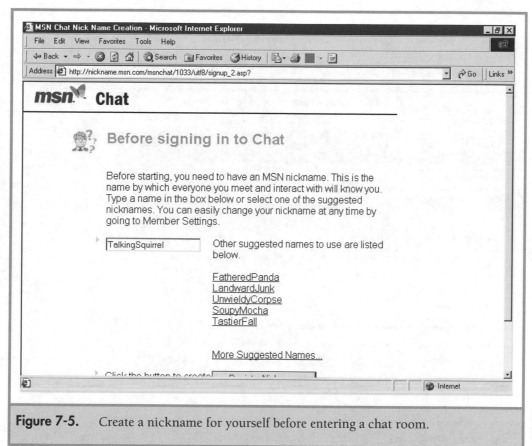

Figure 7-5.   Create a nickname for yourself before entering a chat room.

message "hey, it's great to see you!" makes a nice salutation. But "hey, it's great to see you! :-)" adds a smiling face to the end of that message.

CAUTION

When you exchange text messages in a chat room, you are sending and receiving information over the network. This information is broadcast over the network and is not protected from being viewed by someone who might know how to read data that is being sent over a network. To maintain a level of security while you're chatting, don't share your login name or password for your computer or chat room accounts, or any other private information that you don't want broadcast over the network.

DSL Survival Guide

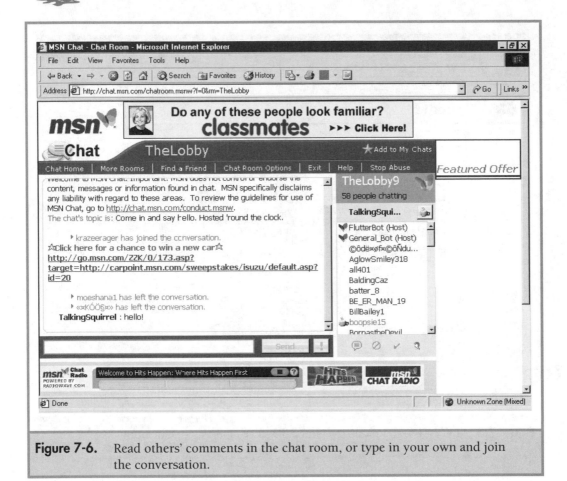

Figure 7-6. Read others' comments in the chat room, or type in your own and join the conversation.

If you're already familiar with emoticons, you may or may not know about forward slash commands for IRC chat rooms. Some chat Web sites also support these commands. You can use a command to view a list of names of others who are in the same chat room, or type a command to change to a new room or channel. Table 7-1 lists a few IRC commands you might find helpful.

Using Messenger for Private Conversations Online

Messenger clients enable you to broadcast messages to more than one person at a time or carry on a one-to-one conversation. Most messenger clients, such as ICQ, AOL Instant

Command	Description	What Others See
/who	See a list of others who are in the same room.	Nothing.
/me	Type this command followed by an action to format a thought with others in the room.	Your user name followed by your comment.
/away	Let others know you're away from your computer.	Your user name followed by the away message.
/list	List all channels available for the IRC server.	Nothing.
/invite	Invite another IRC client to the channel or room.	Nothing. Invitee sees your message.
/kick	Type this command followed by the nickname of the user. If the channel enables users to kick someone out of a room, this command will move the person out of the room.	Nickname of person kicked out of the room followed by the message "has left the room."
/quit	Exit the IRC room or channel.	*Your user name* has left the room.

Table 7-1.   IRC Commands

Messenger, and Yahoo Messenger, enable you to choose a buddy or start a conversation with another person connected to the messenger service. It helps to know the nickname or screen name of the person you want to talk to. However, you can also search for people if you want to start a conversation with a stranger.

In addition to enabling one-to-one conversations, messenger software introduces you to the buddy lists. You can create an individual buddy or group of buddies in your messenger client. Yahoo Messenger has a few additional features that make its messenger program a little more like an IRC chat client. For example, you can invite someone to join your chat or create your own chat room, in addition to using the basic messenger feature of exchanging messages. The following sections show you how to install the AOL, MSN, and Yahoo messengers.

Installing AOL, MSN, and Yahoo Messenger Programs

You can download AOL, MSN, or Yahoo messenger programs from their perspective Web sites. If you don't see a link to messenger services, try searching for "messenger." Download the latest version of the messenger software for your computer. You will be able to exchange

messages with any other computer connected to the messenger service, as long as they're using the same AOL, MSN, Yahoo, or ICQ client. Messenger servers will recognize several versions of the messenger client software, so don't worry about missing friends online if they aren't using the exact same version of the client software as you are.

Double-click the installer application and follow the onscreen instructions to install the instant messaging (aka messenger) software onto your Mac, Windows, or Linux computer. You can install more than one messenger client on a computer. Since each client connects to a different server, you won't have any problems installing more than one client. Although it's possible to run more than one messenger client at a time on your computer, you will see the best network performance if you run one client at any given time. For example, you can install MSN Messenger, shown in Figure 7-7, and AOL Instant Messenger onto the same computer. You can log into the AOL Instant Messenger server, and then start the MSN client and log into the MSN server. It may be easy to confuse which window belongs to which messenger client.

After you have installed a messenger program on your computer, start the messenger application and log into the messenger service. You don't need to set up any special network settings if you want to use a messenger client on your DSL network. Wait for the messenger program to connect to its server on the Internet. If the program is able to successfully connect to the messenger server, you will see a window list appear. You can click the Add or Send button (if you're using Yahoo or MSN Messenger) and type the name of the person you want to send a message to. If you're using AOL Instant Messenger, shown in Figure 7-7, you can click the IM button, and then type the name of the AOL or messenger name you want to send your message to in the IM window's text box. Click the Send button to send your message.

When You're Unavailable

You can reduce the number of instant messages that appear on your screen while you're away from your computer by setting up the messenger client to let people know you're unavailable. For example, choose Options from the Tools menu. Then select the Preferences tab. Select the Show Me As "Away" When I'm Inactive For 5 Minutes check box. You can type the number of minutes into the text box in the Options dialog box. Yahoo Messenger has a drop-down menu located at the bottom of the messenger window. You can choose from I'm Available, Be Right Back, Busy, Not At Home, Not At My Desk, Not In The Office, On The Phone, or On Vacation. Choose your status from the drop-down menu list, and it will appear on your buddy's lists.

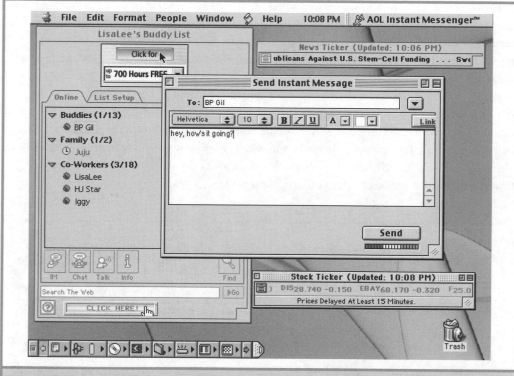

Figure 7-7. Instant Messaging programs enable you to start a one-to-one conversation with another person who has the same messenger program installed on his or her computer on the network.

Replying to a Message

Don't forget you're not alone when you're online. When you log into a messenger service, other users can see you, if the messenger server can see you. The term "see" refers to the window list in the messenger window. Most messenger clients ask you whether you want someone else to add you to their buddy list. However, other online folks can search for you and send a general e-mail to a group of people to try to get an online conversation started.

When you receive a message while you're online, a new messenger window opens. Similarly, when you create an instant message, a new window will open (see Figure 7-8). Any replies or new messages can be viewed or sent from that messenger window. You can exchange messages in one messenger window or several. If you want to save the conversation as a file on your hard drive, choose the Save command from the File menu, and save the document as a text file. You can also copy and paste the text into Notepad (Windows), or SimpleText (Mac OS), or another open text document on a Windows, Mac, or Linux computer.

You can customize the text that you send separately from the text you receive in the AOL Instant Messenger window. Highlight the text you want to format. Then choose a font, font size, font style, and font color from the instant message window. When you click Send, your message will appear in the recipient's messenger window as you formatted it. Choose Preferences from the Edit menu to choose the font and font size you want to use as the default settings for any messages you send or receive.

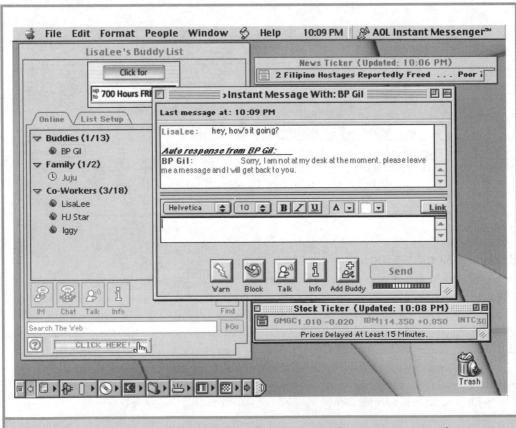

Figure 7-8.   View the conversation in the messenger window. You can save the session as a text or HTML file, or copy and paste it into another text editor application.

Logging In

Messenger clients enable virtually anyone to log into the messenger service. If you have an AOL account, you can use your AOL login with AOL's messenger client to send or receive instant messages online without logging into the AOL service. You can configure the login window, shown in Figure 7-9, to store up to six different messenger login accounts. MSN Messenger enables you to use a passport or Hotmail account to log in. You can read your Hotmail e-mail messages from your MSN Messenger client. If you have signed up for an e-mail account on www.yahoo.com, you can use it as your Yahoo Messenger login account.

SURVIVAL TIP

If you're familiar with formatting links and text with the Hypertext Markup Language (HTML), you may want to try formatting your instant messages with HTML tags. If the instant messaging window supports HTML tabs, you can center, boldface, choose a font, or choose a font size by typing in begin and end tags, such as hello, which will boldface the "hello" text.

Creating a Buddy List

You can add the names of friends or family that use the same messenger server to a buddy list. A *buddy list* is a list of instant messaging accounts for that particular instant messaging service. It's possible for someone to have more than one instant messaging account, so you

Figure 7-9. You can set up a computer to allow several people to log into Messenger, or create multiple accounts for your own use.

may have more than one name in your buddy list for the same person. When you log into the messenger service, you will be able to see whether any of your buddies are connected to the messenger service or not. You can organize the names of your buddies in groups, as shown in Figure 7-10, or keep them all in one list.

AOL Instant Messenger is the most popular instant messaging program of the three widely available ones. If you're using AOL Instant Messenger, perform the following steps to add a buddy:

1. First, select the List Setup tab.

2. Click the Add Buddy button if you want to add another person to your messenger buddy list.

3. Click the Add Group button if you want to create a new group.

4. Click and drag the names from one group to another if you want to organize who's who in your buddy lists.

5. If a buddy is online, click that person's name.

6. Then click the IM or Send button and type a message.

To add a buddy to Yahoo Messenger, perform the following steps:

1. Click the Edit button in the Yahoo Messenger window.

2. Click the Friends/Groups button.

3. Type a name of a new group if you want to add a new group of buddies to your messenger window or edit an existing group.

Messenger Security Issues

Messages exchanged between messenger clients are not encrypted. Text is sent as-is. If you're worried about the security of your messenger connection, you should be careful about what kind of information you send. For example, try not to send any login or password information for your account, and definitely don't send your credit card or bank account information in an instant message.

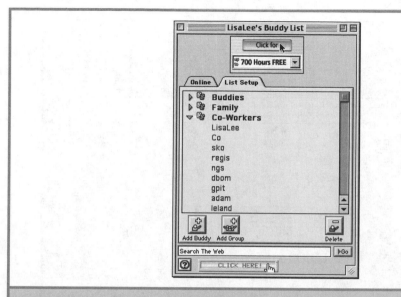

Figure 7-10. Set up a buddy list if you want to find out when a friend is online.

Customizing Stock and News Information

The Yahoo and AOL Messenger programs enable you to view stock and news tickers while chatting with others online. Select the Preferences menu command from the Edit menu to open the Preferences window for AOL Instant Messenger. Then click the Stock Ticker category in the left window list. Type the stock symbol into the text box located at the top of the Stock Ticker Preferences window. Check the Stock Indices you want to view. Then choose the display settings for the ticker. Click OK to save your changes and exit the Preferences window. The stock symbols you entered should appear in the AOL Instant Messenger desktop. Choose Stock Ticker from the Window menu to open the stock ticker window, shown in Figure 7-11.

You can follow similar steps to modify the news ticker. However, you can choose where the news comes from. You can select one of four check boxes to view News, Business, Entertainment, or Sports news in the News Ticker window. Adjust the Display, Refresh, and Display Speed settings from the News Ticker Preferences window. Then click OK to save your changes. Choose News Ticker from the Window menu to open the News Ticker window in the AOL Instant Messenger desktop. You can click the icon located on the left side of the News or Stock Ticker window to view a larger list of news or stock links in a My News or Stock window.

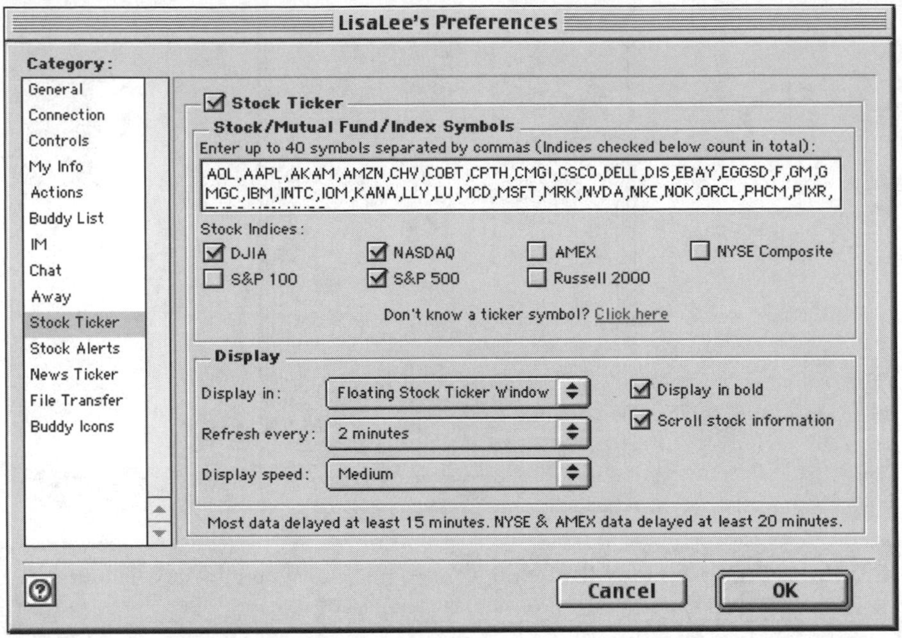

Figure 7-11. AOL Instant Messenger enables you to view stock and news information while you're connected to their services.

Playing Interactive Networked Games

Interactive games can range from chess and card games, like blackjack or poker, to online adventure and action games, like Ultima Online, Quake, or Half Life. Most of these game sites host game servers. You can install the client version of the game on your Macintosh or Windows computer. Then log into the Internet game server over an FTP or HTTP connection to play with others online.

Installing Networked Games

Most online networked games require you to install a client application on your computer in order to connect to the game server. Some network games support peer-to-peer networking; no server is required. However, each client must have the networking feature selected in order to participate in a network game. Depending on the throughput speed of the network, you may be able to support only five or ten simultaneous network players before the network bandwidth makes the game too slow to play over the network.

Many networked games enable you to recognize other computers on the local network that have the network feature enabled. For example, Marathon, which I'm sure is now regarded as an ancient point-and-shoot network game, enables you to see who else is on the network. Once all the players can be viewed online, each person can select their custom settings and gear, and play a game over the network. There are also tamer online game sites, such as the game site on yahoo.com, shown in Figure 7-12. These HTML, Java, and JavaScript games can be fun, and if you don't like one game, there are plenty more to choose from.

SURVIVAL TIP

Networked games may install a large number of files on your hard drive. Three-dimensional graphics and animation require not only a lot of video and processing power but also plenty of disk space. Most game and application installer wizards will show you the amount of disk space required to install the software, and how much available disk space will remain after the installation completes. If you decide to remove a game from your computer, make sure you delete any graphic or data files from your hard drive.

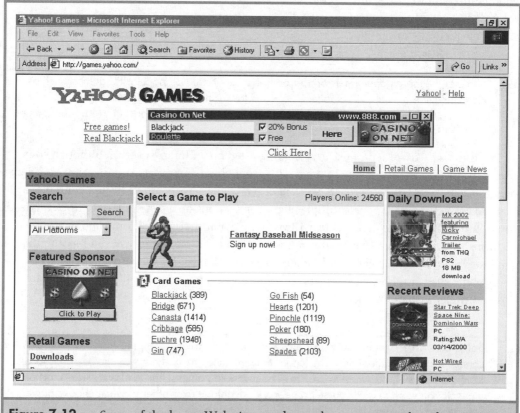

Figure 7-12.   Some of the larger Web sites, such as yahoo.com, provide online games.

Playing Networked Games

There are two kinds of network games you can access on the Internet: single-player and multiplayer games. Single-player games can usually be found on larger Web sites, such as msn.com and yahoo.com. You do not need to pay a fee or log into the Web site to play these HTML, Java, or JavaScript games. However, you should install a compatible browser on your computer before accessing these Web sites. Simply click a link to access a game and follow the onscreen instructions to play them.

NOTE Avid game players may recommend playing network-based games over an SDSL connection, which has a faster upload time than an ADSL line. However, if you prefer to have a faster download time, choose an ADSL connection to the Internet.

Some single-player games, such as those offered by gambling or card game Web sites, may require you to pay a subscription fee or register before you can participate. I don't recommend gambling online. Use your discretion before choosing a Web site that requires you to pay before you can play.

NOTE Some of the more popular network-based games are based on popular PC games, such as Half-Life, Diablo, Diablo 2, Quake, Quake 2, Star Craft, Drakkar, and Halo. Some sites, such as Ultima Online and ea.com, enable you to use a browser to participate in Web-based games.

Multiplayer networked games are usually hosted on an Internet server, although some games enable the client game to interact with other client computers running the same game over the same network to play against each other. Game servers are dedicated computers that are configured to support multiple client connections on a fast network. For example, some game servers are connected to a T3 network connection, which can support up to 45 Mbps. If you have the client software installed on your computer, you can log into the game server and play the game with others logged into the game server over the Internet. Many game sites also host chat servers, enabling gamers to exchange messages and share tips and tricks with each other.

NOTE Some networked games, such as Quake, enable you to view the ping times for any players connected to the game server. The longer the ping time, the farther away the person is located from the server. If you want to play faster networked games, choose players with short ping times. If you want to give yourself a network advantage over other players, choose players with longer ping times.

Problems: Accessing Services

Many of the problems you may encounter with chat, messenger, and game servers may seem oddly similar to access problems to popular FTP, Web, and other online Internet servers. Although there are many chat and game servers on the Internet that are capable of sustaining hundreds of messenger clients or network game players, many can reach their maximum network usage limits during peak hours of the day or if the site is hosting a special event. The best way to work around these server access problems is to log into the server as early as possible and beat the crowd. The following sections describe a few common problems accessing chat and game servers on the network.

Finding a Chat or Messenger Server

If you're using a browser to access a chat or messenger Web page, you won't need to worry about how to find the chat or messenger server on the Internet. The Web page will connect your computer to the appropriate server. If you have not set up a firewall or proxy server on your network, you should not have any problems logging into a chat or messenger server either. Each messenger client is installed to connect to the main AOL, MSN, Yahoo, or ICQ server on the Internet.

An error message may be the first sign that you may have a bad network cable, or you may need to check your network settings to get your computer to connect to the chat, messenger, or game server. Most error messages will explain why the connection failed. If the connection fails, check your software settings for your home area network (HAN) or small office home office (SOHO) network, and then check to see that your network card and any cables are properly connected to the computer.

Checking Your Network Settings

Before changing any settings, take a few minutes to make sure your network connection is active on your computer. You may be able to restore your network connection by simply disabling and reenabling the network connection from the Windows or Mac OS operating system. For example, on a Macintosh computer, you can open the TCP/IP control panel. Press COMMAND - K, or choose the Configurations command from the File menu. Highlight the TCP/IP settings for your DSL network, and then click the Make Active button. Then close the TCP/IP control panel. If your network settings changed, you will see a dialog box appear, indicating that your network settings have changed. Click OK and try starting Messenger again.

Connection Problems? Try Another Computer

If this is the first time you've tried to run chat, messenger, or a network game on a computer, you may want to try removing and reinstalling the software if you're having problems getting these new programs to recognize the network. If you have a second computer that can work with messenger and chat, try connecting it to your network to see whether it can reach the Internet server via your DSL modem.

You can reset the network settings for a network interface card by performing the following steps on a Windows 2000 or Windows XP computer.

1. Choose Network And Dial-Up Connections from the Start | Settings menu. The Network And Dial-Up window will open on a Windows 2000 computer. Double-click the My Network Places icon on a Windows XP computer, and the select the View Network Connections icon.

2. Right-click the Ethernet device connected to your DSL network.

3. Choose Disable from the shortcut menu. Wait for the Ethernet card to disconnect from the network.

4. Right-click the Ethernet icon again, and choose Enable from the shortcut menu.

5. Start AOL or Yahoo Messenger and see whether you can connect to the messenger server on the network.

Checking Messenger Settings

Some messenger programs rely on a browser's network connection to the Internet. If your browser is able to get on the Web, you should have no problems chatting online, provided your browser has plenty of memory available to support the messenger software. If you want to check the connection settings for AOL Instant Messenger, you open the Connection Preferences window (shown in Figure 7-13). Perform the following steps to open this window.

1. Click the Setup button in the login window, or choose the Preferences command from the Edit menu.

2. Select Connection from the Category window list.

3. View the Host Port in the Connection Preferences window. If you have a proxy server set up on your DSL network, select the Connect Using Proxy Server checkbox.

4. Type the host name of the proxy server into the Host text box.

5. Choose a Protocol, SOCKS 4, SOCKS 5, or HTTPS from the Protocol section of the Preferences window. If the proxy server requires you to log in, type the login name and password information in the Proxy Authentication text fields. Click OK to save your changes.

Other messenger programs may or may not have custom connection settings that you can view or change. In most cases, the messenger program will work if your browser connection works. Open a browser window and visit www.yahoo.com, www.msn.com, or www.icq.com. If you can access the Web servers for these messenger server hosts, you should also be able to access their messenger servers using the appropriate messenger client.

Messenger Service Problems

Interactive services such as instant messaging, chat, and network-based games work best on a stable, reliable network. If the interactive service's performance is slow, or if there is a problem with your local network connection to the Internet, your online friends may see

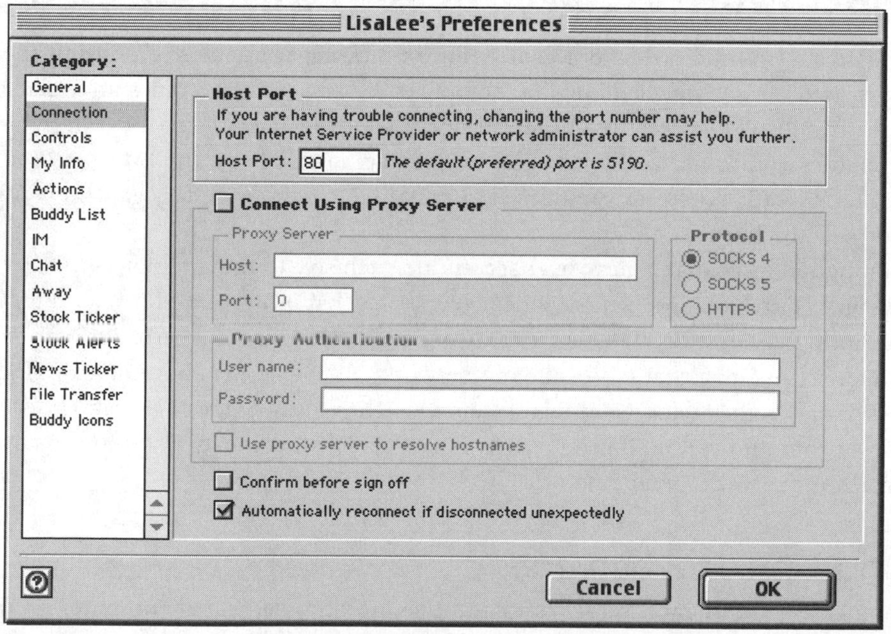

Figure 7-13. You can view or set the Host port for AOL Instant Messenger from the Connection Preferences window.

you appear and then disappear from an instant message server, chat room, or network game. You may need to constantly log in, only to get kicked out.

In general, interactive services are fairly reliable when you're accessing them from a DSL network. However, network problems can prevent you from accessing these services. If this occurs, don't panic. There are several things you can attempt to identify whether the source of the problem is on your network or it is a problem with the interactive service. These processes are explained in more detail in Chapter 15. The point I want to make here is that it's possible for an interactive service to lose its connection to the Internet, too. If that's the case, you might want to visit their Web site to find out when the service is expected to be back online.

Networked Game Problems

Some games rely on an IP address in order to recognize game players on different networks. If you have a Network Address Translator set up on your local area network, you may be able to play games only with other players on your local network. Again, your mileage may vary, depending on the network game you're trying to play.

Solutions: Backup Services and Intranet Servers

One way to stay in touch with your chat, game, or messenger buddies is to install another chat or instant messaging client on your computer. If one service becomes unavailable, you and your friends can switch to a different one. Installing a secondary chat or messaging client enables you to use a different chat or messaging server on the Internet. You can choose an alternative network game site as a backup in case the primary game server goes down or gets too busy.

Although most chat and messenger servers are exclusive to the Internet, some services enable you to purchase or download a demo copy of a chat or messenger server to try out on your local network. If you have two or more avid chat or messenger users, you may want to try setting up a chat server on your network to see whether your home or office network users might prefer using this system to exchange short messages, and bolster interactive communication. If productivity isn't a concern, you may also want to consider adding a game server to your network.

Setting Up Local Servers

Chat, messenger, and game servers should be set up on a dedicated computer on the network. Most server software will run on Unix or Linux operating systems. However, you can also install some servers on Windows or Macintosh computers. Check the documentation for the software to see what the recommended server hardware requirements are for each server.

Setting Up a Local Chat Server

Download and install the chat server software from the IRC Web site. If you don't want folks on the Internet to join the chat sessions on your local network, you can configure the chat server to recognize only computers with IP addresses on your local network. However, you can configure the chat server to allow folks on other networks to access your chat server. After you install and set up the chat server software, restart the computer. Then try logging into the chat server from a client computer on your local network. If the connection is successful, try connecting a second computer and exchanging chat messages.

Setting Up a Local Game Server

There are two different kinds of game servers you can set up on your local network. The easier setup is to create your own Web page of games, like the MSN and Sony Web sites shown in Figure 7-14. You can download any of the free interactive games to your local network, and play the games from a local Web server. Another alternative is to set up an interactive game server if you want to try to improve network game performance on your local network.

Interactive game servers will require a fast network connection; disk space; and, preferably, a dedicated computer. Download and install the game server software to your local network. As with the chat servers, you will need to configure the game server to work with a certain number of computer connections. After you have installed the game server, try to log into it using a client computer on the network. If the login is successful, try connecting with a second computer and playing a game. If you are able to play a game on the game server on your local network, your game server has been set up successfully.

Limiting Chat and Game Access

Each computer that participates in a chat or messenger session will be using some portion of the network to send and receive messages. Network game clients that are graphics intensive get around network bottlenecks by installing all the video-intensive graphics on your hard drive. Playing the network-based game won't require as much network bandwidth if each computer doesn't need to send and receive large graphic files over the network. Most networked games are designed to send a minimal amount of information over the network.

Another way you can try to reduce the amount of network traffic dedicated to playing games is to configure the game or chat servers to limit the number of people who can participate at once. You can use a ping time utility to find out how far away each player is located from your network; or, if you know where the other folks on the network are, choose players within close proximity of your network. This can help maintain consistent client and network performance for these particular tasks and improve the overall performance of network game play without blocking other computers from surfing the Web or sending e-mail on your local network.

Figure 7-14. You can access Web games from msn.com, or play interactive multiplayer games on Sony's Web site.

Limiting the Number of Players

Some game and chat servers may allow you to limit how many computers can participate in a network game. Smaller numbers usually mean that network performance will remain somewhat consistent. If you have a fast DSL network connection, you may want to set a higher number of maximum players for your network than if you have a network running below 1 Mbps (such as an iDSL network). In most cases, you will be logging into someone else's network to access their game server. If you're not picky about who you play network games with, find the faster computer; log into the chat, messenger, or network game server; and compare playing a game with two or three users to playing one with more than ten users. If the network performance is roughly the same, the network game server is probably connected to a fast backbone network. You might want to make a list of preferred network game Web sites and share it with others who access your DSL network.

Limiting the Access by Time

Another way to optimize network performance for messenger, chat, and game clients is to configure the server to allow clients to chat only at certain times of the day. For example, if your network performance usually slows down at around 5 or 6 every evening, you may want to let your network users know that they should not run a chat or network game session during this time. If you want to prevent any of your network users from running chat, messaging, or game clients, you can set up a proxy server and not include specific chat and game sites on the list of servers recognized by the proxy.

Additional Resources

Chat, messaging, and network games are some of the most popular activities folks enjoy participating in on the Internet. It's a great way to meet new people and make friends, without requiring travel time or shopping for a new wardrobe. The information presented in this chapter is just the tip of the iceberg for these vast, dynamic technologies. Many of the chat, game, and messenger Web sites are included in this list.

- ✦ www.aol.com
- ✦ www.msn.com
- ✦ www.talkcity.com
- ✦ www.yahoo.com
- ✦ www.station.sony.com
- ✦ www.icq.com
- ✦ www.mirc.co.uk
- ✦ www.igame.net
- ✦ www.ea.com (electronic arts)
- ✦ www.uo.com (ultima online)
- ✦ www.planethalflife.com
- ✦ www.shacknews.com/funk.y?flat=3105+page=1

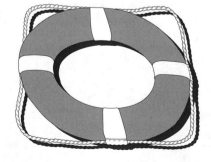

Chapter 8

Setting Up Streaming Media

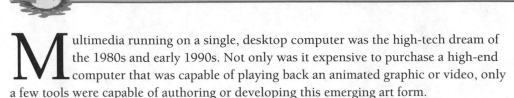

Multimedia running on a single, desktop computer was the high-tech dream of the 1980s and early 1990s. Not only was it expensive to purchase a high-end computer that was capable of playing back an animated graphic or video, only a few tools were capable of authoring or developing this emerging art form.

Today, computers are considerably faster and more affordable. You can play animation, games, and full-motion audio and video with the latest Web browsers. Video, audio, and animation files are stored on Web servers; and when you access these media files from a client computer, the Web server sends a portion of the file to your computer over the network. As you watch the media file, the server sends more and more data until the file playback is complete. You can watch a commercial or a movie trailer, or take a class online by watching and listening to real-time audio and video play over the network. Real Audio, MP3, Flash, animated GIF files, QuickTime, and Windows Media Player files are easy to find and play back over your DSL network.

Although some Web sites enable you to download audio, video, or other multimedia files to your hard drive, streaming media can be restricted from the server so that visitors can only play a file, not download it. If a file is downloaded, it simply points to the larger file located on the Web site. These graphic- and sound-intensive programs require more of a server's network resources compared to regular file servers. Many streaming media servers limit how many users can log in at once. The following list contains a brief description of media files that will be covered in this chapter.

✦ **Streaming audio playback**   Listen to a new song on an album, or to the daily news broadcast over the network. You can install a plug-in file to a browser if you want to listen to real audio files, or use Windows Media Player or the QuickTime player. MP3 files are another popular file format for storing audio.

✦ **Streaming animation**   Macromedia Flash and animated GIF files are a couple of the more popular file formats for sharing animation and interactive multimedia online. Macromedia Flash is the name of the development application and browser plug-in that enables many people to create animation content for the Web.

✦ **Streaming video playback**   Watch the latest movie trailer or commercial on your computer. View video news stories or play full-motion video on your desktop over a network.

Basic Concepts: Audio and Video Over the Web

Streaming media over the Web enables you to play an audio or video file located on a server on your client computer. The media server stores the file, which can range in size from a few megabytes to several hundred megabytes. The client, running a browser program, downloads part of the file from the server over the network. As the media file plays, the video or audio is processed by your computer. You can control playback from your browser, choosing to watch the entire file or stop playback.

Streaming Media Products

There are many streaming media players available for Windows, Macintosh, and Linux computers. This chapter will explain streaming media technologies with the following Windows and Macintosh products. Most of these media players are available for free from the publisher's Web site. Try out as many as you like, and keep the media players that you prefer to use, or that work best on your computer.

✦ **Real Audio**   Download a demo version of the Real Audio player from Real Networks' Web site, www.real.com. Many Web sites, such as www.cdnow.com, enable you to listen to part of a song from an album by playing a Real Audio file. Real Networks also has a streaming media player, Real Video player, that requires you to install a browser plug-in and application on your computer. A demo version is also available from the publisher's Web site.

✦ **iTunes**   The iTunes program is Apple's streaming audio player. It enables you to play streaming audio files over the Web, or to insert an audio CD and convert an audio file on the CD into a digital file on your hard drive. This is a stand-alone application that works independent of a browser program.

✦ **Windows Media Player**   This media player is installed with Windows Me, 2000, and XP. It enables you to play streaming audio or video files if the Windows Media Player plug-in is installed with Internet Explorer or Netscape Navigator. Media can be played or controlled from a separate window from the browser. The program can play a wide range of audio and video file formats, but is available only for Windows computers

✦ **QuickTime Media Player**   Apple's audio and video media player can be installed on Windows or Macintosh computers; and enables you to view streaming audio or video files created in the QuickTime format. The QuickTime plug-in must be installed on the computer in order to play a streaming media file from a browser program.

✦ **Macromedia Flash**   This very popular animation, game, and interactive media player can be downloaded for free from Macromedia's Web site, www.macromedia.com/flash.

Real Audio was one of the first streaming audio technologies to become widely used on the Web. Many Web sites, such as npr.org, www.cnet.com, or www.cdnow.com, posted free sound files on their Web site to enable Web visitors to listen to the latest news, play a song, or watch a video. Figure 8-1 shows the www.npr.org site. You can use the Real Audio player (shown in Figure 8-2), Windows Media Player, or QuickTime to listen to the daily news over the Web. If you have one of these media players installed on your computer, click the link for the media player to play the media file.

You can click the Play button to listen to the news. You can Pause, Stop, Rewind, and Fast Forward the audio file, or just play it. When you first click the Play button, you will wait about a minute or so for the beginning of the media file to download to your computer. The speed of the download will depend on how fast your network connection is, as well as the processing speed of your computer. You should hear audio play about a minute or two after clicking Play.

Figure 8-1.   Listen to news from a browser while you work on your computer.

Figure 8-2. Real Network's Real Audio Player enables you to listen to real audio files, or watch video and audio media over the Web.

As with most things on the Web, speed and network performance can make or break streaming audio or video. The slower the network, the choppier sounding or choppier looking the audio or video will be. However, the faster your connection, the smoother the playback will be. You can use streaming audio to find out how well your DSL and local network can handle playing a streaming audio or video file over the Web. Larger files can be used to find out how long or how much video your network connection can handle for a lot of network packet data. Testing the limits of your network is a good data point to have. However, you should enjoy listening or watching the streaming media you find on the Web.

Setting Up Streaming Media Software

If you're new to playing media files in your Web browser, don't worry. Most Web sites that post media files also show you where to find the browser plug-in file so that you can download and install them on your computer and then view media files when you surf Web sites. The media plug-ins covered in this chapter each come with Macintosh and Windows installer applications. You can download the installer from each media player's Web site. The following sections show you how to get streaming media technology up and running on your Macintosh or Windows computer.

Installing and Setting Up Browser Plug-Ins

You can download the browser plug-in and media files for QuickTime, Windows Media Player, and Real Audio technologies from Apple, Microsoft, or Real Networks' Web sites. Then install one or all of them on your Macintosh or Windows computer. You can download the QuickTime plug-in from Apple's Web site, www.apple.com/quicktime. The Windows Media Player is available from Microsoft's Web site, www.microsoft.com/windows/ windowsmedia, and you can download a free or commercial version of the Real Audio player from Real Networks' Web site, www.real.com.

If you click a Real Audio, Windows Media Player, or QuickTime link on a Web site, but you haven't installed the browser plug-in, you will see an error message appear. This message indicates that you need to download the appropriate browser plug-in if you want to view or listen to the media file. The window shown in Figure 8-3 shows an error message for Windows Media Player. Click the button graphic or text link to go to another Web page to download the Windows Media Player plug-in file, or troubleshoot system requirements or configuration settings for your browser.

You can visit each Web site and download the media player installer from each one. Figure 8-4 shows the download dialog box for the Windows Media Player. Wait for the

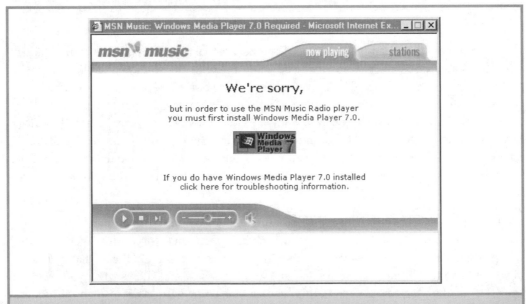

Figure 8-3. Most Web sites will let you know if you need to install a media player on your Macintosh, Windows, or Linux computer.

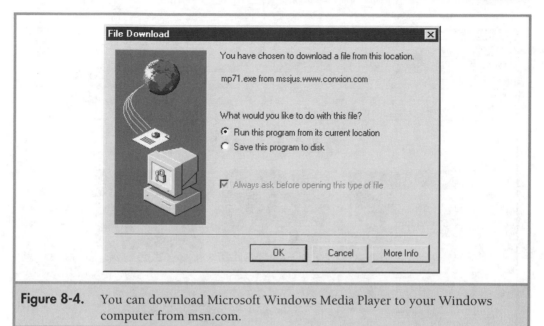

Figure 8-4. You can download Microsoft Windows Media Player to your Windows computer from msn.com.

installer file to download. Then unzip the installer files on your hard drive. Double-click the Setup.exe file, and start the install wizard for the media player. Follow the onscreen instructions to complete the installation. You may need to exit your browser or restart your computer before you can use the installed media players.

Setting Up Network Media Applications

Windows Media Player and QuickTime's media player enable you to set the network connection speed on your computer. This determines the rate the video and audio will be sent to the player application. You can visit Microsoft's Web site to play media files for Windows Media Player. If you have QuickTime installed on your Windows or Macintosh computer, visit Apple's Web site (shown in Figure 8-5) to view or download QuickTime media files.

If you're using Windows Media Player, click the settings link to view the connection rate for the streaming media. On a Mac, you can open the QuickTime control panel to adjust the connection speed. If you have QuickTime installed on your Windows computer, choose Connection Speed from the Edit | Preferences menu. The QuickTime Settings dialog will open. Click the radio button that most closely matches the network connection for your

Figure 8-5. The QuickTime plug-in enables you to view streaming audio or video over the Internet. You can visit Apple's QuickTime Web site to download the QuickTime plug-in.

computer. For example, if you have IDSL, choose 112K Dual ISDN. If you have a 1 Mbps DSL network connection, choose T1. Click the Close box to save your QuickTime settings.

The QuickTime media player enables you to control the media file as it plays in the media player window (see Figure 8-6). Click the Play button to start playing the media file. Click and drag the volume setting on the left side of the window to adjust the audio volume of the media file. Click the Play button a second time to stop playback, or click Pause to stop and start playback as you like. When you've finished viewing or listening to the media file, you can close the media player window.

Analyzing Media Playback

Choose a connection speed setting for the media player. Watch the video and listen to the audio as the media file plays in the media player window. Adjust the size of the video screen, and set the volume to a comfortable listening level. The audio and video should play back smoothly in the media player window. The video may not look as clear as the video on a television.

If you encounter problems playing a particular file, see whether you can download it to your hard drive. If the file plays back smoothly from your drive, you may have network connection problems with the network or the media server. Try playing another media file on a different Web site to see whether the problem persists. If it does, you may want to contact your DSL service provider to see whether there are any known issues with your DSL service and Internet connections or services. If you notice slow playback performance, note the time of day when it occurs. Some networks see traffic peak during the day, while other services may experience peak traffic after 6 P.M. through midnight.

Upgrading Your Video Hardware

Watch the video and audio play back on your computer. There are a few different things to look at when you're watching streaming video. First, the original footage will affect the clarity and smoothness of the playback. Next, the video card or video chipset (if you're using a laptop computer) will determine the maximum colors that can be displayed by the operating system. Finally, the monitor connected to your computer will enable you to view a certain number of colors that can be configured from the Display control panel in Windows or Mac OS X, or the Monitors control panel on a Mac OS 9.

The quality of the streaming video may be affected by one, all, or none of these video hardware components. When I say none, I'm assuming the source material is poor quality. You may want to try changing one of the following software settings to adjust the video or color settings on your computer.

◆ **Calibrate your monitor**   You can use the built-in Windows or Macintosh software to choose a color profile for your computer's monitor. Adjust the way color is displayed on your monitor in order to view correct colors of any onscreen media you want to watch or send to an output device, such as a printer. Open the Display Calibrator Assistant program in Mac OS X to adjust the white point and gamma settings for your

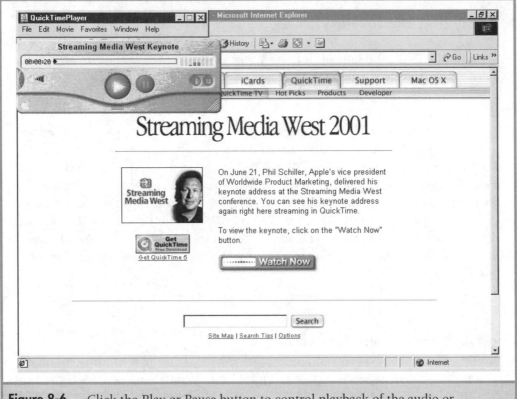

Figure 8-6. Click the Play or Pause button to control playback of the audio or video file.

computer. The ColorSync control panel in Mac OS 9 enables you to select a color management system for the input and output devices connected to your computer. You can choose a color management system on a Windows computer by opening the Display control panel and opening the Advanced options.

✦ **Adjust the color depth** Choose 24-bit color on a Windows system, or Thousands of colors on a Mac OS computer. Most displays are capable of displaying 24-bit color. You can also choose 32-bit color; however, if your monitor isn't capable of displaying more than 24 bits of color, your computer will be spending more processing time working with colors it doesn't necessarily need to process.

✦ **Change the resolution** Selecting a smaller screen size (also called desktop size) will make each pixel larger. But it will require your computer to run faster. You may want to consider choosing a smaller desktop size to see whether it helps improve video or audio media playback performance.

If the software settings aren't capable of improving the quality of the video, you may want to consider upgrading the amount of video memory installed on your computer, or adding a second video card to your computer. If you have a desktop computer, most PC cards available today offer 8–12MB of video memory (see Figure 8-7), which is more than enough for playing back video. If you have a laptop, you may not have too many options available for upgrading your screen or video. However, if your laptop is able to connect to an external display, you may want to view video on a second monitor to see whether the second monitor is capable of displaying more colors than the built-in display on your laptop.

✦ **Video memory**   Some video cards enable you to install additional video memory. Look for a slot on your video card to see whether upgrading video memory may be an option for you to add more color support to a computer system.

✦ **Video graphics card**   If your computer has an unused PCI card slot, you can insert a second video card and connect your monitor to it, or add a second monitor to your computer. Windows and Mac OS enable you move windows between monitors on one huge desktop (that spans both monitors).

Figure 8-7.   You can install a video card in your desktop computer and add a second monitor to your computer system. A PCI video card is shown here.

Playing Streaming Media

Although streaming media files have been around for several years now, setting a player up and playing a source can be either a nightmare or a dream come true. If you have a Pentium III or Power PC G3 or G4 computer, setting up a media player may go a little more smoothly than if you have an older or slower computer. Playing a media file is similar to controlling a VCR recorder or video camera. Simply click the Play button to start downloading the media file from the server. The media file will start playing once the client has received enough data to display in the browser window. The following sections will show you how to navigate audio and video media player controls from a browser using Microsoft's Windows Media Player and Apple's QuickTime player.

Watching Streaming Video

Streaming video files enable you to watch movie clips, commercials, news clips, or presentations in a browser window. Before you can watch a streaming video, you must locate a streaming video file on the Internet. If you have QuickTime installed on your computer, you can find a few of the latest, greatest movie clips, as well as a few audio files you can listen to on Apple's Web site. Open a browser window; go to www.apple.com/quicktime; and then navigate the QuickTime Web pages, and select a link for a QuickTime audio or video file to play. Click a link to start downloading the video file. The QuickTime player controls will appear on the Web page as the video file begins to download to your computer. Figure 8-8 shows the QuickTime player window and button controls for a QuickTime video file embedded on one of Apple's Web pages. You can play, pause, or stop a video by clicking the corresponding control in the media player window. You can also adjust the volume level as the file plays.

Streaming video or audio files are transferred over the network between the server and the client as the file plays on your computer. When you click a link, the server where the file is located downloads part of the audio file to the media player on your computer. Before the media player will actually play the audio file, it waits for one or two buffers to fill up. Each buffer stores part of the audio file. Once the buffers are full, the media player will start playing the audio stream. You should hear the audio play on your computer. As the file plays, the server continues to send the remainder of the audio file to your computer. As the audio file plays, each buffer empties. However, the new data sent from the server fills each newly freed buffer until the audio file completes playback.

NOTE

When you play a media file on your computer, the media player plug-in creates one or two buffers, enabling the client to smoothly play the video on your computer. The faster the network connection, the smoother the media file will play back on your computer.

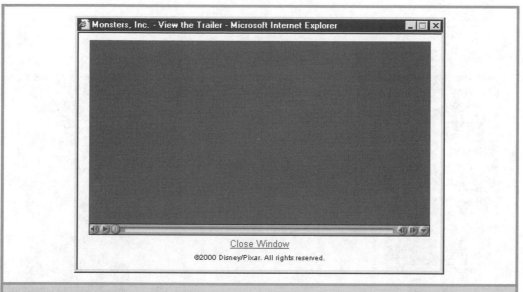

Figure 8-8. Select a QuickTime file to play from Apple's movie trailer Web page.

SURVIVAL TIP

A buffer created by the media player applications represents an amount of memory set aside to store part of a media file as it plays on a computer. Some media players create two buffers for streaming media, alternating between each one as the other fills up with more data.

Listening to Music on the Web

Playing an audio file from a Web site follows virtually the same process as playing a video file, except, of course, there's nothing to see. If you've been reading the news, you may have heard of the MP3 sound file format. It is the most commonly used sound file format for converting, or ripping, a song on an audio CD into a digital audio file. Audio can also be stored along with video in an MPEG or an MPEG 2 file. Before you can listen to an audio file play on your computer, you need to find a Web site where you can download an audio file. Figure 8-9 shows a Web page on msn.com that contains audio files. Navigate the Web pages and click a link containing an audio file to begin downloading the audio to your computer.

The following is a short list of audio file formats available for Windows and Macintosh computers on the Web. Most of these file formats have been available for a few years, and

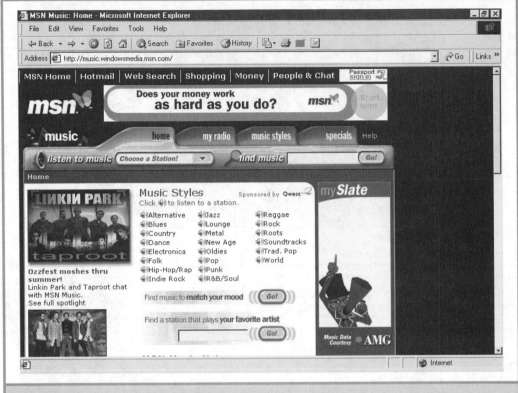

Figure 8-9. You can listen to streaming audio files with Windows Media Player. First, visit a Web site where you can download streaming audio files.

most browsers enable you to play these audio file formats without installing any additional plug-ins.

✦ **MIDI** This is an acronym for *musical instrument digital interface*. These music files are relatively small and enable you to listen to a wide range of songs on your computer.

✦ **SWA** This is the audio file format for Flash files that contain audio. Most Windows and Macintosh browsers enable you to play back SWA audio files.

✦ **MP3** CD-quality audio files are most commonly stored in the MP3 file format. These files can range in size from one to several megabytes. MP3 audio is the same file format as MPEG audio.

✦ **MPEG** Synonymous with MPEG 1, this is the first audio and video file format to become popular on the Web. The quality of MPEG video isn't as clear or smooth as MPEG 2, but there are many files available to download on the Web.

✦ **MPEG 2**   DVD video, and most full-motion video, is edited and broadcast using files stored in this format.

Wait for the file to download to your computer. The audio file will start playing once the buffers in the media player have filled up. Click the volume controls for the media player, and drag the slider control to adjust the volume level of the media player. If you do not hear any sound, check your master volume setting and make sure the volume is not set to mute. Figure 8-10 shows an audio file playing in the Window Media Player on the msn.com Web site. You can also use the QuickTime media player or the Real Audio media player to listen to QuickTime or Real Audio audio files play over the network.

Playing a Windows Media Video File

Microsoft's Windows Media Player can play video files, too (see Figure 8-11). You can find several news clips to watch on Microsoft's Web site, msn.com. Click the news link, and

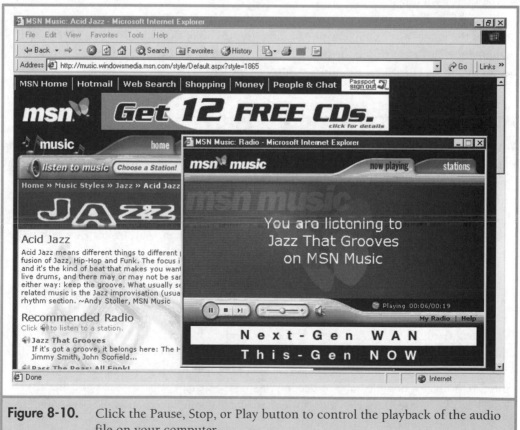

Figure 8-10.   Click the Pause, Stop, or Play button to control the playback of the audio file on your computer.

Converting Audio File Formats

Some media player applications, such as QuickTime Pro, enable you to convert one audio file format into another audio file format. For example, you can open an MP3 file with the QuickTime media player, and then save that audio file as a QuickTime Audio file if you want to modify or combine it with additional tracks of audio. Although the QuickTime media player is available free from Apple, the QuickTime Pro version requires you to pay a nominal fee before you can use the file conversion and digital audio- and video-editing features.

then review and select a video clip to watch. The browser will start Windows Media Player and download the video file from the Web server to your computer. Wait for part of the video file to download to your computer. Then watch the video play back in the Windows Media Player window.

As the file plays, you can move the progress bar in the Media Player window to a specific point in the video. For example, you can jump to the end of the video file by clicking and dragging the slider control in the progress bar to the right. If you want to replay part of the beginning of the clip, move the slider control to the left.

Problems: Playing Media Files

Your browser may already have a media player plug-in file installed for the Windows Media Player, the QuickTime player, Flash, or Real Audio. However, you may visit a Web site that contains media files and get an error message asking you to upgrade to the latest plug-in software. Software, including media plug-in files, generally gets updated once a year. Usually it takes a while for Web sites to create new media files using the latest plug-in version. Be prepared to upgrade your browser to a newer plug-in file if you want to keep watching the latest, greatest video or multimedia content on the Web.

Finding the Latest Plug-In

The best place to download the latest plug-in software is from the software publisher's Web site. Mirror Web sites are Web servers in different locations that contain the same content as the software publisher's Web site. In most cases, you can download the installer application for the plug-in file from a mirror site, as well as from the publisher's site; but if you have problems downloading or decompressing the installer file, try the publisher's Web site. The following sections provide a little more detail about what makes plug-ins different

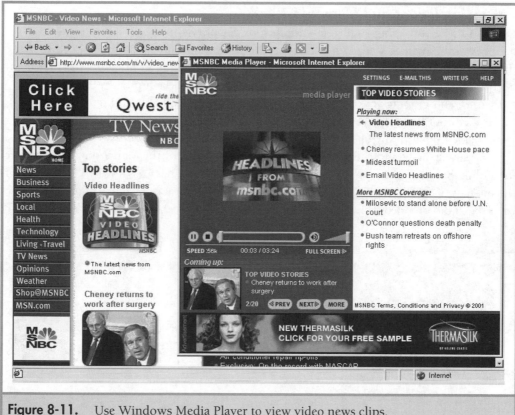

Figure 8-11. Use Windows Media Player to view video news clips.

from each other, and what problems you might encounter after installing or using one with your browser.

Plug-In Compatibility

In most cases, you should download the latest version of a browser plug-in. If you're not sure whether you should install the newest version of a QuickTime, Windows Media Player, Real Audio, or Flash release, you can visit the publisher's message boards to see whether any substantial problems exist with the new release. Most new versions of a plug-in enable you to play files created with previous versions of the software. Generally, compatibility across different versions of plug-ins and media files is not a problem. Although the media player window and controls may change, the media file should play back the same audio and video with a newer, installed plug-in.

Processing Power and Memory Issues

Like most software, plug-in files use application memory—in this case, the browser's memory—to play media files on your computer. The amount of memory needed to play a file depends on the window size of the media file and the number of colors or color depth of the video, or on sample rate for audio. For example, the Flash plug-in file may play animation and graphics created with the Flash authoring application. Figure 8-12 shows Macromedia's Flash Web page, where you can download the Flash plug-in file. You can view Flash animation by visiting a Web site that contains Flash animation.

The larger the window, the greater the number of colors; or the higher the sampling rate for audio, the more memory the plug-in will need in order to play the media file. The size of the file may also require the media player and plug-in to use more memory in order to play back the audio or video. However, if the file is located on a Web server, it may be difficult for

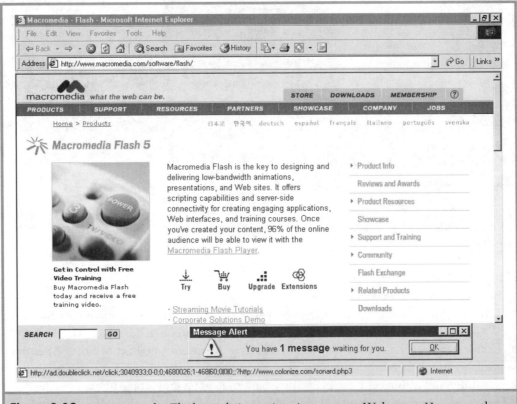

Figure 8-12. Macromedia Flash can bring animation to your Web page. However, the larger the animation, the slower it will play back on the Web.

you to know how much memory to set your browser to. If you see slow performance, or a low memory error message from your Mac browser, you may want to increase the amount of memory to the browser from the dialog that appears when you choose File | Get Info | Memory. If you're using Windows or Linux, you may want to exit any open applications to make more memory available to the browser.

The processor in your computer can also help speed up playback of a media file. However, the processor chip doesn't work alone. It sends data to memory and to your hard drive, as well as to video memory and the network. If you want to compare hardware configurations for your computer, look at the bus speed, as well as the processor speed for the computer. Most of the latest Windows computers have a Pentium III or IV or compatible processor and a bus speed of 100 MHz. Most Macintosh computers have a G3 or G4 processor with a bus speed of 100 MHz.

Viewing HTML Sources

Some Web sites rely on people to post new files that appear on the Web site, while others rely on other computers to grab the latest media files, news, and information. People and computers make mistakes. Sometimes the media file you want to view may be in a different location than the Web page may think. It may be difficult to find the correct location of the file. However, you can view the source code of the HTML page to find out where the file is supposed to be located. Figure 8-13 shows a Web page that contains several graphic images. If you are running an Internet Explorer browser, click the View menu and choose the Source menu command to view the HTML code for the Web page that currently appears in the browser window. Then, put that URL into your browser window to see whether you can fix any typos, or navigate the Web site for the file you're looking for.

Network Solutions: Streaming Media on Your SOHO

In addition to some of the software problems that may make playing a media file a tedious task, the network can also get bogged down and prevent you from viewing smooth video playback. One way to get around this is to download any copyright-free media files to your local file server instead of playing the media file over the Internet. The following sections show you how to monitor streaming media performance on your local network.

Streaming Usage and Network Performance

When files are copied, e-mailed, or received over the network, the overall performance of the network will slow down. Playing a streaming media file will most likely degrade your

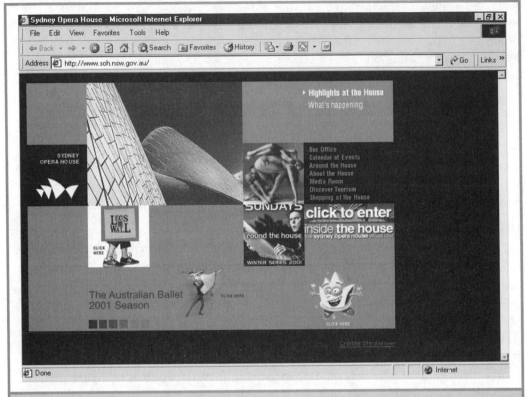

Figure 8-13.   Choose Source from the browser's View menu to view the source code for an HTML file.

network performance if one or two computers are playing media files continuously over the network. Granted, your network performance mileage may vary, depending on whether you've set up network routers, hubs, or special connections to the Internet specially to manage streaming media. If you're working with a vanilla network, running off a simple hub and a 1 Mbps symmetrical DSL connection, you'll encounter network slowdowns in performance as files are downloaded from a Web or an FTP server, or if streaming media files are played over the Internet.

Video, Audio, and Animation Downloads

Before choosing a file to download to your local computer, try viewing it over the Web. Visit a Web page that contains a Windows Media Player, QuickTime, Real Audio, or Flash animation file you want to watch. Wait for the file to download to your computer and watch it play from beginning to end. Figure 8-14 shows a simple Flash animation; each image in the square alternates between showing and hiding on the Web page. If the playback looks all right, you may want to try playing a larger or longer media file.

You can right-click (Windows), or CTRL-click and choose Save Download As from the shortcut menu, to save a media file to your hard drive. Choose a location where you want to save the file on your hard drive. Then wait for the file to download to your computer. Try to pick a 1–4MB file to download. If the media file plays back smoothly from your hard drive, but not over the network, you may want to avoid playing similarly sized media files over the network, and download each one (if possible) before you play it.

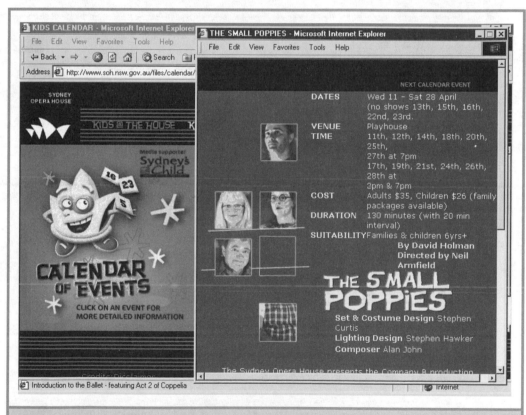

Figure 8-14. Simple animation won't take up a huge amount of network bandwidth. The more objects that move in the animation, the more network bandwidth and processing power you'll need on your computer to play back the file at reasonable performance rates.

Downloading mp3 Files

If you have a computer on your local network set up as a digital jukebox, you may want to download a file and play it on your local hard drive. Many musicians and record companies also post demo songs you can download over the Internet. MP3 is the most common format used for storing CD-quality audio files. You can right-click (Windows) or CTRL-click and choose Save Download As from the shortcut menu to save the MP3 file to your hard drive.

As you convert audio files stored on CD-ROM disks into digital audio files stored on a computer's hard disk, you may want an easier way to add the album and song title information for each audio CD. You can visit a Web site such as cddb.com (shown in Figure 8-15) to search for the album and song title information for any audio CD-ROM disks you may have

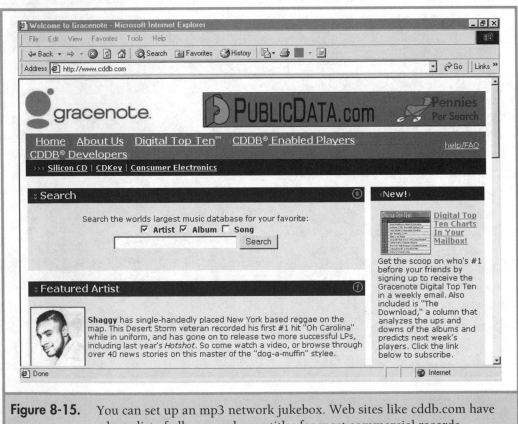

Figure 8-15. You can set up an mp3 network jukebox. Web sites like cddb.com have a huge list of albums and song titles for most commercial records.

mounted on your computer's desktop. The Web site enables you to search for the song title information for a particular musical artist or album.

Limit Access to Web Sites

If you are seeing network performance issues as the direct result of too many computers trying to play media files at the same time, you may want to install Web security software on some of the computers on your network to limit which ones can access streaming media, and reduce the likelihood of network slowdowns due to overloading the network's bandwidth for handling streaming data.

Limiting Browser Access

There are several different software packages available for Windows and Macintosh computers that enable you to limit the Web sites that a computer can access. One of the more popular Web security software packages, KidDesk, is published by Edmark. SurfControl publishes Cyber Patrol and Super Scout, another Web site–filtering software package. The basic task you want to perform with this type of software is to install it onto a computer and then create a list of approved Web sites. When the user tries to visit a Web site that is not on the list of approved sites, a blank page will appear in the browser and a message will let the user know the site is not approved for viewing. You can add or remove sites from the list as you like.

Limit Browser Plug-Ins

If you don't mind playing the role of network administrator, you can remove or uninstall browser plug-ins for media players from some of the computers on your network. You can locate the plug-in files by opening the browser's application folder. Open the Plug-Ins folder and locate the plug-in files for the media player you want to disable.

Removing the plug-in file is a short term solution for limiting computers on your local network from accessing streaming media files on the network. Don't forget that as long as the computer can access and download files from the Internet, someone can always reinstall a browser plug-in after you remove it.

Additional Resources

Streaming media constitute one of the most exciting ways to view the Web. You can listen to music or news clips, or watch a commercial or movie trailer from a browser window. Media files can be large or small in size, although the larger media files can potentially slow down your DSL network. There are a few relatively simple ways you can reduce the number of computers accessing streaming media from your local network. But there is no foolproof, bulletproof way to keep people from being entertained with Web multimedia. You can download the latest media players from the following Web sites, and you can find media files and learn about security issues from the sites toward the bottom of this list.

- ✦ www.apple.com/quicktime
- ✦ www.microsoft.com/windows/windowsmedia
- ✦ www.real.com
- ✦ www.macromedia.com/flash
- ✦ www.npr.org
- ✦ www.msn.com/news
- ✦ www.surfcontrol.com
- ✦ www.kidmark.com

Part III

Working with DSL

Chapter 9

Running Your Home Network

The chapters in this part focus on desktop, laptop, and network issues for a local area network, and for a DSL modem providing a router connection to the DSL provider and to the Internet. Find out how to extend a DSL network by using a wireless access point, or by adding peripherals to a desktop or laptop connected to your DSL network. You may also want to explore connecting your local area network of computers with other electronic devices or appliances in your home or office. Although point-to-point connections are briefly described in Chapter 10, this type of connection is not the focus of the following chapters.

DSL enables your home network to access all the information and services available on the Internet. It can also bring the Internet into your home. For example, if you are on vacation or at a remote site, you can set up a computer on your home network so that you can check on your home or small business with another computer connected to the Internet. You can also expand your home network by setting up a wireless network, or configure a computer to work with television or home automation systems.

- ✦ **Local network services**   Set up your local network to work with different network devices.
- ✦ **Wireless hubs**   Extend your network by adding a wireless hub to your DSL network.
- ✦ **Home automation**   Control the lights, television, digital camera, or other home appliances for your home or office from a networked computer.

Basic Concepts: Designing an Open Network

The term *open network* can represent two characteristics of a network. One definition can be a network that can be accessed from any medium: via modem, over the Internet, or via a wireless connection. The other, more important definition is easy and secure access to the Internet. For example, whether you have a desktop computer or a laptop with a fixed or dynamic network address, when you power on that computer, it should be able to immediately access your e-mail, or any Web pages you want to visit.

One way to provide easy access to your home or office network is to set up a wireless hub. Sony's Wireless Access Point enables any PC or computer device, such as an Aibo robot dog, to connect to other wireless devices connected to the access point, or to the Internet, if the wireless access point is connected to an Internet service provider. Apple's Base Station will work with Apple's AirPort PC cards, which are 802.11b compliant, as well as any other PC running Windows or Linux that has an 802.11b-compatible card.

Although some desktop computers may not be able to access your local network, you won't have to worry about wiring network cable to a computer in order to bring network access to it. Wireless hubs, working with a wireless client, enable you to place a computer up to 100 feet from the hub and access the network wire-free. If you have not set up a wireless network, and your home or office environment is not made up of lead walls or in the middle of a radio broadcast zone, I highly recommend this technology.

The other characteristic of an open network is one that enables Unix, Windows, and Macintosh computers to easily connect to its servers and network services. For some local networks, ones that need to support only Unix or Windows, this might not be an issue. However, if you want to run different operating systems on your client or server computers, it is convenient to use the same login, password, and account information to access any local computers on the network.

Wired and Wireless Networks

Fortunately, there are many options available to you for putting together your home network. You can create a complete, wired network; or start your network with a wired connection to the DSL modem, and then expand it with a wireless hub or with wireless DHCP services. Figure 9-1 shows a diagram containing a wired Ethernet hub connected to a DSL modem. A wireless hub, also called an access point or base station, can connect to one of the Ethernet hubs. Some wireless access point devices ship with software capabilities that enable them to act as DHCP servers.

The biggest difference between wired and wireless networks is that most wireless solutions run at up to 11 Mbps, which is the maximum network bandwidth supported by 802.11b. The actual speed of a wireless network can vary and depends on the connection

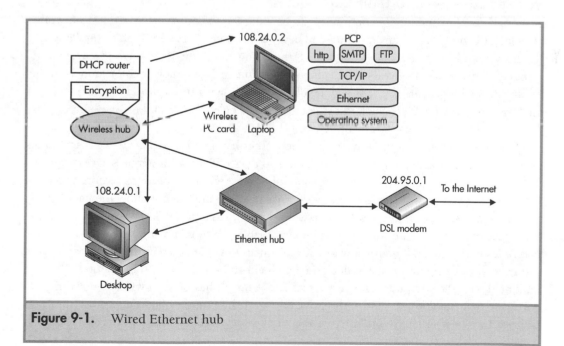

Figure 9-1.   Wired Ethernet hub

speed to the DSL provider, the signal strength between the wireless access point and the wireless PC cards, and the number of devices actively connected and communicating with the wireless access point. Desktop systems with 10/100 Base T or Gigabyte Base T Ethernet can run at much faster network speeds. Wireless networks offer comparable network performance to wired networks in addition to the freedom to compute anywhere you like, especially if you assume that 10 Base T Ethernet cards or chip sets are the most popular and widely used cards on desktops and laptops.

You can connect a Macintosh or a PC to your home or office network. Simply connect one end of a category 5 Ethernet cable to your computer and the other end to the Ethernet hub. If you have more than one computer or need to extend the cable that connects your computer to your DSL modem, you should add an Ethernet hub to your network. An Ethernet hub enables you to connect Windows and Mac OS computers to your network, as well as any printers and devices you want others to access over the network. As previously mentioned, you can also grow your network by connecting a wireless access point to the Ethernet.

If you want to find out more about how to connect a computer to a network, see Chapter 5.

**SURVIVAL
TIP**

Wireless Devices and Their Capabilities

Although desktop and laptop computers can be modified to connect to a wireless network, they lack the mobility of smaller handheld devices. Handheld devices, such as the Palm III, V, and VII, and the clone models made by Handspring and Sony, have become extremely popular over the past few years. The Palm m505 is one of Palm's newer color models in the Palm V form factor. Sony's Clie is a clone of the Palm V, with the addition of a memory stick reader and a jog dial. The latest Clie model has a color screen and enables you to play MP 3 audio files while you're on the go.

Except in the case of the Palm VII and a few other handheld models, wireless capabilities are usually sold separately from the base handheld device. Even with wireless access, except for the Compaq's iPAQ and HandSpring's modules, most wireless solutions require you to subscribe to an exclusive wireless Internet service provider and do not allow the handheld device to function as a node on a local network, but only as a node on the wireless service.

These black-and-white and color handhelds enable you to take your calendar, contacts, and notes with you, and modify any of your information while you're on the go. When you return to your computer, you can dock the handheld and synchronize the data on the handheld with the computer, and vice versa. The Palm VII has built-in wireless network hardware that enables it to send and receive data over the Internet. You must subscribe to Palm's wireless service in order to use the wireless network features on the Palm VII.

The Palm handheld devices may look slightly different from each other, but all use the Palm operating system (Palm OS) and run on a Motorola processor. Since the Palm Pilot was introduced several years ago, many other companies have rolled out handheld devices that can run a wide range of processors and operating systems. Compaq and HP use Microsoft's Windows CE software to run their Pocket PC handhelds. Several companies also provide Linux alternatives for Palm and custom Linux handheld devices. The one thing all these devices have in common is that they can dock with a computer, albeit you will probably need Windows, Linux, or Mac OS to be able to communicate with each device over a serial or USB cable.

Palm and Pocket PC handhelds are covered in this book. Although other devices—such as Research In Motion's Blackberry, Motorola's network pagers, Psion's handhelds, and all the different Linux handhelds—are also growing in popularity, this book will focus on network features in Palm OS and Windows CE. Other handheld software should work similarly if it is capable of docking with a computer and interacting with network data over TCP/IP or Ethernet.

SURVIVAL TIP

To find out more about how to connect your Palm or Pocket PC device to your home network, see Chapter 12.

Setting Up a Wired Device

Chapters 2 and 5 provide more detail on how desktop and laptop computers can be configured with a network interface card, Ethernet cables, and a hub to create a wired Ethernet network. Except for a couple of models, most handheld devices rely on a desktop or laptop computer to bring network data into a handheld device. In order to exchange information between the handheld and the computer, you must place the handheld device in the dock. In most cases, the computer will automatically start to synchronize with the handheld. If it doesn't start to sync automatically, you can press the Sync button on the Palm handhelds. If you have a Pocket PC, you can start the synchronization by choosing the Synchronize command from the File menu in the Active Sync program window.

Handheld devices also require you to insert batteries or charge a built-in battery before you can use them. If you want to connect the handheld to a computer or to a network, you must install the desktop software for the handheld product. For example, if you have a Palm handheld, you can install the Hot Sync and Palm desktop software onto your Windows or Macintosh computer. If you have a Handspring device, you can install the Handspring Hot Sync and desktop software onto your computer. Similarly, if you have a Pocket PC, you can install Microsoft's Active Sync software onto your Windows computer.

Setting Up a Wireless Device

If you have a laptop that has a PC card slot, you may want to consider purchasing a PC card that enables your laptop to connect to a wireless access point or base station. If you have a desktop, you can purchase a PCI wireless Ethernet card to enable your computer to network with the wireless hub. Several companies were involved in creating the 802.11b standard for wireless hubs and cards. If you're worried about purchasing a wireless card that is not able to communicate with other wireless cards or with the wireless hub, purchase wireless products that are 802.11b compliant.

SURVIVAL TIP

To find out more about how to set up a wireless access card with a laptop, see Chapter 11. To find out how to set up a wireless access card with a Compaq Pocket PC, see Chapter 12.

NOTE

The 802.11b standard supports network speeds up to 11 Mbps. A wireless access point costs approximately $300, and each wireless access card, approximately $100. Recently, the 802.11a standard was introduced, which supports network speeds up to 54 Mbps. An 802.11a network access card is estimated to cost around $300, with availability expected sometime in 2002. An 802.11a wireless access point is currently available from Agere Systems, formerly Lucent Technologies, for approximately $1500. This particular wireless access point enables 802.11b and 802.11a wireless access cards to connect to it.

Some Palm and all Handspring models have an expansion port or enable you to connect a modem to the docking connection on its case. The Palm V and some of Handspring's handheld devices enable you to purchase a custom peripheral that attaches to the handheld device. The wireless module enables you to communicate with a wireless service, which you must subscribe to. These wireless services enable you to send and receive e-mail on your handheld while you're out and about. This kind of wireless network connection works separately from your home network.

NOTE

Xircom makes 802.11b expansion module products for Palm, Handspring Visor, and Pocket PC handheld devices. The Xircom Wireless LAN model for the M500 Palm handhelds, and the Xircom SpringPort Wireless Ethernet module, each costs approximately $300. The Xircom CreditCard Wireless Ethernet Adapter for Compaq iPAQ handhelds costs approximately $150.

Other handheld devices, such as the Pocket PC, enable you to connect your handheld device to a wireless hub or access point, such as Compaq's iPaq with a PC card expansion slot. If you purchase a wireless card that supports Windows CE, like a Cisco card, you can access the Internet by connecting your handheld to the wireless hub on your home network.

NOTE

Palm and Pocket PC devices offer different ways to protect the information on your handheld. Palm OS enables you to hide and password-protect memos and information you do not want to share on your handheld or computer. You can create a password for your Pocket PC so that one must be entered in order to view the contents of the handheld. If you have the Pocket PC set up to sync with a particular account on a Windows PC, you can prevent others from viewing your Pocket PC data by logging out of the account when you're not using your Pocket PC.

Setting Up a Base Station

The more traditional ways of designing and wiring a home or office for a wired network were explained in Chapter 3. Don't get me wrong, wired networks are great. In fact, you may want to wire part of your home or office with a faster 100 or gigabyte Base T network if you have a fast DSL service connected to your DSL modem. Regardless of how efficient and reliable wired networks are, wireless networks are almost impossible to pass up. Not only can you move your furniture around your home or office without worrying about losing your Internet access, but you can work outside or move around to a new location without losing your network connections.

The first step in setting up your wireless network is to set up and configure your wireless access point, or hub. This network device is a little more sophisticated than an Ethernet hub, but lacks the full-fledged interface of your computer. In fact, most wireless hubs contain a wireless PC card connected to a power supply and modem. I'm oversimplifying the hardware components to bring out the simple fact that wireless hubs are small, lightweight devices that are easy to plug into an existing network.

Installing Administrator Software

Before you can connect your wireless PC card or PCI card to the wireless access point, you need to connect the access point to your local network. Connect an Ethernet cable from your Ethernet hub to the wireless access point. Then power on the access point. You should see the lights on the access point light up.

You can configure the access point on your local network. Then unplug it and move it to an optimal location in your home or office. Find a location in your home or office that is not near other radio transmissions and is at the center point of your home or office space. The access point will broadcast approximately 150 feet in all directions. The access point will also need to be near an Ethernet hub so that it can access your DSL network connection to the Internet.

Next, install the software onto your computer. Start a computer that's connected to the same network. Insert the CD-ROM that contains the software for the access point and install it onto your computer. The wireless access point will have a custom identification number that you must type into your computer in order to access the device on your network. The illustration shows information for Sony's wireless access point. Log into the access point and view the software features available for your home network.

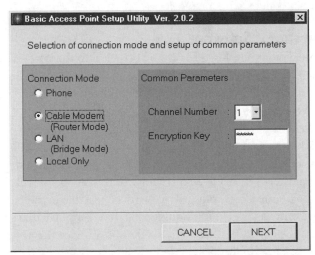

The access point can be configured from a computer that has the administrator software installed. Different access point hardware may require unique information in order for you to configure it over the network. For example, you must have an Apple AirPort card installed on your Macintosh, or a cleverly disguised Linux or Windows software setup in order to access and modify Apple's base station. The illustration shows the options for Sony's wireless access point. In this figure, the Cable Modem option most closely resembles the DSL modem network configuration you will want to use with the Sony wireless access point.

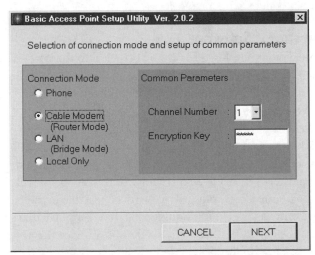

One way to safely limit how many wireless devices can access your network is to require that certain wireless cards be used to access your local network. You can set up a wireless hub to permit only specific ID-numbered wireless cards to connect to the access point. The card can be inserted into any laptop that wants to access the network, provided the network software on each computer is set up correctly for the wireless card.

Setting Up an Apple AirPort Base Station

You must use the software, and sometimes the corresponding computer, to configure the wireless access point on a network. For example, you must use a Macintosh computer to log into Apple's base station and view or customize its settings. The illustration shows the main window of Apple's AirPort Administration Utility application. You can access any Apple base station within range of your AirPort PC card. However, you won't be able to configure non-Apple wireless access points. Click a base station in the window list, shown in the illustration, and then select the Configure button to log into the base station.

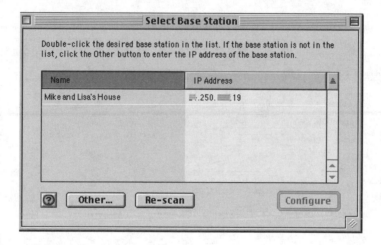

The main window of the base station administrator application consists of four tabs: AirPort, Internet, Network, and Access Control. You can configure the IP address of the base station from the window, activate the DHCP or NAT services, or configure the base station to recognize only particular wireless cards. You can also choose the channel you want to broadcast with. If you don't want to connect the base station to your DSL network, you can set it up as an isolated LAN. This can be helpful if you want to test new hardware or software before adding these elements onto your larger network.

SURVIVAL TIP

You can configure the base station with a fixed IP address. You can also activate the DHCP server feature on the base station so that any computers connected to the base station will not need to have a fixed IP address in order to connect to the local network. Set up the DHCP server so that it does not give out an IP address number that matches any of the static IP addresses. Also, avoid having a second or third computer picking the fixed IP address of the base station. This can cause the DSL modem or network router to send packets to the wrong computer, resulting in a slower and possibly unhappy network.

If you're not sure how you want to set up your base station, the minimal amount of setup you can do is type in the IP addressing information for the base station, and then decide how you want other wireless devices to connect to it. First, configure the IP address for the base station. Click the Internet tab, shown in Figure 9-2. Then type in a valid IP address, a subnet mask, a router address, and DNS servers into the corresponding text boxes. If your network has a domain name, such as flatfishfactory.com, type the domain name into the Domain Name text box.

```
┌──────────────────────────────────────────────────────────┐
│ □ ═══ Configure "Mike and Lisa's House" Base Station ═══ ▤ │
│ ┌────────┬──────────┬─────────┬────────────────┐         │
│ │AirPort │ Internet │ Network │ Access Control │         │
│                                                            │
│  Information in this section describes how your base       │
│  station is connected to the Internet or network.          │
│  For an explanation of each option, use Balloon Help.      │
│                                                            │
│    Connect using: [ Ethernet           ⬍]                  │
│   Configure TCP/IP: [ Manually          ⬍]                 │
│                                                            │
│        IP address:  [▦.250.1▦.19        ]                  │
│       Subnet mask:  [255.255.252.0      ]                  │
│     Router address: [▦.250.▦.1          ]                  │
│       DNS servers:  [▦.1.4.12           ]                  │
│                     [▦.1.4.14           ]                  │
│       Domain name:  [                   ]                  │
│                                                            │
│  [?] [ Optimize Placement... ]      [ Cancel ] [ Update ]  │
└──────────────────────────────────────────────────────────┘
```

Figure 9-2. Setting up a base station is similar to setting up a computer on the network.

Next, configure network access to the base station. Click the Network tab, shown in Figure 9-3, and then select the Enable DHCP Server On Ethernet check box. Also, select the Enable AirPort To Ethernet Bridging check box to enable the base station to route packets to the wireless cards connected to it. Click the Share A Single IP Address radio button if you want the base station to dole out IP addresses as needed, but using the IP address of the base station to represent those computers on the network.

If you want to limit the number of wireless tourists on your network, select the Share A Range Of IP Addresses radio button. Then type a limited range of IP numbers you want to assign to the computers on the wireless network. Once the designated IP addresses have been assigned to the computers on your network, any additional computers will not be able to connect until one of the other computers goes to sleep or disconnects from the network.

After you have typed in the configuration information for the base station, save your changes and exit the administrator utility program. Disconnect the computer from the Ethernet cable, and then insert the wireless PC card into it. Install the software for the PC card onto your laptop or desktop computer. Then try to connect to the base station.

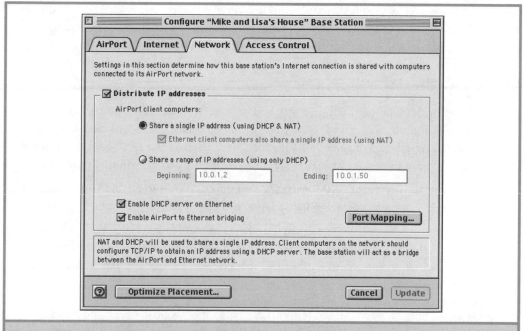

Figure 9-3. Set up the AirPort Administrative software to share one IP address with any other computers connected to the local network.

To find out more about how to connect a laptop with a wireless PC card to a wireless hub, see Chapter 11.

SURVIVAL TIP

Expanding Your Home Network

These next two topics may fall into the category of overextending your computer network into extraneous territory. First, I want to discourage you from connecting your computer network to non-computer-based home networks. Finding a compatible interface for devices that were not designed to work with computers can be tedious if not impossible. That said, the following sections introduce you to a couple of home automation systems that you may want to add to your home or office computer network.

Controlling Your House with Power Outlets

X10 is one of the communications standards for creating home control systems. Many X10-compatible products are available and are designed to be compatible with 110-volt electrical wiring systems. X10 transmitters, receivers, and two–way devices are available. You can also purchase X10 devices that can interface directly with a computer. The following list is a general summary of the components you can use to set up a home automation system using the electrical outlets in your home.

+ **Power outlet adapter**   You can mix and match X10-compatible power outlet adapters and use different adapters to control lights, fans, televisions, and telephones—basically, anything connected to a power outlet. Each device can be set to a unique identification number. The X10 system can support up to 256 unique numbers.

+ **Remote control**   Some X10 kits include a remote control to enable you to control your lights and other power-outlet adapter systems with the press of a button.

+ **Computer interface**   You can purchase X10-compatible hardware with a computer interface if you want to access your home over the Internet. Control consoles are also available that enable you to dial into your home and control appliances and lights over the phone.

Many other home automation systems are fairly inexpensive. However, most lack computer software or hardware controls that would make a power outlet–based network as savvy as a computer network. Before you connect a home automation system to your computer network, be sure to spend several days, if not weeks, on site to make sure the system is running as expected, or as designed. One disadvantage to controlling devices over the network is that you may not be able to hear or see something that may be out of place or need correction as quickly as if you were on location.

SURVIVAL TIP

Having a home network brings the Internet into your home and also enables you to access your home over the Internet. If you plan to install a home automation system, you may want to connect one or more computers to the home automation system. If a system is not being used, you can check its status at home or over the network, and save a little energy by turning the computer off if it does not need to be powered on.

Getting Your Television on the Network

Automating your home can help you get comfortable without having to go from room to room to adjust the lights or turn off an appliance. Another way to bring your home to your computer network is to install a video card on your Mac or PC so that you can watch TV from your computer desktop. You can also install X10-based power systems to power different televisions in different rooms of your home or office as you move from room to room. An IR device enables you to change all the televisions in your home to the same channel, no matter from which room you're watching the television.

In order to control all of the televisions in your home, each one must have an IR device nearby. Also, each television must have a remote control, or infrared port. The IR device broadcasts the channel change from one television to all the other IR devices in the house. This system might come in handy if you want to broadcast a communications meeting or limit the television programs that are viewed in your home or office.

Problems: Configuring Server Access

All of these wireless home systems are intriguing and may be technology you will want to add to your DSL network some day. A bigger problem to solve may be how to set up your network so that you can experiment with what's possible without sacrificing the stability and reliability of your existing network. There are so many ways to set up a network, the following sections explore some of the options for setting a wireless network, and some of their inherent limitations.

Using a Wireless Hub as a DHCP Server

You can set up a wireless hub to assign IP addresses to a limited number of computers or to any computer on the network. This is an easy way to enable anyone within a 150-foot proximity of the base station to access the local network and the Internet. However, choosing

this configuration doesn't prevent computers from having problems accessing the network, nor does it bring any additional security to your network. The following sections describe some of the more likely problems you'll encounter when you set up a wireless hub.

Checking Your Network Settings

The first thing to check if you're unable to connect to the base station is whether it's connected to a power source. Although different access points may use different colored lights to indicate a powered-on state, you should see a green light at the front of the access point if it has received power. Next, make sure the Ethernet cable is completely connected to the wireless hub's Ethernet port, in addition to being connected to the Ethernet hub on your network. Open the network settings on your computer, and make sure your computer is set up to be on the same network as the wireless hub. If you are unable to use a wireless access card with one computer, try connecting to the wireless hub with a different computer.

Limiting Internet Access

Depending on the type of network you choose, you may want to limit the number of computers that can access the DSL modem at once. You can connect a wireless hub to the DSL modem and configure the wireless hub to assign a fixed number of IP addresses to the other computers on the network. If you limit the number of IP addresses to three or five computers, you can more easily monitor network traffic and troubleshoot any problems with the wired or wireless network without overloading the network while you're working on it.

When a Base Station Won't Respond

Setting up a base station or wireless access point can be one of the more tedious, time-consuming tasks you encounter when you bring up your wireless network. Although it's entirely possible to have a speedy installation, at some point, you will encounter some form of troubleshooting that will require you to reset the base station. Apple's base station has soft and hard reset modes. Simply unplug the power to perform a soft reset. The flashing red lights will change to green when the base station has restarted. To perform a hard reset, you'll need to insert a paper clip into the bottom side of the base station. The base station will take a little longer to restart, and any software settings will be deleted, restoring the base station to its default, out-of-the-box state.

Solutions: Designing a Smart Network

The bigger concern for an open network is how to keep uninvited computers out of your network. Keeping people off your network is mainly an issue if you plan to leave one or more computers powered on and connected to the network 24 hours a day. Uninvited guests, also referred to as hackers, can run scripts and software tools to probe a network for network addresses, and then try to guess your login name and password. One way to limit their access to your network is to set up a firewall.

Firewall Solutions

The term *firewall* was originally created to describe a type of wall that could be constructed to prevent a fire from spreading. In the computer world, a firewall can be a hardware device—including a computer or software running on a computer—that enables computers on the local network to access the Internet, but prevents computers on the Internet from visiting your local network. In most cases, a hardware firewall is the best kind of firewall you can set up to protect your network from being compromised by an uninvited guest.

Hardware Firewall Solutions

Check your DSL modem to see whether its firmware has a built-in firewall feature available. Since the DSL modem is the first line of contact with your local network, as shown in Figure 9-4, many DSL modems have a firewall feature built into them, enabling any computers on your network to access the Internet, while preventing computers outside of your DSL network from accessing any computers on your network.

You can configure a computer, a wireless access point, or a DSL modem to function as a hardware firewall for a local area network. In some cases, you may want other computers to send data to computers on your network. For example, if you're connecting to a remote network that requires the external computer to be authenticated, you may need to deactivate the firewall in the DSL modem each time you want to connect to the virtual private network. If you don't want to log into the DSL modem every time you want to access the virtual private network, you can set up a secondary network and set up a personal firewall on the client connecting to the virtual private network.

A local area network can have more than one firewall running at the same time. For example, if the DSL modem has the firewall activated, you can set up an additional level of protection by enabling the encryption feature for a wireless access point. If you want to restrict the wireless access cards that can access the wireless access point, most wireless access points enable you to add each specific wireless access card's MAC address. Using encryption combined with a defined list of wireless access cards can help keep uninvited computers from accessing your wireless network.

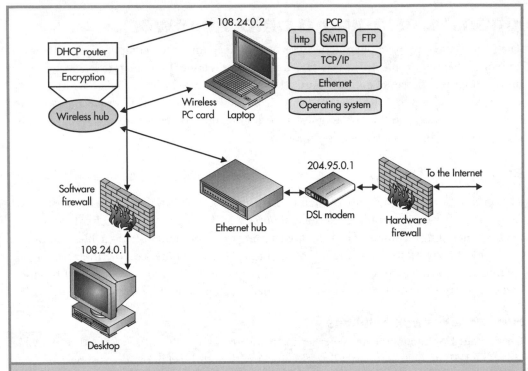

Figure 9-4.   A dedicated firewall can be set up on your home network to keep uninvited guests off your network without requiring an entire PC to be dedicated to the firewall.

To find out how to set up a wireless access card with a wireless access point, see Chapter 11.

SURVIVAL TIP

Software Firewalls

There are few different ways you can set up a software firewall on a computer. One way is to set up a DHCP server to run with encryption turned on. For example, Apple's AirPort base station enables you to activate the Wireless Encryption Protocol on each client. In order for a computer to connect to the DHCP server, it must first provide the encryption code to the wireless access point before it can access any other services on the network.

Another way to monitor network data is to install firewall software on your local computer. Symantec's Norton Personal Firewall, shown in Figure 9-5, is available for

Windows and Mac OS, and enables you to install and activate a firewall on your personal computer. No matter what network you connect to, you can monitor any new or existing network data that is sent from your computer.

Monitoring Network Access

Firewalls aren't the single solution to keep all bad things from getting to your networks. Some of the latest viruses have been attacks on e-mail servers carried out by sending JavaScript, or programs as attachments that when opened create a huge amount of new mail that gets sent out over the Internet. Some Web pages can also include software that can send code that results in random e-mail being sent to or from your computer without your knowing about it.

Running a personal firewall on each local computer can help monitor incoming or outgoing network data. It can help you evaluate software running on a single computer before you put it on your network by monitoring the computer for outgoing data that might be sent to the network. This can help you identify potential network bottlenecks before they get out of hand.

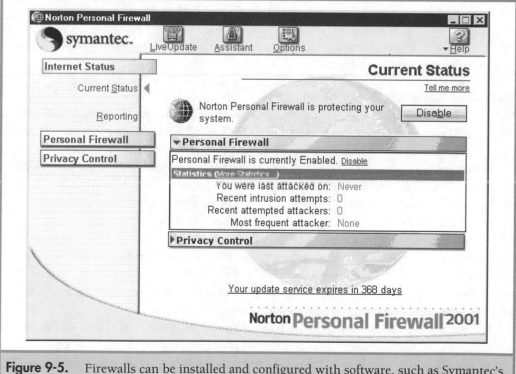

Figure 9-5. Firewalls can be installed and configured with software, such as Symantec's Norton Personal Firewall.

Outgoing Network Information

Outgoing network information is data that a computer sends to another computer on the Internet. Network routers usually do not filter information from leaving a local network, although it is possible to configure the router to prioritize data and send certain types of data out of the network before allowing other types to leave. Any computer may generate outgoing network data: data that leaves the local network for another computer on the Internet. Any application you install on a computer may potentially check to see whether the computer is connected to the Internet. If it is, the software may send data about the computer to the publisher or vendor on a regular basis.

As you install software onto each computer on a network and connect to different Web sites, software firewalls can be configured to warn you or simply to log files that are sent from your computer. Although you may never find yourself casually reading through the logs to look for problematic entries, you can set up a software firewall to notify you if data is leaving your computer from software that you weren't expecting to be running on your computer. Figure 9-6 shows the incoming and outgoing network activity on my computer.

If you install a personal firewall application on each computer, you can configure each computer to prevent outgoing data from being sent from the computer, thus preventing a virus or trojan horse from propagating over the local network. You will want to set up your computer to allow e-mail and browser data to leave your computer and be sent out to the Internet, without allowing extraneous data to be sent out onto the network and potentially generating extraneous network traffic.

Incoming Network Information

Incoming network information is data that a network router and each computer can receive on the local network. When a computer checks for new e-mail messages or loads a Web page, a request is sent to a mail or Web server; and the server, located on the Internet, sends data into the local network to the computer that originated the request. Along with legitimate data, uninvited viruses, trojan horses, and other transient network code can also invite itself past a network router and try to break into a computer on a local network.

If you've read about hackers or heard about hacker attacks on the news, you may have seen how a software virus can bring down a Web site or many network systems, very quickly. Read a little more about network computer "attacks," and you might find that most of the software that visits your computer doesn't really cause any harm. Some people seem to like the challenge of breaking into a system without causing any harm, while others may want to know what kind of data is stored on a computer.

Many types of software can arrive on your computer. Like other software that can run on your computer, malicious software is made up of code. Some code, such as a virus or script, can be triggered by a certain date, or by the presence of another file on your computer.

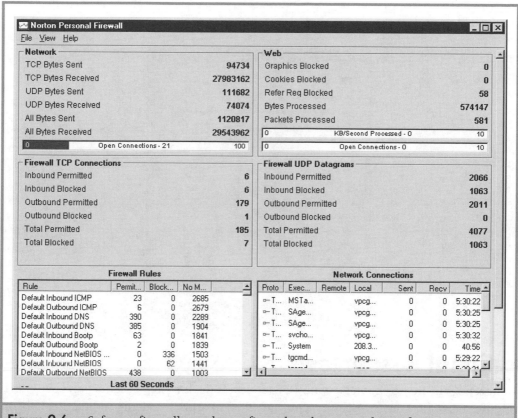

Figure 9-6.   Software firewalls can be configured to show you when information is leaving your computer or being sent to your computer.

Trojan horses are a type of software that may appear to be an e-mail application or text program; but when started, they run a different program, such as virus or a program that, for example, erases your disk.

The whole point of bringing up all these software nightmares is to emphasize the importance of backing up files, especially files that you cannot afford to lose. The other point is to emphasize once again that having a personal firewall installed on the computer on your network can help them run with fewer unexpected problems and also help you track exactly what kind of network data is moving to and from a computer. Windows XP has personal firewall software built into the operating system. The illustration shows the Advanced tab of

the network interface card properties window. Select the top check box to activate the personal firewall.

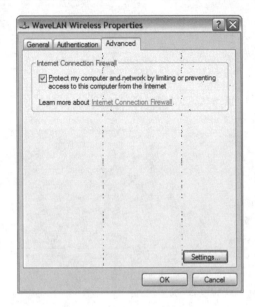

Additional Resources

Connecting the first computer to your DSL modem is the first step in setting up your home or office network. You can easily extend your wired network by adding an Ethernet hub, or extend your network with a wireless access point. The Table 9-1 contains a list of 802.11b card vendors and their URLs.

Wireless Card Vendor	Vendor's Web Site
Apple Computer	www.apple.com
Cisco	www.cisco.com
U.S. Robotics	www.usrobotics.com
Lucent	www.wavelan.com
	www.orinocowireless.com
Xircom	www.xircom.com
Proxim	www.proxim.com
NetGear	www.netgear.com

Table 9-1.   802.11b-Compliant Wireless Access Cards

If you're feeling adventurous, you might want to set up home automation systems to control the lights, the appliances, or even the television sets in your home. There are many different ways you can grow your network to support additional computers and manage a diverse set of tasks. However, as your network grows, so do the number of potential network problems. The following list of URLs leads to some general information about the products and technologies discussed in this chapter:

- www.apple.com
- www.sony.com
- www.x10.com
- innerspan.com
- www.smarthome.com
- www.symantec.com
- www.microsoft.com
- www.cert.org
- www.orinocowireless.com
- www.xircom.com
- www.networkcomputing.com
- www.networkcomputing.com/1201/1201ws1.html
- www.itworld.com
- www.itworld.com/Net/3022/WirelessLANspeedbump756

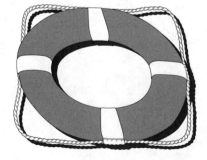

Chapter 10

Desktop Computers and Your DSL Network

The first computer you bring up on your network will most likely be a desktop computer. The term *desktop computer* refers to the standard tower, or rectangular computer box, that connects to a monitor, keyboard, and mouse. Most desktop computers, including Macs, ship with a 10 Base T Ethernet chip set or Ethernet network interface card and network-savvy operating system software so that you can surf Web pages on the Internet and share files with other computers connected to the network.

Desktop computers are great for enabling more than one person to use a computer without affecting any of the other users' files on that computer. You can set up the operating system software to allow more than one person to use a desktop computer. As you set up access to a computer, you may want to consider whether that computer will be powered on and accessible on the network 24 hours a day. DSL networks provide fast access to the Internet, enabling you to view text, media files, and interact with other users connected to the Internet. This chapter shows you how to set up user accounts and access privileges for the computers connected to a local network.

✦ **Creating accounts and passwords** Find out how to create, modify, or detete a user or group account on a Windows, Mac, or Linux computer.

✦ **Directory access** Set up access privileges on Windows, Mac, or Linux computers so that other computers can access shared files on the local network or over a remote network connection.

Basic Concepts: Sharing Information

Computers are powerful machines independent of any network connection. You can develop software, design graphics, and write about all sorts of things on a computer. Connecting a computer to a network enables you to share all that information with other computers without having to take the time to look up a computer's address or copy a file from one computer to another. Instead, you can attach a file to an e-mail message and send it across the world in a matter of seconds.

Sharing information across computers is all well and good. However, the other issue that needs to be addressed is, how do you allow more than one person to use a desktop computer without having to share all their software and hardware settings with everyone else who wants to use that computer? The answer is to create user name and password accounts for each user on a computer. The latest versions of Windows, Mac OS, and Linux enable you to set up login and password accounts for each person who wants to access a computer.

Windows 98, NT, Me, 2000, and XP all enable you to create a range of user accounts that can enable a user to have limited or full access to the computer. You can modify a user account to enable a user to change operating system settings, install programs, or limit the user's access to only save documents to a particular folder that user can access. An administrator account is a special type of account that enables a user to access any file on the computer A computer that can be accessed by multiple users will have at least one administrator account, which is used to create, modify or delete user accounts, and one or more user accounts.

You can also create user and group accounts on a computer server on the local network. This type of account enables a client computer to access a server computer that is connected to the same network. If you set up a Windows NT or 2000 file server on your network, the server will have at least one administrator account and one or more user accounts. You can set up custom file-sharing privileges for each user account on the file or move two or more users into a group and share files with a group of users.

Before you connect a client or server computer on a network, check to see what type of network the Ethernet card supports. If you want to set up the computer as a server, you may want to connect each of your servers to a faster network connection, such as a 100 Base T Ethernet hub and a 100 Base T Ethernet network card installed on the server computer. This network configuration creates a faster network backbone between the hub and the server.

You can attach client computers to the same network using 10 Base T Ethernet cards, or wireless access cards. Most clients, including wireless access points support only up to 11 Mbps. The average network performance of a wireless access card will be within a range of 1 Mbps. Performance of the wired or wireless network will vary, depending on the network bandwidth and throughput of the local area network. You may want to consider setting up a faster wired network if you plan to add wired or wireless computers to the network over time.

Setting Up Administrative Access on a Computer

If you haven't had the time to sit down and plan out your network, you can set up a PC or a Macintosh computer with administrator and user accounts to start with. You can customize user accounts on each computer as you need to accommodate new computers or new users on your network. For example, if you add a wireless access point, you may want to give full Internet access to the wireless computers on your network but configure the desktop systems with a different software configuration.

NOTE

Wireless access points connect to a standard Ethernet port and enable other computers with wireless cards, primarily handhelds and laptops, to connect to the network by connecting to the access point.

Windows, Mac OS, and Linux computers are all capable of sharing files. However, each operating system uses a slightly different implementation of file sharing. In addition to file sharing, Mac OS, for example, also enables you to turn your Mac into a Web-sharing computer. If your local network is hiding behind a firewall, you can also set up a PC or a Macintosh to allow remote access or to connect to a virtual private network over the Internet.

To find out more about network interface cards, go to Chapter 2. To find out more about file sharing, go to Chapter 3.

NOTE

Creating a User Account

As mentioned previously, there are several different ways you can share files on your computer. However, before you can actually share a file, you must log into a computer. Windows and Macintosh computers enable you to create user accounts with different access to levels to the files on your computer. You can use the Windows network connection wizard to create a user account on the computer. On Mac OS 9, you can create user accounts with the Multiple User control panel. Each user account on a Mac OS X computer can have the same general access to the computer. You can select a check box option to grant a user administrator privileges. Figure 10-1 shows the New User window for Mac OS X. You can type in a login name, a password, and a password hint. Then click Save to create a new user account.

The Multiple User control panel enables you to create multiple login and password accounts on a Macintosh computer running Mac OS 9. However, this type of login can be

Creating a Difficult Password

The point of creating a password is to keep other people from guessing it. Try to avoid using consecutive numbers, or words from a dictionary. A good password usually consists of six to eight characters. If you find it difficult to remember passwords, you may want to try substituting numbers for certain letters in a word you might remember. For example, you might use pa55w0rd for your password, substituting the number 5 for the letter s, and the number zero for the letter 0. Also, don't forget to change your password on a regular basis, every two to four months or more frequently. Finally, don't share your password with others. Changing your password often, and not sharing your password, will help keep your account secure.

241

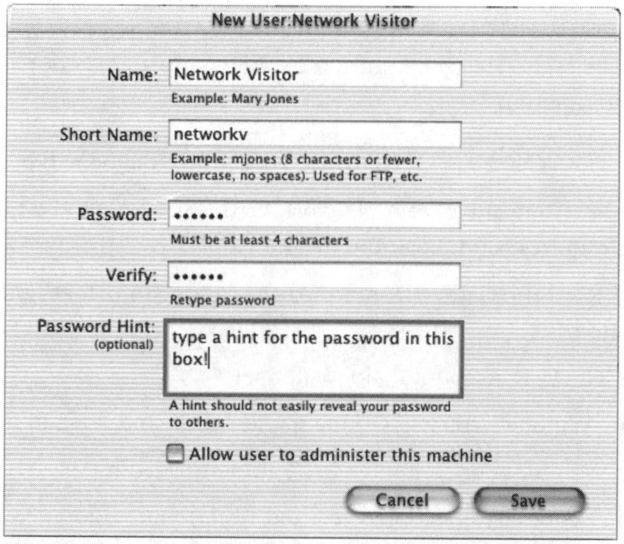

New User:Network Visitor

Name: Network Visitor
Example: Mary Jones

Short Name: networkv
Example: mjones (8 characters or fewer, lowercase, no spaces). Used for FTP, etc.

Password: ••••••
Must be at least 4 characters

Verify: ••••••
Retype password

Password Hint: type a hint for the password in this
(optional) box!

A hint should not easily reveal your password to others.

☐ Allow user to administer this machine

Cancel   Save

Figure 10-1. You can create a generic visitor login and password if the people using the computer system don't mind sharing Web and e-mail information on the same machine.

bypassed if you start up the computer from a CD-ROM or an external hard drive. Windows operating systems also enable you to create more than one login account for a computer. Of course, Unix and Linux also support multiple login accounts.

If you have a Windows NT or 2000 server set up on your network, you can create user login accounts for each computer, or you can create a login account that connects to a network server. In order for someone to log into the Windows NT or 2000 server, that person must have an account on that server in order to log into the client computer. Once the network account is created, a user can log into the Windows network.

To connect a computer to a Windows 2000 server network, perform the following steps.

1. Right-click the My Computer icon and choose Properties from the shortcut menu. The System Properties dialog will open.

2. Click the Network Identification tab in the System Properties dialog.

3. Click the Network ID button. The Network Identification Wizard dialog will open.

4. Click Next. The How Do You Use This Computer? dialog, shown in Figure 10-2, will open.

5. If you want to connect to a 2000 server, select the "This computer is part of a business network, and I use it to connect to other computers at work" radio button. Otherwise, select the "This computer is for home use and is not part of a business network" radio button.

6. Click Next. The What Kind Of Network Do You Use dialog will open.

7. Choose the My Company Uses A Network With A Domain radio button if your 2000 server requires you to log in with a domain.

8. Click Next. Read the Gather Domain And Account Information Before You Proceed dialog.

9. Click Next. The User Account dialog will open.

10. Type in your Windows 2000 server login, password, and domain information.

11. Click Next. Wait for your computer to be authenticated by the server.

12. Finish the network identification setup and restart your computer.

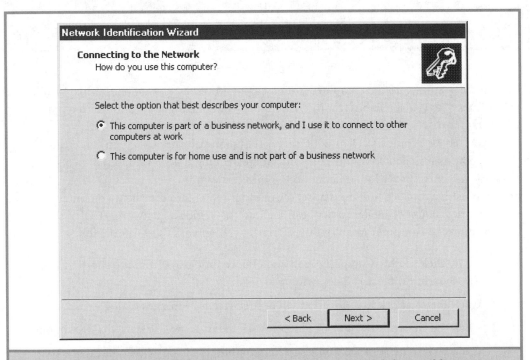

Figure 10-2. Windows 2000 has a network identification wizard that enables you to create login and password accounts that log into a network server.

Creating a New User

Windows, Mac, and Linux computers enable you to create a new user account if you have administrator access privileges assigned to your user account. The two basic components of a user account are a name and password. You can create new users and groups with the Computer Management program installed with Windows 2000. Here's how:

1. Click the Start menu, choose Programs | Administrative Tools, and then select Computer Management. The Computer Management program window, shown in Figure 10-3, will open.

2. Click the Local Users And Groups icon to view the Users and Groups folders for your computer.

3. Click the Users folder in the left window list to view a list of users in the right window list of the Computer Management window.

4. Choose New User from the Action menu to create a new login account on your Windows computer.

5. Right-click a user account to set a new password, rename the account, delete it, or access the properties dialog for the selected user account.

In addition to the login accounts, each computer can be configured to share files. On a Macintosh, the easiest way to share files on your hard drive is to turn on file sharing. On a PC, you can right-click a folder and assign permissions if you want to share it on your local network. Each user can create a login account to enable other computers to connect to the files on their computer. The following list provides a brief description of the each of the different ways a computer can share files on a network:

✦ **File sharing**   You can select a folder on a Windows or Macintosh system and right-click (Windows) or CTRL-click (Mac) to select a sharing option. If you're using Mac OS, you'll need to start file sharing before your can access the Sharing window for a folder.

✦ **Web sharing**   This feature is available to Windows users if you have network access and are using FrontPage. However, this feature more specifically applies to Mac OS 9, which has a Web Sharing control panel, enabling your Mac to become a Web server.

✦ **Program linking**   Windows applications that use OLE or that share data over a network may use program linking to update shared files over the network. This type of file sharing does not require a login or password in order to work properly.

✦ **Remote access** You can create an account enabling other computers to dial into or connect to your computer. On a Windows computer, you can click the Start menu and choose Settings and then Network And Dial-Up Connections to open the Network And Dial-up Connections dialog. Double-click the Add A Network Connection icon, read the introduction, and click Next. Select the Accept Incoming Connections radio button if you want to allow other computers to connect to your computer.

If you don't want to worry about sharing files on someone else's network, consider setting up a dedicated file server on your local network. If you work with other computers on several different networks, you may want to ask the network administrators for those networks if they have a file sharing server set up for general access. If you can post your files to a local server, including a Web server, it will be much easier for others to access those files when your computer is not connected to that network.

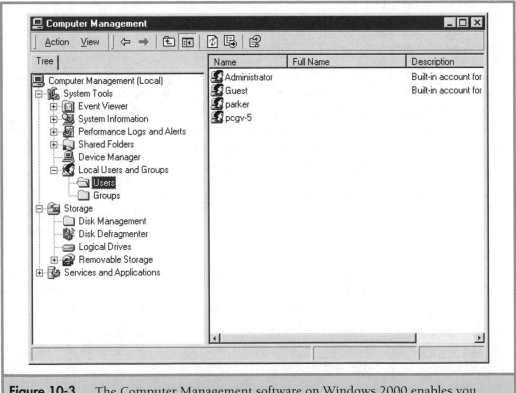

Figure 10-3. The Computer Management software on Windows 2000 enables you to create users and groups who can access your computer.

To find out more about sharing files, refer to Chapter 3.

**SURVIVAL
TIP**

Adding Peripherals to a Computer

Some of the peripherals you might want to connect to your computer and share on a network are devices such as printers, digital cameras, and scanners. Large printers will probably be connected to the network as their own devices. However, you can connect a USB or parallel port printer to a PC, or a USB or serial port printer to a Mac and share it on the network with other computers. In order for another computer to access the printer, the computer must have the printer driver installed. This is usually where some of the cross-platform issues start to bubble up to the surface. For instance, if you have an Apple LaserWriter PostScript printer, you may not be able to print to it with a Windows computer, especially if the printer requires an AppleTalk network connection in order to process a print job.

The first step to getting a printer recognized by your Windows computer on a network is to install the printer software on each computer connected to your network. Next, click the Start menu, choose Settings, and then select Printers. The Printers window will open. Double-click the Add Printer icon, and then click Next. Select the Network Printer radio button. Type the name of the printer or its URL into the appropriate text box, and then follow the on-screen instructions to add the printer to your Windows computer.

If you have a Macintosh computer, you also need to install software for the printer. Open the Chooser program from the Apple menu, and click the printer icon from the left window. If there are any printers that use the selected driver on the network, its name will appear in the right window list. Click the printer name, and then click Create. A desktop printer icon will appear on your desktop, and the selected printer becomes the default printer for your computer.

Hooking up a digital camera or scanner to the network works a little differently. As with most hardware devices, you must install software before you can access or control the camera or scanner. Although some cameras, such as the Logitech QuickCam Pro, shown in Figure 10-4, work only with Windows computers, most consumer digital cameras use a USB or serial cable to connect to a Macintosh or a Windows PC. Most scanners also work with Macs and Windows computers.

If you want to manually control a camera or scanner over the network, your best bet will be to install Timbuktu on the computer that has the camera or scanner connected to it. Timbuktu software enables you to create login and password accounts on a computer and,

Figure 10-4. Install the Macintosh, Linux, or Windows software and then connect the camera, direct-connect printer, or scanner to your computer.

more impressively, control the computer remotely from your local computer desktop. This is an invaluable tool if you need to help a newbie fix his or her computer, find a file, or take a picture with a digital camera connected to the computer.

Using Video to Monitor Your Home or Network

Account logins and passwords work great if you simply want to help keep files organized on the computer. However, if you want to design a smart network, you may want to set up a camera to find out if someone is actually using a particular computer, or if you want to monitor the computer's physical location. Figure 10-5 shows the motion detector feature in the QuickCam Pro software. If you plan to leave a server or client computer on 24 hours a day on your network, you can set up the camera software to create a picture if it notices a change between the newly captured image and the previous one.

Another alternative is to create snapshots at timed intervals. Figure 10-6 shows the Create Pictures and Videos feature of Logitech's QuickCam camera software. Taking pictures at regular intervals might be a better way to track computer usage if the computer is located in an area where there is a lot of foot traffic or if the computer is near a window that may be near other kinds of motion. You can save each set of pictures on your hard drive and burn a CD-ROM of images to create a video archive of computer use if you want to track that kind of information.

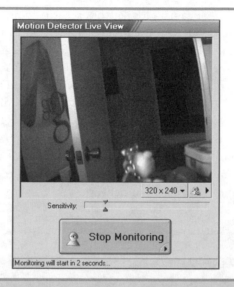

Figure 10-5. Some cameras enable you to capture an image if motion is detected. You can use this feature to find out who is using which computer on your local network.

Figure 10-6. You can position a camera near a computer to monitor access to a computer, see if the computer is running fine, or find out if it has crashed.

If you don't need to use that camera for network security, you can use it to accompany chat sessions or create a short video for friends and family. Some cameras enable you to capture full motion video, in addition to capturing still frame images. You can choose the broadcast feature in the QuickCam software, shown in Figure 10-7, to capture streaming video to your hard drive. Then save the file to your drive and send it in an e-mail message, or post it to your Web site, if you want to share it with a wider audience.

Linux distributions can support printing over a network, as well as image capture with a digital camera. However, you may need to search the Linux Web sites for the best drive to use for a particular digital camera or printer. I haven't had a whole lot of positive experiences to share in this particular area, but don't let that discourage you from hooking up a Linux computer, printer, or digital camera to your network.

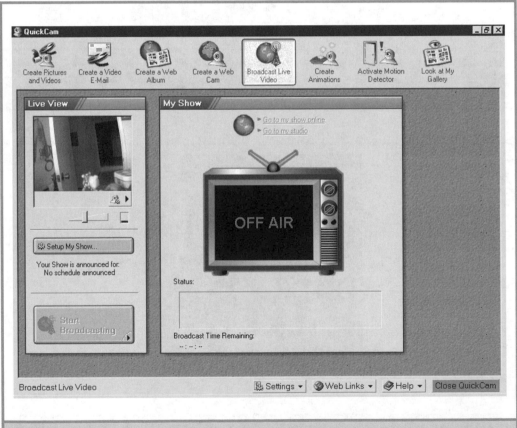

Figure 10-7.   Join a conference call over the Internet by pointing your camera to a Web page.

Problems: Supporting an Open Network

DSL networks can support Macs, Windows PCs, and Linux computers. Most home or office networks will have mostly one type of computer and less of another. If you already have one or two computers hooked up and running on your DSL network, you should be proud. Although you may not be able to share files directly between a Windows PC and a Macintosh computer, you can easily share files between two Windows or Macintosh computers. If I haven't made my point clear, creating a network that enables one computer platform to share files with another easily is not an easy thing to do. Of course, with the right software, like Virtual PC on a Mac, or Dave on a Windows computer, it's much easier to share files, compared to relying only on the Windows or Mac operating system.

Choosing a Standard for Managing Accounts

One way to share files on a network made up of different kinds of computers is to set up a Unix file-sharing server or a File Transfer Protocol (FTP) server. You can also set up a Web server to share both files and information content on the network. Windows 2000 server, Mac OS X server, and Linux distributions offer a wide range of cross-platform compatible network services. See Chapter 13 to find out more about how to set up a server on a local network.

Setting Up Administrative Access

If you're the only person using a desktop or laptop computer, you're the administrator of that computer. If you are responsible for the computers on a home or computer network, you may also be the network administrator. However, you may also have hired a network consultant to perform network administrative tasks for your home or business network.

There are two kinds of administrative access you can set up on a computer. If you're able to access every single file on your computer, including installing and removing any file as you like, you've got administrative privileges. If you want others to also access the files on your computer, you can create one or many user accounts, granting each one limited access to a particular folder or group of folders on the computer's hard drive.

This second type of user access is either a standard or restricted level of access. Restricted access may allow a user to read and possibly modify files in a particular folder, but not copy or delete files from the computer. Standard access may enable a user to install and delete applications and files but not create new users or groups on the computer. As you bring up or design your network, determine what kinds of files may need to be accessed by other users on the network. You may decide to set up a dedicated file server or standardize user account names or login names for users on the local network.

As a network administrator, you may want to limit the amount of disk space available for file sharing by partitioning the drive on the file-sharing server, or limiting the amount of disk space for each folder on the computer. The latter is a little more difficult to accomplish than the former. However, Windows and Macintosh computers can connect to each other directly if files absolutely have to be exchanged between two computers that are not too far away from each other. Choose on of the options from the Network Connection Wizard dialog box if you want to use the serial, parallel, or infrared port to share files. Otherwise, right-click a folder and choose the Sharing command from the shortcuts menu list if you want to share files over the Ethernet network.

Login and Password Accounts for File Sharing

As mentioned previously, different kinds of file sharing enable you to use your computer to create new accounts or change access of another account to accommodate a special connection, such as a serial, parallel, or infrared port connection. If two users want to share information, they can move their computers off the network and share data directly between the two devices. After you choose a port, click Next.

Click a check box to select a user account for the direct connection. The other computer will need to have a login name and password for the user account you select in the Allowed Users dialog in order to connect directly to your computer. Figure 10-8 shows the list of accounts available on the computer.

Click Next and type a name for the direct connection. A new file will appear in the Network And Dialup Connections dialog. You can double-click this file to open the login window that can connect you to another computer.

To find out more about file sharing, refer to Chapter 3.

**SURVIVAL
TIP**

File Security and Internet Access

If you're paranoid about keeping the contents of a file under wraps, you can encrypt a file using a file encryption program, such as PGP (Pretty Good Privacy), or if you're on a Mac, Apple File Security. The Apple File Security program, available only with Mac OS 9, is located in the Security folder of the Applications folder on your hard drive. You can encrypt a file with a password and then send it to someone else or leave it on the hard drive. You must enter the password for the encrypted file in order to view its content.

You can set up a secure shell server on your network if you want any computers connecting to your network to have a registered security key in order to access any computers on the

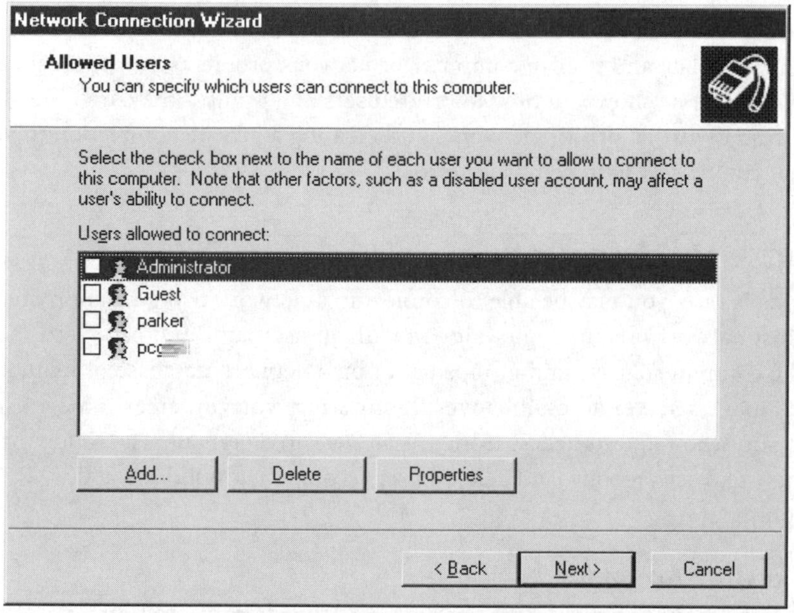

Figure 10-8. Once the file sharing connection is set up, you can choose which users can take advantage of this file sharing direct connection.

network. A secure shell actually consists of three components: secure login (slogin), secure shell (ssh), and scp. Ssh enables you to access a network over a secure connection from a remote location. There are also three different encryption algorithms you can choose from when you use ssh: Blowfish, DES, and IDEA. The latest version of ssh is ssh2. It is currently being defined by the Internet Engineering Task Force (IETF).

Network Solutions:
Connecting to Other Networks

One way to manage each computer, as well as access any servers or Internet services on a local network, is to create a standard set of user and group accounts. A *user account* represents a single user name and password. It should be unique for each person who logs into any computer on the local network. A *group* is a way of organizing one or more users to access a common set of directories on a server, as well as providing a certain level of security by limiting what each group can do on any given computer on the network. Only a user or group with more access privileges, such as an administrator or administrator group, can help isolate and resolve computer or network problems on the local network. The following sections show you how to create users and groups; they are followed by a brief discussion of virtual private networks and creating a private connection to your local network that can be accessed over the Internet.

Defining User Accounts

Although this is rare, you may be able to connect to a network using an anonymous login account. Most networks require you to log in with an username and password that already exists on the computer's users and groups list or on a network database of login accounts. If you want to make a server accessible over the Internet, you can create a new user account for each person who requests access from a Web site, or via e-mail. The following sections show you how to create, modify, and delete a user account on a Windows 2000, XP, Mac OS X, or Linux computer.

Creating a User Account

Creating a user account involves opening the User Management program on a Windows, Linux, or Mac OS computer and then assigning a unique user name and password. Each account can be configured to prompt the user to create a new password on a regular basis. You can also assign access privileges for each user you create on a computer.

Each folder can have read and write access privileges for one user and one group. Read privileges enable a user to copy any file in the folder to his or her computer. Write privileges enable a user to copy files to that folder or delete any files in the folder. If you want to share a folder but not any of its contents, you can allow a user to write to a folder but not read any of its contents. This is more commonly known as a drop box: a folder where any user can submit files but not view any files that have been submitted, unless the user has the appropriate access privileges.

You can share one folder, share several folders, or give the user full access to all software on the computer. Granting a user full access to read and write to any directory on the computer is essentially giving that person administrator access. Whether you're using your own computer or setting up several computers on a network, most users should have very limited access to the files on your computer. Only you or the person responsible for your computer should have full access to all files on the computer.

Creating a Windows NT or 2000 User Account   When you first install Windows NT, 2000, or XP onto a computer, it should have at least one administrator account. You can add, modify, or delete users as you like. To create a user account on a Windows NT or 2000 computer, perform the following steps:

1. Click the Start menu, choose Programs | Administrative Tools, and open the User Manager program.

2. Choose New User from the User menu.

3. Type a user name and password and click the Create button.

Creating a Windows XP User Account   To create a user on a Windows XP computer, perform the following steps. You must be logged into the Windows computer as an administrator in order to create, modify, or delete a user account.

1. Click the Start menu, choose Control Panels, and then open the User Account control panels shown in Figure 10-9.

2. The Users panel displays a list of users on the computer. Click the Advanced tab.

3. Click Advanced in the Advanced user management section of the User Accounts dialog. The Local Users And Groups dialog will open.

4. Click the Users folder located in the left window list of the Local Users And Groups dialog.

5. Choose New User from the Action menu. The New User dialog will open. Type a user name into the User Name text box.

6. Next, type a password into the Password and Confirm Password fields.

7. Check the User Must Change Password At Next Login check box if you want the user to create a new password. Otherwise, check the User Cannot Change Password check box.

8. Finally, click Create. If the password for the user account passes the built-in requirements, the new user account will appear in the Local Users And Groups dialog.

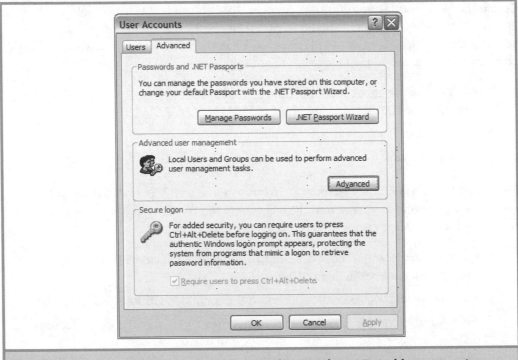

Figure 10-9.   The User Accounts control panel in Windows XP enables you to view
a list of existing users; use the Advanced tab to access additional user
and group settings.

Creating Mac OS 9 Users and Groups   Mac OS 9 enables you to create users and groups
for a Macintosh computer. Since both users and groups are accessible from the same control
panel window, both are covered in this section, instead of two separate sections. Also, the
user and group settings for Mac OS 9 apply to personal file-sharing access privileges. You
can configure separate login accounts for individuals from the Multiple Users control panel.
Perform the following steps to create a new user or group and view the account settings on
a computer running Mac OS 9.

1. Click the Apple menu, choose Control Panels, and select the File Sharing control panel.

2. Select the Users And Groups tab to view a list of users and groups for the Macintosh
   computer. Click New User to create a new user. Select the New Group button to
   create a new group.

3. Double-click a user or group in the window list of the File Sharing window to view
   the settings for the selected user or group.

4. Click the Show pop-up menu to view the Identity, Sharing, and Remote Access settings for each user.

5. Make any changes as you like.

6. Click the Close box of the user or group window to save your changes.

You can add users to a group by first double-clicking a group to open the group window. Then simply click, drag, and drop a user from the File Sharing window onto the group window to add the user to the selected group. You can delete a user or group from a Mac OS 9 computer by selecting the user or group from the window list and clicking Delete in the Users & Groups panel of the File Sharing window.

Creating a Mac OS X User Account   Mac OS X has a Users control panel that enables you to manage user accounts. If you want to manage groups on a Mac OS X computer, you will need to purchase the Mac OS X server product. Perform the following steps to create a new user account on a computer running Mac OS X:

1. Click the Apple menu and choose System Preferences.

2. Double-click the Users icon in the System Preferences window. The Users window will open.

3. Click New User.

4. Type a name and password into the New User window.

5. Mac OS X requires you to also type a hint for the password. This hint will appear if you incorrectly type the password more than three times into the login window.

6. Check the Allow User To Administer This Machine check box if you want to grant the user account administrator privileges.

7. Click OK to save the new user. The new user's name will appear in the window list of the Users window.

Creating a User Account on a Linux Computer   You have more than one way to create a user account on a Linux computer. If the computer has KDE or Gnome installed, you can use one of the KDE or Gnome programs the provide a user interface to create a user name or password for the Linux computer. If you're not sure what distribution is installed on the Linux computer, or if you prefer to use command-line tools to manage user accounts, you can perform the following steps to create a new user account on a Linux computer:

1. Open a terminal window.

2. At the prompt, type the following command to create a new user. In this example, *testuser* is the user name.

```
>useradd <testuser>
```

3. Next, type a password for the user account using the passwd command and the user name. When you press ENTER or RETURN, the new password text will appear at the prompt. Type the password, then press ENTER or RETURN. Then type the password a second time when "Re-enter new password" appears in the terminal window.

```
> passwd <testuser>
New password:
Re-enter new password:
Password changed
```

Modifying a User Account

To modify a user account on a Windows 2000 or Windows XP computer, open the User Account control panel from the Start menu. Double-click a user name to view the account settings for the user. If you want to change the password for a user, select a user from the window list in the User Account window and click Set Password.

You can modify a user account on a Mac OS X computer from the Users window. Click the Apple menu and choose System Preferences. The System Preferences window will open. Double-click the Users icon, and the Users window will open. Select a user from the window list and select the Edit User button. You can modify the user name, password, or hint for the user account.

On a Linux computer, you can change the owner of a directory by using the chown (change owner) command. For example, if you want to change the owner of a directory named docs from root to lisalee, you can type the following command in a terminal window. This changes the owner of the folder named docs from root to lisalee. You can confirm that the owner of the directory has changed by typing **ls –alF** into the prompt. The contents of the directory, along with the name of the owner of each file in the directory, will appear in the terminal window.

```
>chown docs root lisalee
```

Modifying Access Privileges for Files

On a Windows 2000 computer, you can right-click a folder and choose the Sharing command from the shortcuts menu to view the sharing privileges for a particular folder. You can also right-click a folder if you are running Windows XP. The Sharing And Security menu command will take you to the folder properties dialog, which is similar to the properties dialog in Windows 2000. Click the Share This Folder radio button if you want to share the contents of the folder over the network. Then click Permissions to choose the user or group names and allow or deny privileges for the selected folder.

On a Mac OS 9 computer, you can similarly select a folder icon and then choose the Get Info | Sharing command from the File menu. Select the user or groups you want to give access to the selected folder. Then choose the read or write privileges for the contents of the folder. If you want to share all files on a computer, you can select the hard drive icon and then choose Get Info | Sharing from the File menu.

A computer running Mac OS X works similarly to a Mac OS 9 computer. Select a folder in a Finder window. Then choose Show Info from the File menu. Select the Privileges item from the Show pop-up menu. Set the owner of the folder and assign any members or grant everyone access to the selected folder.

You can modify access privileges to files on a computer by using the chmod command. The chmod command enables you to assign read and write access privileges for a file. For example, if you want to modify a text file named chapterfile.doc that is read-only, you can type the following command into a terminal prompt:

```
>chmod chapterfile.doc -w
```

Deleting a User Account

If a user no longer needs to access a computer, you can remove the user account from a computer. On a Windows XP computer, open the User Accounts control panel window and click on the user account you want to remove. Then click Remove. A dialog box will appear asking you if you are sure you want to remove the selected account. Click Yes if you want to delete the account. Click No if you do not want to remove the account from the computer.

On Mac OS X, you can delete a user account from the Users window. Click the Apple menu, select System Preferences and select the Users icon. The Users window will open. Click a user name in the window list. Then click Delete User in the Users window to delete the user from the computer. Mac OS X will ask you if you really want to delete the user. Click Delete to remove the account from the Mac OS X computer. The access privileges and files will be reassigned to any accounts that have administrator privileges.

Monitoring User Accounts

You can use the command-line tools in Windows NT, 2000, or XP to monitor application and network usage on a computer. Sorry, Mac folks, this kind of information is not available with Mac OS 9 or Mac OS X. On a Windows NT, 2000, or XP computer, type **net user**

<user name> into a command-line window. For example, on my computer, if I type **net user lisalee**, the following output appears:

```
C:\Documents and Settings\FFF>net user lisalee
User name                     lisalee
Full Name
Comment
User's comment
Country code                  001 (United States)
Account active                Yes
Account expires               Never

Password last set             3/8/2001 1:02 AM
Password expires              Never
Password changeable           3/9/2001 1:02 AM
Password required             Yes
User may change password      Yes

Workstations allowed          All
Logon script
User profile
Home directory
Last logon                    9/3/2001 1:46 PM

Logon hours allowed           All

Local Group Memberships       *Administrators
Global Group memberships      *None
The command completed successfully.
```

Defining Group Accounts

If you have several different users that regularly access the local network, you can organize access privileges to any computer that you have administrative access to while preserving each user's account by placing users with similar access needs into groups. Most directories on a computer allow only a single user or group to access that file or folder at once. It's all right to have everyone use the same login and password to log into a server. However, if you want to add a level of security to the network and change the account name and password on a regular basis without having to broadcast the login information to the whole company, it's more efficient to create a user account for each computer on the local network, and require each user to change their own password on a regular basis. The following sections show you how to create a new group, modify a group, and delete a group with Windows, Mac OS, and Linux.

Creating a Group Account with Windows XP

Windows 2000 and XP has several groups predefined when you first install the operating system on a computer. The groups you can choose from are Administrators, Backup Operators, Guests, Network Configuration Operators, Power Users, Remote Desktop Users, Replicator, Users, and HelpServiceGroup. The following sections will show you how to create a new group, add a user to an existing group, or delete a group from a computer.

Creating a Windows XP User Acccount   To create a group on a Windows XP computer, perform the following steps. You must be logged into the Windows computer as an administrator in order to create, modify, or delete a user account:

1. Click the Start menu, choose Control Panels, and open the User Account control panel.

2. The Users panel displays a list of users on the computer. Click the Advanced tab.

3. Click Advanced in the Advanced User Management section of the User Accounts window. The Local Users And Groups window will open.

4. Click the Group folder located in the left window list of the Local Users And Groups window, as shown in Figure 10-10.

5. Choose New Group from the Action menu. The New Group window will open. Type a group name into the Group Name text box.

6. Click Create.

If you want to add users to the group, perform the following steps:

1. Double-click the group from the right window list of the Local Users And Groups window.

2. Next, click Add in the group properties dialog. The Select Users dialog will open.

3. Type the names of the users you want to add to the group.

4. Click Check Names to verify that the users' names in the group exist on the computer.

5. Click OK to save your changes to the group.

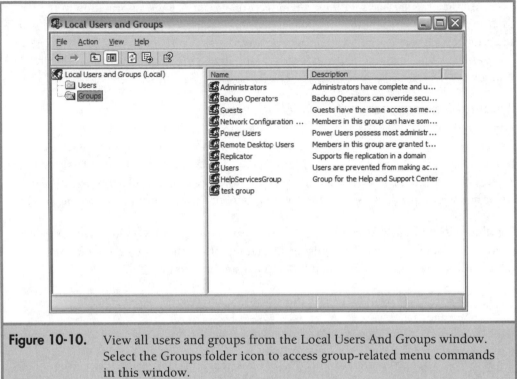

Figure 10-10. View all users and groups from the Local Users And Groups window. Select the Groups folder icon to access group-related menu commands in this window.

Modifying a Group Account

If you are the primary user on a computer, you should add your account to the administrator group. To modify a group from a Windows XP computer, open the Local Users And Groups window. Select the Groups folder from the left window list. Then double-click the group you want to edit from the right window list. The group properties dialog will open. Click Add if you want to add another user to the group, or select an existing user and click Remove to delete a user from a group.

Deleting a Group Account

To remove a group from a Windows XP computer, open the Local Users And Groups dialog. Select the Groups folder from the left window list. Then highlight the group you want to remove from the right window list. Next, select Delete from the Action menu. A dialog box will appear asking you if you want to delete the selected group. Click Yes if you want to remove the group from the computer. Click No if you do not want to delete the group.

Accessing Remote Networks

A DSL modem remains connected to the Internet as long as it is powered on and the DSL service that it is connected to remains active. You can use a network tunneling protocol, such as the Point-to-Point Tunneling Protocol (PPTP), the IP Security (IPsec) protocol, or the Level 2 Tunneling Protocol (L2TP) to connect to a virtual private network (VPN): a remote network that is also connected to the Internet. A VPN can be accessed only if you have an existing login account on the private network. Each protocol provides an encryption and authentication process for gaining access to the VPN. Each client must also have network settings that exactly match those of the virtual private network server in order to connect to the VPN.

VPN software is installed with Windows 2000. However, it is available only as a third-party solution for the Mac OS and Linux operating systems. The general process of connecting to another network involves logging into the network with a valid user account. This process will be the similar on a Mac or Linux system. However, the software interface will have a different user interface than the Windows example that will be used in the following sections.

To find out more about virtual private networks, go to Chapter 17.

**SURVIVAL
TIP**

Setting Up VPN Access

You can create a VPN network connection in Windows 2000 with the Make New Connection icon in the Network And Dial-Up Connections dialog. Click the Start menu, select Settings, and choose Network And Dial-up Connections. The Network Connection Wizard will open. Read the introduction and click Next. Click the Connect To A Private Network Through The Internet radio button and click Next.

The Public Network dialog will appear. Select the Do Not Dial The Initial Connection radio button and click Next. Next, the Destination Address dialog will appear. Type the IP address of the virtual private network or its name into the text box and click Next. The Connection Availability dialog will appear, shown in Figure 10-11. Click a radio button to create the connection for your specific login account or share to it with all other accounts connected to your computer. Click Next to continue to the next wizard screen.

Finally, type a name for the virtual private network connect. Figure 10-12 shows the default name, Virtual Private Connection, Windows will give this connection. Then click Finish. A new icon, shaped like a cloud, will appear in the Network And Dial-up Connections dialog.

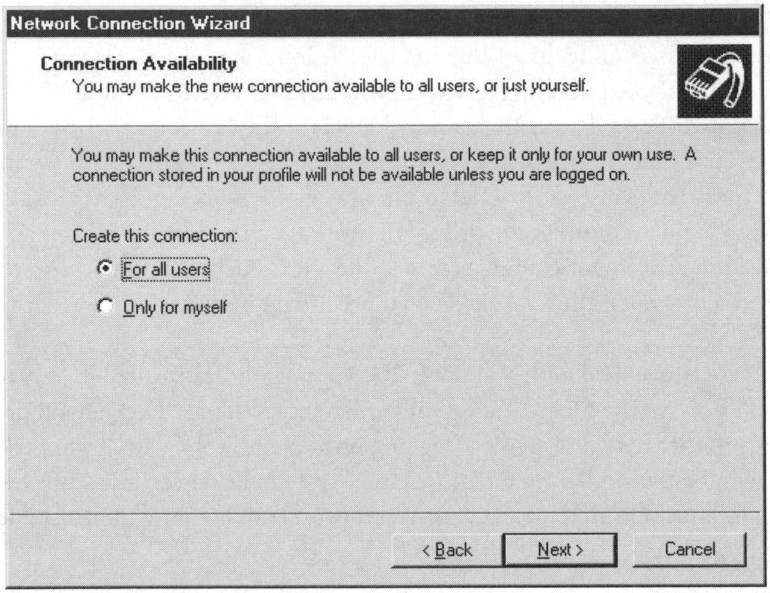

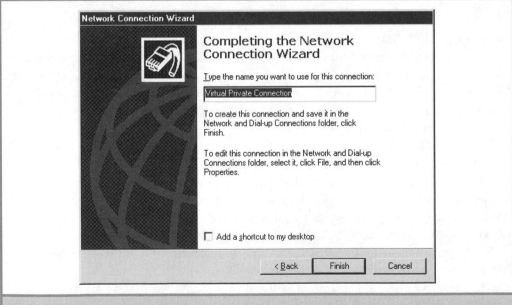

Figure 10-11. Choose which users can access the virtual private network connection.

Figure 10-12. Type a name for the virtual private network connection.

Connecting to the Private Network

Double-click the VPN icon in the Network And Dial-up Connections window. A login window will appear on your desktop. Type your password into the Password text field. Click Connect to connect to the VPN.

A VPN connection works much like a dial-up connection created over the phone line—except, of course, that all of the encryption and authentication is exchanged through a tunneling protocol over the Internet, instead of over a phone line. When you connect to a VPN, the login and account information is encrypted on your computer and sent to the VPN host you typed into the VPN Network Connection Wizard. The account information is decoded by the authentication host, and if the login information matches valid account information on the VPN network, your computer is given access to the VPN. Once connected, your computer interacts with the VPN as if it were another computer on that network. If you plan to use a software application such as a browser while connected to a VPN, it may need to be configured to work with any special settings on the VPN, such as a proxy server, in order to access the Internet.

You can view and modify the VPN settings from one of the five tabs available in the VPN Properties dialog. Click Properties in the login window to customize the settings for the VPN connection. The VPN Properties dialog consists of five tabs: General, Options, Security, Networking, and Sharing. Select the General tab to view or change the VPN address for the VPN connection. Customize the dialing and redialing settings in the Options tab. The Security tab enables you to choose how you are authenticated on the VPN. Most networks will require you to submit a secure password in order to connect to the network. Each VPN connection can have its own custom set of networking protocols. Click the Network tab in the VPN Properties dialog to customize the network protocol settings for the VPN connection.

CAUTION   Be sure to disconnect your computer from the VPN connection after you have completed the tasks you wanted to perform on the virtual network. Leaving the virtual network connected when you're not actively using it leaves both networks vulnerable to network hackers.

Allowing Other Computers to Access Your Network

Network information can also be shared with a second computer that is connected to a primary computer that is actively connected to the Internet, including a VPN connection. Windows has an Internet Connection Sharing feature built into it that enables you to turn a Windows PC into a router. You will need to have a secondary Ethernet card or port available for the computer you want to piggyback onto the primary computer's Internet connection. The following sections will show you how to set up Internet Connection Sharing with Windows 2000.

Setting Up Internet Connection Sharing

The Internet Connection Sharing (ICS)feature in Windows enables you to connect a second computer to a computer that is relies on a PPPoE or router connection to a DSL provider's network. The secondary computer can access the Internet through the same DSL connection. The primary computer, the one running ICS, acts as a router for network traffice intended for the secondary computer. The secondary computer may experience slower network performance compared to the primary computer.

To activate ICS on a Windows 2000 computer, perform the following steps.

1. Click Properties on the VPN login window. The VPN Properties dialog box will open.

2. Select the Sharing tab to view the Internet Connection Sharing settings.

3. Check the Enable Internet Connection Sharing For This Connection check box.

4. Choose the local network connection for the secondary computer you want to connect to the network.

5. Click Settings in the Properties dialog. An Internet Connection Sharing Settings dialog will open.

6. Select the Services tab from the Advanced Settings dialog box. Then check any services you want to activate on the remote network. Click OK to save your changes or choose Cancel to exit the dialog box without saving any changes.

7. Click OK in the Settings and Properties dialogs to return to the desktop.

8. Connect the secondary computer to your primary computer and start the network connection to activate the ICS setup.

The ICS settings are located in a slightly different location on a Windows XP computer. Choose the Advanced tab in the VPN properties dialog box to access the ICS settings mentioned in step 2. Check the Allow other network users to connect through this computer's Internet connection check box to activate the ICS connection for the secondary computer.

Allowing Computers to Dial Into Your Network

You can also set up a computer on your local network to accept incoming connections from another computer on the Internet. The following steps show you how to configure a computer on the local network to allow another computer to access it over a dial-up connection.

1. Double-click the My Network Places icon to open the Network And Dial-up Connections window.

2. Then Double-click the Make New Connection icon in the Network And Dial-up Connections dialog.

3. Click Next in the Network Connection Wizard. Choose the radio button for Accept Incoming Connections. If you're running Windows XP, choose the Set up an advanced connection radio button. Click Next.

4. Select a check box to select a port for the incoming connection. In this example, I chose the built-in modem on my computer. The Incoming Virtual Private Connection dialog will appear.

5. Select the Allow virtual private connections radio button and click Next.

6. Click a check box to select the user accounts you want to make available to the incoming connection. The dial up account will need to match the login account information selected in the Allowed Users dialog in order to connect to your computer.

7. Click Next. The Networking Components dialog will appear. Highlight the TCP/IP Protocols item in the window list. Then click Properties. The Incoming TCP/IP Properties dialog will open, shown in Figure 10-13.

8. Check the Allow Callers To Access My Local Area Network check box.

9. Click a radio button to determine how IP addresses will be assigned to the computers connecting into your virtual private network.

10. Click OK to save your changes.

11. Click Next and type a name for the Incoming Connection. A new icon will appear in the Network And Dial-up Connections dialog. In this example, you will need to connect a phone line to the built-in modem on your computer in order to make the incoming connection work.

12. Click the Incoming Connection icon to set up your computer to accept incoming connections from another computer to your modem.

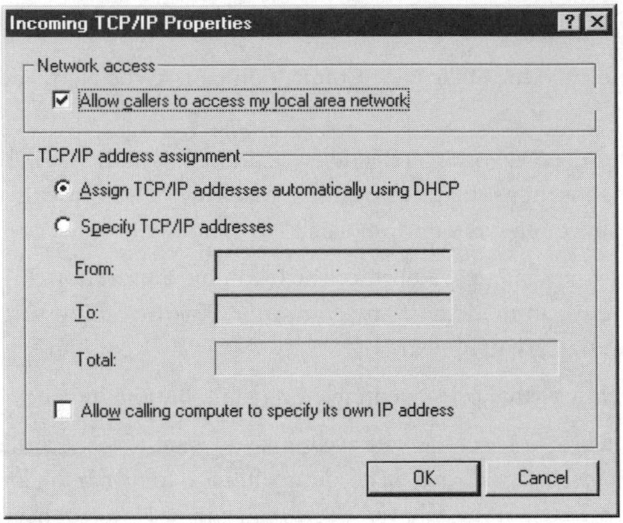

Figure 10-13. You can configure a Windows 2000 computer to allow another to computer to connect to it over a dial-up connection.

Additional Resources

Sharing files, together with setting up your computer to access and share files over the Internet, is a simple, yet complex task. The best way to share information is to set up dedicated file servers with login and password access. However, you can also create peer-to-peer connections between two computers and copy or remove files between them. If you don't want to share everything on your computer, you can restrict access to files or encrypt them. The following links provide a selected list of Web sites that can provide more explanation about the topics discussed in this chapter:

+ www.msn.com

+ www.microsoft.com/windows

+ www.apple.com/macos

+ www.linux.org

+ www.netopia.com

+ www.ssh.com

+ http://www.cert.org/tech_tips/home_networks.html#II-L

Chapter 11

Laptops and Your DSL Network

Laptop computers are growing in popularity as they increasingly rival desktop machines in features and performance. It's even become more common for people to have laptops connected to their home or small business network than desktop computers. Wireless access cards are almost standard features for most laptops. Not only is a wireless network the easiest way to grow your network without having to knock down or drill through a wall, in most instances it's faster than 10 Base T Ethernet. This chapter will show you how to set up and use a Windows or Macintosh laptop computer to share files, print, and do a few interesting tasks with your wireless network.

✦ **Setting up a wireless client** Install and set up a wireless PC card on a Windows notebook or a Macintosh PowerBook computer.

✦ **Sharing information peer to peer over a wireless network** Connect two computers together wirelessly.

✦ **Setting up printer and peripherals** Access and control network devices from a wireless laptop connection.

Basic Concepts: Mobile Computing

Laptops, notebooks, PowerBooks, and iBook computers are just as powerful as most desktop computer systems being manufactured today. One of the obvious differences between the two is that laptops are likely to have a smaller monitor and keyboard. Also, if you're not connected to a power source, the battery supply will limit you to two to six hours of computing time, unless you swap batteries. Even then, you need a power source to connect to if you want to continue to compute without powering off the computer.

The big advantage to working with a laptop computer is that you can take it with you and work on your computer anywhere you like. Before wireless networks were available, the biggest detriment to mobile computing was the absence of the Internet. That's not the case anymore. Wireless access points and wireless access cards enable you to grow your home network without dealing with the expense of wiring your home or testing and troubleshooting cable and connector issues.

NOTE Wireless access cards tend to cost more than a standard 10 Base T Ethernet card. The average wireless access card costs approximately $100. An Ethernet PC card costs approximately $100. A PCI Ethernet card costs approximately $30 to $40. However, you may also want to combine the additional cost of wiring your home or office, including any carpentry costs if you decide to build the Ethernet cabling or hubs into the walls.

Although laptops may not have PCI expansion slots like desktop computers, most laptops have at least one PC card slot you can use to connect an Ethernet or wireless PC card. You can also use the PC card slot to mount Compact Flash and Smart Media cards from digital cameras on your desktop, and copy image files from your camera onto your computer's hard drive. Having one PC card slot may require you to temporarily disconnect from the network if you want to copy some of your digital pictures onto your computer but this exchange is a fairly straightforward task, and I highly recommend setting up a wireless network as your home or office network instead of a wired network.

Connecting to a Wireless Network

You may have a friend or two with a base station or wireless access point set up in their home. Many companies are also starting to support wireless networks. In fact, you may already be working at a company that enables laptop users to connect to the corporate network. Chapter 9 showed you how to set up a wireless access point. The following sections will show you how to connect a laptop to a wireless access point, or base station.

Connecting a Mac to an Apple Base Station

In order to connect to a wireless access point or a base station, you must first install a wireless PC card, including its software, onto your computer. If you have a Macintosh computer, the AirPort software will be installed along with Mac OS 9 on your computer's hard drive. You can insert the AirPort card into your PowerBook's PC card slot, or connect it to the adapter card to install it on a desktop system. Don't forget to connect the internal antenna to the AirPort card.

Once you have installed the AirPort card and set up the AirPort base station, you can start the Airport application. Click the AirPort control strip module located at the bottom of your desktop, and then choose Open AirPort from the control strip module menu. The AirPort window, shown in Figure 11-1, will open. You can view the signal level of the wireless connection in the status area of the window. Click the Settings triangle to view the settings for the card and choose the base station network you want to connect to. You can click the Choose Network pop-up menu to choose a computer-to-computer connection or connect to any nearby base station networks.

If you want to turn your AirPort card and Macintosh computer into a software base station, click the Software Base Station button located in the lower-left corner of the AirPort window. A Base Station Setup window will open, enabling you to configure the network and access control settings for the software base station. This feature can come in handy if you are traveling with other computer users who may want to share data when no network is available.

```
┌─────────────────────────────────────────────────────────────┐
│ □  ▧                    AirPort                          ▤   │
│  ┌─Status────────────────────────────────────────────────┐  │
│  │ FishNet                                                │  │
│  │ Connected to the Internet via Ethernet                 │  │
│  │            Signal level: [████████████████████▌    ]   │  │
│  └────────────────────────────────────────────────────────┘ │
│  ▽ Settings                                                  │
│  ┌─AirPort──────────────────────────────────────────────┐   │
│  │  AirPort: On                      ┌─────────────────┐ │   │
│  │                                   │ Turn AirPort Off│ │   │
│  │                                   └─────────────────┘ │   │
│  │        AirPort ID: 00 30 65 08 D9 E2                  │   │
│  │           □ Allow selection of closed networks        │   │
│  └──────────────────────────────────────────────────────┘   │
│  ┌─AirPort Network──────────────────────────────────────┐   │
│  │  Choose network: [ FishNet                      ▼ ]  │   │
│  │  Base Station ID: 00 60 1D 1E 3E C7                  │   │
│  └──────────────────────────────────────────────────────┘   │
│  ┌─┐ ┌──────────────────────────┐                            │
│  │⊘│ │ Software Base Station...  │                           │
│  └─┘ └──────────────────────────┘                            │
└─────────────────────────────────────────────────────────────┘
```

Figure 11-1.   Apple's AirPort base station enables a computer with a wireless card
to access the Internet from a local network.

Apple's base station enables PCs to connect to a wireless network in addition to Apple's
Macintosh computers. If you have an 802.11-compliant card installed on your PC or older
Macintosh computer (one that doesn't recognize an AirPort card), you can configure each
of these computers to use a wireless connection to access your DSL network.

If you take your computer to work and then back home, you should turn AirPort off
before leaving your current network. You may want to choose the TCP/IP configuration for
the other network from the TCP/IP control panel. Click the Apple menu, choose Control
Panels, and then select TCP/IP to open the control panel. Press COMMAND-K to open the
TCP/IP configurations window. Click the network configuration you want to use. Then
click Make Active. When you arrive within range of the new network, turn AirPort on. The
computer should connect to the new network.

To find out more about how to set up the hardware and software for a wireless access point,
refer to Chapter 9.

NOTE

Connecting to Another Wireless Computer

Another way to create an instant wireless network is to create a connection between two wireless cards. This is more commonly referred to as a peer-to-peer connection. Apple's AirPort software, calls it a Computer to Computer connection. You can select the type of network connection from the Airport program window. If you're using Mac OS X, you can click the AirPort icon in the dock and choose Computer to Computer from the pop-up menu. The Computer to Computer window, shown in Figure 11-2, will open. Type the name and password information for the other computer. Then click OK to connect to it.

To find out more about peer-to-peer network connections, refer to Chapter 3.

**SURVIVAL
TIP**

Each wireless PC card supports up to 11 Mbps. When you create a Computer to Computer wireless connection, the data will be exchanged at the same rate as if it were connected to a wireless access point or a base station. Although the data can travel as fast as 11 Mbps, network data is usually transmitted at 1 Mbps.

NOTE

Computer to Computer

Please enter the following information to create a
Computer to Computer Network:

Name: Mac OS X Computer

Password: •••

Confirm: •••

Channel: Default (1) ⇅

Cancel   OK

Figure 11-2.   A computer configured with a wireless access card can log into another
computer's wireless access card.

After you log into the wireless computer, the AirPort icon in the dock will change to reflect the network connection for your computer. Figure 11-3 shows the Ethernet Properties for Lucent's WaveLAN card on a Windows 2000 a Windows 2000 XP computer. A dual computer icon will appear above the AirPort Signal Strength icon in the dock. If you're running Mac OS 9, the icon in the control strip will change to reflect the peer-to-peer connection.

Configuring IP Settings for a Wireless Card

Whether you have a Macintosh or a PC, you will need to configure your computer to have a valid IP address: either a dynamic IP address assigned by a DHCP server, or a fixed IP address. When you insert a wireless card on a Windows computer, a new network connection will appear in the Network and Dial-up Connections window. You can access the TCP/IP settings and configure the IP addressing information for the wireless card from the wireless access card properties window. To open the properties window, right-click the wireless card icon and choose Properties from its shortcut menu to view and change the network settings for the wireless card.

Select the Internet Protocol (TCP/IP) item from the Ethernet Properties window list. Then select Properties. The TCP/IP Properties dialog will open. Select the Obtain An IP Address Automatically radio button if you have a DHCP server set up on your wireless network. Otherwise, type in a fixed IP address and fill in all the subsequent IP addresses so that your computer can be recognized on the network. Next, right-click the wireless Ethernet icon in the Network And Dial-up Connections and choose Enable from the top of the shortcuts menu. Wait for the wireless card to connect to the network. You should see the lights on the PC card flashing as the connection is established.

You can right-click the same icon in the Network And Dial-up Connections dialog and choose Status if you want to view the network traffic for the wireless card. Some wireless cards install monitoring software. Figure 11-4 shows the Client Manager dialog for Lucent's WaveLAN wireless card. You can view the signal strength and some of the base station settings for your wireless network from the Client Manager dialog.

Configuring DHCP Access

If you do not have a wireless access point or a base station connected to your network, you can create a software base station, like the one mentioned earlier in this chapter. Another alternative is to turn your laptop into a DHCP server. First you must realize that this computer won't be moving out of the network a whole lot. In fact, it will probably be tethered with a wired connection to the rest of your network. The following sections show you how to set up a DHCP server and Network Address Translation on a computer.

Reviewing Setup Options

IP Net Router is a Macintosh software application that enables you to turn a PowerBook or desktop Macintosh into a DHCP server. You can configure this software to act as a router

Figure 11-3. The Properties window for the WaveLAN 802.11b PC card or Windows XP enables you to customize network settings for a wireless card.

on your network or assign IP addresses to other computers on the local network. You can also use it to set up a firewall and filter inbound and outbound packets. Figure 11-5 shows the Interfaces window of the IP Net Router software. This software works so well that it is used in Apple's AirPort products.

You can choose the Gateway command to customize the way network addresses are managed on your local network. For instance, if you check Enable Local NAT the DHCP server will use the IP address of the DHCP computer when network data is sent from any of the computers on your local network. Each computer on your local network address will have its own custom IP address, but all network packets must be routed through the DHCP server before any can arrive at any of the computers that are using the DHCP services on your local network.

Sharing Video over a Wireless Connection

Being able to access a network wirelessly enables you to control network devices, like a camera or scanner connected to another computer, or add a device to your laptop and extend the visible realm of your network. If you have a camera or scanner connected to a desktop computer on your network, you can use software such as Netopia's Timbuktu to connect to the desktop computer and capture an image from a camera. If the camera is set up to capture images automatically, you can log into the desktop computer and open or copy the image files on your laptop computer.

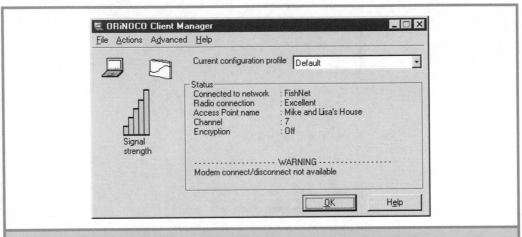

Figure 11-4.   Once your computer is connected to the wireless network, you can view the signal strength of the connection.

If you have a digital video camera, you can connect it to the laptop's 1394 or FireWire port. You can use an application such as iMovie or Adobe Premiere to download the digital video footage to your computer. Then edit and compress the video and share it in an e-mail message or post it to a Web site. One of the greatest advantages to having a mobile computer is that you can work virtually anywhere, and with an Internet connection, you can share your information more easily and faster than ever.

Controlling Other Mobile Devices

I realize the following section is probably not going to be a practical application for your home or office network. However, it is a glimpse of the type of wireless devices that may be created in the future. Each model of the robot dog has a digital camera in its nose to help it get a general sense of direction. The second generation model can capture a digital image, in addition to enabling you to add a wireless PC card to it.

In order to control the Aibo robot wirelessly, you must first take it apart. Disassemble its appendages so that you can insert the PC card into its PC card slot, as shown in Figure 11-5. Then reassemble the robot parts, and power on the device. You can access the Aibo dog using a peer-to-peer connection, using demo mode, or by communicating with a wireless access point.

Problems: Accessing Different Networks

One of the first issues that may have come up while you were setting up your base station or connecting your wireless card to the wireless network may have been related to security. As with wired networks, data sent over a wireless network is not protected. This means that

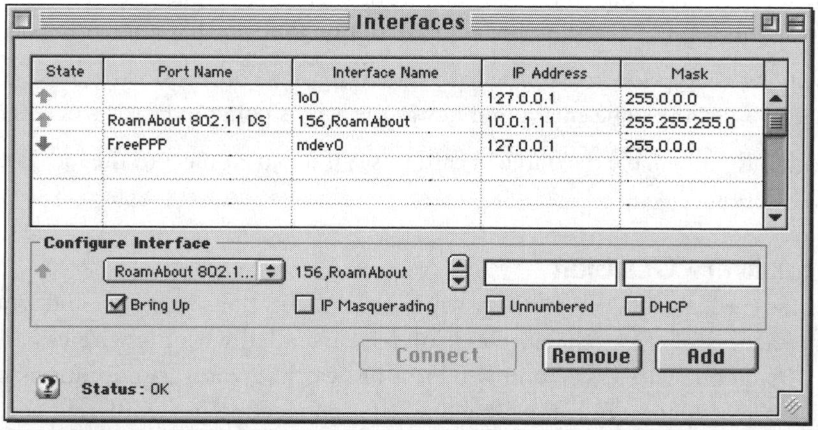

State	Port Name	Interface Name	IP Address	Mask
↑		loO	127.0.0.1	255.0.0.0
↑	RoamAbout 802.11 DS	156,RoamAbout	10.0.1.11	255.255.255.0
↓	FreePPP	mdevO	127.0.0.1	255.0.0.0

Interfaces

Configure Interface

RoamAbout 802.1... ◆ 156,RoamAbout

☑ Bring Up   ☐ IP Masquerading   ☐ Unnumbered   ☐ DHCP

Connect   Remove   Add

(?) Status: OK

Figure 11-5.   You can turn a wireless card into a DHCP router if you have the right
software installed on you computer.

if someone really wanted to sniff the packets being broadcast between the wireless card
and the base station, they could, with the proper computer hardware and software.

Base Station Here, Base Station There

Fortunately, most wireless access points and cards support the Wireless Equivalency
Privacy (WEP) encryption system. You can set up your access point to require encryption
be activated on each wireless client in order to access your wireless network. The broadcast
data will be encrypted as it is sent to and received from each wireless device. This is a great
way to add a level of security to your network. However, if you move between work and
home wireless networks, it can be tedious to switch from one network to another each day.
The following sections show you how to set up the encryption settings on your wireless
client and how to configure a wireless card to communicate with another wireless device.

Creating a Secure Network

If you purchased a wireless access card that support wireless encryption, you can install the
software for the card and set up the encryption features for the card. The following steps show
you how to modify the configuration settings for the WaveLAN or Orinoco wireless card.

1. Click the Start menu, choose Programs, select the Orinoco software folder, and start
   the Client Manager program.

2. Click the Action menu and choose the Edit Configuration command. The Edit
   Configuration window will open.

3. Click the Encryption tab to view the settings. Check the Enable Data Security check box if you want to access a wireless base station that also has encryption activated.

4. Type the encryption key for the base station into one of the Key text boxes. Make sure you use the same encryption key at the access point and each wireless client.

5. Click OK and enable the wireless card to see if it can connect to the local wireless base station.

A Card for Every Occasion

Most wireless cards enable you to create separate configurations for home and work. These settings are accessible from the wireless software installed with the wireless card on the computer. Using one wireless card in two locations works great if both locations have the same wireless access point or compatible ones. If each location has a different access point, and you don't mind purchasing more than one wireless card, you can configure one for work, and the other for home.

You can insert a wireless card into the PC card slot while the Mac or Windows computer is powered on. When you insert the wireless card into a a Windows PC, Windows will automatically loads the TCP/IP settings for that card. On a Mac, you must open the TCP/IP control panel to view or select the IP configuration you want to use with the wireless card connected to your PowerBook or iBook. In some cases, a wireless network may require you to use a specific brand of wireless card in order to have a computer access the wireless network.

Signal Strength and Your Laptop

Although most base stations enable you to connect within a 150-foot range, your mileage may vary depending on whether there are any other wireless broadcast systems and devices. The materials built into the walls of your home or office may also help or hinder the broadcast signal from working better or worse than the advertised 150-foot range. One way to find the limits of your wireless network is to move a laptop that contains a connected, wireless card to different locations in your home or office and view the signal strength meter for the card to determine when the signal starts to weaken and where it tends to be strongest. You might want to set up an additional base station or move the access point to a better location if you want to optimize wireless access in your home or office.

Network Solutions: Staying Connected

Computing on a wireless network works great if you can find a place to sit down, set up your wireless connection, and start working. The connection to the wireless base station should not change or go away unless someone moves the base station to a new location while you're working or the power goes out. The following sections show you how to get your laptop to work with printers connected to your network and how to work with software that accesses data over the Internet.

Accessing Network Devices

Once your laptop connects to a wireless base station, it can send and receive network data as if it were on the wired network. If you have already set up a printer on the wired network, you can continue to send print jobs to it if your laptop is connected over the wireless network. Similarly, you can run streaming media and load Web pages on your laptop using the wireless connection.

Printing on a Wireless Network

If you're using a Macintosh computer, click the Apple icon in the menu bar and select the Chooser application. The Chooser window, as seen in Figure 11-6, will open. Select a printer drive from the list of icons on the left. Then click a printer name from the right window list.

Windows users can click the Start menu, choose Settings, and select the Printers menu item to open the Printers window. Double-click the Add Printer icon to create a new printer for your computer. Or choose Print from your word processing or Web browser program, and select a printer from the Print dialog box.

Surfing the Web

You can test your wireless connection by trying to access an external Web site. For example, type www.apple.com to see if your laptop can load a Web page from a Web server located outside of your local network. If you have a Web site set up on your intranet, type the URL for the local Web server and see if the pages load in the browser window. If you're able to surf the Web on the wireless network as you would on the wired network, you have successfully connected your laptop to the wireless network.

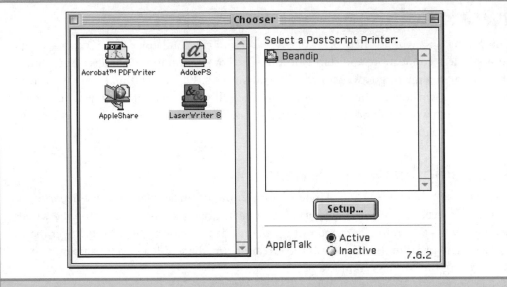

Figure 11-6. If the printer is connected to the same Ethernet network as the wireless access point, you can access the printer with a wireless access card.

Additional Resources

The first laptop and notebook computers weighed over ten pounds and offered slow processing in addition to short battery life. Not only are today's laptops, notebooks, and PowerBooks designed to rival desktop computers with high-resolution graphics and fast processor and bus speeds, but these mobile machines enable you to access the Internet over a wireless connection. This chapter showed you how to get connected to a wireless network. You may want to visit some of the Web sites listed here to find out more about wireless network computing.

- ✦ www.apple.com/airport
- ✦ www.ibm.com
- ✦ www.sony.com
- ✦ www.orinocowireless.com
- ✦ www.manginphotography.com/sptshtr20.html
- ✦ www.attws.com

Chapter 12

Handheld Devices and Your DSL Network

O ver the past few years, handheld devices have literally sprung up from all different industries, including, of course the computing industry. Handheld devices enable you to compute in the palm of your hand at home or at work, and many hospitals, insurance companies, classrooms, and businesses are adding these devices to their list of supported computing tools to boost productivity and keep their business chugging along. The following topics will be discussed in this chapter, which will focus on the Palm and Pocket PC handheld devices:

✦ **Docked devices**   Most handheld devices, such as the Palm handhelds and all their clones, can dock to a computer.

✦ **Networked devices**   You can turn a Palm or Pocket PC into a wired or wireless network device to share information with friends, family, and business associates. The Palm VII is Palm's wireless handheld that can instantly connect to a wireless network that you can subscribe to for a monthly fee.

✦ **Pocket PC**   Microsoft designed the operating system software for these handheld devices. Out of the box, these models can easily synchronize information with Windows applications such as Microsoft Outlook. They can also be set up to work with wired or wireless networks.

Basic Concepts of Handheld Devices

Today's handheld devices enable you to write, or tap your memos, tasks, address, phone numbers, and appointments into a battery-powered rectangular-shaped device. Most of the front area of the device is dedicated to screen real estate. But you're also bound to find a few buttons on the side and front of the device. The stylus, which is shaped like a pen but has no ink, can be used to tap on a software keyboard on the screen or to draw alphanumeric characters on the screen to input characters into the device. Some handhelds have a full-alphabet hardware keyboard in addition to a stylus.

Besides a screen, a stylus, and a power supply, handhelds have few components in common. Like computers, handhelds have platforms. Handhelds of a given platform, such as a Palm device or a Pocket PC device, share some common elements, such as hardware designs, processors, operating systems, and applications. Palm handhelds are probably more similar to each other than to desktop computers or other handheld devices.

A Short History of Handhelds

Palm introduced the first Palm Pilot in 1996, and among its many easy-to-use features was its capability to dock to a computer and synchronize the memo, contact, calendar, and task information on the Palm handheld with the Palm desktop software installed on your Mac or

Windows PC. The first Palm device, the Palm 1000, ran off alkaline batteries, came with a docking station, and enabled you to carry your personal data with you and synchronize it with a computer. About a year later, the Palm Professional model replaced the 1000 and 5000 models. In 1998, Palm introduced the Palm III handheld. Like its predecessors, it ran Palm OS and used a handwriting recognition system called *graffiti* to input data into the device. It came with 2MB of memory, which soon grew to 8MB. Most Palm models today have 8MB of memory.

Over the years, Palm has introduced more models, such as the Palm V, shown in Figure 12-1. Most models can also support external wired and wireless modems. A few clone makers have also entered the market, such as IBM, Qualcomm, Handspring, and Sony. Each of the clone models, like Palm's handhelds, uses a Motorola Dragonball processor and Palm OS software. The application bundle varies from model to model. Except for a few changes to the hardware, such as the expansion slot on Handspring devices, and the job dial and memory stick slot on Sony's Clie devices, the clone models are virtually identical to Palm's handhelds. However, some models, like the Sony Clie, dock only with Windows PCs, whereas Palm and Handspring models dock with Windows and Macintosh computers.

Microsoft introduced its first operating system for handheld devices a few years ago: Windows CE. The first Windows CE devices had small color screens with miniature keyboards and were fairly popular, albeit expensive. A few handhelds that supported handwriting recognition were introduced by Philips and HP; they used the 2.0 version of the Windows CE operating system. About a year later, Compaq and Hewlett-Packard introduced the first Pocket PC devices based on Windows CE 3.0; these are not only easier to use than the first handhelds but were fully network compatible with wired and wireless networks.

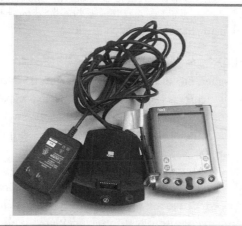

Figure 12-1. Like most handheld devices, the Palm V docks to your computer, enabling you to store its contents on your PC, and vice versa.

One distinct difference between the Pocket PC and Palm devices is that Pocket PC models can use different processors and hardware ports and also run the Windows CE operating system. Compaq's iPAQ is similar to Apple's Newton, a handheld device that many consider to be the first true, albeit heavy, handheld device. Both use Intel's ARM RISC (reduced instruction set computer) processor, which is a popular, low-power reduced instruction set processor. Many high-end IBM servers, as well as all of Apple's desktop towers, iMacs, and Powerbook computers use RISC processors. Hewlett-Packard's Jornada uses a processor made by Hitachi. Both models can include 32MB or more of memory, and all models can dock to a PC.

In contrast, the Motorola dragonball processor, used in the Palm devices, is a CISC (complex instruction set computer) processor. There are many scientific and technical debates over which of the two types of processor is faster. But most computers, as well as consumer devices, are making the transition to RISC processors.

As when using the Palm devices, you can use a stylus to select and enter data with the Pocket PC devices. Black-and-white and color models are available, as are a growing number of applications. Microsoft includes mini-versions of Excel, Word, and Outlook for the Pocket PC, and they work great as a desktop companion to a Windows computer that runs Outlook and the Microsoft Office application suite.

NOTE The first handheld devices were not designed to connect directly to the network. Apple's Newton, for example, was capable of synchronizing only with a serial cable connected to a Mac or Windows computer. Similarly, the Palm handhelds were designed to use an analog modem or to dock with a computer in order to access a network. In order to fully connect to an Ethernet network, you need to be able to connect an Ethernet card and connector, or a wireless Ethernet card to a handheld device. Newer handheld models are more likely to support this additional network hardware than are older devices.

Palm Handheld Models

The Palm V is a slightly smaller, sleeker version of the Palm III. Not only does it have a nicer screen, which displays clearer, crisper graphics, it is also capable of connecting to an external modem in addition to several third-party add-ons, such as Omnisky's wireless modem. The first Palm V model to ship had 2MB of memory. Palm soon shipped an 8MB model and called it the Palm Vx.

The Palm VII was introduced in 1999. It was the first wireless handheld for Palm, using Web clipping technology to enable the device to access wireless services. The Palm VII is slightly larger and a little heavier than a Palm III. It has 2MB of memory and comes with all the docking and handwriting recognition features available with all Palm models.

In 2000, Palm introduced its first model that sported a color screen, the Palm IIIc. Although Palm OS and the color screen are capable of displaying colors, the IIIc did not have many color applications available when it was first released, and Palm OS limited what colors appeared, and where, in applications and in the operating system.

As new models are introduced, each borrows from an existing model. For instance, the Palm m505 is a color Palm V that can dock to a USB port on a PC or Mac. Palm clones also have a few new features. They usually have a unique look, such as Sony's Clie, but not necessarily more memory or a larger screen. Handspring also created a clone of the Palm V. It's called the Edge.

NOTE Handheld devices, also known as personal digital assistants, are often so diverse that it's difficult to know what to like or not like about any particular model. If you're considering purchasing a PDA to connect to your DSL network, look for a PDA that enables you to connect to an Ethernet network. If possible, check to see if the software enables you to rely on a dynamic or static IP address, too.

Palm OS and Web Clippings

Every Palm handheld and Palm clone runs Palm OS. In addition to the Palm clones, a few years ago, Palm licensed its operating system to other companies to make custom handheld phones and other devices primarily for work use. The Palm operating system is responsible for starting up the device and running all the software programs, such as the calendar, memo, and contact list. It also enables applications to access hardware ports, such as the IR port, hardware slots, and each of the buttons on the device. When you wake a Palm device from sleep, you can view the last application screen or press the Application button to view a list of programs installed on the device.

NOTE If you have used a handheld device, you might have noticed that the application and operating system software offer fewer options than on a desktop computer or a laptop. Operating systems are actually a fraction of the size of desktop OSs due to limited space on the handheld device. However, these mobile operating system must be able to manage battery power and power to the display more efficiently than do desktop or laptop computers, to both extend battery life and give the end user as long as possible to use the device.

Palm introduced Web clippings when the Palm VII was introduced in 1998. Web clippings enable a Palm handheld to access a select group of customized Web sites on the Internet. You can download a Web clipping for amazon.com, for example if you want to use wireless modem or a cell phone to connect a Palm handheld to the Internet and shop online. Since then, a few changes have been made to the operating system to make it easier to hook up a phone line or a wireless modem to a handheld device. Palm's m100 and m500 series handhelds are the first products to ship with an additional CD that enables you to install Web clippings on your new Palm handheld, even if it isn't a Palm VII.

You can access Web clippings by tapping the MyPalm icon in the applications window. MyPalm enables your Palm to dial into the Internet with a cellular phone or a traditional phone line to connect to the Internet. Once connected, you can select a Web clipping, such as Yahoo or Amazon, and surf and shop on the Internet.

Pocket PC Models

Casio, Hewlett-Packard, and Compaq have at least two Pocket PC models available today. Each model from each vendor has a slightly different processor, set of features, weight, and shape. But all Pocket PC models have a 320 × 240 desktop resolution, which is noticeably larger than the 160 × 160 desktop resolution of the Palm handhelds. Most models also have 16MB of memory, although some models may have 32MB. The iPAQ boasts the fastest processor, as well as the highest price tag for its color model, but it also happens to be the most popular Pocket PC available today.

NOTE The ARM processor powers Compaq's iPAQ Pocket PC. Years before, Apple worked with an earlier version of the same processor for the Newton when the chip maker was known as Advanced RISC Machines. Today the company is known as ARM Ltd., and its processors are manufactured by Intel.

Each Pocket PC can run Windows CE applications, including multimedia programs such as Windows Media Player and Macromedia Flash. Internet Explorer comes bundled with each Pocket PC, and you can input text using the natural handwriting character recognition software or type out your entries on the built-in keyboard. In addition to using pocket versions of Microsoft Word and Excel, you can also read text files with Microsoft Reader and download and install games, music, and multimedia files. Some models enable you to attach an expansion slot for a Compact Flash or PC card. The expansion slot enables you to run network applications such as e-mail and browser software on your iPAQ and download new data as it arrives or as you surf the Web.

Setting Up a Handheld Device with a Computer

You can install Palm desktop to synchronize and back up the information on your Palm device with a Macintosh or Windows computer. If you have a PocketPC, you can install Active Sync. Both handhelds enable you to update information, install programs, and manage information between your PC and Palm desktops. The following sections show you how to install and set up Palm Desktop and Microsoft Active Sync on a Windows computer.

Installing and Setting Up Palm for the Network

You can insert the CD-ROM that comes with the Palm handheld device. The Palm desktop software consists of the Palm Desktop application, plus Hot Sync, the software that enables a computer to synchronize data with the handheld device, and the Install tool, which you can use to install Palm programs from your PC. After you have run the installer program for the desktop application, you can restart your computer.

After you have installed the Palm desktop software onto your computer, place the Palm handheld in the dock, connect the USB or serial cable from the dock to your computer, and press the Synchronize button on the dock. A Hot Sync dialog box should appear on your computer's desktop, and also on the Palm desktop. Synchronizing data will take a few minutes. When it has finished, the data on your Palm handheld will match the data that appears on your Palm desktop.

If you have a modem module available for your Palm device, you can connect it to the handheld and use it to dial into the Internet. Choose Preferences from the Applications screen on your Palm device and choose Network from the pop-up menu located in the upper-right corner of the Preferences screen. You can select a service (as shown in the illustration) and type your user name, password, and phone number into the appropriate text fields. Then click Connect.

Palm Desktop for Windows has a few extra features that you won't find on the Mac version of Palm desktop. For example, the Palm Desktop version for Windows enables you to synchronize your expense reports with Microsoft Excel. The Macintosh version of Palm Desktop does not enable you to view any expense information. Palm's latest version of its desktop software, Palm Desktop 4.0, is the latest version of Palm Desktop available for Windows. This version of Palm Desktop has a Mail Setup program and enables you to synchronize e-mail on your PC so that you can view it on your Palm handheld.

Click the Details button of the Network preferences screen if you want to customize the type of network connection, idle timeout, Query DNS, and IP address behavior when connecting to the remote network. Although you won't be able to use a static IP address for your Palm handheld, you can click the script button if the Internet service provider you're connecting to requires a custom script in order to allow a computer to connect to the Internet.

You can use a modem with your Palm handheld if you want to download e-mail while you're on the go. If you take a laptop along with you, you do not need to set up the Network preferences settings. You can simply dock to the computer to update e-mail, Web, calendar, or other files on your Palm when you press the Synchronize button.

Installing and Setting Up a Pocket PC

As with the Palm handhelds, all of the bundled software comes preinstalled on the Pocket PC. One or more CD-ROM disks will also come with the Pocket PC. You will need to insert the Microsoft Active Sync CD-ROM into your computer and install Active Sync on the computer you want to dock the Pocket PC device.

Follow the onscreen instructions to install Active Sync onto your Windows computer, and choose the serial or USB port the Pocket PC dock is connected to. Click the File menu of the Active Sync software and choose the Synchronize command. The default setting for the iPAQ is to update the Pocket PC device whenever new data arrives in Outlook on the PC.

Most Pocket PC models use a lithium ion battery, not regular AA or AAA batteries. Depending on how you use your Pocket PC, you may get several hours or several days of use before recharging the battery. However, for optimal battery life, dock the Pocket PC whenever you can. Another thing to keep in mind when evaluating battery life of your Pocket PC is whether any additional modules or expansion devices are connected to it. You can install software for the Cisco wireless card on the Pocket PC and then access the network wirelessly as long as you are within range of a wireless access point to the network.

There are two different kinds of wireless network cards you can use with a PocketPC. If you want to connect your Pocket PC to your DSL network's wireless access point, you will want to insert an 802.11 PC card into the Pocket PC expansion slot and configure the PC card with an IP address for your home or office network. If you want to have 24 × 7 wireless access to the Internet, you can purchase a wireless modem, such as Omnisky's Wireless Air Card for Compaq's iPAQ Pocket PC. This type of service requires you to subscribe to the wireless service provider and pay a monthly service fee. If you purchase a wireless modem, you can configure your Pocket PC to dial into your home or office network. However, it will not be able to connect to a wireless access point in the same way that an 802.11 wireless card will be able to put your Pocket PC on the network.

Connecting Handheld Devices to the Network

Both the Palm and the Pocket PC can access data on the Internet via your computer. The Pocket PC is capable of supporting static or dynamic Ethernet address configurations. However, the Palm, or rather Palm OS, supports only dial-up connections to a network. The illustration shows the Outlook summary page for the Pocket PC device. One of the nice things about Compaq's iPAQ is that it was able to synchronize with my PC right after I installed Active Sync. The contents of the Today page update whenever Outlook receives new data on the PC.

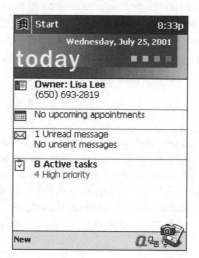

Problems: Updating Information on Your Handheld

Palm and Pocket PC devices should be able to synchronize data with a PC, regardless of the network setting you add or change for an expansion network card. The docking experience is generally trouble-free if you have installed either the software that came bundled with the

handheld device or the latest version of desktop and synchronization software available from Palm, Handspring, Sony, Microsoft, Casio, HP, or Compaq.

In addition to discussing issues related to upgrading and running network features on your Palm or Pocket PC, the following sections will show you how to set up a PC to work with both Palm and Pocket PC devices, or more than one of either device. Setting up a PC to allow more than one Palm or Pocket PC to dock can be helpful for setting up a dedicated PC docking station on your home or office network or a PC that might be shared with two or more family members or co-workers.

Configuring Handhelds to Update Information

Most files you install or work with on a Palm device end with the filename extension of .prc. When you install the Palm Desktop software, an update folder is created. It contains Palm OS software that you can install onto any Palm handheld. If Palm releases a new version of Palm OS, you can upgrade most Palm models, or rather, all models except for the m100 series, and take advantage of the newer features in the latest Palm OS.

If you have a clone model of Palm device, you will need to download your Palm desktop and, if supported, operating system upgrades from the clone vendor's Web site. For example, if you have a Handspring Visor, you can visit Handspring's Web site to upgrade your Palm desktop software on your Windows or Macintosh computer. However, Handspring's models do not support upgrading the operating system, so you won't find any Palm OS upgrades on the Handspring Web site.

CAUTION Not all versions of Palm OS will work with any particular hardware model. Generally, newer operating systems will work with any previously released hardware, but only the latest operating system will be able to work with the latest hardware model. For example, Palm OS 3, which shipped with the Palm IIIc, can be upgraded to Palm OS 4. However, the m500 series models require Palm OS 4.0.1 in order to synchronize with the Palm desktop software. Be sure not to put an older version of Palm OS onto a newer hardware model.

The operating system, Windows CE, as well as applications, can be upgraded on a Pocket PC much as Palm devices can receive upgrades. You can add or remove programs using the Active Sync software on your PC. If you click the File menu and choose Explore, you can navigate the file system on the Pocket PC from your Windows desktop. This provides an easy way to copy files between your desktop PC and Pocket PC. You can also access files in the operating system and create a complete backup of all the software on the device directly from your PC.

**SURVIVAL
TIP**

You can use only one device at a time with any single serial or USB port on your computer. If you encounter problems syncing or connecting a dock or device to a computer, check the software settings on your PC to make sure there are no other device drivers, such as a printer, running that may be using the same serial or USB port.

Configuring Pocket PCs to Update Browser Information

Pocket PC and Palm handhelds can download Web pages from a computer if the computer is connected to the network. AvantGo is one of the more popular and easy-to-use applications for performing this task. Whenever you dock and synchronize data between your handheld and desktop, AvantGo accesses its Web server on the Internet and sends the latest pages from any number of Web sites to your Palm or Pocket PC.

In order to use AvantGo, you must first install the AvantGo software onto your Palm or Pocket PC. The AG Connect (Palm) or Avant Go Connection (Pocket PC) software enables you to type in the name of the AvantGo server you want to use to synchronize network data. After the Avant Go software is installed, you can access the AG Connect icon from the Home page on the Palm device. If you have a Pocket PC, you can select the Start menu, choose Settings, and then select the Connections tab. Double-click the Avant Go Connection icon if you want to change the server settings, as shown in the illustration.

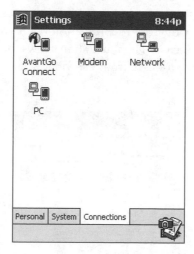

To navigate Web pages, click the AvantGo icon on your home page (Palm), or on the Internet Explorer icon on the Programs page (Pocket PC). The Web sites that appear on the AvantGo page can be customized if you create an account on AvantGo's Web site. Click a link to read more about a news headline or Web page topic. Click the Home icon to return to the AvantGo home page. You can navigate the pages you've visited by clicking the back and forward buttons in the menu bar of your Palm or Pocket PC device.

Avoiding Conflicts

There are a couple different but common scenarios that you may adopt in using your handheld device. You may take it with you to work at the beginning of the day and then home at the end of the day. The problem with this scenario is that if you have a home network and want to access your work network remotely or access information on the Web, you will have to manually change the network settings every time you change from one network to the other.

The second common scenario is that you have one PDA for work and a second for home. You can set up your PC to synchronize with both devices. However, if there are other PDAs that also need to access the Internet from your home or office network, you may need to create some kind of administrative or user account on one or more computers to keep each PDA's information stored but not accessible on the desktop computer.

Working with More Than One Network

You can view the IP information for each network card that has had its software installed on your Palm or Pocket PC. Click the Identification tab if you want to view more information about the network card. The illustration shows the Network Settings for the Pocket PC. Double-click a network card from the window list. The IP settings window will appear on screen.

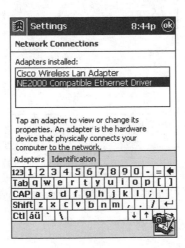

Click Use Server-Assigned IP Address as shown in the illustration, if your home or office network has a DHCP server set up on the network. Select Use Specific IP Address if you want to type in a unique IP address, subnet mask, and default gateway for the local network. If your home and work networks share the network settings, you will not need to change the network settings if you move your handheld device from one network to the other. If you do not want to constantly reconfigure the network software settings for the card, you may want to consider using separate network cards for home and work.

Setting Up Multiple Accounts

You can give each device a unique name when you first synchronize information with a computer. First, you need to assign a name for the Palm or Pocket PC handheld. Check to make sure the desktop software does not already have a setup with the same name. Then perform the following steps to name your Pocket PC device.

Click the Start menu, choose Settings, and click the System settings tab on a Pocket PC device.

1. Tap the About icon and view the name of the device.

2. Tap the Device ID tab in the About Settings screen.

3. Type the name of the Pocket PC into the Device Name text box.

4. Click OK to save your changes and return to the Settings screen.

NOTE Both Palm and Pocket PC devices can be configured to override data on a computer or vice versa. Open the Palm desktop software on your computer. Choose Custom from the Hotsync menu. Then highlight an option from the window list and select a radio button if you want to synchronize files between both devices, have one device override the other, or do nothing for the selected conduit when the devices are synchronized. If you have a Pocket PC, you can set it to warn you if the data on the handheld does not match what's on the PC or if the data being sent to the Pocket PC is too large to store on the device.

The first time you synchronize the Palm device to the computer, the Palm desktop software will ask you to type a name for the Palm handheld device. Type a unique name for each device. If you want to set up the Palm handheld to send the synchronized information to a different computer on the network, tap the HotSync program and tap the menu icon. Choose LANSync preferences and tap the LANSync setting. Next, choose Primary PC Setup and type the PC name and IP address into the Primary PC Setup window. Test the network docking connection and see if your computer is capable of receiving the latest information from your PDA over the network.

Wired and Wireless Solutions

As you add new devices onto your home or office network, you may want to work with a handheld device over a wired network first to see how you like the software and network performance and then switch over to a wireless network and compare the network and software performance on the wireless network to that on the wired network. In most cases, either kind of network should have similar performance on the handheld. However, environmental conditions may skew wired network to perform better than wireless networks, or vice versa. The following sections take a closer look at setting up and running wired and wireless solutions for handheld devices.

Pocket PC Network Solutions

Don't get me wrong. A Palm handheld device with Web Clipping technology is a great wireless solution if you want 24 × 7 Internet access to the Internet while you're on the go. However, if you have a wireless network set up on your home or office DSL network, it's a little more practical to plug a wireless PC card into an expansion slot and access the

Internet, or your local network, while you're moving around in your home or office. The following sections will show you how to set up a Pocket PC to navigate Web data and connect to a wireless network with an 802.11b wireless PC card. 802.11b wireless cards are also available for Palm and Handspring visor handheld devices.

Wireless and Wired Web Access with a Pocket PC

Internet Explorer 3.0 is installed with Windows CE 3.0 on Pocket PC handheld devices. This pocket version of Internet Explorer enables you to view HTML Web pages that are downloaded to the Pocket PC over a docked connection using the AvantGo software to pick the Web pages to download off the Internet. The illustration shows the main page of Internet Explorer on a Compaq iPAQ. As when using a standard browser, you can view text and graphics and click a link to go a related Web page. However, unlike when using the full-featured browsers on computers, you won't be able to run Perl or JavaScript code on your Pocket PC, although you can play a Flash or Windows Media Player file.

If you click a link, the Web page that has been downloaded to your Pocket PC will appear onscreen. At the bottom of the screen, you'll find a menu bar, shown in the illustration. The house icon will return you to the home page if you click it. The View and Tools menus enable you to choose a menu command for the browser. You can click the folder icon to choose a favorite Web page or click the Refresh icon (two arrows drawn in a circle) to reload

the page. You can view HTML Web pages on the Pocket PC. However, the browser is not a fully functional browser like the one installed on your Windows or Macintosh computer.

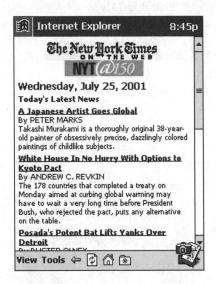

Once you've set up your Pocket PC to connect to your local wireless network, you might want to test your network connection by updating your AvantGo Web pages. You can view the AvantGo server information on a Pocket PC by selecting the AvantGo icon in the Connections screen of the Settings screen. The AvantGo Connect screen will appear. You can add a new server, view a server's properties, or remove a server from the Server settings window list.

If you want to use a full-featured browser, you may be disappointed with the Web browsing experience on a Palm or Pocket PC. Most of the Web pages created for these handheld devices are primarily made up of text, due to the relatively small amount of screen real estate available to each Web page. However, if you like to catch up on the latest news, it's great to be able to be able to pick and choose the Web sites you want to tap into while you're waiting for a meeting to start, or waiting in line for a meal.

Setting Up a Pocket PC for a Wireless Network

You can install software for a wireless card onto your Pocket PC device. Then configure the card to connect to your local wireless access point. As mentioned previously, a wireless card enables you to access your local network as long as you're in range of the access point. If you're out of range, or if your wireless access point is not available, you will not be able to check your e-mail or create a meeting over the wireless connection.

Palm and Handspring Visor handhelds can also connect to 802.11b wireless access points if equipped with an 802.11b wireless access card module.

NOTE

Insert the CD-ROM for the wireless card into your PC. Dock the Pocket PC and start the installer application. Follow the onscreen instructions to copy the network and wireless PC card software from the CD onto your Pocket PC device. Then attach the expansion card adapter and insert the wireless card into the expansion slot. Click the Start menu and choose Programs. You may need to double-click a folder icon such as the Cisco icons shown in the illustration to view the applications for the wireless card.

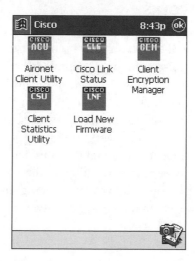

To configure the wireless card, double-click the Client software for the wireless card. A new program screen should open. The illustration shows the Aironet Client screen for the Cisco Wireless PC card. Click each of the items in the Property window list and enter the settings for your wireless access point. Click OK to save your changes.

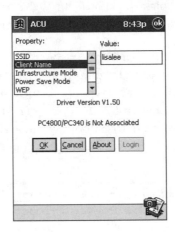

Now you're ready to test out your wireless network access. Try sending yourself an e-mail message. You may also want to try loading a Web page. If the device is unable to connect to the network, you will see an error message appear, indicating that the connection to the network could not be established. Recheck your network settings for the card and see if you can connect to the wireless network using the same PC card connected to a laptop or desktop computer.

Accessing the Networks

Like desktop and laptop computers, most of today's handheld devices work perfectly well with wired networks. For a handheld device, this means the dock that tethers the handheld device to the Ethernet network also relies on a computer's having a fast network connection to bring data to the handheld device. However, one of the problems of setting up a wired network is setting up a hub and installing all the cables that must travel from the hub to each room to which you want to grant Internet access. Wireless access points are an affordable alternative to setting and using a wired network for Pocket PC devices. If you have a Palm handheld, you can purchase a modem cable and use your cell phone or landline phone to dial into a wireless or wired service provider. Although these two wireless solutions are not similar in any way, they offer two alternatives for bringing Internet access to handheld devices that will be sharing the computers on your network.

Using Web Clippings on a Palm Handheld

Palm has a mobile Internet kit designed to bring the Web clipping technology in the Palm VII to the Palm III, IIIx, IIIxe, m100 series, IIIc, or V series models. The latest m500 series Palms can also work with Web clippings. In order to install the Web clipping software, you must have a Windows computer (sorry, Mac folks), and a cell phone that's capable of working with the Web clipping data. You can view a complete list of supported cell phones by visiting the Palm.Net Web site, or my.palm.com.

Web clippings enable you to subscribe to Palm's wireless service. You can connect to hundreds of sites over the wireless connection and surf the Web, look for the nearest ATM, or perform an e-commerce transaction from your Palm handheld. You can work with the set of Web clippings that is installed with the Web clipping software or add additional Web clippings by downloading them from Palm's Web site.

Configuring Network Settings on a Pocket PC

Compaq's iPAQPocket PC handheld and some Handspring devices can be configured to connect to a local area network using the same network information, such as an IP address and gateway, as the desktop or laptop computers are configured on your network. To access the network settings on a Pocket PC, perform the following steps:

1. Choose Settings from the Start menu.

2. Click the Connections tab to view the list of network drivers installed on your Pocket PC.

3. Double-click the Ethernet icon to view the network configuration information for your Pocket PC.

4. If you want to view the IP address information for the network card, double-click the network device from the window list in the Settings window.

5. Type the network settings for the Pocket PC and tap on the OK button to save your settings.

The Palm VII, and any of the Palm handhelds with Web clippings installed, are like most other handhelds that work with wireless networks, Each device connects to the Internet directly using a particular wireless Internet service provider. If you want an alternative way to access your e-mail or Web pages from a wireless handheld device, you may want to consider using the Palm VII, or the Research in Motion Blackberry device. However, if you want to use a handheld wireless device to access services on a local network as well as on the Internet, you may want to take a closer look at Compaq's iPAQ or at Handspring's 802.11b solution.

Additional Resources

Network-savvy handheld devices are beginning to become more and more familiar to both home and business networks. They enable you to carry a subset of information with you wherever you go. The following Web sites provide additional information about Palm and Pocket PC mobile devices.

- ✦ www.palm.com
- ✦ www.compaq.com
- ✦ www.hp.com
- ✦ www.sony.com
- ✦ www.cisco.com
- ✦ www.pocketpc.com
- ✦ www.hp.com/jornada
- ✦ www.microsoft.com/mobile
- ✦ www.arm.com
- ✦ www.omnisky.com
- ✦ www.redhat.com/embedded

Chapter 13

Running File- and Web-Sharing Servers

Whether you have one or many computers connected to your DSL network, you can install, configure, and activate e-mail, backup, file sharing, Web sharing or other network services by setting up a dedicated server computer. There are many kinds of network services you can activate or install onto a Windows, Macintosh, or Linux computer to enhance a local area network. In most cases, one operating system offers similar, and in some cases, the same services as another operating system. Apple's Mac OS X server, for example, installs the Apache web server on a Mac, while there are also Linux distributions for the Power PC processor that can also run the Apache Web server on a Macintosh computer.

A *file server* is probably the most common server you'll find running on a local area network. A file server enables you to store a copy of one or more files that can be accessed by one or several client computers on the local network or the Internet. If your computer should cease to function, you can always restore any information stored on the file server and be up and running much faster than if you had to recreate the original data files from scratch.

A file server enables a computer to share one or more files with other computers connected to the network. The hardware for most file servers consists of beefed-up PCs or Macs with fast processors, large hard drives, and possibly a backup mechanism such as a DVD or tape drive. A special application enables the computer to host multiple network connections and provide other computers on the local network with access to its files. The server's administrator creates separate user accounts and organizes them into groups to define which files and folders each user can access on the file server.

A *Web server* is another type of server commonly found on a local area network. A Web server enables you to set up your own Web site and share your Web pages over the Internet from your DSL network. As an alternative, you can create a test Web site that's accessible only from your internal network. Web sharing is similar to file sharing, except the computer shares files specifically made for a Web browser and any browser-savvy applications. Other types of servers you may want to set up are backup, media, streaming media, and cross-platform-compatible servers. The following topics will be discussed in this chapter. Although Linux, Mac OS 9, and Mac OS X file and Web servers are discussed, this chapter focuses on the server products in the Microsoft Windows 2000 server.

- ✦ **Share Web files**   Set up a file or Web server on your Mac, Windows, or Linux computer

- ✦ **Back up files on the server**   Create a simple or dynamic backup system for your networked computers

- ✦ **Share multimedia files**   Add a multimedia server to your network

Basic Concepts: What Is a Server?

A server consists of both hardware and software. It is designed to store or host information and to allow many computers to connect to it at the same time. If you've used a browser, you may not have realized that the browser was downloading Web pages from a Web server. The essential hardware for a server is not all that different from that for any other desktop computer, except that a server may require more space for hard drives, and expansion ports to support multiple network connections. Windows, Mac OS, and Linux all enable you to activate server software on your computer if you want to share data with other computers on the network.

Before adding a server to your network, consider the type of computer you will be using to run the server and the amount of network traffic that will be moving into and out of the server. If you have a relatively slow computer available, such as a Macintosh computer with a 603 or 604 Power PC processor, you may want to use it as a print server or a file server. If the file or print server won't be exposed to a lot of printer or file downloading network traffic, installing it on a slower computer allows you to add a service to the local network without having to invest in newer, faster computer hardware. If you are familiar with Linux, you may want to install Linux for PPC onto an older Mac model. If faster hardware is available, you might want to use it to host file or print services that will attract a higher amount of network traffic.

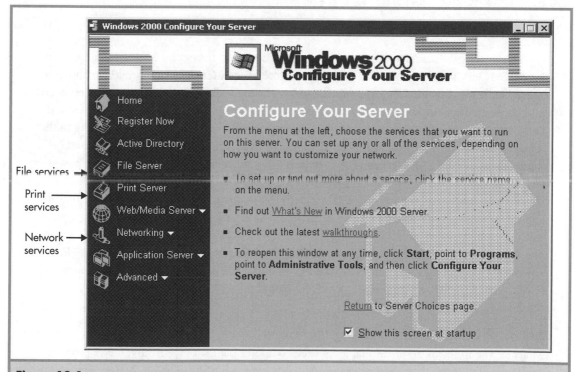

Figure 13-1. Windows 2000 Server enables you to configure a PC to host file, print, and other networking services.

Server Hardware and Software

The computer hardware you choose for a file server will depend on how many client computers you expect to connect to it at any given time. If you decide to set up a computer that is too slow (referring to the computer hardware in general) to handle two or more simultaneous client computer connections, the server may be too slow to be usable. If you plan on only two or three people accessing a computer server, you may not need to purchase a huge drive, or a fast computer to use as a file server. However you will need to make sure the computer has enough disk space and adequate hardware performance to be useful as a server. If you plan to grow the number of computers connected to the network, consider using a desktop computer with plenty of room for additional hard drives and Ethernet PCI cards as the computer for running a server that will get heavy network interaction. For most local area networks with less than fifty to a hundred clients, or users, you can use a desktop or laptop computer to host a single server, such as a file, Web, or mail services for the local network.

SURVIVAL TIP

Although you can run more than one server on a computer, the server will provide its best performance running one specific type of service.

Most network interface card vendors develop Ethernet drivers for Linux, Windows, and Mac OS. If you want to convert a PC or Macintosh computer to a server, adding hardware shouldn't be too difficult. The larger the file server, the more disks, network cards, and hardware will be needed to support a limited number of client computers. In addition to what's in the computer, you should also make sure the server is located in a cool place (I'm referring to the temperature of the room, here, not the decorum). If you want to reduce the likelihood of losing data on the file server, you may also want to connect it to an uninterruptible power supply (UPS).

Next to hardware, the most critical element for a network server is the software that will run on it. Most server programs rely on the networking capabilities of the operating system, as well as the stability of the operating system, in order to run reliably on a network. Linux and Mac OS X, which are Unix-based operating systems, are probably the most cost-effective solutions if your budget is cost-sensitive and you want to add a network server to your network. If you want to set up a server easily, consider installing a Windows 2000, Mac OS 9, or Mac OS X server.

Server Products and Computer Platforms

Many server applications are available for each computer platform. Generally, server programs cost quite a bit more than the average word processing application. The price varies, depending on the number of users that can simultaneously access the server, as well as the features available in the server. Some of the names in Table 13-1 may look familiar, while others may be new. The table contains a list of server products, matching them to the platform on which they run, and the client platforms that can access each one.

Server Product	Server Platform and Description	Client Platform
NetBEUI	Windows personal file sharing. This software is installed on Windows 98, Me, NT, 2000, and XP clients	Windows
NetBIOS	Windows Basic Input and Output System. Windows installs NetBIOS information with each network interface card.	Windows
WINS	Windows name server. Replaces DNS server on a network and uses NETBIOS to translate computer names to IP addresses.	Windows
File Sharing	Apple Mac OS 9 and Mac OS X personal file sharing	Mac OS 9, Mac OS X
AppleShare, AppleShare IP	Apple Mac OS 9 and Mac OS X file server	Macintosh over AppleShare, or Mac, Windows, and Linux over IP
FTP server	Linux, Mac OS X, Windows 2000 file server	Windows, Mac, Linux, Unix
Apache	Linux, Unix, and Mac OS X web server	Windows, Mac, Linux with a Web browser
Personal Web Sharing	Mac OS 9 client web server	Windows, Mac, Linux with a Web browser
Windows Exchange Server	Windows e-mail server	Windows or Macintosh computers running Outlook, Entourage, or Outlook Express
Windows 2000 Web Server	Windows web server	Windows, Mac, Linux with a Web browser
Windows 2000 Terminal Server	Remote access or application server level access terminal server	Windows, Mac OS, or Linux
Windows 2000 Media Server Windows 2000 Streaming Media Server	Audio and video media server	Windows Media Player for Windows or Macintosh

Table 13-1.   File Server Products and Computer Platforms

Choosing Network Services

Mac OS X, Unix, and Windows 2000 server operating systems enable you to host networking services, such as a DHCP server or a router, from a PC or Macintosh computer. These services can be custom installed on a PC or Mac after the Windows 2000 server or Mac OS X server software has been installed on the computer. Figure 13-2 shows the Server Configuration window in Windows 2000 Server. Click a link from the left side of the Configuration window to add DHCP server, router, domain name server, or remote access server software to the PC.

If you're running Mac OS 9, you can purchase third-party software to turn your Mac into an IP address, domain name, or router server on the network. You may want to consider upgrading to Mac OS X Server if you have Macintosh hardware that meets Mac OS X Server's hardware requirements. Apple sells server desktop computer models bundled with Mac OS X Server software. These desktop server computers have larger-sized hard drives than the workstation, or client Mac OS X computer models.

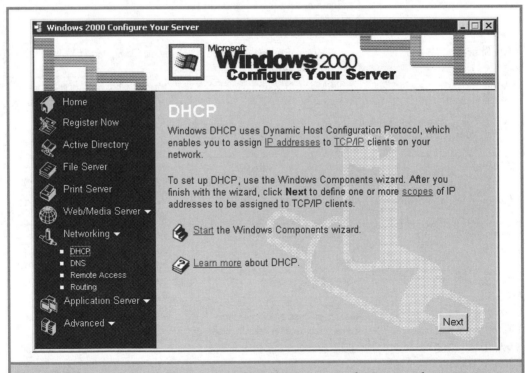

Figure 13-2.   You can configure a Windows 2000 server to host network services such as routing, remote access, domain name services, and Ethernet IP address services.

CAUTION

An advantage of setting up computers on a network is that if one computer fails, the rest of the network will continue to run. On your local network, avoid taking down the entire network infrastructure if one computer stops working or fails to connect to the network. This condition is called a single point of failure and can happen if you have one computer set up to host the file sharing, e-mail, and Web servers on the local network. If that one computer loses its connection to the network, the other computers will lose access to all file servers on the network.

Sharing Files on an FTP Server

One of the most common servers to set up is a file-sharing server. Linux and other Unix operating systems enable you to install an FTP server, shown in Figure 13-3, as part of the workstation operating system configuration. Windows and Mac OS client operating systems enable you to turn on personal file sharing to allow other Windows or Macs to access the client computer over a network connection.

SURVIVAL TIP

To find out more about personal file sharing, go to the section on peer-to-peer networks in Chapter 3.

The biggest problem with personal file sharing is that other computers cannot access the files on a computer if it is powered off or not connected to the network. A dedicated file server can remain on 24 hours a day on your local network or on the Internet. You can set up a Mac OS X server or Linux computer to run an FTP server. If you want to add FTP services to a Mac OS X or Linux computer, you must first install any networking software for the operating system onto the computer and then install the FTP server software. You can configure the FTP server with user or group accounts to allow client computers to access it with a user name and password. Start the FTP server to share the files on the Mac OS X server or Linux computer with other computers connected to the network. Any Windows, Mac, or Linux client can access files from it on the network. Figure 13-3 shows the Fetch program running on a Mac to access files stored on a Unix server situated on the Internet.

SURVIVAL TIP

You can also configure a Windows 2000 server or Mac OS 9 computer to host file sharing services. Windows and Mac OS file servers will be explained in more detail in the following sections in this chapter.

```
┌──────────────────────────────────────────────────────┐
│           ▨▨▨▨  New Connection...  ▨▨▨▨               │
│  Enter host name, userid, and password (or            │
│  choose from the shortcut menu):                      │
│                                                        │
│  Host:      ┌────────────────────────────────┐        │
│             │ spies.com                       │        │
│             └────────────────────────────────┘        │
│  User ID:   ┌────────────────────────────────┐        │
│             │ lisalee                         │        │
│             └────────────────────────────────┘        │
│  Password:  ┌────────────────────────────────┐        │
│             │ ●●●●●●●●●●                       │        │
│             └────────────────────────────────┘        │
│  Directory: ┌────────────────────────────────┐        │
│             │                                 │        │
│             └────────────────────────────────┘        │
│  Shortcuts: ▼      [ Cancel ]    [  OK  ]             │
└──────────────────────────────────────────────────────┘
```

Figure 13-3.   Access files on a Unix server with a File Transfer Protocol (FTP) client program.

CAUTION   FTP servers are fairly easy to set up on a local network. The most difficult administrative task is to create user accounts and groups to grant access to files on the server. Once you put that FTP server on the Internet, you will want to set up IP packet monitoring software and check for potential security problems that may result from hackers sniffing packets going to the FTP server. One way to increase network security to an FTP server is to set up a Secure Shell (SSH) server on the computer and require passwords for every account that can log into the server. FTP and SSH are available for Linux and Mac OS X servers.

You can log into an FTP server from your local computer using a client application, such as Fetch on a Mac or an FTP client for Windows. You can also use a terminal window to access an FTP server. In order to put or get files onto the FTP server, you must type Unix commands into the terminal window. When you access an FTP server from a client computer, you can view each of the files in your login directory, as shown in Figure 13-4. You can also move, copy, or delete files on an FTP server if you have been granted permission to perform these tasks. The Put command enables you to copy a file up to the FTP server, and the Get command enables you to download files.

If the server is running an Apache Web server in addition to an FTP server, which is a common configuration for Unix computers, you can create a Web folder and set up a Web site on your local network, or intranet. Figure 13-5 shows the index.html file in a Web directory on a Unix server accessed with an FTP client program. Although I don't recommend running a file server on the same computer as a Web server, you may want to set up such a computer if you want to test upgrades to an operating system or test some Web pages before posting them on a more critical computer on the network.

Client-Server Web Sharing Services

There are two basic kinds of Web servers. The first is a standard HTML server. In order to update Web data on this kind of server, you can manually edit each HTML text file, or you

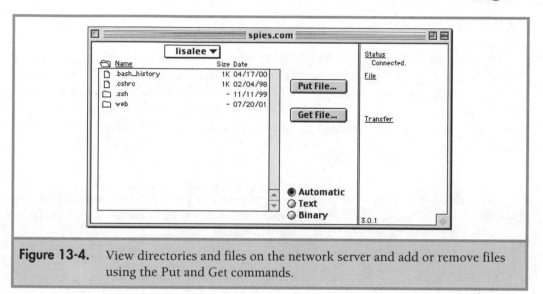

Figure 13-4. View directories and files on the network server and add or remove files using the Put and Get commands.

can run a script to update multiple text files as new data becomes available and place the newer information in one of your Web pages.

The other type of Web server dynamically updates. Active Server Pages and Java Server Pages are two of the more popular forms of database-backed Web sites on the Internet today. Applications or scripts running on the Web server can access data stored in a database server to update the content on the Web pages stored on the Web server. The database server may

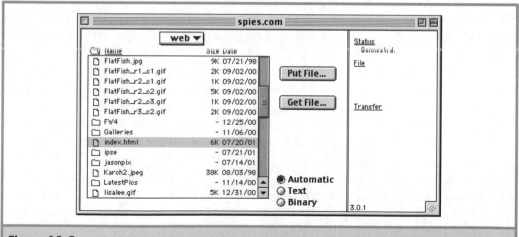

Figure 13-5. Fetch on the Mac enables you to add files by dragging and dropping them into a directory window list.

also have applications or scripts that run regularly to gather information from other Web servers on the Internet or from other databases on the local network.

The advantage of having a database running behind the scenes with a Web server is that dynamic data can easily be added or updated to a Web page without the need to rewrite any HTML, JavaScript, or other code located in files stored on the Web server. If you have never set up a Web server before, set up a traditional HTML server first, then learn how to design dynamically updating Web pages and compare setup and maintenance efforts for each kind of Web site.

NOTE   You can share Web pages on a computer by activating the personal Web sharing software on a Mac or Windows computer. One of the limitations of sharing files is that the files are available only when the computer is on and connected to the network.

Windows 2000 servers and Linux computers can host Web sharing services if you install and run the Apache server on the Linux computer, or the Windows 2000 Web server on a Windows 2000 server. A Mac OS X server can also host Web sharing services. If you use either Web server as a client computer in addition to the Web sharing services, the computer will be sharing Web files over a peer to peer connection with other client computers on the network. For best results, do not use a Web server as a client computer on the network.

Peer-to-Peer Web Sharing Services

An alternative to setting up a dedicated Web server on the local network is activating the personal Web sharing software on a Macintosh computer. Although you can leave on a Macintosh personal Web sharing server 24 hours a day, it is not recommended to use the personal Web sharing software as a dedicated Web server solution for the Internet or the local network. However, personal Web sharing servers are great for sharing Web pages that are in development.

Mac OS 9 and Mac OS X enable you to run a personal Web server from your computer. This is yet another way you can post new Web pages to the network, without having to worry about fixing bugs or breaking the more critical, larger Web server on the network. Figure 13-6 shows the Web Sharing control panel in Mac OS 9. If you want access the Web pages on the Web sharing server, type the IP address of the computer into a browser application running on any client computer connected to the same network as the Web server.

If you have installed a Windows 2000 server on a PC, you can turn it into a dedicated Web server on your network. You can set up a Windows Web server so that users can type a name to access the Web server or type an IP address. For best results, assign a static IP address to

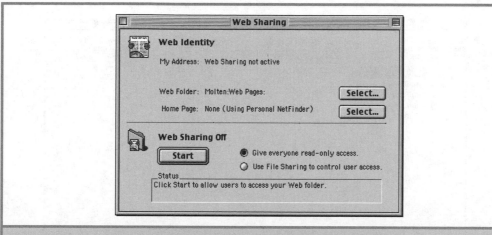

Figure 13-6. Open the Web Sharing control panel to turn your Mac into a Web server and let others view your Web pages over the Internet.

the Web server. Perform the following steps to install the Web server software onto a computer running Windows 2000 Server.

1. Install Windows 2000 server onto a PC.

2. Click the Start menu and then select Configure Your Server from the Administrative Tools menu list.

3. Click the Web Server link in the Windows 2000 Configure Your Server window and follow the onscreen instructions to install the Web server software.

4. Select a set of Web pages you want to work with from the Internet Information Services window shown in Figure 13-7.

A Web server enables a computer to share HTML files with other computers that have pointed their browser to your uniform resource locator (URL). By setting up a dedicated Web server, you can reduce the likelihood that other software running on that computer will cause it to crash or become inaccessible to the network.

Once you've installed the Web server software, you can start it. Navigate the files in the Web server directories installed on your Windows 2000 server. The Web server will create folders to store temporary files, and it will create associated Web files in accordance with the configuration settings for your Web server, as shown in Figure 13-8. Once you have copied the Web pages you want to share onto the Web server, check to make sure the Web sharing services are actively running on the Web server. Then open a browser application on a Windows, Mac, or Linux computer and try to view a Web page stored on the Web server.

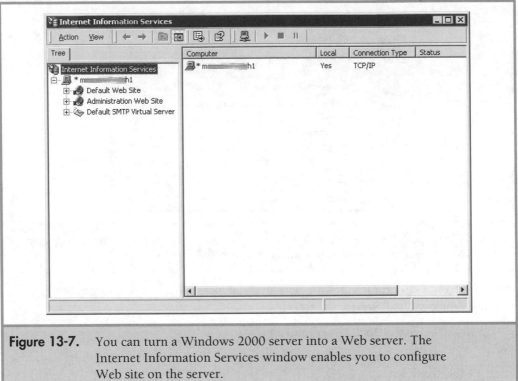

Figure 13-7. You can turn a Windows 2000 server into a Web server. The Internet Information Services window enables you to configure Web site on the server.

Backing Up Your Server

If you're going to add file and Web servers to your network, you will probably already have a backup server running on your network. If you haven't covered this base on your network, you should seriously consider it. A backup is often the fastest way to restore a network server or client software if the computer should experience a hardware or software failure or a virus attack. The following sections summarize some of the features you might want to consider when it comes to backing up the server system on your network.

Backup Options

Retrospect, published by Dantz Development Corporation, is one of the easiest-to-use backup software programs available for Windows and Macintosh computers. If you want to back up files on a Unix machine, you can use the tar and gzip programs that are installed with Linux distributions. The main purpose in creating a backup is to identify computers and data that need to be backed up on the network and store them on an external storage device. Figure 13-9 shows the Configure screen of Retrospect Express, which is a bundled lite version of the full Retrospect Remote software.

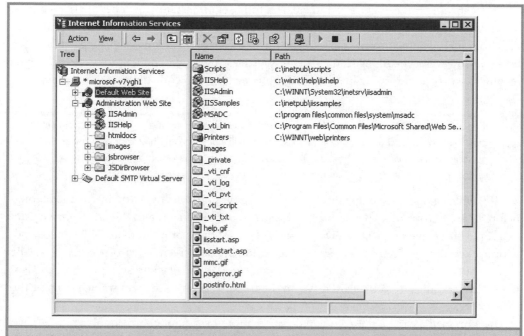

Figure 13-8. The Windows 2000 server creates a set of default Web files when you install the Web server software.

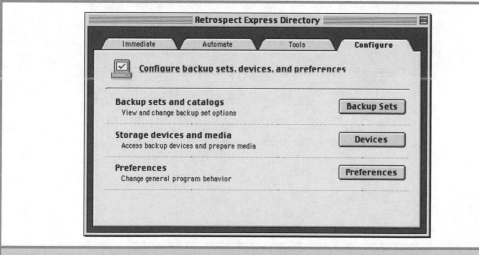

Figure 13-9. Some backup applications, like Retrospect Remote, enable you to create a simple backup or catalog multiple backups to all kinds of storage devices.

Retrospect Remote enables you to create a full backup instantly or schedule regular backups on a daily, weekly, or monthly basis. You can have your network users manually copy files from their computers onto the file server if you want particular files to be logged in to the backup. However, scheduling regular backups enables you to work more productively without having to worry about losing files because someone forgot to copy them to the file server.

SURVIVAL TIP If you don't want to wait for a full backup for each computer on the network, you can set up an incremental backup. An incremental backup will back up only files that are newer than the previous backup or the full backup. You can also set up some backup programs to exclude folders on a server or client computer.

If you designate one computer to store backup files on your network, it won't take long before its hard drive fills up with backup files. You can attach a removable media drive, such as a Zip or Jaz drive or a CD-R, CD-RW, or DVD-RAM drive or point to an FTP site to send your backup files to. Figure 13-10 shows the Backup Media screen in Retrospect Express. Click a radio button to select the type of media connected to your backup system. You can also manually copy files from the hard drive on the backup server to the removable media or the FTP server.

Backup media can be reused if you do not want to keep a long-term archive of the files on your network. Be careful not to copy corrupted data or virus-infected files to the backup. Otherwise, your backup will be rendered useless. You may, however, want to rotate backup media from day to day, or week to week, if you don't think the amount of backup information will change too dramatically until the new media are rotated into the backup schedule. Figure 13-11 shows the rotating media screen for Retrospect Express.

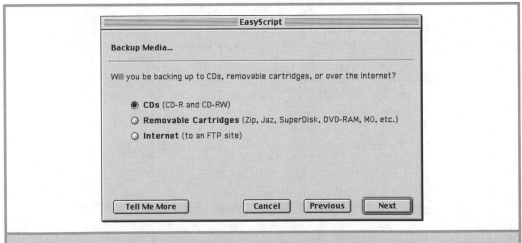

Figure 13-10.   You can connect a wide range of devices to your computer to store backup files for one or several computers on the network.

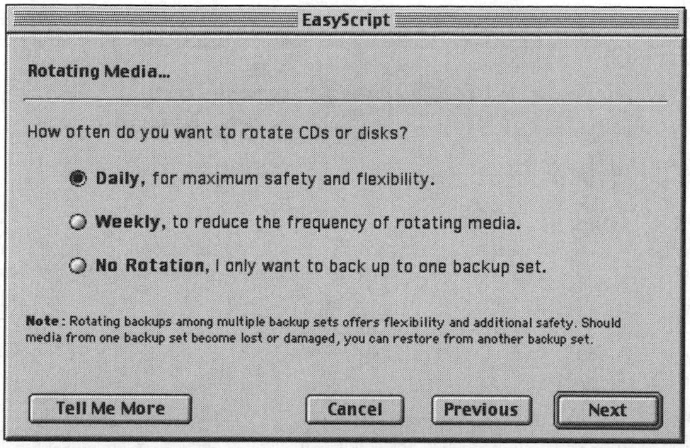

Figure 13-11. Set up regular backups on the backup server. If no files change on a computer, no new files are added to the backup media.

Windows and Mac File Servers

If you want to set up a dedicated file server, you can purchase Apple's Mac OS X server, AppleShare IP 6.3 software, or Windows 2000 Server software (see Figure 13-12) to share files between Linux, Macs and Windows computers connected to the same network. You will find many similarities between a personal file sharing computer and one that runs a dedicated file server. File servers enable you to store files on a computer that can be accessed by everyone else connected to the network.

Setting up a file server involves two general steps. Installing and activating the file sharing software, and creating users and groups that will access the files stored on the file server. The person responsible for installing and adding users and groups becomes the administrator of the file server. As users request access to the server, the administrator can create a user name and password for person. If there are many users accessing the server, the administrator may want to organize the file server so that there are general areas for storing applications, documents, and private folders where any user can add, or drop a folder to any other user who can access the file server. The file server administrator can also be responsible for backing up files on the server, managing disk space, and user access privileges on the file server, as well as removing any users or groups as users or groups change or leave the network.

Problems: Accessing and Managing Servers

Setting up and running a server with Windows, Mac, or Linux software running on a reliable hardware system is usually problem free. Problems that arise are usually related to aging hardware, power failures, problems with too many users accessing the same server at

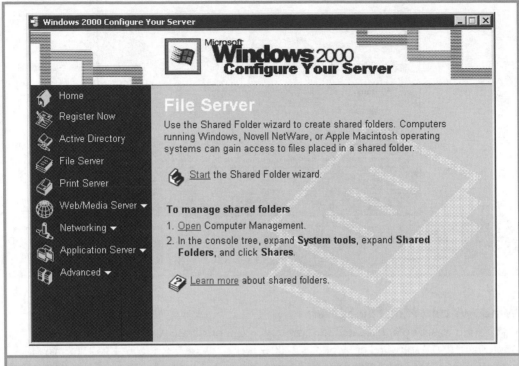

Figure 13-12. Set up a file server with a Windows 2000 Server computer.

once, or lack of disk space to store user data on the computer. If the server is not immediately accessible, you may need to spend some time isolating the cause of the server problem. The following sections discuss some of the problems you may encounter when running a server on a local or remote network.

Configuring Server Accounts

If you have a small group of users with constantly changing membership or tasks, you may be asked to set up specific access privileges for each person in the group as they start or stop different projects. The whole point of creating group access on a server is to afford those who are in a group permission to see certain files and to keep others from accessing those same files.

Administrative Access over the Network

When you set up a file server, it should be accessible from any other computer connected to the network. As different people access your network and use the server, you will need to create new accounts and delete old ones. You may also need to install virus or firewall software to help keep uninvited hackers from visiting your computer.

Mac OS X Server and Mac OS X enable you to create administrative or user accounts and groups that can be accessed over the Internet or remotely over a phone line. If the server is running Windows 2000, you can install a terminal server to enable a client computer to log into the server with administrator privileges. Windows terminal servers can be configured to allow remote access, enabling full access to the Windows system, or applications access, enabling limited access to specific programs installed on the terminal server. Linux, Windows, and Macintosh computers can also use a virtual network client if you want to install a common tool on all computers on your network.

Troubleshooting Access to Servers

Networks can be incredibly reliable or, occasionally, flaky. A network is working well when every computer can access the Internet, in addition to any local computers or printers on the network. When you cannot access one or all of these services, the network may not have been configured correctly, the DHCP server may have run out of IP addresses, or an Ethernet cable may have gone bad. If you have set up your server so that other computers can access it via your local network or remotely, you should be able to continue to access it, unless its hardware or software fails or the network hardware that connects it to other computers fails for some reason.

Troubleshooting network problems can take a bit of time, especially if you have dozens of computers connected to your local network. One of the best ways to approach network troubleshooting is to keep a list of known network issues, along with a list of network configurations, cables, and software settings to check. To find out more about troubleshooting computers, go to Part IV, "Troubleshooting DSL."

Some of the more common network problems that occur on a network involve IP addressing. For example, if a network relies on static IP addresses and a new computer wants to join the local network, but all the static IP addresses are in use, the new computer will not be able to access the Internet from the DSL network. Conversely, if a DHCP server is configured to only give out a certain number of IP addresses and all of the allocable addresses have been assigned, a new computer attempting to join the network will be unsuccessful until another computer disconnects from the network. One of the most common configuration problems arises when two computers are configured with the same static IP address. If two computers share the same IP address, the network router will not know which computer to send network data to. This can result is slower network performance or poor network performance for the two computers that are using the same IP address. Windows and Mac OS usually warn you if you enter an IP address that is already in use on the network. However, the operating system won't prevent the computer from trying to connect to the network.

Problems with Remote Administration

A server on your network may not be physically located near you. You may have a server set up off-site to improve network accessibility, to maintain service if, for instance, the power goes out at your office, or to keep a server system running for others who may use your network outside of your home or office. The biggest problem with remote servers is that if you have problems accessing the remote computer, you can't tell whether it crashed due to a software problem or someone has manually powered it off accidentally at the remote location.

SURVIVAL TIP

Some computers enable you to connect hardware controls so that you can power a computer off and on over the Internet. If you have a remote computer on your network, this type of hardware device may come to your rescue if you want to access or reset your computer after a power failure, or if you are unable to access the computer over the network.

Solutions for Sharing Files Across Platforms

If you're not sure which server you want to set up on the local network, pick a server that best meets the short term needs of the client computers on the local network. Install the server software and set up administrator, user, and if needed, group accounts on the server. Access the server from one or more different client operating systems and applications to see that the server is capable of providing adequate network performance. Allow the server to run for several days and if you like, several weeks. If the server software appears to perform consistently and reliably, you may want to keep it up and running on the local network. If it performs erratically or does not provide the services you expected, choose a different server solution and install and configure it to run on the local network. The following sections review a selected group of servers you can install on a Windows, Mac, or Linux computer.

Comparing Server Platforms

Windows 2000, Linux, and Mac OS X servers are capable of hosting a number of network services. Each is relatively easy to use, as far as servers go, and all provide services that are generally stable, reliable, and secure. Before you set up a server on your local network consider the client computers that will need to connect to it and what kinds of network services those client computers will need in general on the local network. The following tables contain a list of server features available for Mac OS X (see Table 13-2), Windows 2000 (see Table 13-3), and the Red Hat 7 Linux distribution (see Table 13-4). The column on the far right lists the client application needed in order to access a particular network service.

Service	Description	Client Program
File server	Share text or graphics files with Windows 2000 file server. Print server also available.	Windows, Mac, or Linux operating system
Web server	Host Web pages.	Windows, Mac, or Linux browser, such as Internet Explorer or Netscape Navigator
Media server	Share streaming audio or video files over the network.	Windows Media Player for Windows or Mac OS
Terminal server	Provide remote log in access to the Windows 2000 server. Manage a server from a remote network.	Windows 2000 or Windows XP
Network servers	Host a DHCP, router, or Windows Name Server.	Windows, Mac, or Linux
Mail server	Microsoft Exchange Server enables Windows or Macintosh computers running Outlook (Windows), Entourage (Mac), or Outlook Express (Windows or Mac) to send or receive e-mail messages. It can host mail services that support POP, SMTP, and IMAP.	Windows running Outlook or Outlook Express or Macintosh running Entourage, Outlook, or Outlook Express
Database server	Run a Structured Query Language (SQL) database server for database client applications or web applications.	Windows, Mac, or Linux database client or web browser

Table 13-2.   Windows 2000 Services

Service	Description	Client Program
File server	Share text and graphics files as an FTP TCP/IP or Apple Fileshare (AFP) Protocol server. Terminal services are also supported. You can use a telnet client to access the terminal server installed on the Linux computer.	Windows, Mac, or Linux operating system
Web server	Apache web server. Share HTML web pages. Also supports SSL, PHP, MySQL, JavaServer Pages, Java Servlets, Perl, Mac CGI, and Caching Web Proxy services.	Windows, Mac, or Linux computer running Netscape Navigator or Internet Explorer

Table 13-3.   Mac OS X Services

Service	Description	Client Program
Media server	QuickTime streaming server. Share audio and video files.	Windows or Macintosh computer running QuickTime Player
Network server	DHCP, DNS, and SLP services. Server Admin (TCP/IP), SSH, NetBoot services, NetInfo, and LDAP services.	Windows, Mac, or Linux operating system
Mail server	Host e-mail services that support POP, SMTP, and IMAP.	Windows, Mac, or Linux computer running an e-mail client that supports POP, SMTP, or IMAP
Print server	Printer sharing services for all platforms.	Windows or Macintosh operating system

Table 13-3. Mac OS X Services (*continued*)

Service	Description	Client Program
File server	Share text and graphics files by running an FTP server on the Linux computer. Terminal services are also supported. You can use a telnet client to access the terminal server installed on the Linux computer.	FTP client program on a Windows, Mac, or Linux computer
Web server	Apache web server. Share HTML web pages. Also supports SSL, PHP, MySQL, JavaServer Pages, Java Servlets, Perl, Mac CGI, and Caching Web Proxy services.	Netscape Navigator on a Linux system, or Windows or Mac, or browser, such as IE or Netscape
Mail server	Host e-mail services that support POP, SMTP, and IMAP.	E-mail client program that support POP, SMTP, or IMAP
Network server	Host dynamic IP addressing with a DHCP server.	Windows, Mac, or Linux operating system
Name server	Collect and broadcast computer names and IP addresses with a Domain Name Server.	Windows, Mac, or Linux operating system
Database erver	Share data with an SQL database client application or as shared data with a web site.	Windows, Mac, or Linux database client or web browser

Table 13-4. Red Hat Linux Services

Installing Windows 2000 Terminal Server

A terminal server enables you to log into a remote server and access software controls as if you were sitting in front of that computer. Linux and Mac OS X servers provide this form of access through a telnet server. If the telnet server is running, you can run a telnet program installed on a Windows, Mac OS, or Linux client and log into the server over a local or remote network connection. Windows 2000 server has a terminal server feature that provides services similar to the telnet server.

One way you can use a terminal server is to install it alongside any other Windows 2000 server, such as a file or Web server. If you install the remote administration mode of the terminal server, you can manage a server remotely should any problems occur with the server. For example, you can set up a backup server along with a terminal server on the same computer. If you want to monitor or access backed up files over the local network, simply log in as the remote administrator and check the backup file directories to see if the latest scheduled backups have been running.

There are two ways you can configure a Windows 2000 terminal server: with remote or applications level access. Remote access allows you to access all Windows settings and any applications installed on the computer. Applications server mode enables you to access specific programs installed on the computer from a Windows, Mac, or Linux system. The following steps show you how to install the Terminal Services for Remote Administration mode on a Windows 2000 server:

1. Open the Configure Your Server window and click the Terminal Services link, located below the Application Server section of the main window.

2. Read the onscreen information about the terminal services and click Start if you want to set up a terminal server on your Windows 2000 computer. A terminal server can be used to set up different access levels to a computer, in addition to hosting file sharing, Web sharing, or media sharing services.

3. Select the Application Server link from the Configuration window. The Windows Components wizard, shown in Figure 13-13, will open. Check the Terminal Services check box and click Next.

4. The Terminal Services Setup window will appear.

5. Select Remote Administration Mode, as shown in Figure 13-14, if you want to set up administrator accounts for this server on the network.

As mentioned previously, you can set up a terminal server so that only certain applications installed on the Windows 2000 server are accessible remotely. This mode is called Application Server mode. Perform the following steps to set up the terminal server to run in Application Server mode.

1. Open the Configure Your Server window and click on the Terminal Services link.

2. Click Next and follow the remaining onscreen instructions to set up the terminal server.

3. Wait for the files to install on your Windows 2000 Server.

4. Create administrator and user accounts on the computer and log into each account and see which files and folders you can limit or open access to on the server.

If you're able to use the terminal services from your local network, you should be able to access it remotely from another network connecting to the terminal server over the Internet.

After the terminal server has been installed, reboot the computer and log into the terminal server. If you're running the file server or the Web server, start each service. Then log out of the server and leave the computer powered on. Test the servers by accessing the file and Web servers with a Windows client computer that is also connected to the same network. Log into each server as a standard user account and copy and remove files from the server. Then log into the same server with your terminal server administrator account.

Setting Up Media Servers

Another kind of server you can set up on your network is a media server. Media and streaming media servers tend to require more network bandwidth in order to serve audio or video files

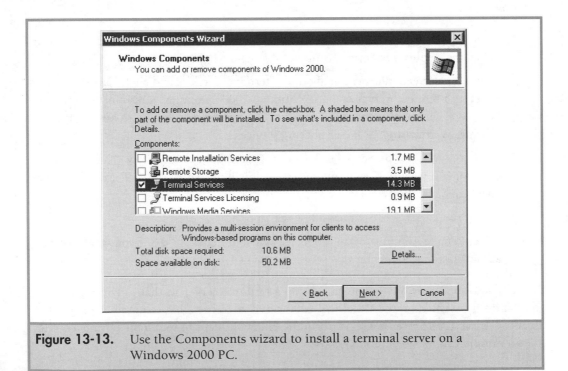

Figure 13-13. Use the Components wizard to install a terminal server on a Windows 2000 PC.

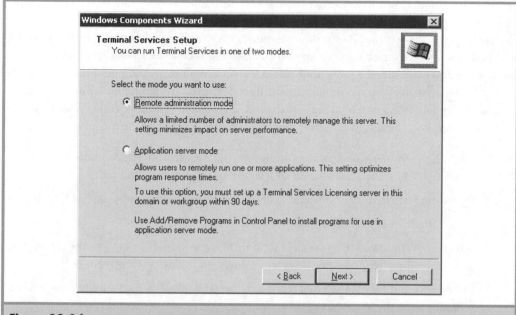

Figure 13-14. Select the Remote Administration mode option to enable you to log into the Windows 2000 server over the Internet.

to their clients. Windows 2000 Server enables you to set up a media server or a streaming media server on a PC. Media servers enable you to copy or play audio and video multimedia files on a client computer on your network. You can either view a media file by opening it from the server or copy one or more files to your local computer's hard drive.

If you want to share media files but do not want each media file to be copied to every computer on your network, you can set up a streaming media file server. Streaming media enables a client running a browser to view animation and video media files by downloading part of the media file over the network. The actual file is never copied to the client.

SURVIVAL TIP To find out more about accessing a media server using a browser application on a client computer, go to Chapter 8.

Setting Up a Streaming Media Server

If you like creating multimedia files, you can set up a media file server to share files over the Internet. You may also find QuickTime, MPEG, or MP3 media files as you surf the network. If you stumble upon a media file that allows you to create a copy and share it on your own network, you can add the media file to your local network. Playing media files from a local server will usually result in smoother playback performance than if you need to rely on an Internet connection to access that same file.

You can set up server access to allow computers on your network to view streaming video and audio in a browser or set up a streaming media server with a Windows 2000 computer. You can embed a streaming media file on a Web page and post it to a Linux or Mac OS X Apache Web server, or you can set up a dedicated streaming media server with a computer that has Windows 2000 Server installed. If you have Windows 2000 server installed on a computer, you can install the streaming media server by performing the following steps.

1. Click the Start menu and choose Configure Your Server from the Administrative Tools menu list. Click the Media Server link in the configuration window.

2. Select the Streaming Media Server. The Windows Components Wizard will open.

3. Check the Windows Media Services checkbox.

4. Select the Windows Media Services item from the window list to view the amount of disk space the streaming media server requires on the network server.

5. Click Next and follow the onscreen instructions to install the streaming media server software onto the Windows 2000 server.

6. Start the server software on the computer and try to access and play a streaming media file from the media server to see whether you can successfully play it on your desktop or laptop computer.

Media Files and Media Players

New versions of media player software arrive at least once a year. Most newer versions are capable of playing media files created with previous versions of the media software. As newer media players become available, you may need to add newer versions of media files that will work only with the latest version of the media player. If you have access to a free media player, such as Windows Media Player, you may want to set up a Web page or a shortcut to Microsoft's media player server so that those visiting your Web site can download the latest media player, which will enable them to view the media files they download from your media servers. Table 13-5 contains a list of media files, along with the media players you can use to view or edit the media files.

To find out more about streaming media files, go to Chapter 8.

SURVIVAL TIP

Media Files	Media Players
Audio .wmp files	Windows Media Player
Video .wmp files	Windows Media Player
MPEG 2 video files	Windows Media Player
Motion graphics and animation	Macromedia Flash Player
Shockwave Flash audio files	Macromedia Flash Player
QuickTime audio and video files	QuickTime Media Player
MP3 audio files	Windows Media Player, QuickTime Player

Table 13-5. Media Files and the Media Players That Can Be Used to Modify Them or Play Them Back

Setting Up a Windows 2000 Print Server

If you have one or two printers on your local network and want to be able to reprioritize print jobs or start or stop any print jobs that are being sent to a printer, you can configure a Windows 2000 Server computer to act as a print server on a network. Any document that is sent to the printer will first arrive at the print server. If a print job has problems printing or for some reason can't be processed by the printer, you can go to the print server and remove the print job, allowing other documents to proceed that are waiting in line to be printed.

You can set up a print server from the Configure Your Server window by performing the following steps.

1. Click the Start menu, choose Administrative Tools, and choose Configure Your Server to open the Configure Your Server window.

2. Click the Print Server link to view a brief description of the print server.

3. Click the Start link to add a local or network printer to the print server.

4. Click the Manage Printers link to view any printers that are already configured with the Windows PC.

After you complete the print server installation, use another computer to send a print job to the printer that is connected to the print server. You may want to try stopping or pausing the print job from another computer on the network to test different software features of the print server.

Sharing Files Across Platforms

If you have FTP software installed on a Linux computer, you can host an FTP server on the local network. Windows, Mac OS, and Linux systems are all capable of accessing an FTP server if you install an FTP client program. Setting up an FTP server is probably the easiest way to share files across Mac, Windows, and Unix computer platforms. You can also set up a Web server on the local network to create a cross-platform file-sharing server.

A Windows 2000 server can make a great Mac and Windows-friendly file server. Any Windows or Mac OS client computers can store or access files stored on the Windows 2000 server. Use the Choose or Network Browser to access a file server on a Mac OS 9 computer. You can open a browser window and type \\<*name of file server*> in the Address text field to access a Windows file server on the local network.

NOTE

If you want to add more security to a Macintosh connecting to a Windows 2000 file server, you can install Microsoft's User Authentication Module (UAM) file on each Macintosh computer. UAM provides a Mac with a more secure connection with a Windows 2000 file server. Figure 13-15 shows the UAM file you can install on a Mac.

Apple's AppleShare server software can turn a Mac OS 9 computer into a file share server. Sharing files is a two-step process. First identify the files you want to share, and then move them into a folder on the server's hard drive. Then configure the users and groups and the access privileges you want each user to have for the server. Table 13-6 lists some of the cross-platform file server products available. You can also share files with Windows, Mac OS, and Linux computers with a Mac OS X file server.

NOTE

If you have a Macintosh computer running AppleShare and AppleShare IP server software, you can install Thursby's TSSTalk on a Windows computer to access the Macintosh file server.

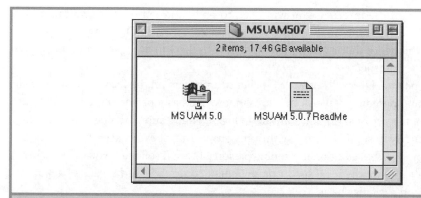

Figure 13-15. Install the MS UAM file on a Macintosh file server to enable a Macintosh computer to access Windows 2000 files on a network.

Servers and Security Issues

If you have a firewall set up on the local network, computers located outside the local network will not be able to access servers connected to the local network. This is a good thing if you only want client computers on the local network to access these servers. However, if you want

Product	Client Platform
Mac OS 9 AppleShare IP Server Mac OS X Server	Software runs on Mac OS 9. Any IP-configured computer such as a Mac OS 9, Mac OS X, Windows, Unix, or Linux client can log into the AppleShare server.
Windows 2000 Server	Windows 95, 98, NT, 2000, XP can connect to the Windows host. Macs and Linux computers running the appropriate browser or other client software can also connect to a Windows 2000 server.
Linux FTP Server Apache Web Server	Various Linux distributions such as Red Hat, SuSE, Caldera, and Mandrake can install a Linux client. Windows and Mac OS clients can also connect to this Unix-based server. Any of these platforms running a telnet or ftp client or a browser can connect to the FTP or Web server.

Table 13-6. Cross-Platform File Server Software Products

to host a web server on the Internet, you will need to open a hole in the firewall to allow network traffic to flow from the Internet into the local area network. Opening up your local network to Internet network traffic can potentially allow hackers to access computers on your local network via the Internet.

You can install personal firewall software on client computers on the local network to help monitor incoming and outgoing network traffic. Windows XP has a personal firewall built into it. You can configure the personal firewall software to log incoming and outgoing network traffic. Check the logs regularly to see if you can identify any suspicious network activity entering or leaving the client computer. In addition to running personal firewall software, you can also install virus protection software on the local server or any client computers and create a backup of any important files on a regular basis.

If a server or client computer crashes or reboots, check the computer for any viruses or trojan horses before bringing the client or server back up on the network. In order a trojan horse to run on a computer, it must first terminate the running application it wants to replace. Therefore the computer must crash or reboot in order for the trojan horse to run on a computer. Of course, computer hardware and software that is free of viruses and trojan horses can also crash. Be sure to check the computer logs, and the creation and modification dates of any software that become problematic after a computer exhibits odd behavior after being connected to a network.

Additional Resources

As your home or business network grows, one of the best ways to minimize file duplication and optimize your network's performance is to add dedicated file, web, or media servers to your local network. This chapter touched on a few possible servers you can add to your DSL network. You can find out more about DSL hosting services and server products at the following Web sites:

+ www.microsoft.com/windows

+ www.microsoft.com/windows2000/server

+ www.apple.com/macosxserver

+ www.apple.com/macosx

+ www.linux.org

+ www.redhat.com

+ www.xo.com

Part IV

Troubleshooting DSL

Chapter 14

Reviewing Your Network and Account Information

Troubleshooting computers connected to a DSL network is not much different than troubleshooting computers connected to other star hub–based networks or broadband networks. Telephone company– and phone-line–related problems, of course, will be unique to your home or office location and telephone line service provider. A computer network that relies on DSL service for its Internet connection follows the same processes for gathering information about network problems, and troubleshooting and solving network problems as other computer networks. Finding the root cause of a network problem can take time, or the problem may mysteriously solve itself. The chapters in this part review your DSL account information as a starting point for troubleshooting networks, computers, and virtual network connections.

It's possible to set up a home or office network that requires minimal maintenance and monitoring. This can be a small network with one or two computers and a printer. Unfortunately, it is pretty common to spend quite a bit of time troubleshooting network issues when you first bring up a local area network. There are four general steps you can follow to help diagnose and repair network problems: First, identify the problem. Then isolate it to one or two computers on the network. Then determine what needs to be done to fix the network problem. Finally, test the computers and other network services after you have implemented the fix.

The following chapters show you how to troubleshoot networks, computers, and virtual private network connections. This chapter shows you how to review your DSL account information and use it to review and troubleshoot your network setup. Knowing how the computers on your network are configured can help you more efficiently identify a network problem.

- ✦ **DSL modem and firmware information**   Review the features of your DSL modem.

- ✦ **Troubleshoot DSL modem connections**   If you have a point-to-point, bridged, or router connection, take a look at potential connection issues and ways to troubleshoot and solve them.

- ✦ **Modify your DSL account**   Access your DSL account settings on your service provider's Web site and customize your DSL account.

DSL Account Basic Concepts

DSL service providers can offer a range of plans, contracts, or packages for home and business owners. In addition to the DSL modem, each service provider provides some form of Web-based access for your e-mail accounts. In most cases, you will not get to choose the DSL modem that gets installed in your home or office. However, you can work with your

DSL provider to configure, troubleshoot, and if necessary replace your DSL modem. The following sections introduce you to some of the modem characteristics commonly found in basic and advanced DSL modems, and they describe a couple of different scenarios for Web accounts offered with basic or advanced DSL service.

Identifying Your DSL Modem

DSL modems come in many makes and models, with varying features. Most providers have a basic package designed for one computer or IP address that relies on a DSL modem to create and sustain a Point-to-Point Protocol over Ethernet connection to the Internet. DSL packages that support multiple computers use a DSL modem that can act as a router or bridge to the local computers on your home or business network. These larger-scale packages are capable of supporting static or dynamic IP addresses on your local network.

A Brief Tour of DSL Modems

Three basic kinds of DSL modems are available. The type of DSL modem that is installed depends on the type of DSL service you subscribe to. The following list provides a short description of each of the three kinds of DSL modems that may be installed with a DSL service:

✦ **Point-to-point**   A basic DSL modem that enables one or two computers to create a point-to-point connection to the DSL provider's network.

✦ **Router**   A more sophisticated DSL modem that can have a limited or wide range of network-related features. The DSL modem router acts as the gateway to the Internet for the local network. Most DSL modem routers also have firewall, DHCP, and filtering options.

✦ **Bridge**   A type of DSL modem that joins a local network with the DSL provider's network.

Setting Up a PPPoE Connection

DSL modems all look pretty much the same. Most DSL modems are no larger than traditional analog modems, except DSL modems have Ethernet and phone line ports, in addition to several lights on the front panel. Basic models can look nearly identical to advanced models. Figure 14-1 shows an Alcatel DSL modem, which is a dial-up DSL modem for a basic account. Figure 14-2 shows the Flowpoint DSL modem, which provides a router connection to the Internet. At a glance both models look similar, but they work quite differently from each other.

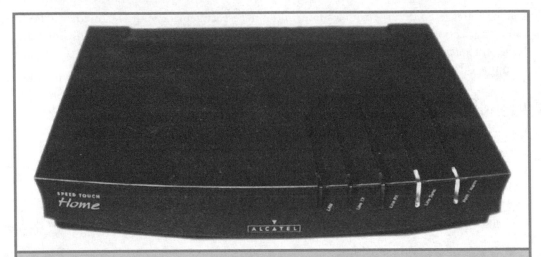

Figure 14-1. The Alcatel Speed Touch modem enables you to connect to a basic DSL service over a point-to-point connection.

Both units have a power supply, phone and Ethernet connection ports at the rear of the modem, and several lights located on the front of the box. You won't really know what kinds of features are available on a modem unless you visit the DSL modem vendor's Web site and review the modem's product information.

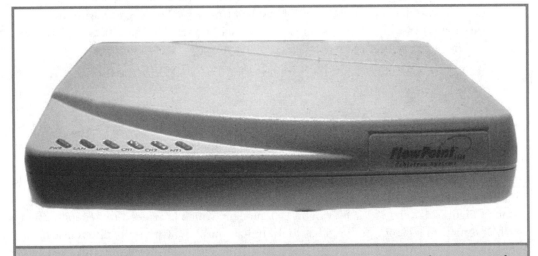

Figure 14-2. This Flowpoint DSL modem provides a router connection to the Internet and can be configured with additional features, such as a firewall or DHCP server.

The DSL provider will install the DSL modem and connect it to the phone line in your home or office. If your phone line uses a splitterless service, look for a filter (see Figure 14-3) connected to each voice phone line. To recap, a splittterless service enables the DSL provider to set up DSL services without requiring the local phone company (CO) to modify the copper wire to your home or office. The DSL line will not require any modification. However, each voice, fax or phone-reliant device will need to have a splitter installed on the phone line in order to work with the splitterless DSL service. Take a look at how the technician installs the splitter and make note of which connector the DSL line is plugged into. If the phone company has installed a splitter in your home's or office's phone box, you will not need to install a filter for the DSL or voice connection.

Depending on the type of plan you sign up for, you may need to connect your computer on your own or walk through the setup process with the technician. After your DSL modem has been installed, visit the DSL provider's Web site and create an account there. Some providers require you to phone in from the DSL line as part of the authentication process. Another way of activating a DSL modem is to type in an activation code for your account from the provider's Web site.

After you have created your DSL account for a PPPoE connection, you need to set up your computer to dial into the DSL service (see Figure 14-4). Most newer operating systems, such as Windows XP, and Mac OS X, have PPPoE software installed along with the operating

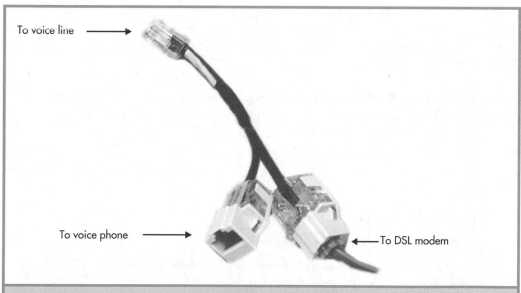

To voice line ⟶

To voice phone ⟶   ⟵ To DSL modem

Figure 14-3.   Splitterless DSL services do not require the DSL connection to be modified. however, this particular splitter must be added to each telephone or voice-reliant device connected to a phone line in the home or office.

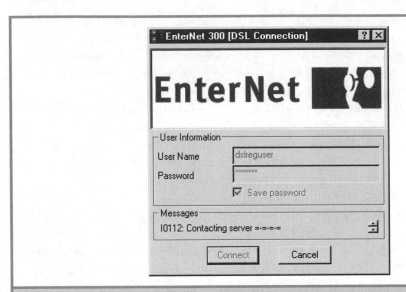

Figure 14-4. The first time you access the Internet with your DSL modem, you may need to authenticate your phone line and account with your DSL service provider.

system. You can easily configure a computer to connect to a DSL provider's PPPoE service using these versions of Windows and Mac OS. However you may also need to install the DSL service provider's custom PPPoE application onto the computer regardless of the operating system installed on the computer.

Accessing Windows XP PPPoE Software Settings   You can use the network connection wizard to create the initial PPPoE settings on the Windows XP computer. Double-click the My Network places icon, and then double-click the Create a new network icon in the Network Connections window to start the network connection wizard. Follow the onscreen instructions to configure your PPPoE connection. To access the PPPoE settings on a Windows XP computer, perform the following steps.

1. Click on Start to view the Start menu.

2. Select Control Panel from the Start menu.

3. Choose PPPoE Service from the Control Panel window. Windows XP will connect the computer to the DSL service provider.

Accessing Mac OS X PPPoE Software Settings   You can set up and modify the PPPoE settings from the Network settings window in Mac OS X. You may want to compare the account information for the DSL service to the settings on the Mac OS X computer. To configure PPPoE on a Mac OS X computer, perform the following steps.

1. Click on the System Preferences icon in the Dock or choose System Preferences from the Apple menu.

2. Click on the Network icon. The Network window will open.

3. Select the PPPoE tab in the Network window. The PPPoE settings will appear in the Network window.

4. Check the Connect using PPPoE check box.

5. Type in the service provider, PPPoE service name, account name and password for the DSL account and configure the PPPoE settings for your DSL provider.

6. Click on the PPPoE Options button to view Session and Advanced Options. Check a checkbox to activate any option you like. Then click OK to save your changes.

7. Click on the Save button to save your changes.

8. Click on the Close box to exit the Network settings window.

On a Windows computer, you can set up a dial-up network connection similar to creating a remote access account. If you have a Macintosh computer, you can create a dial-up account using Apple's Remote Access control panel or set up your DSL account with third-party PPP over Ethernet software. Although the DSL provider enables you to connect to the Internet 24 hours a day, you may be required to type in your login name and password if your computer connection is inactive for some period of time.

CAUTION   Different DSL vendors provide different DSL modems for their customers. Before signing up for a service, make sure your computer meets the system requirements for the service plan you're signing up for. The system requirements can help determine whether your computer is compatible with the DSL modem that will be installed in your home or office.

Setting Up a DSL Router or Bridge

You can connect a single computer directly to a DSL modem, or connect a small network of computers to a DSL modem router via a star topology hub. Both types of DSL modem configurations can connect a computer to the Internet. The DSL modem enables any computer that can be recognized by the DSL provider's network to access the Internet. Power on the DSL modem to activate the router or bridge connection. The DSL provider usually programs the IP address for the router or bridge into the DSL modem. If this IP address changes, you will need to log into the DSL modem and change the IP address settings for the router or bridge.

Once the DSL modem is powered on, you can set up one or more computers to access the Internet. You must type a valid static IP address or set up the DSL modem to assign a DHCP address to each computer on the local network. When the computer powers on, it will be connected to the network. Start a browser program and visit a Web site on the Internet to test the DSL connection to the Internet.

Connecting Your DSL Modem to the Internet

After you have created your DSL account for a PPPoE connection, you need to set up your computer to dial into the DSL service. On a Windows computer, you can set up a dial-up network connection much as you would create a remote access account. If you have a Macintosh computer, you can create a dial-up account using Apple's Remote Access control panel or set up your DSL account with third-party PPP over Ethernet software.

Your Windows or Macintosh computer should be configured to accept a dynamic IP address. Each time your computer dials into the DSL service, the DSL provider will assign your computer a new IP address, which enables your computer to complete its connection to the Internet. Once a computer is connected to the Internet, you can test the connection by trying to load a Web page, or by sending yourself an e-mail message.

NOTE

A PPPoE connection is a point-to-point connection to the DSL provider's network. While the modem and computer remain powered on, the DSL service may require you to enter your login name and password if your computer connection becomes inactive for some period of time.

If you have a DSL modem that is set up to function as a bridge or router (like the unit shown in earlier Figure 14-2), you should be able to power on the modem and connect it to the hub on your network. You can view the lights on the DSL modem case to see if any network activity is able to cause the light to blink. Some modems indicate that network traffic is reaching a hub or modem by flashing an indicator light. If none of the lights on the modem are lit, you may want to check the power supply connection and make sure the modem is connected to a power source.

CAUTION Some DSL service providers enable you to use a regular voice phone to dial into your account. This is a backup dial-up account that you can use if you want to check your e-mail while you're away from your home or office network.

A DSL modem that connects as a router or bridge to the DSL provider's network does not require any computer on your network to dial up to establish a connection. If you have a single computer connected to the DSL modem, it remains connected to the network as long as it is powered on. If the DSL modem is connected to a star hub, each of the computers can access the Internet via the DSL modem/router.

In order for a computer to access the Internet via a DSL modem/router, it must have a unique IP address. If you subscribed to a DSL package that provides a static IP address, type the IP address into the computer you want to connect to the Internet. If the DSL account works with a dynamic IP address supplied by the DSL provider, you must configure the computer with the DSL provider's DHCP configuration before the computer can connect to the DSL provider's network.

CAUTION Check your DSL provider's terms and conditions to find out if your account is capable of allowing more than one computer to share the DSL modem account to access the Internet. Some providers may not mind, while others may discourage sharing an account.

If you want to set up a DHCP server for the local network, you may need to check with your service provider to find out if your DSL modem is set up as a DHCP server. If it is, make sure the local network does not have another DHCP running. You want only one DHCP server running on the local network. You need to configure the network settings for a Windows or Macintosh computer to be recognized by the Ethernet network.

If you have a Windows 2000 computer, you can view the TCP/IP settings for the Ethernet card by performing the following steps.

1. Right-click the Ethernet network interface card icon and choose Properties from the shortcut menu.

2. Select Internet Protocol (TCP/IP) from the window list.

3. Click the Properties button. If the DSL modem is configured to assign an IP address, click the Obtain an IP Address Automatically radio button.

4. Click OK in each of the windows to save your changes.

The following steps show you how to access the DHCP settings on a Mac OS 9 computer.

1. Open the TCP/IP control panel.

2. Choose Ethernet from the Connect Via pop-up menu located at the top of the TCP/IP control panel window.

3. Choose DHCP from the Configure pop-up menu.

4. Click the Close box of the control panel window and then click Save in the dialog box.

Testing Your Internet Connection

There are many ways to check the hardware aspects of your network connection. The first thing to do is to make sure the DSL modem and each computer connected to it, as well as any network devices located on the network, are powered on. Some Ethernet cards have a green or red indicator light. Usually, that it lights up signifies that the card can communicate with the hub or that it is receiving network data. Some hubs also have a green light that blinks when network traffic passes through a port in the hub.

NOTE   If you have a Windows, Mac OS X, or Linux computer, you can ping the DSL modem to see if it is running. Type **ping *<IP address of the DSL modem>*.** Press ENTER or RETURN and wait for the DSL modem to respond to the ping. If it doesn't respond, you may need to reset the DSL mode or check the network cabling going to the modem.

The best way to test your Internet network connection is to start an application that can access another computer on the Internet. For instance, you can start AOL Instant Messenger and see if you can send a message to one of your online buddies. Another way to test your network connection is to start a browser program and try loading a Web site, such as www.cnn.com. You can also send an e-mail message to yourself. If each of these tests meets with success, your computer is all set to work on the Internet.

While your computer is powered on, the network actively recognizes it. Some computers support a sleep, or low-power, mode. You can press the SPACEBAR or move the mouse to wake a computer from sleep. If you want the computer to be aware of network activity while it is asleep, you can configure the sleep options to reconnect to a server or wake from sleep if the computer receives information over the network. You can also set the computer to disable network connections while it is sleeping. If you have your computer in this mode, the computer must be on in order for e-mail applications to check automatically for new messages.

When you're not using your computer, I recommend putting it into standby (Windows) or sleep (Macintosh) mode or powering it off. When a computer is asleep, or in standby mode, the operating system and programs remain on, but the computer is no longer recognized by the network.

Checking Your DSL Account Information

Most DSL providers rely on their installation technicians to set up your computer and make sure it can connect to the Internet when they set up your DSL modem. However, not all providers may do this. Some providers have self-install plans, where the technician is only responsible for setting up the modem and providing PPPoE driver software for your computer. If you have problems getting a computer to connect to the Internet, pull out your DSL account information and make sure you've entered the correct network information into your computer before you call the DSL provider's support team.

Reviewing Billing and Network Information

Before the phone company or DSL provider sets up an appointment with you to install your DSL service, you should receive some sort of account summary. The type of account, along with any IP address, e-mail, or hosting information will be in this e-mail document. Review the billing information and check to see if the account that you have signed up for matches the services and billing information on the DSL provider's letter or Web site.

The information for your DSL account may consist of some of the items in the following list. The wide area network (WAN) information pertains to the IP information for the DSL provider. The local area network (LAN) is your account information:

✦ **WAN information**   This may consist of one or two IP addresses unique to the provider. You may need to use these IP addresses if you have another local network router that you want to connect to the DSL provider's network

✦ **LAN information**   This information can applied to any computer on your network. You might want to try mapping your account information to each computer on your local network to see how much of your DSL account will be online.

✦ **DHCP IP address range**   This includes IP addresses that will be dynamically allocated by the DSL modem to computers on the local network.

✦ **Static IP address range**   This includes IP addresses you can enter into each computer to manually configure it.

✦ **Router LAN address**   If your DSL modem can be configured as a router, this is the IP address of the DSL modem. You can input this address as the default Gateway (Windows), or Router Address (Mac) on each computer on your local network.

✦ **Subnet mask**   Type this number into each computer on your local network so that it will be recognized by the DSL provider's network.

✦ **Domain name servers**   Most service providers make available two domain name server addresses for each account. Type both into each computer's TCP/IP control panel. These name servers are used by computers on the local network to locate other computers on the Internet.

✦ **E-mail server information**   Most DSL plans provide at least one e-mail address as part of the basic plan. There is usually a limit to the amount of e-mail you can store on the provider's mail server. You can set up your e-mail application to delete messages after they have been downloaded from your mail server. Most mail clients are set up to send and receive e-mail with POP3 and SMTP protocols on the mail server. You may also be able to download newsgroup messages from a news server to your hard drive.

✦ **SMTP and POP3**   The SMTP mail server setting enables you to send e-mail from your computer and the DSL provider's mail server to other mail servers on the Internet. The POP3 mail setting enables you to receive e-mail received by the DSL provider's mail server. You can enter these mail server settings into each e-mail account you create in an e-mail application, such as Outlook, Entourage, Netscape Messenger, or Eudora.

✦ **News**   A newsgroup is an online message board. There are thousands of newsgroups you can visit and post messages to from the Internet. If newsgroup services are available as part of your service plan, you can enter the name of the news server into your browser or newsgroup application.

SURVIVAL TIP

The safest way to connect your DSL Ethernet modem and computer together is to power off each device and then connect them together, either directly or to a hub. Power on the DSL modem and the computer in no particular order. Then try to connect to the Internet. Once the two devices are connected, you can power off the computer when you've finished using it, but you can leave the modem on. If the DSL modem is also connected to a USB or parallel port, connect the USB or parallel cable to the computer and then connect the USB device to the Ethernet port on the DSL modem.

Logging into Your DSL Web Account

Web access services vary from one DSL provider to another. Some providers enable you to view your billing information, customize your e-mail account settings, or add new DSL services to your plan. When you sign up for your DSL account, you should receive a URL to your DSL provider's Web site. Login requirements will vary from site to site. Some providers may require you to log in with your mail account information, while others may require you to create a separate e-mail account to access your DSL account information and settings.

To log into your DSL account, visit your provider's Web site. Follow the onscreen instructions and either create a new account or type a valid login and password. If your login is successful, you should see a main menu page. The settings available on this page will vary from provider to provider. You should be able to access your e-mail account, read support information for the service provider, and view account options or provider specials. Some provider Web sites enable you to visit message boards or chat rooms hosted by the provider if you want to participate in online support or help others troubleshoot their DSL problems.

Problems with Your DSL Account

Your DSL account represents information about you, combined with a set of IP addressing information that can put your computers on the Internet. For the most part, this information will not change unless you move, change your name, or change your DSL plan. However, it is possible for your DSL billing or IP addressing information to change without your request or as the result of more than one person calling the provider to make changes.

Aside from tracking the written information on your account, as you use your DSL service, you may encounter new phone-related issues that may need to be addressed by either the phone company or the service provider. Some of the potential problems you may encounter may be related to other systems in your home or office, such as a phone-based security system, or a wiring problem in one room. The following sections describe a few problems that you may find as you use your DSL services.

DSL and Your Home Phone System

Your DSL connection to the Internet relies on the phone line installed in your home or office. Before you sign up with a DSL provider, you should talk to the DSL service provider to find out what types of DSL service are available to your site. If your home or office has an alarm system, you should let the DSL provider know before you choose a subscription or have the splitter installed. If the quality of the voice phone seems to suffer significantly after the installation, check with the DSL provider. Depending on the installation policies of the service provider, you may need to pay an additional fee to remove the DSL equipment. The following sections highlight a few sources of connection and compatibility problems with your DSL service and your home's or office's phone system.

Connection and Performance Problems

Your DSL-based Internet connection is only as reliable as the phone lines that are wired into your home or office. If the voice phone system at your site is unreliable, chances are your DSL line will not be reliable either. Some of the symptoms you may experience include slow network performance and error messages indicating problems connecting to an Internet server, such as a mail server or a Web site.

If you pick up your voice phone (and I don't mean a wireless one), you should hear a clear dial tone. If you hear static, that particular phone line may have poor reception, or the local phone system may be under repair or have some other problem. In general, the quality of your voice phone line should not change after the phone line has been split to support DSL. If you notice problems with the quality of your voice phone after the DSL modem has been installed, you will probably need to call your local phone company (your incumbent local exchange carrier, or ILEC) to take a look at the DSL installation and diagnose the state of the phone line and connection.

In addition to the phone company, your DSL-based Internet connection relies on the computers and equipment owned by the DSL service provider to keep your local computer or local network connected to the Internet. Depending on whether you've signed up with a local phone company or a DSL provider, you may need to call one or two different companies to track down the status of your DSL network should problems arise.

SURVIVAL TIP

If your modem or computer is on and seems to be working fine, but neither device is responding to network activity, power off each device. Then power both devices back on again. Resetting the modem and computer can help renew the IP address for each device.

Compatibility Issues with Phone Alarm Systems and DSL Services

Depending on the type of alarm you have installed, you may need to rewire the cable that connects the alarm system to the DSL jack, or you may not need to do anything at all. When a DSL service is installed in your home or office, the technicians only focus on bringing up the Internet connection to your location. Some providers may require the technician to also set up and connect a computer to the Internet before leaving. If you have a security or communications system installed on your home phone line, it's up to you to make sure it's still running properly after the phone company and DSL provider have split the line and installed the DSL modem.

Solutions for Your DSL Account

After you have set up your DSL account and connected one or more computers to the Internet, monitor the network performance and reliability of the DSL services on your computer or local network. If the DSL service meets your needs and provides reliable Internet access, you may want to upgrade your DSL service to support additional computers or host a server on your local network. The following sections provide a few suggestions for modifying your DSL account.

Changing Your DSL Account

After you've tested your Internet connection, you may want to customize your account password, or personalize your e-mail settings. Most DSL providers give you access to a Web account in addition to your DSL and mail accounts. Account services vary from provider to provider. If you're not sure how to access your Web account, you can probably find out by visiting your DSL service provider's Web site. The following sections will show you how to change your DSL account options and settings.

Changing Modems

Most DSL providers do not offer much of a variety of modems to choose from. Also, DSL modems are not like computers: new models are not introduced on a regular basis. However, DSL modems are changing as existing services change and new DSL services are brought online. If the DSL modem that's installed in your home is having problems establishing a reliable connection, or if it has some sort of software conflict with your PC or Mac, contact the DSL service provider's support center online. They will try to troubleshoot the connection or compatibility problems with your current setup, and if another modem is available, they may be able to substitute it to see if it solves the problem.

A more likely scenario is that you want to grow your DSL service from a basic service to a more sophisticated local area network connection. This type of service upgrade will probably involve changing a point-to-point DSL modem to a DSL modem that can serve as a router or bridge to the Internet. Check with your DSL service provider to find out how to upgrade your DSL service and potentially upgrade your modem, too.

Reconfiguring Your Modem

Most DSL modems that provide router and bridge functions enable you to log into the modem over the local network, or over the Internet. Your DSL provider can also access the settings in the DSL modem and customize your local network setup if you do not want to manually change the DSL modem settings. To log into the DSL modem, you will need the user name and password for the modem. You can get this information from your DSL service provider.

Log into the DSL modem from your local network. You can use a telnet application on a Windows, Linux, or Macintosh computer to log into the modem, which uses a command line interface. Type **help** to view a list of commands for the modem. You can view or modify its settings, as well as save or delete settings. For example, you can turn the firewall, DHCP, or NAT features on or off by typing the appropriate commands into the telnet window. Be careful! If you want to modify the DSL modem settings, be sure to write down the current settings before changing anything. It is possible to misconfigure the modem and prevent your local network from accessing the Internet.

Hosting a Web Server on Your DSL Network

You may also want to grow your network by hosting a file, Web, print, or mail server. Before you sign up with a DSL service provider, check to see if the provider allows you to run 24-hour host servers from your local network. Some providers or plans may not provide this option, and others may require you to upgrade your subscription to the DSL provider to access some of these services. Some providers may embrace Web hosting and offer e-commerce solutions for Web servers, enabling your Web site to process electronic purchases.

Upgrading Network Services

If you decide to grow the number of computers on your home or office network, you may eventually hit a wall or two (sorry for the pun)! Setting up one computer to connect to the DSL modem is fairly straightforward. If you don't mind extending a cable through a hallway, or across a doorway, it can be pretty easy to set up your first computer with the DSL modem. However, if you want to reduce the probability of having someone pull an Ethernet cable out of a hub, or your computer, or the DSL modem, you will need to either tape down Ethernet cables or have these cables installed inside the walls of your home or office. Fortunately, if you don't want to choose a wired networking solution, you have the option to go wireless, too.

Rewiring Part of Your Home

Whether you decide to build the Ethernet cable and hubs into the walls of your home or office is up to you. Opening a wall to pass cables along or through walls can be an expensive, if not messy, job. Be sure to review the blueprints for your home or office before attempting to punch a hole into or through a wall. It's possible to do more harm than good if you mistakenly punch a hole in a load-bearing wall or beam.

At least part of your home network will be wired. In order to connect your DSL modem to a local network, you'll need at least three Ethernet cables, one to connect the DSL modem to the star hub, another to connect a computer to the hub, and a third to connect the base station to the hub. You may also have a printer connected to the star hub, in addition to other computers, such as servers or network bridges or routers.

One thing to keep in mind when wiring your home or office is to try to keep the length of each cable to a minimum. Keeping the overall distance of the network to a moderate amount of wiring can help your network run more reliably. Of course, this doesn't mean you should make a cable too short and risk breaking or losing the connection to the network interface card or hub.

Setting Up Wireless Internet Access

Wireless networks were introduced a few years ago and have become extremely popular for both home and business networks. A wireless network requires a wireless hub, or access point. Apple's Base Station was one of the first wireless hubs introduced, along with the iBook in 1999. The wireless access point can be connected to an Ethernet star hub or to a phone line. Each computer must have a wireless PC card that is compatible with the software in the wireless hub in order to connect to it and access the network.

The wireless access point has a general range of about 100–150 feet. There is no limit to the number of wireless clients that can connect to it at once. You can monitor the performance of the wireless network and decide whether a second hub might need to be set up on the network. The wireless signal does not have to have a direct path between the access point and the client. Wireless devices use radio frequencies, which are not blocked by walls or other objects that may be located between the wireless client and its server.

Features vary between wireless access products. Most access points offer a single level of security, known as WEP (Wireless Encryption Protocol). This form of security can be easy to break. An eight-digit code is required from each wireless client in order to connect to the access point. If an uninvited computer is able to guess that eight-digit code, it can easily join your network.

Some wireless access points can also be configured as DHCP servers. If you decide to set up a DHCP server on your local network, make sure there are no other DHCP servers running on the same network. For example, you may need to log into your DSL modem and deactivate the DHCP service in the modem before you activate the DHCP server in the wireless access point.

SURVIVAL TIP   To find out more about how to set up a wireless access point, go to Chapter 10. To find out more about how to set up a wireless client to connect to a wireless access point, go to Chapter 11.

Additional Resources

Although DSL accounts and services vary from provider to provider, most providers enable you to choose a starter account and add on features or change modems as your home or office network changes or grows. Check with your DSL service provider to see what kind of plans, accounts, and account options are available for your DSL service. The following list of Web addresses may provide additional information for you to research or compare your DSL modem and services to other providers:

- ✦ www.dsl-modem-internet-access.com
- ✦ www.xo.com
- ✦ www.pacbell.com
- ✦ www.sbc.com
- ✦ www.broadcom.com
- ✦ www.earthlink.net
- ✦ www.aol.com
- ✦ www.msn.com
- ✦ www.telocity.com

Chapter 15

Troubleshooting a DSL Network

If you have connected to the Internet with a modem or an online service like America Online, you have probably experienced a network problem. You may have noticed a slowdown in network performance or visited a Web site that may have been working fine the day before but today is no longer accessible on the network. Having so many computers connected together is bound to introduce intermittent problems, such as a hard drive or network cable failure, or not surprisingly, computers crashing while connected to the network. Because networks contain so many hardware and software components, this chapter focuses on network connection troubleshooting, including the following topics:

✦ **DSL modem settings**   Identify common problems and solutions for your network's DSL Internet connection and for each local computer's connection to the local network.

✦ **Network connections**   Identify and isolate common hardware and software network problems with PCs and Macintosh computers.

✦ **Computer network settings**   Review, modify, and test network settings on Linux, Windows, and Macintosh computers.

Basic Concepts for Troubleshooting Networks

Network problems can be caused by something big or small. There's no telling whether what your computer is experiencing might be a part of a brownout or a software conflict between your computer and another device connected on your local network. Network problems can start without your knowing it. It's an obvious problem only when it prevents your computer from being recognized by your local network or accessing the Internet.

If you take a step back from the confusion or surprise, the first question you might ask when your computer loses its connection to the Internet is, "Where do I begin to troubleshoot this problem?" This chapter will introduce you to many common network problems and show you how to use network tools to troubleshoot and solve them.

Characterizing a Network Problem

The general process you can follow to troubleshoot a network problem is to first collect information. Then try to isolate the problem to a particular network device. Once the problem is identified, then you can try to identify the best solution for the problem.

In most cases, the problem can be isolated to a single computer, such as a defective network interface card or an incorrect network software setting. If a single computer is affected by the network problem, other computers on the network may experience problems communicating with it. However, only that computer has network problems, and other computers should still be able to access the Internet. Another possible scenario is a network router failure. Most of the computers connected to that router will lose access to other local networks, and potentially the Internet, too. Both types of failure involve a single network device that failed; however, the symptoms are unique for each type of failure.

Common Network Problems

Troubleshooting a network problem involves gathering information about the problem, isolating the problem to either the local network or the Internet, and then isolating the problem to a specific network cable or computer. If the network was previously working problem-free, and each computer on the network was correctly configured, a recent change may be the root cause of the network problem. Once you've found the source of the problem, you can implement a solution. The following list contains a few of the more frequent network problems you may encounter with your home or office network, plus a few questions that may help you troubleshoot the cause of a network problem.

+ **Cable connection**   Is the network cable defective? Is it properly connected to the network hub and the computer?

+ **Network card**   Is the network card properly installed in the computer? Is the software for the card installed? Does the card work installed in a different computer?

+ **Network or Internet settings**   Does the computer have the correct TCP/IP network settings for the local network? Is all the network software installed for the operating system?

+ **Incompatible hardware or software**   Does the computer connect to the network with different hardware?

Before a network problem occurs, you should spend some time observing the network performance of a healthy network. You might want to note which computers you've observed and note the download and upload rates to a local file or Web server to begin to characterize your network. You should also keep a list of computers on your network and note how much memory, how much disk space, and what type of network interface card is in each one.

If a problem occurs with a specific computer, make a note of it. If a problem consistently reoccurs on the same computer, this may help troubleshoot whether the source of the problem is software- or hardware-related. You might want to keep a separate log of hardware and software upgrades performed on each computer, too.

Losing Access to Your Local Network

Another common scenario is when a computer may be running perfectly on your local network. All of a sudden, it will not be able to access the local network printer or share files

with another computer on the network. Before you change anything, take a look at the physical network connections connecting your computer to the DSL modem or to a local star hub. Disconnect and reconnect each end of the Ethernet cable. If the network connection is restored, it's possible the cable may have become separated from the network interface card or hub connector.

Stepping away from potential network hardware problems, it is possible that the computer's IP address may not be recognized by the network router. You can reset the IP address on your Windows computer by performing the following steps with Windows 2000 or XP:

1. Click the Start menu and choose the Run command from the menu list.

2. Type **cmd** into the Open text box in the Run window.

3. Wait for the command window to open.

4. Type **ipconfig/release** at the prompt (see Figure 15-1). You should see a message indicating that the IP address for the computer has been released. If you're using Windows 98, type **winipcfg** instead of **ipconfig**.

5. To get a new IP address assigned to your computer, type **ipconfig/renew** at the prompt.

6. The new IP address information for your computer should appear in the command window, as shown in Figure 15-1.

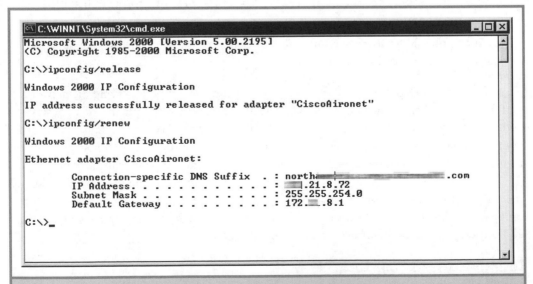

Figure 15-1. Using the Windows 2000 ipconfig tool to release and renew the IP address for a computer.

NOTE

Although most hubs and network cables share a common RJ-45 connector interface, some network hubs and cards may not be as stable or compatible with your computer's hardware or operating system software as other network hubs and network interface cards. If you notice intermittent problems with a local network's performance after installing a new network hub, you may want to remove the new hub to see if the problem goes away. If it does, you may have identified a brand of network device that you might want to use with caution in your home or office network. Check the manufacturer's Web site to see if there are any known compatibility issues with your computer or its operating system. You may need to download newer software drivers to see if this may fix the incompatibilities with the network interface card.

If your computer is running Mac OS 9, perform the folowing steps to access the TCP/IP settings.

1. Click the Apple menu, choose Control Panels, and then select TCP/IP. The TCP/IP control panel will open.

2. Press COMMAND-K. A list of network configurations will appear.

3. If you have only one network configuration, its name will appear in the TCP/IP configuration window.

4. Click the network configuration in the window list.

5. Click Make Active. Finally, close the TCP/IP control panel.

If the network connection is restored, you can continue to compute on the network. If the ipconfig or TCP/IP commands do not get your computer reconnected to the network, consider shutting down your computer and then powering it back on.

Losing Access to Other Platforms on Your Network

One of the easier conditions to troubleshoot is a card or cable connection problem on the local network. It's possible for each computer on the local network to access the Internet successfully but not be able to access another computer on the local network. One way to test the local network configuration is to activate personal file sharing on a Mac or Windows computer and see if you can copy a file from the file-shared computer to a second computer on the network.

The file sharing feature on Macs and Windows computers can be set up to work with the Internet Protocol. However, the default protocols for each platform are not set up using the Internet Protocol. Macs use AppleTalk to enable file sharing services over the network. Windows computer use the NetBEUI protocol to enable file sharing between two Windows computers. By default, both brands of file sharing will work only with the local network.

If you're running Mac OS 9 or Mac OS X, you can check the IP checkbox to share your computer's files over the Internet, or over multiple networks using the Internet Protocol.

If you can access the network settings on each computer, first, make sure each computer has a unique IP address. Next, check to see if there is a DHCP server responsible for assigning IP addresses on the network. Check the IP address range of the DHCP server. If the server is configured to assign a limited number of IP addresses, check to see if all of the addresses have been given out. If this is the case, a new computer will not be able to connect to the local network because the DHCP server has run out of addresses to give out. If other computers are powered on and connected to the network but are not currently being used, power one or all of them off to free an IP address.

Internet Access Problems

It might not surprise you that your DSL connection will be only as reliable as your voice phone line. Point-to-point, router, and bridged DSL modem connections can experience problems either gaining a connection or keeping a connection with the DSL service provider. Problems with your local phone company's phone lines may also affect your DSL connection. However, your DSL Internet connection can also fail, whether the voice phone works or not.

If your computer is unable to access the Internet, perform the following steps to power off and on the computer and the DSL modem.

1. Power off your DSL modem and leave it off for a few minutes.

2. Shut down the computer and then restart it.

3. Power on the DSL modem and the computer.

4. Try to access the Internet by loading a Web page or sending an e-mail message.

If you are able to access the Internet, problem's solved. If you still can't connect, you may want to fall back to a dial-up connection and check to see if your DSL provider has scheduled a network downtime for maintenance, or if the DSL service is experiencing problems in your area.

Finding the Root Cause of a Network Problem

It's relatively easy to troubleshoot network problems if you have one or two computers and possibly a printer connected to your local network. It's even easier if you have administrator privileges on each computer. If a network setting needs to be corrected or changed on a computer, you can quickly address any network changes you might want to make without having to worry about finding the owner of the computer.

After you have gathered information about the network problem, you may need to isolate the problem and find its root cause. The three methods of troubleshooting that will be explained in this chapter are tracking changes, isolating techniques, and systematic trial-and-error methods. The biggest advantage you can have when troubleshooting a network is being familiar with its configuration. If you know what hardware and software are installed and running on each computer, you can track what hardware or software components are changing and determine whether the network problem was the result of a change to a computer or network device.

Creating a Network Map

The first step is to document your network by creating a network map and noting what types of network interface cards, hubs, routers, printers, operating systems, and applications are installed on your local network. Use the network map to track the physical and logical information on your network. Depending on how you like to organize and track your network information, you may also want to note what processor, network card, and operating system are installed on each computer.

A network map, such as the one shown in Figure 15-2, combined with any other hardware or software information you can document for your network, enables you to keep track of all the devices connected to your network. You might also want to label each computer, printer, and other network device and list the hardware and software configurations in plain view and note the network configuration on the label. If a problem should occur, you can check the map, labels, and any documentation about the hardware and software on that computer and track any issues that may reoccur over time.

As you change hardware and software on the network, monitor the computers and the network after the upgrade has been performed. If a network problem occurs as the direct result of one of the changes you have made, you can revert the computer to use the previous version of software installed on that computer.

Using the ping Command

The ping tool, available on Windows, Mac OS X, and Linux computers, can be used to find out your client computer's IP address or another computer's IP address on a network. You can use the ping command to find out if a computer is actively connected to the network or not. If a network error occurs with a particular IP address, you can use ping to locate the computer with that IP address on your local network.

Sometimes more than one computer may cause a network problem to occur. You can use the ping command to identify any computers that may have crashed or become disconnected from the network, as well as locate computers that are actively connected on the network. The divide-and-conquer method of troubleshooting is the process of isolating active versus

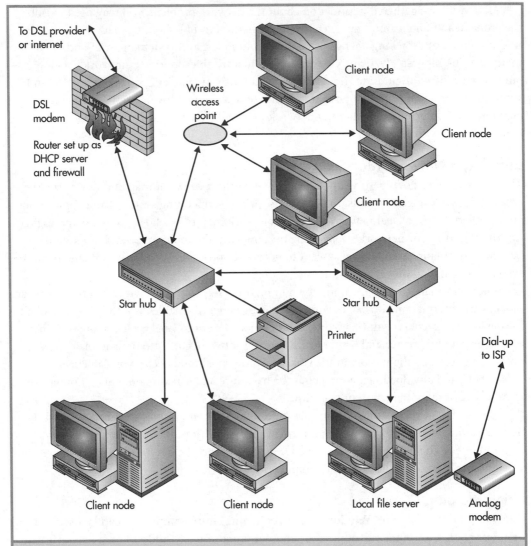

To DSL provider
or internet

DSL
modem

Router set up as
DHCP server
and firewall

Wireless
access
point

Client node

Client node

Client node

Star hub

Star hub

Printer

Dial-up
to ISP

Client node

Client node

Local file server

Analog
modem

Figure 15-2. Create a physical map of your network and show the logical flow of data through the network.

inactive computers on a network. On a Windows 2000 or XP computer, you can perform the following steps to use the ping command to see if another computer is actively connected to the network.

1. Open a command window by clicking the Start menu and then choosing Run.

2. Type **cmd** in the Open text box, and wait for the command window to open.

3. Type **ping** *<name of the computer>* at the prompt.

SURVIVAL TIP

Windows, Mac OS X, and Linux enable you to view the command options for ping, traceroute, or other command-line network tools. Type **ping –help** in the command or terminal window to view the help options for the ping command.

To find out your computer's name on Windows 2000, perform the following steps.

1. Right-click My Computer and choose Properties. The System Properties window will open.

2. Clickthe Network Identification tab. The Network Identification panel will appear in the System Properties window.

3. Click the Properties button. The computer name appears in the Computer Name text box of the Identification Changes window.

On a Windows XP computer, choose the Computer Name tab in the System Properties window to view the computer's name information. The computer's name appears in the Full computer name text field, below the Computer description text box. Type a description of the computer into the Computer description text box. Click the Change button to change the name of the computer.

To find the IP address of a computer named cloudnine, perform the following steps on a Windows 2000 or XP computer.

1. Type **ping cloudnine** in the command or terminal window.

2. The ping command will show the IP address of your computer if it can be located on the network.

3. On a Windows 2000 or XP computer, the following information will appear:

```
Ping Statistics for 10.0.1.1:
Packets: Sent = 2, Received = 0, Lost = 2 (100% loss)
Approximate round trip times in milli-seconds:
Minimum = 0ms, Maximum = 0ms, Average = 0ms
```

NOTE

You can use the ping command to ping a known local IP address on the network. When you ping another computer that is actively connected to the network, it will send a reply. Each reply will show the IP address of the computer and the round-trip time for the ping. The number of packets sent should match the number of packets received by your computer. The ping command will work only if the name lookup service is available for the network. If the DSL modem is off, or if the domain name servers for the DSL service are down, the ping command will not work. When you ping your own computer, it sends and receives the ping command, so it can't reply. That's why the packets sent were not received, and both packets are lost.

Using the Traceroute Program

Find out how far away another computer is located in relation to your computer using the Traceroute command. Windows, Mac OS X, and Linux all have this command preinstalled. Perform the following steps on a Windows 2000 or Windows XP computer to trace the network path of a computer on the local network.

1. Open a command (Windows) or Terminal window.

2. Type **tracert** *<IP address>* (see Figure 15-3) or **tracert** *<computer name>*.

```
C:\WINNT\System32\cmd.exe                                          _ □ ✕
C:\>tracert 208.38.145.48

Tracing route to 208.38.145.48 over a maximum of 30 hops

  1    <10 ms   <10 ms    10 ms  w249.z208037140.sjc-ca.dsl.cnc.net [208.37.140.2
49]
  2     40 ms    30 ms    40 ms  w001.z208177225.sjc-ca.dsl.cnc.net [208.177.225.
1]
  3     30 ms    30 ms    30 ms  a3-0d1.web1.sjc-ca.us.xo.net [205.158.11.25]
  4     30 ms    30 ms    30 ms  p2-0.tran2.scl-ca.us.xo.net [64.0.0.129]
  5     30 ms    30 ms    40 ms  ge4-0.edge1.scl-ca.us.xo.net [64.220.0.54]
  6     30 ms    30 ms    40 ms  p5-0.snjpca1-cr1.bbnplanet.net [4.24.234.17]
  7     30 ms    40 ms    30 ms  p1-0.snjpca1-br1.bbnplanet.net [4.24.9.133]
  8     30 ms    40 ms    30 ms  p9-0.snjpca1-br2.bbnplanet.net [4.24.9.130]
  9     40 ms    40 ms    40 ms  p2-0.lsanca2-br2.bbnplanet.net [4.24.8.26]
 10     81 ms    80 ms    80 ms  p9-0.crtntx1-br2.bbnplanet.net [4.24.5.62]
 11    120 ms   120 ms   111 ms  so-4-2-0.atlnga1-br2.bbnplanet.net [4.24.6.41]
 12    110 ms   120 ms   120 ms  so-7-0-0.atlnga1-br1.bbnplanet.net [4.24.10.33]

 13    110 ms   130 ms   120 ms  p1-0.atlnga1-cr1.bbnplanet.net [4.24.7.234]
 14    111 ms   110 ms   120 ms  p0-0.aperian8.bbnplanet.net [4.24.186.10]
 15      *                  *    Request timed out.
 16      *       ^C
C:\>_
```

Figure 15-3.   Open a command window in Windows 2000 and use the tracert command to list the routers on the network path between your computer and the target computer.

By default, traceroute will make 30 hops, one hop representing one computer on the network, or stop if it locates the other computer on the network. On a Mac OS X or Linux computer, you can run the Traceroute tool by first opening a terminal window. Then use the Traceroute command instead of tracert in step 2.

The Traceroute command will start tracing the IP address from your computer and list each hop as it traces the connection to the target computer. Figure 15-3 shows 14 hops, followed by a time-out for the fifteenth request. The timeout indicates that the computer is not available. Traceroute will continue to find the next hop if it encounters a request time out. If you decide you want to end the trace, press CTRL-C to end the session.

Checking Network Server Logs

Another way to track what a computer has been processing is to tell it to log its activities in a text file. A log enables you to read what the computer thinks it has sent or received over the network. A log can help determine whether a particular network problem is affecting a particular computer or not. Windows, Mac OS X, and Linux computers have a limited amount of network information that starts when a network connection is established and continues until you either log out, put the computer to sleep, or shut down the system.

Some network programs create their own logs of network activity. Norton's Personal Firewall software, for example, enables you to select what specific type of network information you want to add to the log file. If the personal firewall is enabled, it will track which incoming and outgoing network data has been allowed or denied access to your computer. This can be helpful for tracking down network-borne viruses, worms, and Trojan horses that may have infiltrated your network.

On a Windows 2000 computer, you can create a log that monitors one or several computer tasks. The Performance window contains a system monitor item and Performance Logs and Alerts components. The following steps show you how to create a log using the Performance program:

1. Click the Start menu, select Programs | Administrative Tools and then choose Performance.

2. Uncollapse the Performance Logs and Alerts list (see Figure 15-4).

3. Right-click a log file and choose New Log Settings from the shortcuts menu list.

4. Type a name for the log and click OK. The main log window will open.

5. Click the General tab and then click the Add button. The Select Counters window will open.

6. Click the Performance Object drop-down menu to choose a performance object. If you want to monitor the network, you might want to select TCP or Network Interface from the menu list.

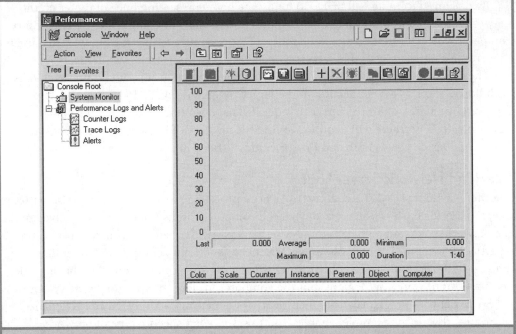

Figure 15-4. The Performance program in Windows 2000 enables you to log system information and view it in the System Monitor window.

7. Select a counter from the window list located in the lower-left corner of the Select Counters window. For example, choose Connection Failures if you want Windows to log its TCP connection failures. Click the Add button to add the criterion to the log file. A list of counters will appear in the main log window.

8. Click the Log Files tab to choose a location for the log file to be stored on your hard drive. You can also customize the way log files are named from the Log Files panel.

9. Select the Schedule tab to define how you want to log file to be created and how or when you want to stop capturing data to the log file.

10. Click OK to save your changes and create the log.

11. To view the log data in the performance window, click System Monitor. Then click the View Log Data icon (looks like a cylinder) at the top of the System Monitor window. Select the log file and view its contents in the Performance window.

You can view each log file by selecting the Counter Log icon from the Performance window list on the left. Right-click the log to access its shortcuts menu. Choose Stop if you want the log to stop capturing data.

Monitoring Transfer Statistics

You can also pick a computer that you suspect might be the cause of a network problem, and check its network settings to see how it is interacting with the network. A computer must also process other tasks while it is sending and receiving data over a network. Sometimes a computer may appear to have slow network performance. However, the cause of the problem might be that the computer has a shortage of resources, such as disk space, memory, or processing power. You can take a look at what a computer is spending its time processing, check the amount of available disk space, and inspect network settings, in addition to checking each computer's network connections.

If you're not sure whether the computer is having problems interpreting network data, you can view the network statistics for the Ethernet card. Figure 15-5 shows the Network Utility window for Mac OS X. To open this window, double-click the Macintosh HD icon, and then click the Application icon that appears at the top of the directory window. Locate and double-click the Network Utility application in the Applications window. The Network Utility window will open. Click the Info panel and choose the Ethernet card from the pop-up menu located at the top of the info panel. Look for any Send Errors or Recv Errors in the Transfer Statistics area of the Info panel (as seen in Figure 15-5).

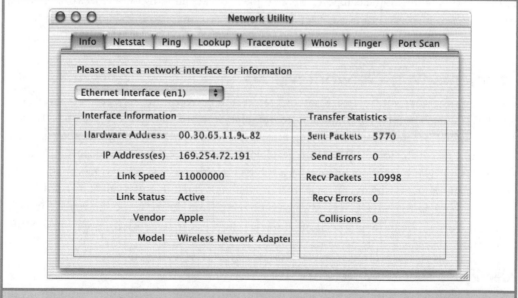

Figure 15-5. The Network Utility window enables you to monitor the number of incoming and outgoing packets on your network.

On a Windows or Linux computer, you can view network information for a network interface card. Right-click the My Network Places icon. The Network and Dial-up Connections window will open. Right-click the network device icon located in the this window. Choose Status from the shortcuts menu. A status window for the network interface will open. The Connection status, duration, and speed appear at the top of the window, and the Activity of Sent and Received packets appears at the bottom of the status window.

If there are no errors and your computer is capable of sending and receiving packets, then your computer is probably not having any problems processing network packets. If you see errors, check a second or third computer connected to the same network to see if they are also having problems sending and receiving packets. If other computers are not having any problems processing packets, the problem may be on the DSL provider's network, or the DSL modem or router may be configured incorrectly on the external network.

Problems Accessing Network Configurations

One of the biggest advantages of troubleshooting network problems in your home or office is that you can physically access each computer on the local network. Although it's possible to set up remote access software on Windows and Macintosh computers, it's difficult to troubleshoot network problems quickly if you cannot log into a networked computer, listen to the drive spinning on the computer, or see if the lights are blinking on the network interface card. You may also need to use a specific network tool to help troubleshoot a problem. The following sections describe some common networking problems.

Problems with Network Media

As you put together your network, choose cables and network interface cards that are fairly similar. Having a similar configuration on the same network can give you the opportunity to swap cables or cards if you are trying to isolate a network problem with a cable, a connector, or a hub. Some of the more perplexing network problems can occur when a particular hardware component, such as a cable or a card, has a software incompatibility with another network device. If a network problem is related to a particular piece of hardware, you can remove that hardware component from the network and replace it with one that works. The following sections show you how to use network programs to identify a computer that has lost its network connection.

Identifying Your Local Network

If one or several computer on your local network fail to connect with any computers on the Internet, you may want to find out if your local network's name server is actively connected to the network. If the name server becomes unavailable to the network, the computers on your local network will not be able to locate or communicate with computers located on an external network. Whether you have a point-to-point connection or a router-based connection, most service providers supply you with two domain server IP addresses for each computer account. If the primary name server loses its network connection, your computer will look for the secondary name server to try to resolve the IP address of the target computer.

The nslookup command in Windows enables you to locate the name and IP address of your local network's name server or a name server on a different network. You must open a command window in order to use the nslookup command. You can also type **nslookup** in a Linux or Mac OS X terminal window. Mac OS X also enables you to access the nslookup command from the Network Utility window, shown in Figure 15-6.

To view your local name server information, type **nslookup** at the prompt. On a Windows 2000 computer, the command window will show the server name and IP address. For example, if I type **nslookup**, my computer returns the following information in the

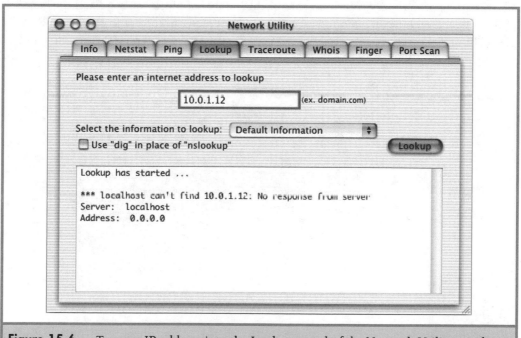

Figure 15-6.   Type an IP address into the Lookup panel of the Network Utility window to locate another computer on the network.

command window. The default server value is the name of the name server. The IP address of your DSL account should match the address returned by nslookup:

```
Default Server: Hudson.concentric.net
Address: 207.155.183.72
```

Pinging Your DSL Gateway

If the name server isn't the culprit preventing your computers from accessing the network, check to see that the DSL provider's gateway IP address is online. You can use the ping command, mentioned in the previous section, to see whether the gateway address responds to your network request. Figure 15-7 shows the Ping panel of the Network Utility in Mac OS X. Type the IP address of the DSL modem into the text box. Then click Ping to send your network requests out to the network. The results of the ping request appear in the bottom window of the Ping panel.

As mentioned previously, ping is also available with Windows and Linux systems. On a Windows 2000 computer, open a command window and type **ping** followed by the IP address at the prompt. If you want to change the number of pings you send and the length of the timeout, add the –n option to set the number of requests and –w to set the timeout period in milliseconds. For example, **ping –n 2 –w 20 10.0.1.1** will ping the IP address of 10.0.1.1 for 20 milliseconds, for a count of two times.

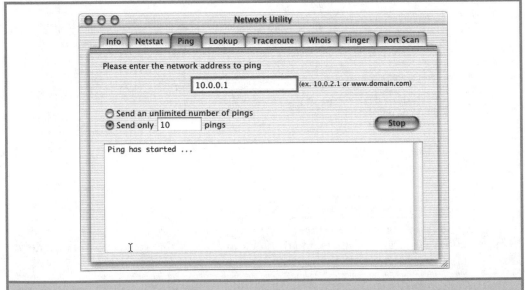

Figure 15-7. Type the IP address of the DSL modem and the DSL provider's Internet gateway address to see if these devices are actively connected to the network.

CAUTION

When dot coms were booming, some mischievous hackers created a malicious attack known as a denial of service attack. Many computers were set up to ping specific, highly visible Web sites, such as cnn.com and amazon.com. Each Web site received so many requests that legitimate Web surfers could not access these Web sites. A side effect of the denial of service attacks is that many of these Web servers are set up not to respond to ping requests. If you try to ping a well-known Web site, don't be surprised if you don't get a ping reply, even though you can successfully load a Web page for that Web site with a browser.

If the DSL modem functions as a router on your network, you might want to check to see that it is properly connected to your local star hub. If that doesn't do the trick, try powering it off and then on again to see if you can ping from another computer on your network. If the DSL gateway remains inaccessible from the local network, contact your DSL service provider to find out if there are any known problems with the DSL service in your area. If the DSL service is unavailable, the support representative can have the local phone company or DSL provider try to repair the problem.

Checking the Status of Your Local Network

The DSL service shares the same phone line as your voice phone service. It's possible for your DSL network to lose Internet access if your local voice line becomes unavailable. If you notice your DSL network slowing down in performance, or if you lose Internet access altogether, first try searching for the name server, then try to ping the gateway address for your network. If the system appears to be up and running, pick up your phone line to see if you can hear a dial tone. If you hear line noise, or if you hear something different from what you would normally hear, you might want to check with your phone company to see if they are working on your phone lines. If the phone lines in your area are generally reliable, then I would not suspect a DSL Internet connection problem to be due to a problem with the voice line or phone line.

If you've checked the DSL provider's network servers to make sure they're running properly, you might want to take a look at the routing information for your local network. Figure 15-8 shows the Netstat panel of the Mac OS X Network Utility window. Click the Display Routing Table Information radio button. Then click the Netstat button to view the routing tables for the computer.

On a Windows computer, you can type **netstat –r** in a command window to view the routing table information for your network. Although each platform will show slightly different information about routing tables, you should see network destination, gateway, and interface information for each device that appears in the routing table. You can check the IP addresses that appear in the routing table to see that each IP address is valid. If all addresses are valid, you may want to investigate to see if a potential software setting conflict is the cause of the network problem.

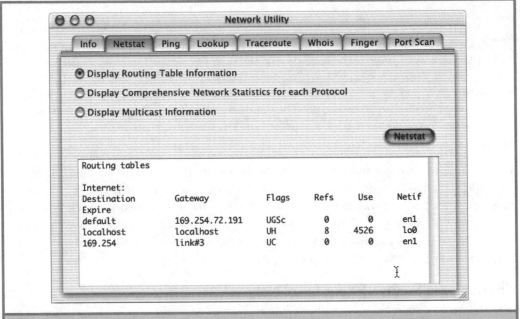

Figure 15-8. Select the Display Routing Table Information radio button in the Netstat window of Mac OS X to view the routing table information for your local network.

You can type the **netstat –a** command to view the state of the active protocols on the computer:

```
C:\>netstat -a
Active Connections
   Proto  Local Address          Foreign Address        State
   TCP    pc505:epmap            vpcg505.test.com:0   LISTENING
   TCP    pc505:test-ds      vpcg505.test.com:0   LISTENING
   TCP    pc505:641              vpcg505.test.com:0   LISTENING
   TCP    pc505:653              vpcg505.test.com:0   LISTENING
   TCP    pc505:1027             vpcg505.test.com:0   LISTENING
   TCP    pc505:1028             vpcg505.test.com:0   LISTENING
```

If you want to view more detailed statistics about the computer's network connection, type **netstat –s** to view the network statistics for your computer. Focus on the IP information and look for errors for packets that have been sent or received:

```
C:\>netstat -s
IP Statistics
  Packets Received                   = 117622
  Received Header Errors             = 0
  Received Address Errors            = 280
  Datagrams Forwarded                = 0
  Unknown Protocols Received         = 0
  Received Packets Discarded         = 11776
  Received Packets Delivered         = 103474
  Output Requests                    = 108373
  Routing Discards                   = 0
  Discarded Output Packets           = 0
  Output Packet No Route             = 0
  Reassembly Required                = 3644
  Reassembly Successful              = 1334
  Reassembly Failures                = 14
  Datagrams Successfully Fragmented  = 65
  Datagrams Failing Fragmentation    = 0
  Fragments Created                  = 130
ICMP Statistics

                           Received      Sent
  Messages                 501           427
  Errors                   0             0
  Destination Unreachable  217           70
  Time Exceeded            21            3
  Parameter Problems       0             0
  Source Quenches          0             0
  Redirects                0             0
  Echos                    0             354
  Echo Replies             263           0
  Timestamps               0             0
```

```
     Timestamp Replies          0            0
     Address Masks              0            0
     Address Mask Replies       0            0
 TCP Statistics
     Active Opens                      = 2944
     Passive Opens                     = 28
     Failed Connection Attempts        = 300
     Reset Connections                 = 516
     Current Connections               = 0
     Segments Received                 = 63343
     Segments Sent                     = 53716
     Segments Retransmitted            = 650
 UDP Statistics
     Datagrams Received    = 39173
     No Ports              = 950
     Receive Errors        = 8
     Datagrams Sent        = 53527
```

Checking for IP Address and Network Setting Conflicts

If your network uses a combination of static and dynamic IP addresses to grant Internet access to computers on your network, be sure each computer with a static IP address has a unique address. If an IP address is used with more than one computer, network traffic flow and resolution conflicts may cause your network to perform slowly or prevent a computer from accessing another device on the network.

If the DSL modem is configured as a router or bridge to the Internet and the local area network has a lot of network activity, you may encounter slow network performance as a result of packet collisions occurring on the network. Packet collisions occur when two network cards transmit signals over the network at one time. The network cable can handle only one signal at a time. As packets are transmitted over the network, each one keeps trying to get onto the information superhighway. Whenever two packets try to join the network at the same time, a network collision occurs.

NOTE

The DSL modem will have its own IP address if it is configured to act as a network router or bridge. When a computer connects to the Internet using a DSL modem and a point-to-point connection, the DSL modem does not have its own IP address. If there is a lot of network traffic between the DSL provider and your computer, the PPPoE DSL modem will not filter any network traffic from reaching your computer.

You can check the IP address settings on a Windows computer by opening the Internet Protocol window from the Network interface's Properties window. If you're using Mac OS 9, you can click the Apple menu, select Control Panels, and choose TCP/IP. On a Mac OS X computer, open the Settings panel and click the Network icon. If you're running Linux, open the network configurator or linuxconf program or ping your local host name to view your computer's IP address.

NOTE   A star hub topology network enables you to extend your network by attaching a second hub to the first hub. This is called *cascading* a network. If your DSL modem acts as a router or a bridge, you can grow your local network by adding a hub or two to each room you want to compute in. Be sure to monitor your network as it grows. If you add a hub and a few computers to your local network and then start seeing a new crop of network issues appear, you may want to take a closer look at your network design and the logical flow of data to find out if you have too many hubs and computers on the local network.

Checking Hardware Connections for Remote Servers

A network map can help you test a network remotely. If you suspect that a server or network computer has lost its network connection, you can use the network map to systematically move from one computer to the next to find out which ones may be affected by the network problem. In some cases, a power outage or system crash may prevent a remote computer from being accessed. If this is the case, you will need to visit the remote location personally and reboot the system or have someone at the remote site check on the suspect computers.

Network Security

A DSL service provider is responsible for providing the DSL connection to the Internet. However, any security for your computer or local network is solely your responsibility. If you're not sure how secure your network is, you can purchase an antivirus program such as Symantec's Norton Anti-Virus, or McAfee Virus Scan. You can also visit sites on the Web such as housecall.antivirus.com if you do not want to purchase an antivirus package.Even if you rely on virus protection software to guard your system, it's still possible your computer may become infected with a virus, worm, or trojan horse. If your computer system starts to behave erratically and rebooting it or shutting it down doesn't help, you may want to take the time to back up any documents you don't want to erase and reformat the computer's hard drive. Then reinstall a new operating system and any system software from their original disks or restore an image of a disk from CD-ROM.

Resetting Network Services

Your DSL service enables your computer to access computers outside your local network. You can subscribe to an online service if you want to set up a Web server remotely on their networked computers, or you can set up the Web pages on a computer on your local network to test them before you share them with the world. Your DSL modem can also be a network server. The features of the modem vary depending on what the DSL provider has installed in your home or office. The following sections show you how to access a DSL modem router and a network server located on the Internet.

Accessing and Resetting Your DSL Modem

A DSL modem router is actually colocated on your local network and the Internet. The DSL router is the gateway to the Internet for your local network. You can ping or view routing table information to locate the IP address for your DSL modem.

If you can ping the DSL modem, you can use the telnet application to log into it. You will need a login name and password to log into your DSL modem. The interface for a DSL modem is a command-line interface. You can type **help** at the prompt of the telnet window to view the commands available for the DSL modem. The command set varies from vendor to vendor.

Most routers will have a set of commands that enable you to view or change configuration information for the DSL modem. You can log in, change your password, and then log out of a DSL modem router or use the getconfig command to view the network profiles. Some routers may also have ping, Traceroute, and network statistic tools you can use to monitor network traffic flowing through the DSL router. If the DSL modem has a reboot command, type it at the prompt and wait for the modem to reboot. You can also power off the modem if you want to reset the hardware.

Accessing and Resetting a Network Server

A file server, MP3 digital jukebox, or Web server may have problems staying on the network, especially if it's getting a lot of traffic. If all the software settings and packet information look correct, you may want to reboot the computer to see if it can be recognized on the network. If the problem goes away, it's possible the network server may have been the source of the network problems. Log an entry to your network map to remind yourself to look at this computer at some future point in time.

Another way to check and reset a computer is to set up the server as a Windows 2000 server running a terminal server. A terminal server enables you to log into the computer server as if you were running it on your desktop computer. You can copy, delete, and remove files from a terminal server in addition to being able to restart the server.

Applying Network Solutions

Although I have mentioned solutions and troubleshooting processes throughout this chapter, the following sections show you how to replace network hardware components. A better practice is to hold off on making any sudden decisions to try to fix a network. Plan for a solution and then implement it on your network. The last sections show you how to look for network processes on a computer and how to reset a network server.

Correcting Network Hardware Problems

There are several steps you can take to try to isolate the trouble spot in your local network. First, check your network connections, and make sure each computer is recognized by the network. Start a browser or e-mail application and see if you can load a Web page or send yourself an e-mail message on each computer. If you're unable to reach the Internet, then there may be a problem with your computer or your network's configuration. There may also be a problem with the DSL modem, or the DSL service. If your DSL connection fails and you have a traditional telco account you can dial into with a 56 Kbps modem, you might want to see if your DSL service provider is experiencing problems with their network.

Testing and Replacing Cables

Network interface cards and network cables are pretty reliable. If you don't stretch the cable or pull on the Ethernet connector while the computer is running, the computer should stay connected to the local area network as long as your DSL service remains up and running. If you suspect a network cable is not properly bringing the network to a computer, you can do one of these things:

✦ Check the lights on the Ethernet card and the hub.

✦ Disconnect and reconnect the Ethernet connector on the computer.

✦ Disconnect and reconnect the Ethernet connector on the hub.

✦ Swap the Ethernet cable with another cable that you know works.

Some Ethernet cards have a green or red light to indicate that the connection to the hub is functioning. If you don't see any lights, this may indicate that the network cable is not doing its job. If the first task on this list corrects the computer's network connection, the connector may not have been completely connected to the computer. Similarly, if the connection to the hub works fine after you reconnect the cable, the connector may have wiggled loose. If reconnecting the cable doesn't help, try replacing it with a new cable or a cable that is known to work perfectly with your network. Also, if the computer has a second Ethernet card, you can change the configuration of the computer to the second card and see if the computer reconnects to the network.

Upgrading Hardware

It's not easy to draw a line to define where the network ends and the computer begins. The network interface card, hard drive, memory, monitor, and keyboard are as much a part of the network as the network cables and hubs. Most computers will be configured to have a network interface card installed in the computer. If the card fails to communicate with the network, it's possible that it may need to be replaced but before you yank anything out of the computer, you should take a quick look at the other components on the computer first.

Most of the latest computers have a 10–20GB hard drive, which should be more than enough room for average Web surfers to get their work done. Most computers also use virtual memory, a disk-based memory management solution that you can configure in Windows and Mac OS 9. The amount of disk space reserved for virtual memory is usually set to be at least as much as the amount of physical memory installed on the computer. On occasion, a hard drive may fill up with files and some application may not be able to access the network because there is nowhere to store new application or operating system data on the drive.

On a Linux or Mac OS X system, you can type **ls** to view a list of files in the current directory of the hard drive. Figure 15-9 shows the root directory for my login name llee using the command **ls –alF**. The ls command has several options, which you can view by typing **ls –help**. In Figure 15-9, the directory name appears on the right, and the access privileges are shown on the far left side of the window. The size of each directory appears in the middle column beside the date information. You may want to consider upgrading a hard drive if you notice that network problems are related to a computer's hard drive filling up as the result of sending or receiving network data.

If you want to view the amount of available disk space on the drive, you can type **df –k** in Mac OS X or Linux. The df command represents the disk free command. The results of the disk free command appear at the bottom of the terminal window shown in Figure 15-9. The disk name appears on the right side of the window, and the capacity appears in the column immediately to the left of it. Review the amount of used and available disk space. If the available disk space become zero, you will need to back up files onto another drive or CD-R discs to free up disk space so that other programs can run on the computer.

On a Windows computer, you can right-click the My Computer icon and choose Explore from the shortcut menu. You can navigate your hard drive by selecting a directory from the left window list and viewing directory information from the right window list. To view the size of a directory, right-click the folder icon and choose Properties. The Size field displays the size of the selected folder. To view the amount of used and available disk space for a

```
● ● ●                      /bin/tcsh  (ttyp1)
[localhost:~] llee% ls -alF
total 64
drwxr-xr-x  15 llee   staff     466 Apr  6 19:24 ./
drwxr-xr-x   6 root   wheel     160 Jun 17 18:46 ../
-rw-r--r--   1 llee   staff       3 Nov 14  2000 .CFUserTextEncoding
-rw-rw-rw-   1 llee   staff    6148 Apr  6 19:24 .DS_Store
-rw-rw-rw-   1 llee   staff   20480 Apr  6 19:24 .FBCIndex
drwxrwxrwx   3 llee   staff     264 Apr  6 19:24 .FBCLockFolder/
drwx------   8 llee   staff     264 Jul 21 14:10 .Trash/
drwx------  13 llee   staff     398 Jul 21 14:24 Desktop/
drwx------   4 llee   staff     264 Apr 19 17:33 Documents/
drwx------  21 llee   staff     670 Apr 19 17:28 Library/
drwx------   4 llee   staff     264 Apr  6 19:24 Movies/
drwx------   4 llee   staff     264 Apr  6 19:24 Music/
drwx------   4 llee   staff     264 Apr  6 19:24 Pictures/
drwxr-xr-x   4 llee   staff     264 Apr  6 19:24 Public/
drwxr-xr-x   4 llee   staff     264 Feb 13 16:31 Sites/
[localhost:~] llee% df -k
Filesystem        1K-blocks     Used   Avail Capacity  Mounted on
/dev/disk0s9       25259188  9024360 16234828    35%   /
devfs                    32       32       0   100%   /dev
fdesc                     1        1       0   100%   /dev
<volfs>                 512      512       0   100%   /.vol
/dev/disk0s10        589104     2187  586917     0%   /Volumes/Boot Partition
automount -fstab [226]     0        0       0   100%   /Network/Servers
/dev/disk1             4832     3302    1530    68%   /Volumes/iTunes Installer
[localhost:~] llee%
[localhost:~] llee% ▮
```

Figure 15-9.   Check the files on your local computer's drive, in addition to any other network computers, to see how much free disk space is available.

particular hard drive, right-click the drive icon you want to check and choose Properties. The Properties window for the disk will appear. You can view the amounts of used and free disk space on the drive.

Viewing Server Processes

If all the hardware systems on a computer appear to be running smoothly, you can take a quick peek at some of the network processes running on a computer. It's possible that the

computer might think it's busy processing a network task, when the network data has already been delivered to the computer. Figure 15-10 shows the results of the top command for a Mac OS X computer. Type **top** in a terminal window to view a list of current processes running on the computer. You can also use this command on a Linux or Unix computer. The PID is the Process ID. The first process on the list is top command, which we just ran. It's currently taking up the most CPU time.

If you don't want that process to run, you can use the kill command to end it. Type **kill –9 top** or **kill –9 772** to kill the process ID for top. Typing in the name of the process may result in deleting more than one running instance of a process (that's a bad thing). If you use the specific PID number to kill a process, you kill only a single process. If a program freezes, or is not responding, you can look for its PID number and kill the nonresponsive process. You can also exit an application by killing its processes. However, the kinder, gentler way to exit an application is to choose the Exit (Windows) or Quit (Mac) command from the application's File menu.

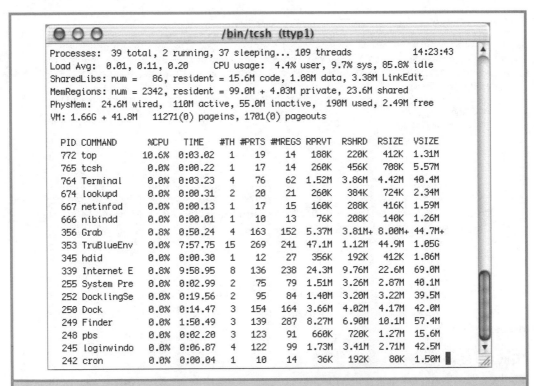

Figure 15-10.   In Mac OS X, you can view currently running processes by typing the **top** command into a terminal window.

At the top of the results for the top command, you can view the CPU usage, the amount of physical memory installed and used, and the amount of virtual memory configured for the computer. In the VM row, the number of pageins or pageouts should not be zero. A zero value would indicate that data stored in virtual memory is not properly being managed on the disk.

Testing Network Access

I have a really hard time admitting I watch TV for a living and an even harder time trying to explain how I'm paid to watch TV over a network connection. Testing network access is as simple as connecting to the Internet and accessing a variety of services with your computer. As you use these services, network performance should remain consistent with each service you access. If you access a fast server, it should remain fast. Similarly, if you access a slow server, it should remain slow. If your computer hiccups and intermittently loses its network connection, this might point to a problem with either your network cable or your network card. As you test your network, takes notes of the network behavior you observe, and try these same tasks again on a different computer to see if the problem is reproducible. If it is reproducible, you may need to apply your newly learned troubleshooting skills to find and fix the network problem.

Testing Cables and Cards

The best way to test a network card is to connect it to the local network and use it. You can activate file sharing on another computer and try copying files between two computers. If the copied files can be opened after being transferred over the network, that's a good sign. Next, try to load several Web pages that you're familiar with and see if you have any problems loading the URL. If Web pages load correctly, you might want to try playing back streaming audio or video to see how the network card processes streamed data. Subtle network card incompatibilities may be acceptable to some computer users and not others. For example, the computer may not be able to process streaming media as smoothly as another computer on the same network.

Testing Network Hardware and Software Upgrades

As you add new computers and network devices to your network, try to use each device after connecting it to the network. Make sure any drivers or application upgrades can be run on the computer and that the computer can access the Internet. If you don't observe any problems, you can continue to use the computer on your local network. However, be on the lookout for any new network problems that may occur. If a new problem occurs due to an incompatibility with the new hardware or software, be prepared to revert to a different network card or remove the upgrade from the computer.

Additional Resources

Knowing the types of computers, network hardware, and DSL hardware you have and being familiar with their firmware settings can help you troubleshoot your network most efficiently. If a problem occurs on your local network, you can follow a general process of identifying, and if relevant, reproducing the problem. Then you can isolate it to a particular hardware or software component running on the network. Because a network enables a multitude of computers to interact with each other, if one computer loses its network connection, it can have a small, big, or delayed effect on other computers that may interact with the problem computer. The following list of Web addresses contains additional resources and information about network troubleshooting.

- www.k12.hi.us/~network/1999/41200nettrbleshoot
- www.pmg.com/nai_basics.htm
- compnetworking.about.com/cs/troubleshooting
- onenetworks.comms.agilent.com/network/troubleshootingbook.asp
- freepctech.com/pc/002/networks010.shtml
- www.bris.ac.uk/is/selfhelp/supportstaff/nwtroubleshooting.html
- www.microsoft.com/mobile/pocketpc/stepbystep/network.asp
- www.practicallynetworked.com/support/troubleshoot_wireless.htm
- personal.bellsouth.net/sdf/h/b/hburgiss/dsl/survival

Chapter 16

Troubleshooting Networked Computers

The most complex device on the network is a computer. Usually it's a reliable network machine, but sometimes it can be the source of a network problem. In addition to sharing the same hardware constructs as the network routers, hubs, and switches that help run the network, a computer can run a variety of operating systems and network applications. In addition to software, a computer relies on a processor, a hard drive, a monitor, and a variety of peripherals that enable you to expand the capabilities of your computer and share them with other computers on the network. The following computer-related troubleshooting topics will be discussed in more detail in this chapter.

✦ **Network card drivers**   Each network interface card has a unique software driver that is installed with the operating system. The network drive enables the operating system on a computer to talk to the network interface card.

✦ **Operating system settings**   There are several network settings you must correctly enter into the control panel or properties dialog boxes of the operating system in order to have the network recognize a computer. In addition to these settings, the operating system has tools that enable you to monitor the processes and resources currently being used by the computer.

✦ **Applications and network tools**   Most network problems will bubble up to the network applications that run on a computer. The operating system and network software help communicate network error messages to the browser, e-mail application, or network program running on a computer.

Basic Concepts: Troubleshooting Networked Computers

Troubleshooting a network, including a computer, requires following a somewhat rigid process of identifying a problem, isolating the cause of the problem, and then implementing a solution. Just as you maintain the network map mentioned in the previous chapter, you should keep a log of all the hardware and software components of each computer on the local network. If a problem occurs with a particular computer, you can compare the actual network settings to the documented settings and make any corrections, if needed.

If all problems were that easy to solve, everyone would be running a local network in their home. In addition to tracking the software and hardware installed on each computer, you should also include any hardware or software upgrades performed on the system. Log the version number and filename, and include the date when the system received the upgrade. Depending on how your users use the computer, you may have to provide training for any new software features, such as upgrading from Windows 2000 to Windows XP, or from Mac OS 9 to Mac OS X.

Checking Hardware and Software Settings

Whip out that network map and computer log book, and get ready to check what's on the computer systems on the network. Okay, if you have only one computer, you won't need a network map. The following sections show you how to find out what version of the operating system is running on a Windows or Mac OS computer.

Checking a Windows Configuration

There are many different ways you view your operating system information on Windows XP or 2000. The easiest way to view the version of Windows running on a PC is to perform the following steps.

1. Right-click the My Computer icon and choose Properties from the shortcut menu.

2. Select the General tab. The operating system version appears in the upper-right corner of the General panel of the System Properties dialog box.

If you have administrator access to your Windows 2000 computer and want to see a more detailed system summary like the window shown in Figure 16-1, perform the following steps.

1. Click the Start menu, choose Programs | Administrative Tools, and select Computer Management.

2. The Computer Management window will open on your desktop.

3. Click the System Summary folder from the left window list to view the system information for your PC.

Another set of data to keep in your log is the amount of physical memory installed in the computer, as well as the amount of virtual memory allocated on the computer. The entries at the bottom of the System Summary page list the Total and Available amounts of memory for the computer. The Page File Space indicates how much of the virtual memory disk space is currently in use.

Checking a Mac OS Configuration

You can find out what version of Macintosh operating system is running in any of a few different ways. The easiest way to find out is to choose About This Computer from the Apple menu. You can also select the System file icon located in the System folder and press COMMAND-I to view the version number of the system file. The most informative source of system information resides in the Apple System Profiler application, shown in Figure 16-2. The Apple System Profiler application is installed with Mac OS 9 and Mac OS X. On a

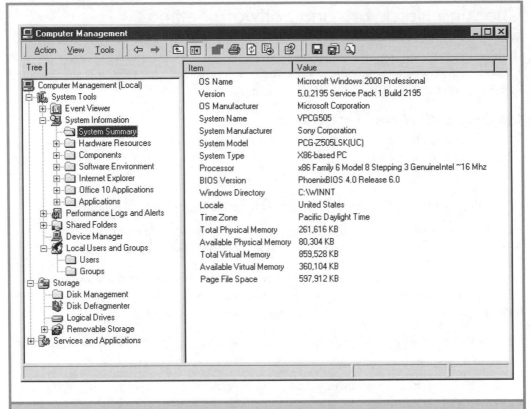

Figure 16-1. You can view the operating system settings for your computer in the Windows 2000 Computer Management window.

Mac OS 9 computer, choose Apple System Profiler from the Apple menu. Perform the following steps to open the Apple System Profiler program in Mac OS X.

1. Double-click the hard drive icon.

2. Click the Applications icon in the Finder window.

3. Double-click the Apple System Profiler application in the Finder window. The Apple System Profiler application will open on your desktop, as shown in Figure 16-2.

4. Click a triangle to the left of one of the items in the System Profile panel. Additional information for that item will appear in the System Profile window. For example, I clicked the triangle beside Network Overview to see the Ethernet cards installed on the iMac in the System Profile panel.

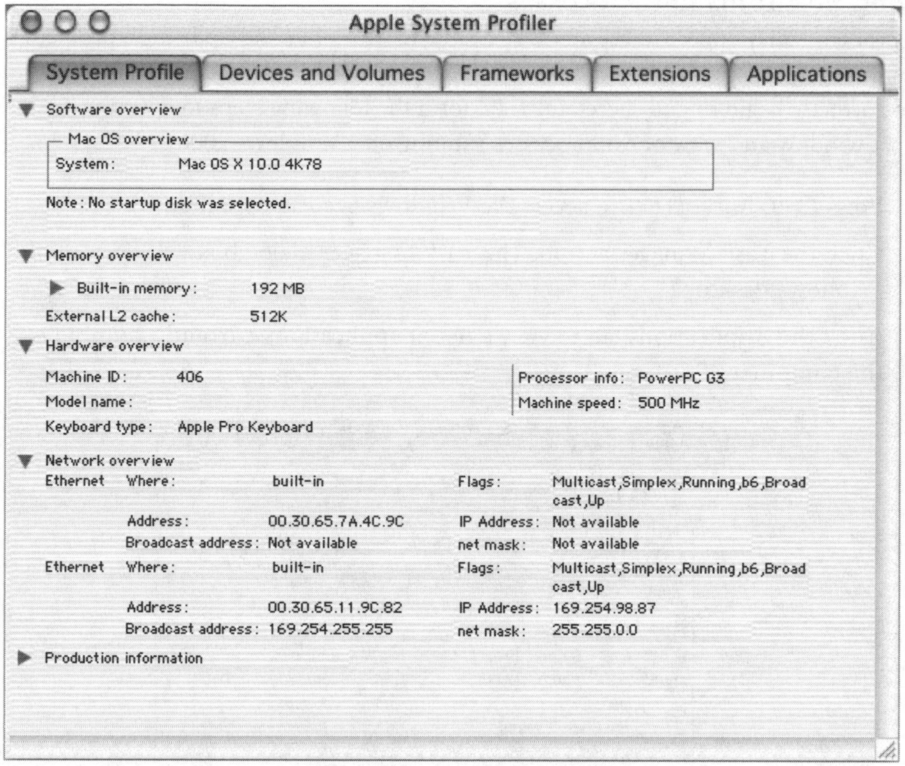

Apple System Profiler

| System Profile | Devices and Volumes | Frameworks | Extensions | Applications |

▼ Software overview

```
┌─ Mac OS overview ──────────────────────────────────────────────┐
│  System:      Mac OS X 10.0 4K78                                │
└────────────────────────────────────────────────────────────────┘
```

Note: No startup disk was selected.

▼ Memory overview

  ▶ Built-in memory: 192 MB

External L2 cache: 512K

▼ Hardware overview

Machine ID: 406   Processor info: PowerPC G3

Model name: Machine speed: 500 MHz

Keyboard type: Apple Pro Keyboard

▼ Network overview

Ethernet	Where:	built-in	Flags:	Multicast,Simplex,Running,b6,Broadcast,Up
	Address:	00.30.65.7A.4C.9C	IP Address:	Not available
	Broadcast address:	Not available	net mask:	Not available
Ethernet	Where:	built-in	Flags:	Multicast,Simplex,Running,b6,Broadcast,Up
	Address:	00.30.65.11.9C.82	IP Address:	169.254.98.87
	Broadcast address:	169.254.255.255	net mask:	255.255.0.0

▶ Production information

Figure 16-2. Open the Apple System Profiler application to view the operating system and network hardware and software information for your Macintosh computer.

NOTE If you're running Mac OS 9, you can click the Apple menu and select About This Computer from the menu list. The About This Computer window will open. You can view the version of the operating system, as well as the amounts of physical memory, virtual memory, and memory allocated to each program currently running.

After you have identified the version of the operating system, review the IP address information for the network interface card and make sure a valid IP address, subnet mask, gateway, and domain name server are input into the Internet Protocol window (Windows), TCP/IP (Mac OS 9), Network Settings (Mac OS X), or LinuxConf (Linux) on each computer. Make sure a unique IP address is assigned to each computer. If a DHCP server is responsible for assigning IP addresses over the network, make sure the server has enough IP addresses to allocate to each computer that needs to be connected to the local network.

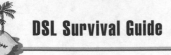

Viewing Programs and Processes

Some problems may appear to be caused by a slow network but end up being a problem with the computer. There may be a problem with the application or a network process may not be able to correctly begin or end successfully. Perform the following steps to open the Task Manager window and view or exit processes running on a Windows 2000 or XP system.

1. Press CTRL-ALT-DELETE to access the Windows Security window.

2. Click the Task Manager button. The Task Manager dialog box will open on the Windows desktop.

3. Click the Applications tab to view a list of applications currently running on the computer.

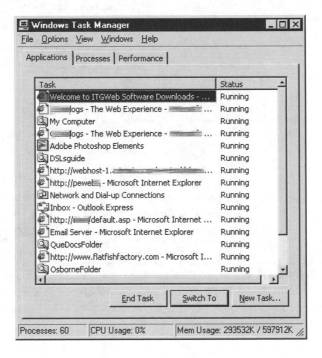

4. Click the Task item, located at the top of the window list; the applications will sort alphabetically.

5. If an application is having problems communicating with the network, the application's status changes from Running to another state, such as Waiting or Stopped.

6. Click a task to select it.

7. If you want to kill, or end, a task, highlight it and click the End Task button. Windows will ask you if you really want to delete the task.

8. Click OK, and the application will be terminated from the Task Manager dialog.

9. Click the Processes tab in the Task Manager dialog to view a list of current processes running on the computer (see Figure 16-3, which also shows the Macintosh equivalent window). The Process panel consists of the name of the process, the Process ID, the CPU being used (for single-or multiprocessor computers) for a particular process, the amount of processor time used by the process, and the memory usage for the process.

SURVIVAL TIP

If your programs are working problem free on your computer, there's no need to end a program or process. However, if you are running several programs and your computer won't shut down, you can try opening the Task Manager dialog, selecting each application, and clicking the End Task button for each one.

Viewing CPU and Memory Usage

Choose the Performance tab in the Task Manager dialog to view the CPU and memory usage information for the computer (see Figure 16-4). If the processor shows activity while no applications are running on the computer, the operating system may be keeping the processor

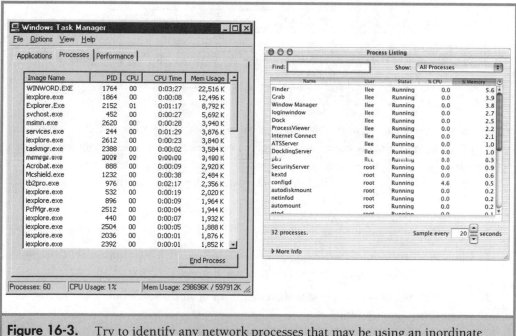

Figure 16-3. Try to identify any network processes that may be using an inordinate amount of CPU cycles or memory.

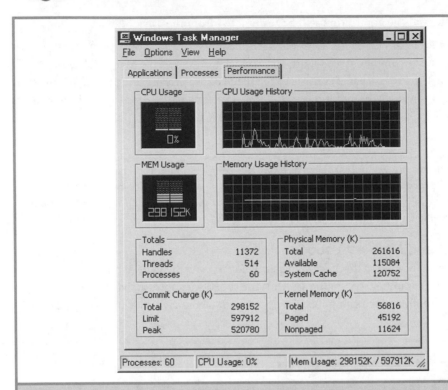

Figure 16-4.   View CPU and memory usage in the performance panel for the Windows
Task Manager dialog box.

busy. In order to manage network tasks, the computer must use the processor. If no processor
cycles are available to process incoming or outgoing network packets, the computer may exhibit
slow performance or display an error message indicating that the computer is busy.

If you want to view more detailed information about how your computer interacts with
its system components, perform the following steps.

1. Open the Component Services window.

2. Click the Start menu, choose Programs | Administrative Tools, and select Component
   Services. The Component Services window will open.

3. Click the uncollapse icon beside the Event Viewer in the left window list of the
   Component Services window.

4. Select the System icon, as shown in Figure 16-5.

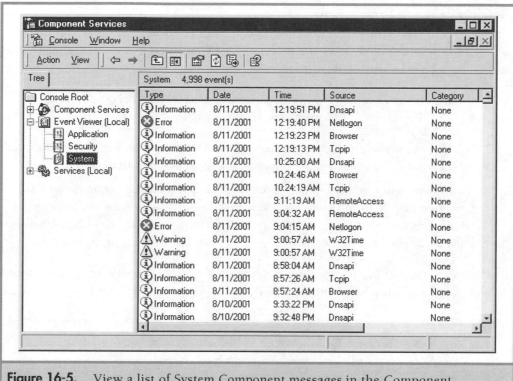

Figure 16-5. View a list of System Component messages in the Component Services window.

If you take a closer look at the files in the Component Services window, you might find entries in the Source column labeled Tcpip. Double-click an entry in the Component Services window to view more detailed information for that item. The Event Properties window will open. You can read about the system event in the Description field and view Byte or Word data for that event in the bottom portion of the Event Properties dialog.

Checking Browser Network Settings

The compute hardware and software specified in the network settings provide the crucial information that enables a network to recognize your computer. However, network applications may have additional settings you may need to customize in order to allow your computer to be properly connected to the network. The following sections show you a few settings you can check or reset in Internet Explorer.

Viewing Browser Preferences

Some of the browser settings that can affect a computer's performance are the home page and cache settings. On a Windows computer, you can view these settings from the Internet Options dialog box by performing the following steps.

1. Open an Internet Explorer window, click the Tools menu and choose Internet Options. The Internet Options dialog, shown in Figure 16-6, will open.

2. If it isn't already selected, click the General tab. The general settings are divided into three sections: the Home Page, Temporary Internet Files, and History.

3. If you want your browser to open faster, click the Use Blank button in the Internet Options dialog. This will open a blank page whenever you create a new browser window on your desktop. If you place a URL in the Address text box, the Web page must load before you can access any menus or window controls in the browser.

The browser caches images from any Web pages it loads. This enables the client to load the Web page faster when you return to a Web site. The cache files in Internet Explorer are

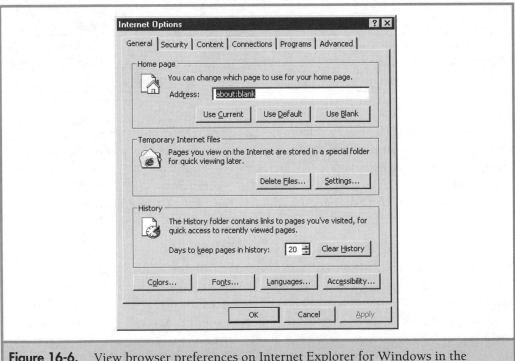

Figure 16-6.   View browser preferences on Internet Explorer for Windows in the Internet Options dialog box.

stored in the Temporary Internet files section of the General panel of the Internet Options dialog. Click the Settings button to view the cached files stored on your hard drive.

At the bottom of the General panel, you can set the number of pages that can be stored in the browser's history list. The history list enables you to navigate to any previously visited Web sites. If you want to clear the URLs stored in the browser's history list, click Clear History.

If you have a Macintosh computer running Internet Explorer 5, start the browser program and choose Preferences from the Edit menu. The Internet Explorer preferences dialog will open. The dialog is divided into two sections, a window list on the left and a larger pane on the right. The items in the left window list are divided into several categories: Web Browser, Forms AutoFill, Receiving Files, Network, and E-Mail.

To modify the cache settings, uncollapse the Web Browser category and select the Advanced item from the left window list. The cache settings appear in the middle of the right panel of the preferences dialog. You can customize how often a cached page is updated by selecting one of the radio buttons in the Update pages area of the Cache settings. Type a number into the Size text box to set the size of the cache. Select the Change Location button if you want to move the location of the browser cache to a different location on your hard drive.

Removing Cached Browser Data

Sometimes a browser may perform slowly if there are too many cached files stored on the disk. Most browsers, such as Internet Explorer and Netscape Navigator have a cache settings that you can clear. The following sections show you how to clear the cache settings with Internet Explorer for Windows and Mac OS.

Perform the following steps to clear the cache settings for Internet Explorer 6 for Windows.

1. Open the Internet Options dialog of Internet Explorer. Right-click on the Internet Explorer icon on the desktop.

2. Select the General tab in the Internet Options dialog box.

3. Click the Delete Files button if you want to remove all the cached files from the hard drive.

4. Click the Settings button if you want to view more options for modifying the cache settings, as shown in Figure 16-7. Select View Files to view a list of cache files on the hard drive. You can manually deleted some or all of these cache files from the Explorer window. Click on the Close box of the Explorer window to return to the Settings window. Then click OK to save your changes.

5. Click OK in the Internet Properties window to save your changes.

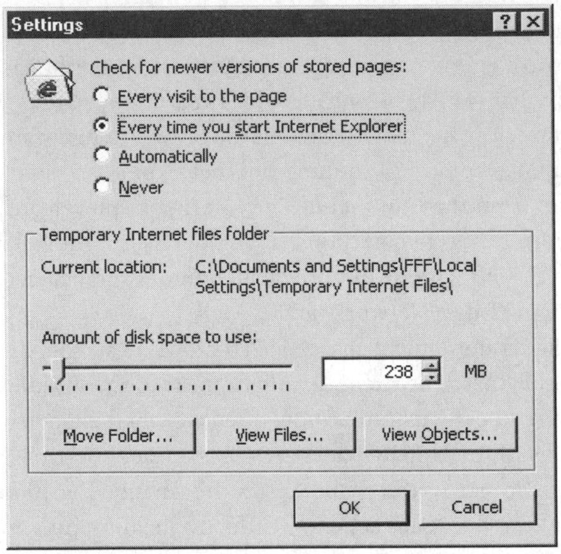

Figure 16-7. You can adjust several cache-related settings from the Internet Options dialog box of Internet Explorer 6 for Windows.

You can customize how frequently pages are stored in the cache, change the amount of disk space that will be used to store cached files from the Web sites you visit, or delete or move individual files stored in the cache.

You can clear the cache settings for Internet Explorer 5 on a Macintosh by performing the following steps.

1. Choose Preferences from the Edit menu. The Internet Explorer preferences window will open.

2. Select Advanced from the Web Browser category.

3. Then click the Empty Now button in the cache settings area of the Advanced settings panel.

4. Exit Internet Explorer to save your changes.

Restart the browser and visit a Web site. If the Web site contains graphical images, it may take a little longer to load the entire Web page.

Checking System Resources

In order for a browser to navigate Web sites, the computer must be properly configured so that other computers on the network can recognize and interact with it. You may want to check the network settings or the availability of the computer's system resources to make sure the computer is properly set up for the network.

To check the network identification of a Windows 2000 computer, perform the following steps.

1. Right-click the My Computer icon and choose Properties. The System Properties dialog, shown in Figure 16-8 will open.

2. Select the Network Identification tab to view the full computer name and domain information.

3. If any of these settings does not match your local network settings, click the Properties button to change the domain settings.

4. Click the Network ID button to create a new login or network ID for the computer.

Aside from entering the IP address information into the TCP/IP control panel, you don't need to make any special changes to the network settings on a Macintosh computer in order for it to be recognized on a Windows network. However, you may want to take a look at the

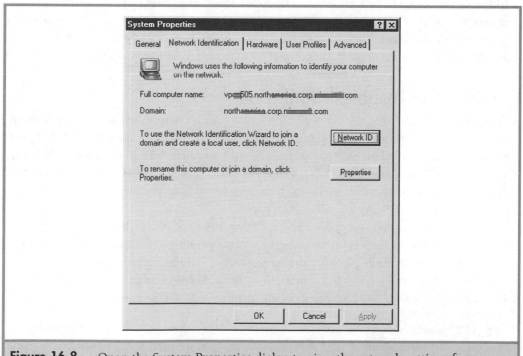

Figure 16-8.   Open the System Properties dialog to view the network settings for a Windows 2000 computer.

memory configuration and the amount of available disk space on each Macintosh computer to make sure the browser and other network applications have plenty of resources available to do their work.

If you're using Mac OS 9, open the About This Computer window to view the memory settings for Mac OS. The version of the operating system appears at the top of this window followed by the amount of physical and virtual memory available on the machine. A list of applications appears at the bottom of the window list. The progress bar to the right of each application indicates the amount of memory each one is using.

Isolating Networked Computer Problems

The process for troubleshooting a computer is similar to the processes you can use to troubleshoot a network. Setting up a computer and documenting each computer's configuration can help reduce the amount of time it takes to troubleshoot a computer problem or a network problem. Next, you'll need to isolate whether the source of a problem is hardware or software.

Hardware and software have a tight relationship; one can't work properly without the other. Before pulling a card, cable, or hard drive out of a computer, first check the operating system settings for the network, memory, and available disk space. Depending on the type of problem, you may also want to run a few applications to check the integrity of the hardware components installed on the computer. The following sections show you how to apply the network troubleshooting methods discussed in Chapter 15 to troubleshoot a computer system.

Choosing a Troubleshooting Method

Tracking down the source of a network problem can be as complicated as tracking down a problem with a computer. First you need to have a general understanding of what hardware and software is installed on each computer, and then you need a short description of what the problem is. Some computer problems tend to have a similar root cause, so if you're new to troubleshooting networks or computers, the more problems you are exposed to, the more familiar you will become with your network.

There are three general processes you can follow to begin troubleshooting a computer problem. One thing to keep in mind as you view settings and try to diagnose the problem on the computer is to abstain from changing any settings unless you absolutely have to. Changing a computer's configuration may affect the reproducibility of the problem. The following list summarizes the troubleshooting methods that will be explained in more detail.

✦ **Hardware and software changes**   Try to find out what the most recent hardware or software changes are that have been made to the computer. If no changes were made, you may want to find out if any changes have been made recently to the network.

- ✦ **Isolate the program error or settings**   Use network applications to try to isolate the problem on the computer. Try to isolate the problem to a combination of settings or identify the programs that may be incompatible with each other.

- ✦ **Look for similar problems online**   If you've isolated the problem to a particular application, operating system, or software or hardware setting, you may want to search the vendor's support Web pages to find out if the vendor or publisher is already aware of the problem. Check to see if an update or fix is available. You may want to consider upgrading hardware or software to fix the problem.

Reviewing Changes to Network Hardware and Software

Any hardware connected to or installed on a computer can potentially be the root cause of a computer problem. Some of the more common hardware upgrades are adding memory, installing a graphics or network card, upgrading a hard drive, or connecting a new monitor. Memory upgrades are very common and for the most part are not the cause of computer or network problems. Memory chips can, however, be the cause of some software instability problems that may manifest themselves as network problems. Occasionally you may receive a memory module that has a defective chip or is not completely compatible with other hardware on your computer.

If your computer won't start up after you install memory, the memory module may not have been properly installed in the computer, or the memory module may be defective. If you notice intermittent hardware or software problems, where the computer freezes or an application crashes after you have changed the memory configuration on a computer, you may want to remove the memory module to see if the problem goes away. Similarly, if you have installed a card or monitor, keep an eye on your computer systems and keep the previous components nearby in case you want to undo the upgrade.

New or upgraded software drivers, operating system components, and software applications can also create new software conflicts with the existing files and settings on a computer. The operating system is probably the most sensitive software component on your computer. When you install software drivers or applications on a computer, be sure these upgrades or new components are compatible with the operating system. Review the software requirements for each upgrade or software installation.

If the software claims to be compatible with your computer, go ahead and install it. After the software is installed, use the software. There's no rush to use the software. However, if the software is incompatible with your system, you will find out sooner rather than later. If you cannot start the program or access a network card, you may want to remove it from the computer. If the software works as expected, you can leave it on the computer and see if any new problems occur as the new software gets more exposure to the computer and the network.

Eliminating Problem-Free Components

The most time-consuming troubleshooting process is isolating the combination of software settings or software components that is causing the problem on the computer. One method for isolating the problem is to consider all the components that are working properly. You can make a short list of reliable hardware and software components. As you review the strong points on the computer, write down any known problem areas with either hardware or software.

The process of elimination requires that you start from a general topic and narrow down the cause of the problem. If following a set of steps can reproduce the problem, take a look at each step and try to determine whether one of the software settings or combination of settings may be causing the problem. Make a note of the settings and version numbers of the programs that are responsible for the problem.

Some problems may start and stop without any interaction from a user. These problems are generally more difficult to isolate. Try to note the times this type of problem occurs and which computers it has been reported on. Try to isolate the problem to a particular operating system or application. It's also possible some problems may occur only during peak network usage times.

Tell a Friend

Some computer problems can be more severe than others. For example, if your computer can't start a browser application, this will be a more severe problem than not being able to open an e-mail attachment. If rebooting your computer, resetting the network settings, and

Before Upgrading . . .

Some upgrades are designed to fix immediate problems for a particular operating system or hardware configuration. If you have a computer that requires a fix for an upgrade, you can install the upgrade. However, you should seriously consider returning to the previous version of the operating system or application before making another upgrade.

When a new operating system or application is first released, you might want to wait at least a few days to see if some of the early adopters or the publisher may be able to document known problems or configurations that may not work with the new product. If an upgrade to an operating system or application is available for download over the Internet, you may want to read any documentation available to find out if the upgrade may or may not be compatible with a particular computer configuration.

reinstalling an application doesn't help solve a computer problem, you may want to try to set up another computer with the same configuration as the problem computer to see if you can reproduce it.

If you can run a different browser and access the Internet, you may be able to find additional troubleshooting information on the hardware vendor or software publisher's Web site. Severe problems that are easily reproducible are usually addressed and fixed as quickly as possible. You may also want to visit an online forum or message board to find out whether other customers have computers experiencing the same problem, and locate additional information about a possible solution.

Simplifying Computer Problems

If you haven't already asked yourself this question, you may be asking it now: Isn't there an easier way to troubleshoot problems? Is there a shortcut to finding and fixing a particular type of problem? I wish I could say yes. But the practical answer is yes and no. This may seem just as convoluted as many troubleshooting adventures you may have, but the reality of troubleshooting is that if you cannot reproduce or isolate the problem, you must choose another approach. One way to find out if a problem might be reproducible on another computer, is to restart the computer and, if necessary, its network connections, and try to reproduce the problem starting from a relatively clean state.

Restarting or Removing Computers from the Network

For most computers starting from a clean slate means powering off the device and then powering it back on. This may sound easier said than done. For example, some handheld devices don't actually power off when you press the power button; they simply go to sleep. Macintosh computers can boot in two different modes, one where system extensions load, and another where they don't load. Windows computers can start up normally, or they can boot into a safe, protected mode. The following list shows you how to reset the hardware and network settings for Windows, Linux, and Macintosh computers.

Restarting a Windows Computer   Perform the following steps to shut down and restart a Windows computer.

1. Click the Start menu and choose Shut Down.

2. Click the drop-down menu in the Shut Down Windows dialog box and choose Shut Down.

3. Click OK and wait for Windows to exit each application, save changes, and display the message indicating that it's okay to power off the computer.

4. Once the computer is powered off, you can remove the network cable from the network interface card, and from the network hub if the problem can be reproduced without a network connection. Otherwise, leave the computer connected to the network, and press the power button on the computer.

Restarting Mac OS 9 and Mac OS X   On Mac OS 9, you can shut down and power on the computer by first choosing the Shutdown command from the Special menu. Wait for the computer to power down. Then press the power button on the keyboard or on the Mac to restart the system. If the computer is running Mac OS X, choose Shutdown from the Apple menu. Wait for Mac OS to exit any open applications, and power off the hardware. Then press the power button to start up the Macintosh computer.

SURVIVAL TIP

If you're running Mac OS 9, you can start up the computer minus the system extension files by holding down the SHIFT key while the computer powers on. You should not see any icons appear on the computer screen before the desktop appears. Software conflicts with extensions are one of the most common causes of hardware and software incompatibilities on Macintosh computers.

Restarting a Linux Computer   If you have KDE or Gnome running as the X Window interface for Linux, perform the following steps to power the computer off and then on.

1. First, log out of the user account. Click on the Log Out button in the Task Bar, and then choose Log Off. The login window will appear.

2. Select the Shut Down button from the login window. A dialog box will appear.

3. Choose Halt and then click Yes to shut down the operating system. Wait for Linux to shut down the computer and then power off the computer.

4. Press the power button to start up the Linux PC.

5. As the computer boots look for any error messages as each process starts. If a network process fails to start, or if any other failures are reported, jot this information down in the computer's log.

Swapping Cables, Network Media, or Network Settings

Another method you can use to isolate a computer problem is to move it to a smaller, controlled, working network where all components are known to work. Connect the problem computer to this network and try to reproduce the problem. If the problem is reproducible on this network, you may want to try swapping out the network interface card and changing the network settings on the computer. The goal of moving the computer to a different network is to make sure the problem is unique to the computer and not dependent on a particular network component.

Implementing and Testing Computer Solutions

The type of problem you find may suggest one or more possible solutions. It's up to you to decide how you want to fix the computer problem. If the problem is hardware related, you may have to replace the hardware component. If software is the source of the problem, the solution may be as simple as installing a fix or reinstalling a software program. On the other hand, you can open up a whole new box of software upgrades, for example, if you need to upgrade your operating system and are not sure if all the programs installed on your hard drive are compatible with the new version of the operating system software. The following sections present a few possible solutions that may help solve some software problems.

Choosing a Solution

You should spend time reviewing each solution before choosing one you want to apply to a computer. Generally, solutions involve some level of risk, time, and cost. Low-risk solutions are changes that will have the least impact on the software and hardware already installed on the computer, as well as little impact on other network systems. A high-risk solution may be your only solution if have an older computer system and a hardware or software upgrade warrants upgrading your computer. Time and cost are somewhat self-explanatory. If you don't want to take the time to learn a new operating system or computer platform or don't want to pay for an upgrade, those solutions will fall to the bottom of your list of preferred solutions.

Choosing a Solution for PPPoE

Troubleshooting a computer connected to a DSL modem configured with a PPPoE connection is similar to troubleshooting any other network connection. In most cases, there will be only one or two computers involved with the PPPoE connection instead of a whole network. The DSL modem for the point-to-point connection should provide a direct connection to the DSL provider's network. Since you won't have to worry about local network configurations, the most likely problem with a point-to-point connection will be with software configurations on the computer, the integrity of the DSL modem, or the DSL service provider. The following list contains a few hardware and software settings to check with the DSL PPPoE connection.

- ✦ **Check cables**   Disconnect and reconnect the Ethernet cable connecting the computer to the DSL modem. If you suspect the cable may be faulty, swap it with another Ethernet cable that is known to work.

- ✦ **Check DSL modem**   Check the DSL modem and make sure it is powered on. You can reset the DSL modem by powering it off and then on again.

✦ **Check network settings** Open the TCP/IP settings for computer's operating system and make sure the computer has the correct settings for the DSL network. In most cases, the DSL network will want to assign an IP address to the computer.

Short-Term Solutions

Before you decide whether you need to repair or upgrade a hardware or software component on your computer, you might want to try adding preventive maintenance software or adjusting virtual memory settings to see if this helps improve the computer's performance. Of course, if these solutions have nothing in common with the problem you're trying to solve, you may need to revisit the solutions on your short list and pick a solution.

Adding a Personal Firewall to Each Computer Computer software can become unstable if a virus or a trojan horse accesses your computer and modifies the software on your computer. If you have not set up a firewall on your local network, you may want to set up personal firewalls on a few of the computers on your network. Figure 16-9 shows the firewall log for Symantec's Norton Personal Firewall software. The Macintosh and PC versions of this software enable you to log any data that leaves your computer or arrives over the network. If the firewall cannot recognize incoming data, it will be denied access to your hard drive. Personal firewall sofware can be helpful if a virus or trojan horse has victimized your computer in the past. However,

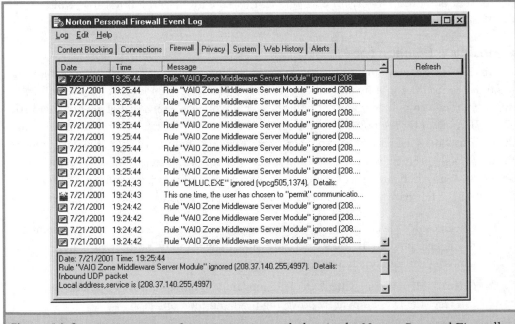

Figure 16-9. You can view the outgoing network data in the Norton Personal Firewall Event Log dialog box.

adding a personal firewall to each computer on the network may cause more problems than it solves. If you create specific rules for each machine to follow, a personal firewall is much easier to work with, compared to configuring it from scratch.

Changing Virtual Memory Settings   Windows, Linux, and Mac OS computers use virtual memory to enable the computer to grow the amount of memory available to the computer as you start applications and open and modify documents. The virtual memory information is stored in a swap file on your hard drive. Linux systems require you to format a separate partition that is used to store virtual memory information. Windows and Macintosh computers, by contrast, create the swap file on the main disk partition, alongside all the other files on your hard drive. If you have a Windows computer with a large hard drive, you can reconfigure the drive into two separate partitions. Then move the bulk of the virtual memory disk space to the second partition. Windows 2000 and Macintosh computers enable you to access and customize virtual memory settings.

If you have a Mac OS 9 computer, perform the following steps to view or modify virtual memory settings.

1. Click the Apple menu, choose Control Panels, and select Memory. The Virtual Memory settings are located in the middle section of the Memory control panel window.

2. Select the On radio button if virtual memory is Off.

3. Type a number into the text box to set the amount of virtual memory for your computer. Virtual memory works slightly differently on Mac OS 9 than on Mac OS X. The optimal setting for the computer is usually 1MB of memory over the amount of physical memory installed. However, if you have more than 100MB of memory installed with Mac OS 9 and plenty of memory to run the applications you want to use, you can leave virtual memory off. Some applications are not compatible with virtual memory, so you may want to turn this setting off to see if this solves a software problem on a Macintosh computer.

4. Click on the Close box of the Memory control panel to save your changes.

5. Restart the Macintosh computer to activate any changes made to the virtual memory settings.

Mac OS X keeps its virtual memory settings unattainable. Virtual memory is always on in Mac OS X, and there is no easy way to turn it off. However, you can type the **top** command into a terminal window to view the amount of virtual memory allocated on your hard disk. Mac OS X is smart about the way it allocates virtual memory. It can grow or shrink the size of the swap file on the hard drive to increase or decrease the amount of virtual memory available to the system. The virtual memory–related output from the top command will look like the following.

```
PhysMem: 24.6 M wired, 110M active, 55.0M inactive, 190 M used, 2.49 M free
VM: 1.66G + 41.8 MB  11271(0) pageins, 1701(0) pageouts
```

You can view the amount of available disk space by opening a Finder window. If the amount of virtual memory is more than 80 percent of the available disk space on your hard drive, the Macintosh may experience slower overall performance. Press the Q key to exit the top tool and return to the command prompt in the terminal window.

You can also type the **vm_stat** command in a terminal window in Mac OS X to view a snapshot of the virtual memory behavior. The vm_stat command can be used to show virtual memory statistics. The vm_stat command can be used to view pages of virtual of memory information as they move in to and out of physical memory onto your hard drive. The pageout value shown in the next example conveys the number of 4096-byte pages that have migrated from physical memory to the hard drive. The pagein value indicates the number of pages moved from memory to the disk. Pages that have recently moved from the disk to physical memory are defined as active pages.

If you notice a high number of pageouts, you may want to consider upgrading the amount of physical memory installed on your system. The number of pageins should not be zero. If the pagein value appears as zero, you may have run out of available disk space on the computer's hard drive.

```
[localhost:~] llee% vm_stat 30
Mach Virtual Memory Statistics: (page size of 4096 bytes, cache hits 36%)
   free active inac wire    faults     copy zerofill reactive  pageins
   620  28191 14100 6241    231177     16031  117522    24173     8951
pageout
307
```

If you want to view or modify the virtual memory settings on a Windows 2000 or XP computer, perform the following steps.

1. Right-click the My Computer icon and choose Properties. The System Properties dialog box will open.

2. Select the Advanced tab, shown in Figure 16-10. This dialog enables you to access operating system preferences for system startup and environment variables for applications and operating system settings for the computer.

3. Click the Performance Options button in the Advanced panel of the System Properties dialog box. The Performance Options dialog box will open. Figure 16-11 shows the Performance options dialog box for Windows 2000. It contains an Application Response section and a Virtual Memory section. The same window in Windows XP contains two panels: Visual Effects and Advanced. Click the Advanced tab to view the virtual memory settings for a Windows XP system.

4. Click a radio button in the Application Response area to determine whether Windows should provide faster performance for applications or background services, such as printing or checking e-mail.

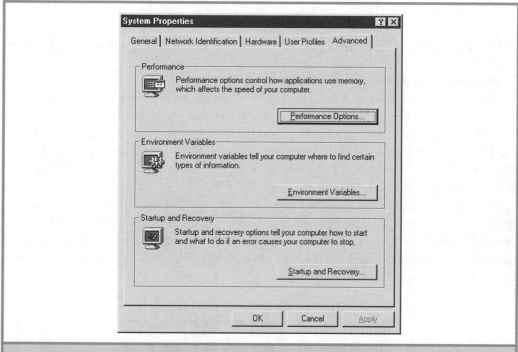

Figure 16-10. On a Windows 2000 computer, open the System Properties dialog box and select the Advanced panel to access the virtual memory settings.

5. View the amount of virtual memory configured for the computer in the Virtual Memory section of the dialog.

6. Click the Change button to modify the virtual memory settings. The Virtual Memory dialog, shown in Figure 16-11, will open. A list of hard drive partitions will appear in the window list at the top of the dialog. Below that, the size of each page of virtual memory appears.

7. Select a drive from the window list and view the size of the virtual memory swap disk. Type a number into the text box to change the size of the VM swap file.

8. Click Set to save your changes.

9. Next, review the recommended amount of virtual memory in the Total Paging File Size For All Drives section of the Virtual Memory dialog.

10. If you want to change the virtual memory allocation on a disk, click a disk in the window list and type a new value into the Initial Size and Maximum Size text boxes. The minimum size can be below the currently allocated amount of disk space for virtual memory. You should set the maximum size above the recommended amount of virtual memory.

11. Click OK to save your changes.

12. Click OK in the System Properties dialog to save your changes and return to the desktop. Then restart your computer to activate the revised virtual memory settings.

Upgrading Hardware or Software

Windows and Mac OS have disk verification software bundled with each operating system. You can run Disk Cleanup and disk Defragmenter with Windows 2000. Apple provides Disk First Aid for both Mac OS 9 and Mac OS X (see Figure 16-12). Both applications can locate and fix most errors that may be found with the file system on each hard drive. The Windows software will also try to optimize the placement of the files on the hard drive. This can improve the performance of the hard drive.

If the hard disk, network, and operating system tools are not able to provide a solution to the computer problem affecting a computer, you may want to find out if there are any hardware upgrade options for each component or for the computer. Computers are generally growing faster and becoming more affordable. If you cannot find a solution for a computer problem, you may want to consider replacing the computer with a new computer system.

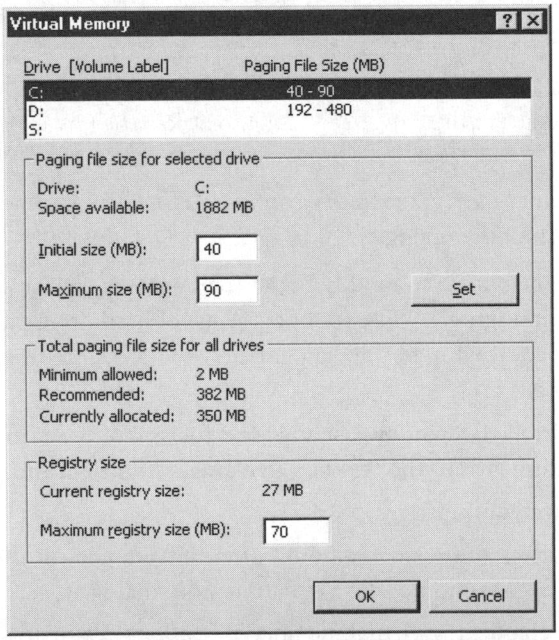

Figure 16-11. The Virtual Memory dialog box gives you access to the virtual memory settings for the computer.

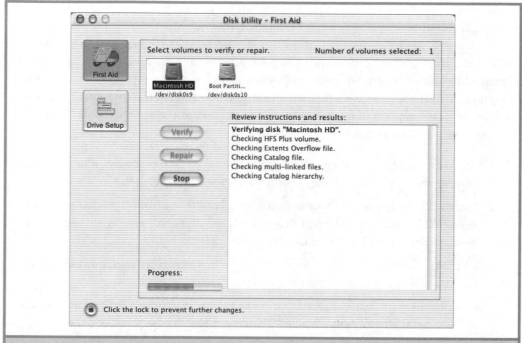

Figure 16-12. Apple's Disk First Aid enables you to check a computer's hard drive for errors. Windows 2000 has a similar program that runs if your computer was not shut down properly.

Reformatting and Reinstalling the Software

If a computer problem doesn't seem to have a root cause, or if you don't think you can spend time identifying the root cause, you can back up any critical documents from the computer and reformat the hard drive. Then reinstall the operating system, any network drivers, and your applications onto the computer. Some computer manufacturers, such as Apple, Sony, and Hewlett-Packard, include master CD-ROM discs that enable you to restore a computer to its original operating system, application bundle, and software driver configuration.

Testing a Network Computer Solution

One way to preempt a computer problem is to test it out on your network. Testing a computer takes time, and if you want to find out if a software or hardware upgrade will be problem free, you'll need to think of a few different things to try out while you're using the system. If you want to test your computer effectively on a network, prioritize the services that are most important to you or to the person who will be using the computer. For most client computers, the browser and e-mail applications will need to be able to access the Internet and communicate with servers located on the Internet.

If interactive or streaming media programs are also popular applications on the network, you should use these applications on a computer after installing a hardware or software upgrade. The following list outlines some of the programs you may want to test on a networked computer. If an application has a problem opening or running on the computer, you may want to check the amount of memory allocated to it, check the version number of the program, and consider reinstalling it.

1. **Browser**   Visit a Web site with Internet Explorer or Netscape Navigator and see if you can view the text and graphics on a Web page and click a link.

2. **E-mail**   Send and receive your e-mail from a browser or from an e-mail application, such as Outlook. You may want to attach a file to an e-mail message to see if your computer can download the attachment and open the file.

3. **FTP**   Log into an FTP server and upload a file to the server. Then download and see if your computer can open the file correctly.

4. **Download files**   Visit a Web site that contains large PDF or image files and download one or several files to your computer. Try to open each file on your computer.

5. **Instant messaging**   Send a message to an online friend. Send messages back and forth and note any unexpected disconnections from the message server.

6. **QuickTime or Media Player**   If the computer has a QuickTime or Windows Media Player plug-in installed with a browser, visit a Web page that contains streaming media files and play a video or audio file over the Internet connection. Watch the file as it plays back and note slow performance or unexpected disconnections from the media server. You may also want to visit a Real Audio or Flash Web site and try playing back a Real Audio file or a Flash file on the computer.

Controlling Computers on a Network

If you don't want to learn how to script to schedule a backup, you can install remote software, such as Timbuktu, or Virtual Network Client. Timbuktu is available for Macs and Windows. Virtual Network Client is available for Macs, Windows, and Unix systems, including Linux. You can log into a computer over the network and manually control it using this type of application.

Timbuktu

Timbuktu enables you to view the desktop of your Windows or Mac computer remotely over a local or remote network connection. It's a commercial product, but if you prefer hands-on control of your computers, you may want to consider seriously adding this tool to your network.

In order to use Timbuktu, you must install it on the computer you are using, as well as the computer you want to control. You can create login accounts on each computer or enter the IP address of the computer and use an Windows or File Sharing login name to access the computer (see Figure 16-13). Performance over the network can be slow, so don't expect to control your PC as if it were your local computer. In some cases, you may need to reconfigure your computer's IP settings, but that depends on what you're trying to accomplish by controlling the other computer.

Virtual Network Computing

Virtual Network Computing, or VNC, is another network-control application available for multiple platforms. It is distributed for free as part of the GNU General Public License, which is also used by Unix, parts of Linux, and the Unix compilers and tools. It is made up of a server and a client (or viewer). Both can run under Unix, Windows, Macintosh, or Windows CE. You can log into another computer connected to the network running VNC and control it from your desktop over the network. Go to www.uk.research.att.com/vnc/index.html if you want to download and test-drive this software on your network.

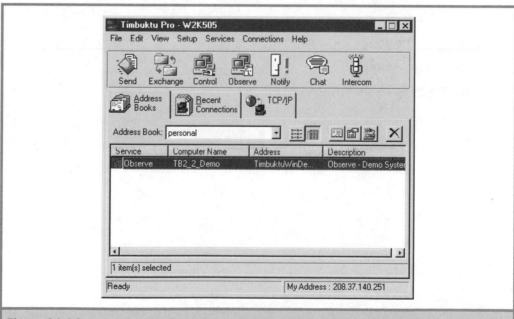

Figure 16-13. You can perform tasks remotely on a Windows PC or a Macintosh using Timbuktu.

Additional Resources

Each year computers become faster and more affordable, with faster network cards, and most important, more fun to use with a network. It's almost impossible to keep track of all the different kinds of past, present, and future computer models. Some of the URLs listed here will take you to a few of the more popular PC/Windows solutions. In addition to troubleshooting computers on the network, this chapter also introduces you to virtual network clients and remote control software solutions for local area networks. Feel free to visit any of the following URLs to find out more about computers and remote software programs.

◆ www.dell.com

◆ www.compaq.com

◆ www.hp.com

◆ www.sony.com

◆ www.apple.com

◆ www.macosxhints.com

◆ www.allosx.com

◆ www.zdnet.com

◆ www.efficient.com

◆ www.netopia.com

◆ www.uk.research.att.com/vnc/index.html

Chapter 17

Troubleshooting VPN Connections

Many companies have adopted virtual private networks to enable their workers to access the company's private network over the Internet, using a DSL service. The term *virtual private network (VPN)* describes the network connection between one computer on your home or office network that is connected over the Internet to a private network of computers. Once the computer connects to the private network, it can send and receive data with other computers on that network over the VPN connection.

Accessing a virtual private network over a DSL network enables one computer to join another network with the fast network speed of a DSL connection. The network data exchanged between the two networks is processed and protected by a tunneling protocol. The IP address of your computer contacts the virtual network, and your login account on the virtual network is authenticated. When the connection is created, the tunneling protocol establishes a connection between the computer's IP address and the VPN server located on the corporate network.

Accessing a private network over the Internet requires each client computer on a local network to have a specific combination of account and network settings on a client computer. You may also need to de-activate the firewall protecting the local network in order to communicate with other computers on the VPN. Establishing the proper account and network settings to enable the two computers on the Internet to communicate with each other is an inevitable troubleshooting topic.

Other troubleshooting areas include customizing your computer's settings to work properly on the private network, and a few ways to check whether a network service is available on the private network. The following topics will be explained in more detail in this chapter. Although it is possible to connect an entire local network of computers to a private network, this chapter focuses on a single-computer connection to a virtual private network.

✦ **Virtual private networks**   Find out how a client computer connects to a virtual private network.

✦ **VPN over PPTP**   Learn how to connect a Windows PC to a virtual private network using PPTP, Windows 2000, and a router connection to a DSL service.

✦ **Troubleshoot a VPN connection**   If a client computer is unable to connect to a VPN, find out how you can check client network settings and dialing settings, and try a few other things to identify the failure point of the VPN connection.

Basic Concepts of Virtual Private Networks

As the first broadband connections became available a few years ago, virtual private network connections were set up by some corporations so that employees could access the corporate network on the road or from home. Over the years, VPNs have replaced the dial-up modem connection to the corporate network.

The first implementations of virtual private networks had some network security skeptics worried about maintaining the privacy of the VPN connection. Microsoft's first VPN implementation in Windows NT was thought to leave a computer too vulnerable to security attacks. Some companies hesitated to open up their networks to broadband connections. However, as more and more people subscribe to broadband services, and as operating systems refine their VPN network protocols, more and more companies are supporting virtual private network access.

What Is a Virtual Private Network?

A virtual private network connection is a connection created between the client computer on a local network and a VPN server, using the Internet as the network connection. A computer on a local network can access the Internet with the DSL modem, and the DSL modem's router can create a connection over the Internet to the corporate network. Once connected, the computer on the local network can freely access other computers on the corporate network. The following list provides a list of terms and definitions that will be discussed in more detail in this chapter:

+ **Client computer**   A desktop or laptop computer connected over a wired or wireless network interface card to a local network. The client computer can initiate or end the VPN connection.

+ **Tunneling protocol**   A type of network protocol that can be created between two computers connected to a network. The protocol usually provides a level of security and privacy by encrypting the user's data; and it can encapsulate other network protocols, enabling two computers to send and receive network data.

+ **DSL modem**   A point-to-point, router, or bridged modem that connects a local network to the DSL provider's Internet services.

✦ **VPN connection**   A network connection where the Internet is used to transfer data between a client computer and a VPN server located on a corporate network.

✦ **Corporate VPN server**   A computer running VPN server software. If a client computer has a valid login and password, the VPN server can authenticate the client and grant it access to the corporate network. The corporate server can initiate or end the VPN connection.

✦ **Corporate network**   A large or small network with Internet access limited by a firewall. Remote access can be obtained by dialing into a computer on the network, or by logging into a specially configured server that is connected to the Internet.

Tunneling Protocols

A *tunneling protocol* is a type of network protocol that enables two computers to send and receive data over a secure connection. Tunneling enables two network access points to exchange protocols over a network connection. The tunnels do not need to be encrypted; but when a tunnel is encrypted, it establishes a secure connection between your computer and the virtual private network. A computer client on a local network can log into the VPN server as shown in Figure 17-1. A client computer can also connect to a VPN using a PPPoE DSL modem.

The connection shown in Figure 17-1 relies on a DSL modem router to establish the connection to the Intenret. The client computer is responsible for starting and ending your computer's connection to the VPN network. Once connected, your computer can access other computers on the remote network. PPTP, IP Sec, and L2TP are a few different protocols that can be used to bring the corporate network into your home. The following sections explain these two protocols in more detail.

In order to access the private network, a telecommuter must have the correct network tunneling protocol installed on his or her computer, as well as a valid user account on the private network. As protocols and operating system upgrades became available for Windows, Mac OS, and Linux, many of the security issues were addressed, and more and more telecommuters and workaholics began using virtual private network connections to enable them to access a corporate network from home or from a remote office.

The PPTP Protocol

PPTP is an acronym for Point-to-Point Tunneling Protocol. The PPTP Forum, a group of companies led by Microsoft and US Robotics, developed it. A VPN server, set on a local or remote corporate network, can host PPTP connections. To get to the remote network, the VPN client computer contacts the DSL modem, which contacts the VPN server over the Internet connection. The VPN server authenticates the VPN client. Then the PPTP protocol creates a tunnel between the two peer computers on the local network: the VPN client and the DSL modem. The tunnel completes with a final connection with the VPN server on the remote network.

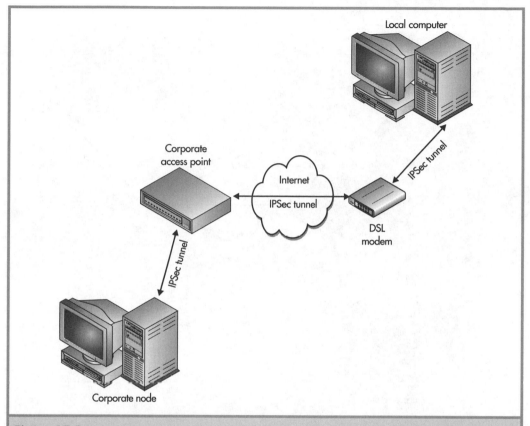

Figure 17-1. A virtual private network creates a custom connection between your computer and a computer on another network.

The DSL modem sends the VPN connection the login information, and if the connection information is valid, a network session is created on the virtual network. Figure 17-2 shows a point-to-point connection with a DSL provider, running concurrently with a VPN connection to a corporate network. This particular service allows the VPN client to work with multiple network channels over the PPPoE connection.

CAUTION   Although it's perfectly fine to work with your VPN connection over long periods of time, be sure to keep the operating system and anti-virus software updated on each computer. This can help reduce the likelihood of exposing your computer to a hacker or virus attack. If you haven't updated your computer's security or operating system software recently, you may want to disconnect the connection to a virtual private network when you are not actively using it. Ending the virtual connection can keep network connections short and discourage hackers from gaining access to your local network or to the corporate network.

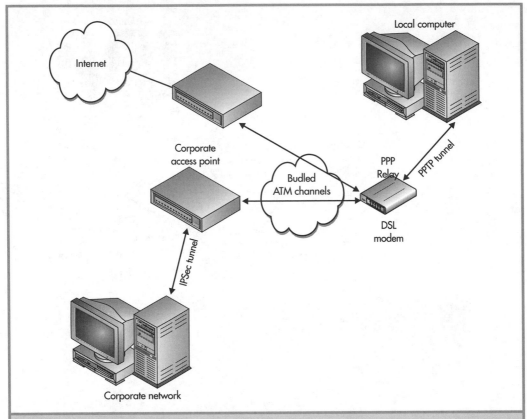

Figure 17-2. The PPPoE modem acts as the gateway to the Internet, as well as to the virtual private network.

PPTP is most commonly used with Windows VPN servers, but it can also be used with Unix servers. NetBEUI, IPX, and TCP/IP protocols are also supported within a PPTP tunnel. In order to create a VPN connection over PPTP, the Windows computer must first already have an Internet connection, and then establish a connection with the VPN server over a TCP connection. The Windows client must know the host name or IP address of the PPTP server in order to create a VPN connection to the private network. When the client disconnects from the VPN network, the client notifies the VPN server, and the server disconnects the session and tears down the tunnel.

The IPsec Protocol

IPsec, short for IP security, is a set of network protocols that can be used to create a VPN connection between two networks. IPsec, created by the Internet Engineering Task Force (IETF), can work with several authentication methods, such as Secure Sockets Layer (SSL), commonly used for e-commerce Web sites; Pretty Good Privacy (PGP), which is used with some e-mail systems; and PKI (public-key infrastructure), which is a system based on digital certificates to create public and private keys to authenticate users attempting to access the virtual private network. IPsec is designed to provide strong network authentication, and it is probably one of the more frequently used protocols for implementing virtual private networks.

The IPsec protocol can enable a VPN server to authenticate, encrypt (scramble data), and exchange a key to determine whether a client should be allowed to access the VPN server. A typical VPN connection using IPsec looks similar to the diagram shown in Figure 17-1, where the tunnel is created between two routers.

Other Tunneling Protocols

Other tunneling protocols can also be used to create a VPN connection over the Internet. The Level 2 Tunneling Protocol (L2TP) can be used to create a VPN connection over the Internet. However, in order to create the connection, an L2TP Access Concentrator (LAC) must be set up on the corporate site, and an L2TP network server (LNS) must be set up on the client site. The L2TP tunnel is created between the LAC and the LNS that enables computers on the client network to access computers on the corporate network. The LAC relies on a radius server, which ISPs commonly use to authenticate their Internet client connections, to authenticate VPN client connections.

Accessing a Virtual Private Network

In order to connect to a virtual private network, the computer on your local network must have the appropriate client software capable of communicating with the VPN server. You will also need to know the host name or IP address of a VPN server that will accept your computer's connection request. In order to connect to the VPN server, your computer will need to provide a valid user name and password to the VPN server.

Creating a VPN connection with Windows

Windows 98, Me, NT, and XP all are capable of creating and connecting to a VPN server over the Internet. The following sets of steps show you how to create, connect, and modify a VPN account with a Windows 2000 computer. Other versions of Windows require a similar set of steps to create a VPN account. Perform the following steps to create a virtual private connection from the Network Connection Wizard in Windows 2000:

1. Right-click the My Network Places icon and choose Properties from the shortcut menu. The Network And Dial-Up Connections window will open.

2. Double-click the Make A New Connection icon to start the Network Connection Wizard.

3. Click Next. The Network Connection Type dialog box will open.

4. To create a virtual private network connection script for a network interface card, select Connect To A Private Network Through The Internet.

5. Follow the onscreen instructions and provide the host name for the VPN server on the corporate or remote network.

6. Click Finish. A VPN icon will appear in the Network And Dial-Up Connections window. This VPN icon represents a VPN account. Double-click this icon to open the login dialog box or initiate the connection to the VPN server.

Once the VPN connection information has been added to the VPN account, click OK to save the changes in the VPN properties window, or click the Close box of the VPN login dialog box. Next, try to connect to a VPN server on the remote network. The following steps show you how:

1. Double-click the VPN icon to open the login dialog box for the VPN connection, as shown in Figure 17-3. Type the user name, password, and domain of the account you want to use to connect to the VPN server.

2. Click the Connect button to send your user name and password to the remote network. Wait for the client to connect to the VPN server.

When the connection is complete, right-click the VPN account icon and choose Status. The VPN status dialog box will open. If the VPN connection is active, your computer will be able to receive and send packets to the virtual private network. You can view the number of sent and received packets in the status dialog box.

NOTE

Your computer relies on the DSL modem to help create the virtual tunnel to the private network. Check the manual for your modem to find out whether the DSL modem or the DSL service can work with static or dynamic IP addresses. Some DSL services can process only static IP addresses, while other services can work with dynamic IP addressing or a network address translator that may mask the IP address of the computer attempting to create a VPN connection.

If the VPN connection fails, you may want to review the settings in the VPN account. Open the VPN login dialog box to access the properties for the VPN connection. To modify the settings for the VPN connection, perform the following steps:

1. Click the Properties button to view the General, Options, Security, and Sharing settings for the VPN connection. Figure 17-4 shows the General panel of the VPN dialog box.

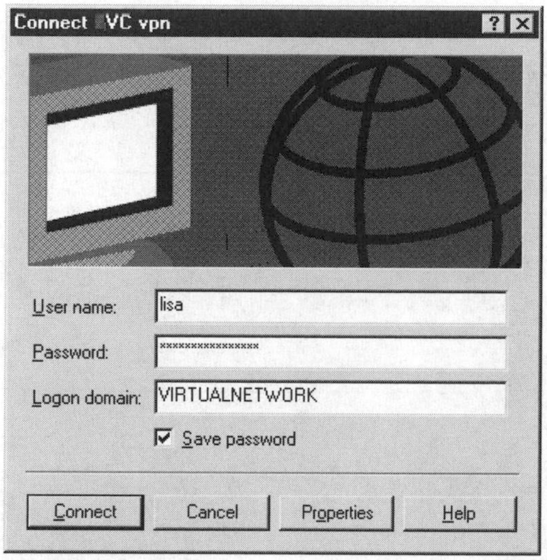

Connect VC vpn

User name: lisa

Password: xxxxxxxxxxxxxxxx

Logon domain: VIRTUALNETWORK

☑ Save password

Connect | Cancel | Properties | Help

Figure 17-3. You can use Windows 2000 to establish a virtual private network connection and log into a remote network.

2. The host name of the VPN connection appears in the text box in the General panel. You can type a different host name in the text field. If you want to access the VPN connection while the connection is active, select the Show Icon In Taskbar When Connected check box, as shown in Figure 17-4.

3. Click OK to save your changes. In order to connect to the virtual network, the computer must first be connected to the Internet.

4. Establish a connection with the DSL service, using PPPoE, a router, or a bridged connection. Click the Connect button in the login dialog.

5. Type a user name and password in the login dialog, and then click Connect. Two or three dialog boxes will appear, indicating the equivalent of dialing, logging in, and connecting to the VPN server on the corporate network.

6. Once your computer has connected to the virtual network, the VPN icon will appear on the taskbar. Try accessing a Web page located on the intranet of the corporate network to test your VPN connection.

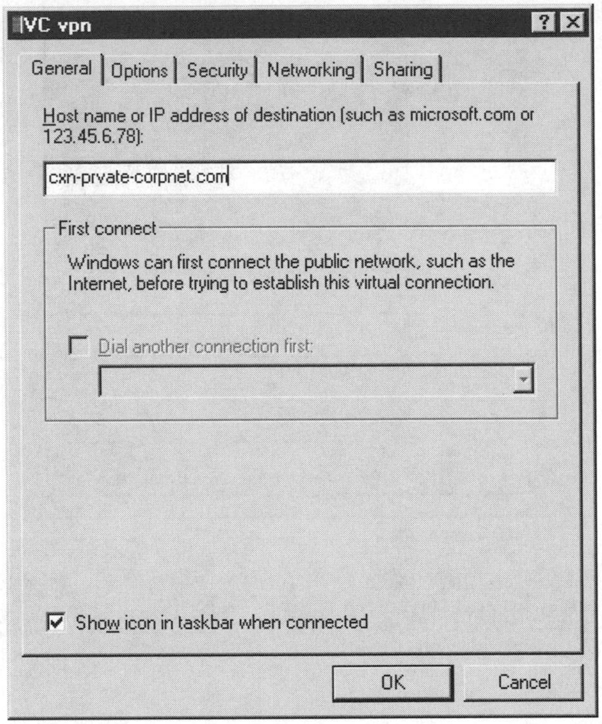

Figure 17-4. Type the name of the VPN connection into the VPN connection properties dialog.

Creating a VPN Connection with Mac OS

Creating a VPN account and connecting to a VPN on a Mac will follow the same general steps as for Windows 2000. However, the VPN software is not built into Mac OS 9 or Mac OS X. You will need to purchase VPN software for a Mac and then learn how to configure the software to dial into the corporate network. There are several PPTP solutions for the Mac.

Wind River Systems publishes PPPoE software products for Macs and Windows computers. MacPoET is the name of their Macintosh product, and WinPoET is the name of their Windows product. Efficient Networks also provides a Mac version of EnterNet, their PPPoE product. You can download the software by visiting each publisher's Web site. I don't have any particular application to recommend at this time. You may want to contact the network administrator of the remote network to find out the VPN client software that works best with the Mac, Windows, or Linux system connected to your DSL network.

You can navigate the network a little easier if you use the same computer platform as the majority of the computers that are connected to the VPN network.

NOTE

Creating a VPN Connection with Linux

Like Mac OS, Linux does not have a PPTP solution built into it. You can download and install PPPoE from Roaring Penguin Software. rp-pppoe is a great Linux solution if you have a DSL modem that requires you to access the DSL service over a point-to-point connection. You can download, install, and experiment with one or more of the PPTP solutions available for Linux. Most tunneling protocols are available for Unix and Linux.

If you don't want to set up a VPN server on your local network, you may want to consider setting up a secure HTTP (HTTPS) connection or see whether secure shell access is available on your network. HTTPS is not a tunneling protocol like PPTP or IPsec. It's a variation on the HTTP protocol most commonly used with e-commerce Web sites. Both HTTP and HTTPS are installed with most Linux distributions, and they enable you to view Web pages, access e-mail, and telnet to other computers on the network. However, these alternatives do not offer the full accessibility to a network that a VPN connection can provide.

Problems Accessing a Virtual Private Network

In order to create the connection, the VPN service on the private network needs to be able to receive incoming requests for connections. The VPN connection is similar to a point-to-point connection, except more security is involved in the VPN connection. Because the virtual connection relies on the Internet, the connection speed of the DSL service and reliability of the Internet access will determine how quickly you can get around the private network. The following sections review a few settings and configuration problems that frequently occur with a VPN connection.

Checking Your Client Settings

First, make sure the VPN services are available on the network you are trying to connect to. Then review the VPN settings on your local computer. The VPN server may be expecting more information than the client connection is sending. If this occurs, the VPN server will not allow the client to connect to the remote network.

Checking Dialing Settings

Windows 2000 enables you to view and customize the dialing settings for a VPN account. If the computer was unable to establish a successful connection to the private network, you may want to make sure the expected login information is available in the connection dialog box, and that the connection is not redialing automatically or hanging up prematurely. The following steps show you how to access and review the dialing settings options:

1. Double-click the VPN icon in the Network And Dial-Up Connections dialog box. The VPN login dialog box will open. If the client starts a connection to the VPN server, click Stop. Then right-click the VPN icon and choose Properties. The VPN properties dialog box will open. You can check the VPN client connection settings from the various panels in this dialog box.

2. Click the Options tab to view the dialing options for the VPN connection (see Figure 17-5). Select the Display Progress While Connecting check box. If the client is not able to connect to the VPN server, you will be able to see where the connection is timing out or failing.

3. If the VPN server requires a user name and password, select the Prompt For Name And Password, Certificate, Etc. check box. This will bring up the login dialog box shown earlier in Figure 17-3. If the Windows network requires a domain name, select the Include Windows Logon Domain check box. An additional Domain Name text box will appear in the login dialog box that opens in step 1.

4. Deselect the Redial If Line Is Dropped check box. Then click OK. Double-click the VPN icon to view the login dialog.

5. Type your username and password into the login dialog. If the VPN network requires a domain, type a domain name into the login dialog; otherwise, leave this field empty.

6. Click Connect to connect your client to the corporate network.

Checking Security Settings

Virtual private networks can potentially leave a corporate network open to Internet hackers. In order to break into the remote network, the hacker needs to have a valid username and password. There are many hacker tools that can be used to find a password for a login account. One way to add a level of security to a network is to require all users to change their passwords on a regular basis.

The VPN connection should require a password from the client in order to connect. If the VPN client is not able to connect, make sure the security settings on the client are set up

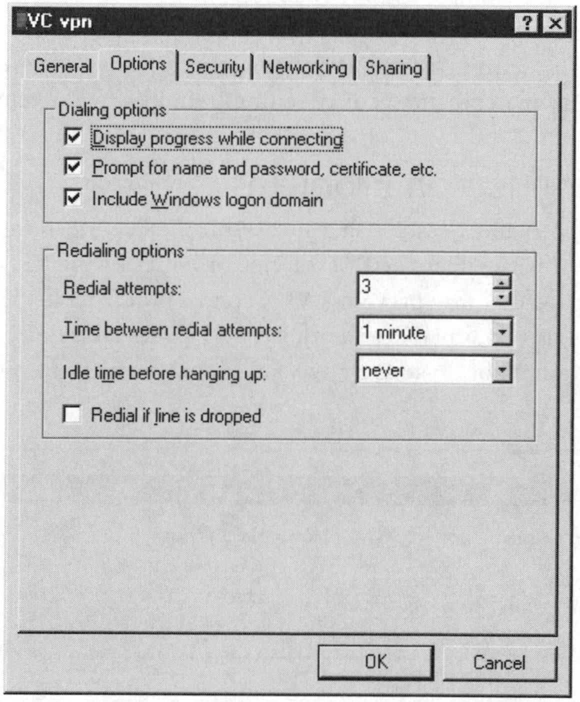

Figure 17-5. View the dialing options in the VPN properties dialog box.

to match the security settings on the VPN service. To check the security settings on a Windows 2000 VPN connection, perform the following steps:

1. Double-click the VPN icon in the Network And Dial-Up Connections dialog box. The VPN Properties dialog box will open.

2. Click the Security tab and view the Security Options for the VPN connection, shown in Figure 17-6.

3. If the VPN server requires data encryption, check select Require Data Encryption (Disconnect If None) check box.

4. Choose the security method for validating your account password.

5. Click OK to save your changes. Click Connect to log into the VPN server.

If the connection fails, contact your VPN administrator to find out the correct client security settings needed to connect to the corporate network. If you have instructions for configuring the security settings for the VPN client, check the security settings and make sure your VPN account matches the security settings required by the remote network.

Identifying Connection Problems

Assuming you have been able to establish a successful VPN connection, you may encounter a connection problem with either the DSL service provider or the VPN server. There are many possible scenarios that may prevent a VPN connection from being successful. If one particular VPN server is not available and other VPN servers are available, try another VPN connection. If you are not able to access any VPN servers, you might want to e-mail a

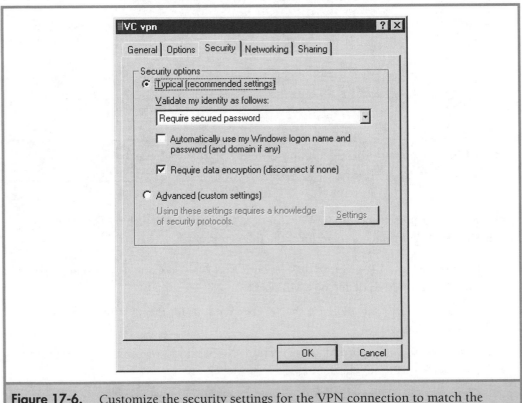

Figure 17-6.   Customize the security settings for the VPN connection to match the virtual network server to which the computer will connect.

co-worker to see whether the IT folks have taken VPN access down on the corporate network. If the corporate network is alive and well, you may want to visit your DSL provider's Web site to see whether there are any reported or known service issues in your area.

Reviewing VPN Errors on Windows 2000

Some VPN connections require that a computer already have IP access to the VPN server via the Internet. If your computer is not connected to the DSL service and you try to initiate a VPN connection, you may see the error message shown in Figure 17-7. Click Cancel, and connect your computer to the DSL service. Then start the VPN connection.

If a client computer has problems connecting to a virtual private network, there are several settings you can check to make sure the computer is properly connected to the local network, the DSL modem, and the Internet. What follows is a short list of hardware and software settings you can check to make sure the computer is properly configured:

✦ **Check the network cables**   Make sure the network cable is properly connected to the computer and to the Ethernet hub.

✦ **Check the local Ethernet connection**   Verify that the computer can communicate with the network interface card. Make sure the computer has the appropriate IP address settings for the local network. You may want to try disabling and enabling the network settings for the operating system, or restarting the computer to make sure the selected network settings are being used by the computer.

✦ **Check the DSL modem**   Look at the network cable connection to the DSL modem, and the connection to the Ethernet hub or to the local computer. If the DSL modem does not seem to be responding to network activity, try powering it off and back on.

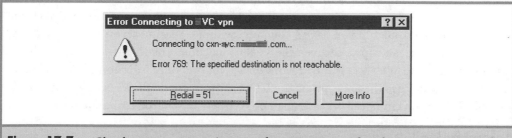

Figure 17-7.   Check your computer's network connection and make sure it is active if you see this error message.

✦ **Check the Internet connection**   Start a browser application, and see whether the computer can load a Web page. If the connection to the Internet seems to be working correctly, you should be able to connect to the virtual private network.

✦ **Check access to the VPN network**   Once the computer has established a connection to the virtual private network, try viewing a Web page from a Web server located on the intranet.

Avoiding a Slow VPN Connection

The amount of Internet-bound traffic on your local network can affect the performance of a VPN connection running on the same network. If you are having problems connecting to the VPN server, check your network, to see whether another computer is creating a lot of network traffic by sending or receiving a large amount of e-mail, or copying files to or from the Internet. You may need to wait for the network traffic to subside before reconnecting to the VPN service if you want to avoid working on a slow network.

Virtual Private Network Solutions

While your computer is connected to the virtual private network, you can access the network services on the remote network. You should be able to access the mail, Web, database, and file servers on the corporate network. Access to the Internet will require you to use any special settings that a computer on the corporate network may need to access Internet computers, such as configuring your browser to work with a proxy server. You may also need to provide a user name and a password for each server you access on the remote network.

Using Your VPN Connection

Before you start diving into any intensive computing processes, you may want to test the speed of your VPN network connection and see whether you can access a general Web site on the corporate intranet. If you have a computer with file-sharing access on, you may want to see whether you can copy a file over the VPN connection. The following sections show you how e-mail and Web access might work on a Windows-only VPN connection. If a Mac or Linux computer has the appropriate tunneling software, once the VPN connection is created, the Mac or Linux can access e-mail or Web services on the corporate network.

Accessing Mail

You should not need to change your mail account settings to access e-mail on the corporate network. For example, if you have a laptop computer that you use at work and at home, you can use the same mail account configuration to access your e-mail from work or from home using the VPN connection. Start a mail application that will work with the mail server on the corporate network. If Outlook is the standard on the corporate network, start Outlook after you have established the VPN connection. The mail program may automatically check for mail.

Depending on how the corporate mail system is configured, you may need to log into the mail server before you can access any new mail messages. You can also click the Send/Receive button to check for new messages. If your mail system uses the Microsoft Exchange Server, you can access your calendar in addition to your public e-mail files.

Accessing Intranet and Internet sites

You may not need to make any changes to your browser to view Web pages over a VPN connection. If the corporate network has intranet Web sites, you should be able to access these Web sites without modifying the browser settings. Some corporate networks may require a browser to point to a proxy server on the network in order to access Web sites on the Internet.

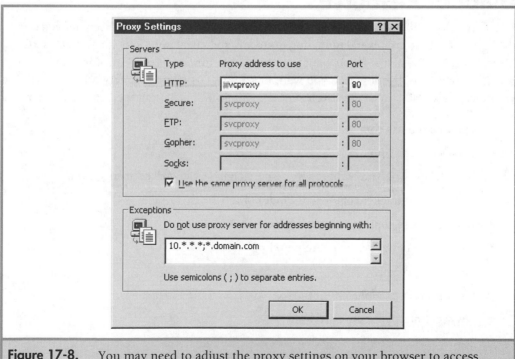

Figure 17-8. You may need to adjust the proxy settings on your browser to access Web sites on a corporate intranet.

Figure 17-8 shows the proxy settings you can configure from the Internet Options dialog box in Internet Explorer 5. However, these same steps can also be applied to Internet Explorer 6, the default browser for Windows XP.

If there are specific domain names or IP addresses on the corporate network, they can be accessed without a proxy. To access the proxy settings, perform the following steps:

1. Open the Internet Options, Connections, LAN settings window in Internet Explorer for Windows.

2. Click the Advanced button, located at the bottom of the Local Area Network (LAN) Settings dialog box.

3. Type the IP information in the Exceptions text field. For example, you can type 10.*.*.* if you want to include all computers on the intranet that have an IP address that starts with 10. You can also configure different proxy servers for different network protocols.

Additional Resources

DSL networks enable you to connect to another private network that is also connected to the Internet. There are several tunneling protocols and client solutions for Windows PCs, Macs, and Linux systems. If you want to review other tunneling solutions for your virtual private network connection, or if you want to set up a virtual private network server on your local network, you can research all the possibilities by visiting the URLs listed here.

+ www.dslreports.com

+ www.efficient.com

+ http://www.wrs.com/ivasion/www.xsense.com/Service/driver_mac_b.html

+ www.versiontracker.com/macosx/index.shtml

+ www.itpapers.com/cgi/SubcatIT.pl?scid=245

+ tiki-lounge.com/~ben/software/pptp.html

+ poptop.lineo.com

+ www.scooter.cx/alpha/pptp.html

+ www.counterpane.com/pptp.html

Index

INTERNATIONAL CONTACT INFORMATION

AUSTRALIA
McGraw-Hill Book Company Australia Pty. Ltd.
TEL +61-2-9417-9899
FAX +61-2-9417-5687
http://www.mcgraw-hill.com.au
books-it_sydney@mcgraw-hill.com

CANADA
McGraw-Hill Ryerson Ltd.
TEL +905-430-5000
FAX +905-430-5020
http://www.mcgrawhill.ca

**GREECE, MIDDLE EAST,
NORTHERN AFRICA**
McGraw-Hill Hellas
TEL +30-1-656-0990-3-4
FAX +30-1-654-5525

MEXICO (Also serving Latin America)
McGraw-Hill Interamericana Editores S.A. de C.V.
TEL +525-117-1583
FAX +525-117-1589
http://www.mcgraw-hill.com.mx
fernando_castellanos@mcgraw-hill.com

SINGAPORE (Serving Asia)
McGraw-Hill Book Company
TEL +65-863-1580
FAX +65-862-3354
http://www.mcgraw-hill.com.sg
mghasia@mcgraw-hill.com

SOUTH AFRICA
McGraw-Hill South Africa
TEL +27-11-622-7512
FAX +27-11-622-9045
robyn_swanepoel@mcgraw-hill.com

**UNITED KINGDOM & EUROPE
(Excluding Southern Europe)**
McGraw-Hill Education Europe
TEL +44-1-628-502500
FAX +44-1-628-770224
http://www.mcgraw-hill.co.uk
computing_neurope@mcgraw-hill.com

ALL OTHER INQUIRIES Contact:
Osborne/McGraw-Hill
TEL +1-510-549-6600
FAX +1-510-883-7600
http://www.osborne.com
omg_international@mcgraw-hill.com